Cambridge Studies in Social Anthropology

General Editor: Jack Goody

24

THE PALM AND THE PLEIADES

OTHER TITLES IN THE SERIES

The Palm and the Pleiades

INITIATION AND COSMOLOGY IN NORTHWEST AMAZONIA

STEPHEN HUGH-JONES
Lecturer in Social Anthropology, University of Cambridge

CAMBRIDGE UNIVERSITY PRESS

CAMBRIDGE
LONDON   NEW YORK   NEW ROCHELLE
MELBOURNE   SYDNEY

Published by the Press Syndicate of the University of Cambridge
The Pitt Building, Trumpington Street, Cambridge CB2 1RP
296 Beaconsfield Parade, Middle Park, Melbourne 3206, Australia

First published 1979

Printed in Great Britain at the
University Press, Cambridge

Library of Congress Cataloguing in Publication Data
Hugh-Jones, Stephen, 1945–
The Palm and the Pleiades.
(Cambridge studies in social anthropology; 24)
Based on the author's thesis, Cambridge University,
1974, which was presented under title: Male
initiation and cosmology among the Barasana Indians
of the Vaupés area of Colombia.
Bibliography: p.
Includes index.
1. Barasana Indians – Rites and ceremonies.
2. Barasana Indians – Religion and mythology.
3. Indians of South America – Colombia – Rites and ceremonies.
4. Indians of South America – Colombia – Religion and
mythology. I. Title.
F2270.2.B27H83   390'.098   78–5533
ISBN 0 521 21952 3

FOR LEO AND TOM

CONTENTS

Contents

TABLES AND FIGURES

MAPS AND PLATES

Maps

Plates
Between pp. 40 and 41

The publisher and the author gratefully acknowledge the permission of Brian Moser to reproduce Plates 1, 3 and 4, and of Akademische Druck- und Verlagsanstalt to reproduce Plate 2, which first appeared in Koch-Grünberg (1909–10) *Zwei Jahre unter den Indianern*, Vol. I, p. 315.

x

PREFACE

This book is an amended version of my doctoral thesis entitled 'Male Initiation and Cosmology among the Barasana Indians of the Vaupés Area of Colombia'. The thesis, submitted in May 1974, was based on fieldwork carried out in Colombia between September 1968 and December 1970 under the auspices of Cambridge University. Of this time, approximately twenty-two months was spent in the field.

This field research formed part of a larger project of study of Indian groups in the Vaupés region and involved myself, my wife Christine and Peter Silverwood-Cope. The project was directed by Professor Sir Edmund Leach and financed by a grant from the Social Science Research Council. This support is gratefully acknowledged.

My first encounter with the Indians of the Vaupés came from reading Wallace's *A Narrative of Travels on the Amazon and Río Negro* as a boy interested in exploration and natural history. On leaving school, I travelled to Colombia and headed for Mitu, a small frontier town and capital of the Vaupés. There I spent a month living with the nearby Cubeo Indians. This short visit was enough to persuade me both that I wanted to do anthropological research and that I should return to the Vaupés, specifically to the Río Pirá-paraná. Unlike the Cubeo, the Indians there had remained largely isolated from the activities of missionaries and marginal to the rubber economy that dominated the rest of the Colombian Vaupés. The reports of the few travellers and missionaries to enter the river showed that its Indians still retained most aspects of the traditional culture once common to the region as a whole.

In 1967, when I graduated at University, Amazonia was an anthropological *terra incognita*, especially for English anthropologists with their traditional focus on Africa and Asia. One of the objectives of our research was simply to fill an important gap in the ethnographic knowledge of Amazonia. With the exception of Goldman's pioneering work amongst the Cubeo (Goldman 1963), no extended study based on participant observation over a long period of time had ever been undertaken for any of the Tukanoan groups of Northwest Amazonia. Our intention was to study one such group in depth and, in conjunction with Peter Silverwood-Cope, to examine the reported 'symbiotic' relationship between the Tukanoans and their nomadic Makú neighbours.

At this time also, the structuralist anthropology of Claude Lévi-Strauss, in particular as applied to the study of myth, had already had a major impact upon anthropological theory in England. But whilst the theoretical ideas were familiar enough, the ethnographic basis on which they were founded was not. The three volumes of *Mythologiques* that had appeared contained not only a general theory of myth but also an extended discussion of South American Indian ethnography, some of it culled from sources of doubtful quality. Our second objective, and one more directly related to the theme of this book, was to provide an empirical test for some of the grand generalisations that Lévi-Strauss had offered concerning the structure of South American Indian mythology and its relation to Indian thought and culture. The Vaupés, lying well outside the Central Brazilian culture area that forms the focal point of Lévi-Strauss's work on Amerindian myth, appeared to be an ideal location for such a test. Lévi-Strauss himself had only given passing consideration to the myths from this area.

The river Pirá-paraná, choked with dangerous rapids and inhabited by Indians who, till recently, had a reputation for fierceness, is a refuge area. During the rubber boom at the turn of the century and, to a lesser extent, during the Second World War when natural rubber was once again in great demand, the Indians suffered heavily at the hands of Colombian rubber gatherers. Houses were burned, women were abused and the men were carried away by force to work for white *patrones*. Initially, the Indians reacted with violence and later moved away from the main rivers to the side streams and headwaters. From after the war until the late 1960s, when the first Catholic and Protestant mission outposts were established in their midst, the Indians remained more or less isolated, receiving only sporadic visits from rubber gatherers and itinerant missionaries.

After an initial survey trip down the entire length of the Pirá-paraná, and including a stay amongst the Makuna of Caño Komeyaka, my wife and I established ourselves in a Barasana longhouse on Caño Colorado where we were based for the rest of our time in the field. Our hosts, though overtly friendly, were extremely suspicious of our presence and understandably unwilling to allow us to approach them too closely and become intimate with their culture. In order to overcome their suspicions and to avoid the stereotyped relations that Indians maintain with outsiders, we tried as far as possible to adapt ourselves to the Barasana way of life. We lived inside the longhouse, ate only the food that they ate, observed their food taboos and other restrictions, dressed like them and worked with them in the daily tasks of house building, agriculture, hunting and fishing.

All our research was carried out in the Barasana language which we had to learn without the aid of interpreters or written materials. The few Indians who spoke Spanish knew only enough to conduct a basic relationship of trade. Initially, our life was physically and emotionally strenuous but as our command of the language increased and as we became familiar with our hosts and they with us, it became more and more pleasant and rewarding. As time passed, the Barasana with whom we lived became firm friends, generous with their food, their care and their time. They tolerated our mistakes, encouraged us as we learned and did their best to help us in our work. Living and working in such close contact carried with it both advantages and disadvantages. It meant that we understood things, not only because we saw them and were told about them, but also because we practised them daily. We came to know one community and its neighbours in depth. But what we gained in depth, we sacrificed in breadth. Because it took so long to establish a working relationship in one area and because we knew that it would be equally difficult elsewhere, we avoided travel except in the company of our hosts. Only towards the end of our stay did my wife go off alone to work with a Tatuyo group, affines of the Barasana, and we never visited all the Barasana longhouses, let alone all those of the other Pirá-paraná Indians.

Barasana society is rigidly divided along lines of sex. Men and women use different doors to their house, spend most of their waking lives apart from each other and are periodically and forcefully reminded of their separateness by the Yurupary rites that form the subject of this book. Working amongst them as a married couple was a distinct advantage. Minimally, it established that, in spite of being a foreign man, I was relatively safe and had not come there to take their women. It meant that we were recognised as being mature enough to be fully incorporated into adult life even though our lack of children was the subject of ribald comments. But most important of all, it meant that we became familiar with Barasana society from the point of view of both sexes. Though we never specifically divided topics of research between us, the nature of the society itself imposed a division in our work. Though my wife was barred from secret male ritual, she was able to talk freely with the men and to discuss topics normally kept secret from women. But, for me, the world of women was relatively closed.

Many people have helped me in my research and in the preparation of this book. My greatest thanks go to the people of Caño Colorado, especially those of Bosco's house who took us in, fed us and taught us, all with generosity and good humour. In particular, I should like to record my gratitude to Bosco, Pau, Pasico and Maximilliano, my teachers. Hereafter, in order to protect my informants, I have changed their names.

Professor Sir Edmund Leach, as teacher, supervisor, colleague and friend, has given me unfailing support, advice and encouragement ever since I first went to Amazonia some fourteen years ago. My warmest thanks are due to him.

Many people made our work in Colombia not only possible but also more enjoyable. Special thanks are due to Professor Gerado Reichel-Dolmatoff for his advice and encouragement; to Dr F. Marquez-Yanez and others of the Instituto Colombiano de Antropología who gave official support and who helped in many other ways besides; to the University of the Andes who provided office space and other facilities; to Dr F. Medem who offered hospitality and encouragement and who identified animals; to Mr and Mrs Alec Bright, the Bahamón family, Nina de Friedemann, Horacio and Isobel Calle and many more.

We received help, advice and hospitality from many individuals connected with the Javerian Mission of Yarumal and the Summer Institute of Linguistics. Special thanks are due to Monseñor Bellarmino Corréa and Padre Manuel Elorza of the Prefectura Apostólica del Vaupés and to Joel and Nancy Stolte and Richard and Connie Smith of the Summer Institute of Linguistics. We owe also

a special debt to George DeVoucalla and fellow pilots of the SIL
for their skill, courage and helpfulness.

A number of people have read my Ph.D. thesis and offered advice,
suggestions and helpful criticism which I have tried to incorporate
in this book. My thanks to Professor J. Pitt-Rivers and Dr P. Rivière,
my thesis examiners, to Professor C. Lévi-Strauss, and to Kaj Århem,
Bernard Arcand, Ellen Basso, Patrice Bidou, Irving Goldman, Jean
Jackson, Pierre-Yves Jacopin, Joanna Kaplan, Tom Langdon, Peter
Silverwood-Cope and Terry Turner. Thanks also to Professor J.
Goody for encouragement and for allowing me time to write.

Finally I must thank my wife Christine for her fundamental
contributions to every aspect of this work. We planned our research
together, worked together in the field and pooled all our data. In
writing this book, I have drawn freely on data from her notebooks
and constantly discussed aspects of my work with her, and she has
given up her time and work to enable me to write.

Cambridge   S.H.-J
August 1977

ORTHOGRAPHY

The Barasana orthography used in this book follows that developed by Richard Smith (n.d.) of the Summer Institute of Linguistics. This orthography uses symbols chosen to conform to that of Colombian Spanish. For English readers I have substituted the symbols 'h' and 'ny' for 'j' and 'ñ'; I have also not used the symbol 'q' as it has the same value as 'k' which I use instead of 'c'.

Vowels

Un-nasalised		*Nasalised*
a	as in mask	ã
e	as in egg	ẽ
i	as in ink	ĩ
o	as in orange	õ
u	as in scoop	ũ
ʉ	similar to German ü	ʉ̃

Consonants

b	similar to buy but with prenasalisation (mb)
k	as in kite
d	prenasalised as in and
g	as in go but with prenasalisation (ng)
h	as in house
m	as in man (phonologically a variant of b, conditioned by a contiguous nasalised vowel)
n	as in nose (phonologically a variant of d, conditioned by a contiguous nasalised vowel)
ng	as in tongue (phonologically a variant of g, conditioned by a contiguous nasalised vowel)
ny	as in Spanish mañana (phonologically a variant of y, conditioned by a contiguous nasalised vowel)
p	as in pen
r	between r and l in English
s	similar to English ts as in boats
t	as in time
w	as in wine
y	as in yam

Where animals, plants, musical instruments, and the sun and moon act as people in the context of myth and ritual, I have used capital letters.

PART I

The rites in context

1

Introduction

Despite both the importance and elaborate development of ritual amongst the Indian societies of lowland South America, this topic has received surprisingly little attention in the ethnographic literature. Today, there exists a substantial body of monographic studies of a number of different Amerindian societies, most of which focus upon kinship and social organisation. In addition, Lévi-Strauss (1968, 1970, 1971, 1973) has published a massive cross-cultural study of North and South American Indian mythology unparalleled in the anthropological literature for any other part of the world. Yet to date, there is hardly a single account or analysis of ritual amongst lowland South American Indians that is comparable in scope or detail with those published on African, Asian and Australasian societies. Most accounts of Amerindian rituals form part of a wider, more general, ethnographic study and as such tend to be both highly superficial and often one-sided. To me, this neglect of ritual represents a distortion of the ethnographic reality of South American Indians, at least from a native point of view. On the one hand, one of the most interesting and significant features of these societies is that, unlike some of the anthropologists who study them, they do not see their kinship, marriage and social organisation in isolation from a wider religious and cosmological order. On the other hand, it appears to be through ritual that the elaborate mythological systems of these people acquire their meaning as an active force and organising principle in daily life. This study is intended to redress the balance and to go some way towards filling an ethnographic vacuum. Its focus is upon a particular ritual complex, known in the ethnographic literature as the Yurupary cult, amongst the Barasana Indians, a Tukanoan-speaking group living in the Vaupés region of Colombia.

3

The Yurupary cult, like other secret men's cults widespread amongst lowland South American Indian groups, centres on the use of sacred musical instruments that women and children are forbidden to see. These cults serve to express and to reinforce a fundamental division between the sexes that permeates almost every aspect of society. The cult embraces all adult men, new members being incorporated through rites of initiation at which they are shown the Yurupary instruments for the first time. Yurupary rites are thus rites of initiation but, as I shall show, they are much more than this. They are also the highest expression of the religious life of the Barasana and their neighbours and as such have no single or simple interpretation. I shall describe and analyse these rites and their associated mythology and, by setting them selectively in their wider ethnographic context, attempt to gain an insight into Barasana society, religion and cosmology more generally. I hope to show that such an approach represents a valid and useful way of studying religion and one which achieves results that would not perhaps be gained from a broader descriptive study.

In addition to being a contribution to ethnography, this study is also an exercise in the interpretation of ritual and myth. I have attempted to integrate structuralist analysis, in particular Lévi-Straussian analysis of myth, with more conventional approaches to the study of religion and cosmology in such a way as to construct a unified system around the religious thought of a single society. I seek to show how one ritual can be analysed with reference to others and to a body of myth, and to show how ritual mediates between mythic thought and social action.

The Yurupary cult

The first account of the Yurupary cult comes from the writings of Alfred Russel Wallace (1889 : 241–2), who travelled up the Vaupés river in 1850. Following him, nearly every traveller, missionary and ethnologist to visit the Vaupés region has described Yurupary rites and recorded Yurupary myths, and a variety of interpretations, some of them highly fanciful, have been offered for the cult.

Until the recent past, the Catholic and Protestant missionaries who worked in the Vaupés believed that the cult of Yurupary was the cult of the Devil and they went to considerable lengths to suppress it. They burned the longhouses, or malocas, which play an integral

role in the cult, destroyed feather ornaments and other items of
ritual equipment and exposed the instruments to women and children.
Some measure of the importance of the cult to the Vaupés Indians
is given by the fact that in 1883, when the missionaries exposed
sacred Yurupary masks to women and children at a church service,
the Indians rose in revolt and temporarily expelled them from the
region. Unfortunately, many elements of this intolerant attitude
still persist amongst members of both the Catholic and Protestant
missions that work in the area today. I would like to believe that
this book would enhance respect and understanding for the Indians'
religion, but I fear that, unless the missionaries realise the criminal
folly of their present way of thinking, it may instead be used to
further the process of ethnocide, a fear expressed by the Barasana
themselves.

   In the ethnographic literature on the Vaupés, there are numerous
accounts of Yurupary rituals amongst the different Arawakan and
Tukanoan groups living in the region (see appendix 1). Unfortunately,
most of these accounts are highly superficial, but at least in terms of
gross features it appears that the rites are broadly similar to those
of the Barasana. Usually, forest or cultivated fruit is taken into the
maloca or longhouse to the sound of the Yurupary instruments,
whilst women and children are required either to flee to the forest
or gardens or to remain secluded in a screened-off area at the rear
of the house. The men play the instruments in the house all day and
there follows a dance at which the women are present. Sometimes
the men whip each other (and the women), and sometimes ritualised
intersexual aggression is expressed. My own study of the Barasana
shows that there are two different kinds of Yurupary rite, one much
more extended and much more sacred than the other. This more
elaborate rite appears to have occurred amongst at least some other
Tukanoan groups but has never been properly described before. I
shall argue that it would be impossible to understand fully the shorter,
less sacred, rites without knowledge of the longer rite upon which
they are modelled and for which they act as a preparatory phase in
a process of initiation. One of the objects of this book is simply to
present, for the first time, an accurate and detailed account of
Yurupary rites as a basis for interpretation. What I show in my
analysis is that many aspects of the rites are only comprehensible in
the light of a careful examination of details of their spatio-temporal
structuring, of the dress and age of the participants, and so on.

In addition to these accounts of Yurupary rites, there also exists a large body of myths, recorded from different Indian groups in the Vaupés–Içana region, which tell of a culture hero called Yurupary or of other characters identifiable with him (see appendix 2). A theme common to most of these stories is that of the hero being burned alive on a fire, often as a punishment for an act of cannibalism. From the ashes of this fire springs a paxiuba palm (*Iriartea exorrhiza*) which is subsequently cut up into sections to make the Yurupary instruments. Another theme, equally common, tells how the women stole the Yurupary instruments from the men so that the social order was reversed, the men becoming like women and the women achieving political dominance over the men. Only when the men were able to get back the instruments was the 'normal' order restored. In this book, I present a corpus of myths recorded amongst the Barasana and their neighbours in the Pirá-paraná area. Although none of them concerns a character called Yurupary, and although some of them appear superficially to be very different from the classic Yurupary myths, I shall argue that they can be treated as variants and transformations of them. I use these myths as an integral part of my analysis of Barasana Yurupary rites, showing that unless myth is systematically related to rite, many features of the rites remain inexplicable. This reflects the Barasana viewpoint, for most explanations that they give of whole rites or elements within them are couched in terms of myth or make reference to mythic knowledge. Such explanations are not simply 'charters' for ritual action; myths are understood at a deeper level, by shamans and ritual specialists, and are used to give meaning and potency to the rites.

Throughout this study, I have tried to make as full use as possible of these published accounts of Yurupary rites and myths. I have done so in part to supplement and extend my own data, particularly in the area of myth where, following Lévi-Strauss, I take the view that one myth can only be properly understood in the light of other variants. In this respect, my study is only the preliminary groundwork for a more thorough and extensive analysis of Yurupary myths which I hope to undertake at a later date. But also, by relating my own data and analysis to that of other writers, I hope that this study will be seen not only as a contribution to the ethnography of the Barasana and their neighbours but also as a contribution to the ethnography of Northwest Amazonia more generally.

The word Yurupary (Iuruparí, Juruparí, etc.) comes from the

Introduction

Tupian Lingua Geral or Nheêngatu, a lingua franca once widely
spoken along the Río Negro and its affluents. Various writers,
principally Schaden (1959 : 149–53) and Goldman (1963 : 192,
255), have objected to the use of this term in anthropological literature, pointing out that it is a term used by Indians only in conversation with outsiders, and often as an apparent explanation for
anything taboo, secret or mysterious designed to avoid further
questions, and that its meaning is tainted by having been identified
with the Christian Devil.

The term is generally used in three related ways: first, to refer to
the sacred musical instruments that are taboo to women and children;
second, as a blanket name for a variety of mythical characters,
many of whom do indeed have much in common with one another,
but each of whom has a proper name in the language of the group
that tells the myth; and third, when used in phrases such as 'the
Yurupary cult', to refer both to the instruments and also to the
beliefs and practices that go with them. Used in the first sense, I
can see no great objection to the term as a label for a cross-cultural
phenomenon — it is simply a useful shorthand for the more cumbersome 'sacred flutes and trumpets'. From the evidence available and
as I hope to show, there does seem to be something fundamentally
the same about these instruments, the context in which they are
used and the beliefs associated with them, over a very wide area of
Northwest Amazonia (map 1 shows the rough extent of the area
in which the Yurupary cult occurs). In this book, I shall use the
term Yurupary in this shorthand sense to mean 'sacred flutes and
trumpets taboo to women' that are used (a) within a roughly defined
geographical area and (b) in the context of initiation into a secret
men's cult of which they form the focus.[1] But I shall use the Barasana
term *He* (pronounced like 'hen' without the 'n') to refer to the
Barasana instruments in particular.

Used as a name for a mythical hero, the term is more problematic.
To identify the heroes of Yurupary myths with the Christian Devil
is an error that cannot be too strongly condemned in the light of
the crimes to which it has led. This error was recognised by the
Bishop of Amazonas back in 1909 (Costa cit. Schaden 1959 : 151)
but his words appear to have gone unheeded. Leaving aside the

---

1 In other words I would not, for example, include Tikuna sacred trumpets used in the
context of rites of first menstruation, nor the sacred flutes used in the Xingu area of
Central Brazil.

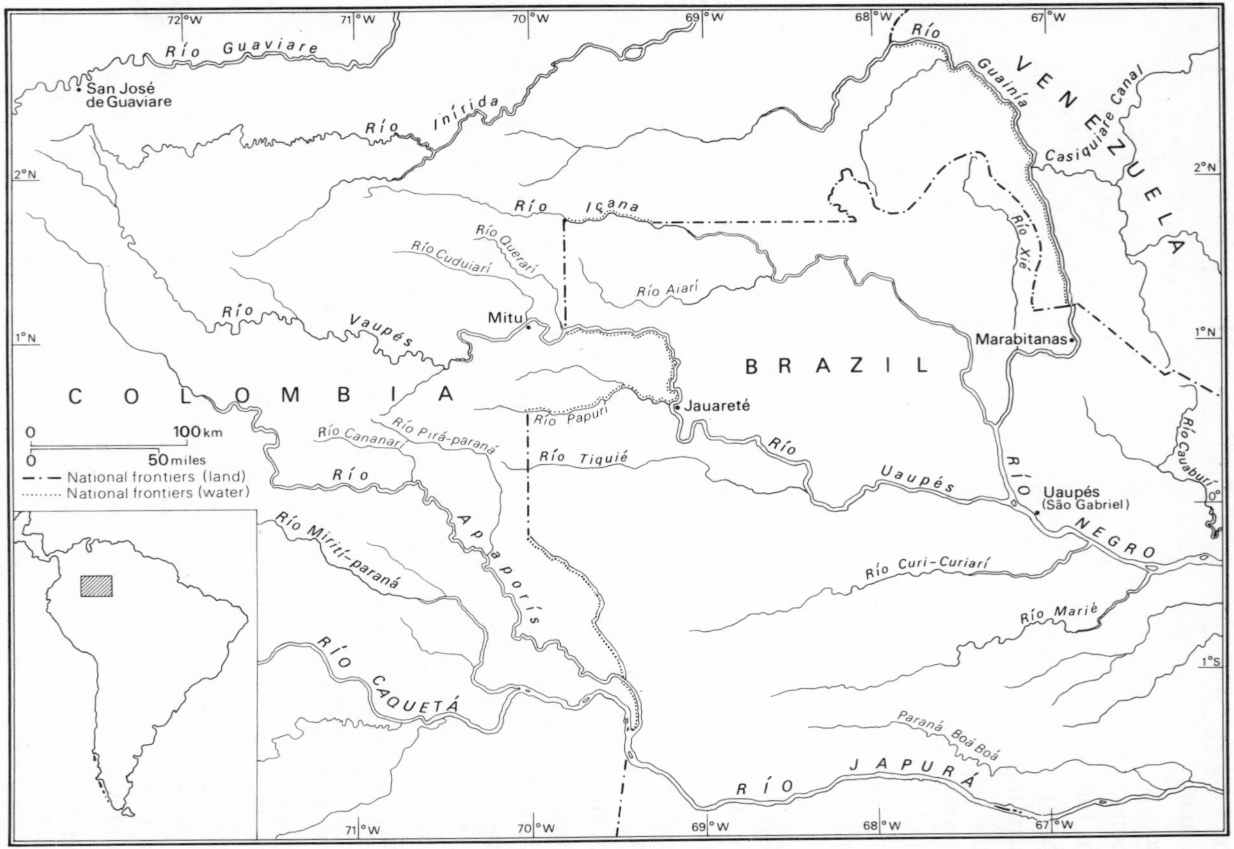

Map 1 Northwest Amazonia: the area of the Yuruparý cult

confusions of missionaries, there still exists a considerable body of
myths about someone to whom those who recorded them rightly
or wrongly assigned the name Yurupary. These myths are close
variants of one another in spite of coming from societies widely
separated in space. They are also close variants of other myths
concerning characters whose names are given in the original language
of the people who told them. All these myths come from a single
geographic area and one in which the Indian cultures are, or were,
strikingly similar to one another. In view of this, and leaving aside
the Devil, I see no great objection to calling these myths Yurupary
myths, nor to calling their heroes Yurupary, provided that it is
understood that these heroes are not identical and that each has
his own proper name. But when I refer to the characters of Barasana
myth, I shall use their proper names.

The term *He* is polysemic and the whole of this book could be
said to be an extended exploration of its various meanings. In its most
restricted sense, the term refers in particular to the sacred flutes and
trumpets; more widely, it is perhaps best translated as 'ancestral'
and refers to the past, to the spirit world and to the world of myth.
At its widest range, it implies a whole conception of the cosmos and
of the place of human society within it. The Barasana have an unusually rich and varied corpus of myths which are treated with
considerable respect and which form the basis of shamanic knowledge
and power. The myths describe the establishment of an ordered
cosmos and the creation of human society within it; the human social
order is seen as part of this wider order, as timeless and changeless
and beyond the immediate control of human agency — it is, or should
be, as it was created in the past. The *He* state implies a state of being
prior to, and now parallel with, human existence. Originally everything
was *He* and the pre-human, man—animal characters of myth are the
He People from whom human beings developed by a process of
transformation. The *He* People and the *He* state, wherein lies the
power of creation and order, are thus set in the distant past. But it
is also an ever-changeless present that encapsulates human society
and which exists as another aspect of reality, another world. When
He is viewed as the past, human society is in danger of becoming
increasingly distant and separated from this wider reality and source
of life — the effects of this time must be overcome. As the present,
this other world is seen as separated in space; human society is in
danger of becoming out of phase with this other reality and spatial

separation must be mediated. The *He* state is known through myth; it is experienced and manipulated through ritual and controlled through spatial and temporal metaphor.

At birth, people leave the *He* state and become human, ontogeny repeating phylogeny; at death, people once again enter the *He* state and become ancestors to be reborn at future births. In life, people enter into involuntary contact with the *He* state through dreaming and illness, through menstruation and childbirth and through the deaths of others. All such contact is uncontrolled and dangerous. It is also possible to enter into voluntary and controlled contact with the *He* state and to experience it directly. The power and position of the shaman lies precisely in his ability to experience and manipulate the *He* state at will; such people are seen as living on two planes of existence simultaneously. Other men can enter into contact with the *He* state through rituals at which the shamans act as mediators. Though all rituals involve such voluntary contact, it is during the rites at which *He* instruments are used that this contact is achieved to its fullest extent. The *He* instruments represent the living dead, the first ancestors of humanity. This regular and controlled contact with the other world, which gives power to control life and which ensures the continuance of society in a healthy and ordered state, is reserved for adult men. Its complement lies in female fertility and powers of reproduction. Women ensure the reproduction of people; men ensure the reproduction of society.

It is impossible for me to summarise adequately the main propositions of Barasana religious thought — I attempt to give some idea of this in the pages that follow. Nor is it really possible to summarise the main themes of my analysis of Barasana *He* rituals. Two points will emerge from my analysis which explain in part why this is so. First, these rites, which are not simply rites of initiation but total religious phenomena, have no simple explanation. Rather they must be explained at a number of different levels and along a number of different axes. Secondly and related to this point, these explanations should ideally be given simultaneously, for they are all there simultaneously in the multidimensional nature of the rites themselves. But because writing involves a linear presentation, they must be taken in sequence. What I have done is to present my analysis in a sequence which is to some extent arbitrary, but to raise at the start a number of interrelated themes which are then explored from a number of different points of view using different aspects of the same set of data.

In order to give some idea of my method of analysis and of the different themes that I explore within it, I shall briefly summarise the contents of the different chapters of this book and the way in which they are interrelated.

The book is divided into five parts together with a preface and appendixes. Part I is intended to set Barasana *He* rites in their wider ethnographic and theoretical context. Parts II and V contain the basic data upon which the argument is based. I found that to attempt to describe and analyse the rites at the same time was cumbersome and the result unreadable. I have therefore tried to keep description and analysis separate. In part II, the rites are described in detail but commentary and explanation are kept to a minimum. In part V, a number of myths are presented, again without commentary or explanation. In part III, the rites described in part II are analysed and explained. The analysis draws heavily upon the myths and also upon explanatory data that is introduced at this point. In order to fully understand the argument, frequent cross-reference must be made to both part II and to part V. The fact that the myths are given as an extended appendix at the end does not in any way mean that they are considered less important. Part IV, the conclusion, is divided into two sections: the first relates my description and analysis of Barasana Yurupary rites to those of other writers on the Vaupés area and attempts to draw together some of the major propositions of Barasana religious thought; the second is devoted to a discussion of anthropological approaches to myth and ritual in terms of some of the general points that emerge from my analysis.

Chapter 2 provides a brief ethnographic sketch of Indian society in the Pirá-paraná region and places *He* rites in the context of other rituals and of Barasana society at large. It is not intended as a balanced or exhaustive account of Barasana society. Chapter 3 describes one kind of *He* rite, called Fruit House, and sets it in the context of an initiatory process that culminates in another kind of rite, called *He* House, described in chapter 4. Fruit House, it is argued, reproduces the structure of *He* House in a reduced and attenuated form. Chapter 5 focusses upon the different categories of actors that take part in the rites. The significance of the maloca as ritual space is discussed in relation to the different age-grades of the participants and it is argued that the microstructure of the maloca with its people reproduces the macrostructure of society and the cosmos. The role of the shaman as mediator is examined and the theme of open and closed bodily orifices is raised, first in relation to shamanic power and then in relation to female reproduction. Shamans and initiates, it is argued, are like menstruating women, and men's *He*, their instruments, are seen to be equivalent and complementary to female powers of reproduction. The theme of dominance and submission between the sexes is also raised and discussed.

Chapters 6, 7 and 8 focus on the dominant and polysemic ritual symbols used in the rites. Chapter 6 examines the *He* instruments in terms of the world they embody, in terms of their role as mediators parallel to that of shamans, in terms of their correlation with the structure of the longhouse group and of society at large and in terms of the way they are used during the rites. The *He* represent the body of the first ancestor who comes to adopt the initiates as his sons. It is through this process that macro- and microstructure are made coterminous, thus ensuring the continuity of society along principles established in the mythic past. The *He* instruments, as predominantly masculine symbols, are thus concerned with continuity and immortality.

Chapter 7 examines the symbolism of a gourd of beeswax that is used in the rites. This gourd, never before mentioned in relation to the Yurupary cult, is shown to be crucial for its understanding and of equal importance to that of the Yurupary instruments to which, as a predominantly female symbol, it stands in a complementary relation. Although women are excluded from the rites, the female element is represented by this symbol. In particular, this gourd is connected with female powers of reproduction which men lost when they took back the Yurupary instruments stolen by the women in the mythic past. Female reproduction, dependent upon periodicity and bodily openness, is reintroduced into male society in symbolic form during the rites. This clarifies the periodic nature of *He* rites and the presence of female symbols in an exclusive men's cult. Menstruation is shown to be associated with a change of skin; the power to change skins is contained within the wax gourd and is in turn related to the theme of rebirth and immortality. It is the combination of the *He* instruments with the gourd of wax that underlies much of the significance of *He* rites. This combination expresses simultaneously the make-up of the human body, sexual reproduction, the interdependence of men and women in productive activities, the complementary relation between the seasons and the creation and structure of the cosmos itself.

Introduction

In chapter 8, the symbolism of hair, whipping and tobacco is examined in relation to the themes of open and closed body orifices, death and rebirth by swallowing and regurgitation, destruction and creation as associated with the two sexes and growth and aggression. Also, fire and water are shown to be in a complementary relation, expressed in terms of the two sexes and of the *He* instruments and gourd of wax that represent them. In chapter 9, the spatio-temporal structuring of the rites is related to that of myth to display the theme of symbolic death and rebirth. It is argued that the rites imply that whereas women create children, it is men who create adult men and the society they represent. This power of creation is in turn related to the forest fruits that are used in the rites. Finally, in chapter 10, it is argued that during the rites, the sun and moon, the ultimate representatives of the *He* state from which all life derives, are brought, in symbolic form, into the house. This is in turn related to Lévi-Strauss's arguments concerning bull-roarers and the 'instruments of darkness', and the 'rotten and burned worlds', a predominant theme of the first two volumes of his analysis of Amerindian mythology (1970, 1973).

Myth and ritual

In his comparative study of Amerindian mythology, Lévi-Strauss does not attempt a systematic analysis of myths from the Vaupés region. With reference to the myth of origin of the cult of Yurupary, he writes:

Many variants of this myth are on record . . . I do not propose to examine them in detail, since they seem to belong to a different mythological *genre* from that of the more popular tales — comparatively homogenous in tone and inspiration — that I am bringing together here to provide the subject-matter for my investigation. It would seem that some early inquirers in the Amazon basin, prominent among whom were Barbosa Rodrigues, Amorim and Stradelli, were still able to find esoteric texts belonging to a learned tradition, and comparable in this connection to those discovered more recently by Nimuendaju and Cadogan among the southern Guarani. Unfortunately, we have little or no knowledge of the old native communities which once lived along the middle and lower Amazon. The laconic evidence supplied by Orellana, who sailed down the river as far as the estuary in 1541–2, and still more so the existence of oral traditions, whose extreme complexity, artificial composition and mystical tone suggest that they must be attributed to schools of sages and learned men, argue in favour of a much higher level of religious, social and political organisation than anything that has been observed since. The study of these previous documents, which are the remnants of a genuine civilization common to the whole of the Amazon basin, would require a volume in itself and would involve the use of special methods in which philology and archaeology . . . would have to play a part. Such a study may one day be possible (1973 : 271–2)

In carrying out field research amongst the Barasana, we had two principal objectives in mind. The first was to make a general ethnographic study of a still relatively unacculturated Tukanoan-speaking Indian population. Our second objective was to examine some of Lévi-Strauss's ideas on mythology, especially on South American Indian mythology, in the light of a detailed body of ethnographic data, including a corpus of myths, collected with this in mind. Many of the ethnographic sources on which Lévi-Strauss's studies of myth are based are fragmentary and sometimes misleading and most of them pre-date his general theories concerning myth and totemic thought. Our aim was to collect data with this kind of analysis in mind, but to refrain from actually reading *Mythologiques* until both our field research and the preliminary stages of our analysis were complete.[2] In addition to the more usual topics of ethnographic enquiry, we therefore paid particular attention to knowledge about the natural world, animals, plants, stars and seasons, and to the kind of 'implicit mythology' that is revealed in such things as hunting, fishing, gardening and food preparation, eating arrangements and manufacturing processes, as well as in ritual and ceremony.

This book represents the first statement of the results of this research. Focussing as it does upon ritual and explicit or narrative myth, it is complemented by my wife's book (C. Hugh-Jones 1979), which focusses upon the 'implicit myth' mentioned above. My aim in this book has not been to analyse Barasana myth itself, but to use myth along with other kinds of data to elucidate the organisational features and symbolism of ritual. My approach to both myth and ritual is essentially structuralist. In my analysis I have drawn both upon Lévi-Strauss's method of analysis as applied to myth, and also upon some of his findings with regard to Amerindian mythology. Reciprocally I have tried to indicate, in the text and in notes, where my findings

2 We did, however, use Lévi-Strauss's *Mythologiques* as a compendium of myths which we read to the Barasana for their amusement. In so doing, we not only obtained a number of Barasana myths, given as the correct versions of myths that other societies 'did not know properly', but also gained many insights into the way the Barasana themselves think about their myths.

14

with regard to Barasana myth and ritual symbolism are in accord with those of Lévi-Strauss for other parts of lowland South America. Without first conducting a detailed analysis of Barasana myth, it would be premature to offer anything more than some tentative remarks upon the applicability of Lévi-Strauss's methods and conclusions to my data from the Barasana. My agreements and reservations will become clear in the pages that follow. In general terms, and in spite of Lévi-Strauss's reservations concerning Yurupary myths quoted above, it does appear that myths from the Vaupés region are by and large close variants or transformations of those that form the subject of Lévi-Strauss's enquiry. The story of Manioc-stick Anaconda (M.6.A), to give but one example, contains within one myth many of the themes that form the backbone of the first two and a half volumes of *Mythologiques*. I find in particular, that his arguments concerning the 'instruments of darkness' (see especially Lévi-Strauss 1973 : 359–475) appear to be confirmed empirically by my data from the Barasana.

Where I differ most strongly from Lévi-Strauss lies in the area of cross-cultural comparison. Lévi-Strauss is concerned to outline the syntax of South American mythology as a whole (1970 : 7–8): he is concerned less with what myths mean than with how they convey this meaning. His argument is that whilst different myths serve different purposes and have different meanings in particular social and cultural contexts, their internal organisation is subject to laws that have universal validity, at least within the area from which the myths he studies derive. I am concerned rather to examine myths within a single socio-cultural context and to elucidate their meanings within it. I am therefore concerned as much with what myths mean as with how they mean it. I shall try to show that, to a considerable extent, Barasana myths can only be understood when they are systematically related to ritual and that it is in the context of ritual that their potential meaning is made actual. Reciprocally, I shall show that many features of Barasana ritual can only be understood in relation to myth.

Lévi-Strauss has proposed three rules for the interpretation of myth which I quote:

1. A myth must never be interpreted on one level only. No privileged explanation exists, for any myth consists in an *inter-relation* of several explanatory levels.

15

2. A myth must never be interpreted individually, but in its relationship to other myths which, taken together, constitute a transformation group.

3. A group of myths must never be interpreted alone, but by reference: (a) to other groups of myths; and (b) to the ethnography of the societies in which they originate. For, if the myths transform each other, a relation of the same type links (on a transversal axis) the different levels involved in the evolution of all social life. These levels range from the forms of techno-economic activity to the systems of representations, and include economic exchanges, political and familial structures, aesthetic expression, ritual practices, and religious beliefs. (1977 : 65)

Throughout this book, I try to apply these rules to the interpretation of myth, but I shall try also to extend them to the interpretation of ritual. I shall show that when considering a myth given as explanation for a ritual, this myth must be considered in relation to other myths that are neither given as explanations nor make any explicit reference to the rite concerned. I shall show that there is no single level at which Barasana Yurupary rites can be interpreted but that the different levels of interpretation can be systematically interrelated. I shall show that Barasana initiation rites must be considered in relation to one another and in relation to other rites. Finally, I shall show that neither myth nor rite can be fully understood unless each is considered within the total ethnographic context from which it derives.

But having said this, it becomes clear that this book is in some ways but the groundwork and preliminary outline of a much more ambitious project. A proper analysis of Yurupary myths alone would indeed require a volume to itself; having analysed Yurupary rites as a process of initiation, the analysis could then be extended to include other rites of passage, notably those of birth and death; and having done this, and in view of the striking similarities between the Yurupary cult and other secret men's cults and their associated mythology from elsewhere in Amazonia, a comparative study might one day be possible.

Finally, a word or two should be said about the circumstances under which these Yurupary rites were observed. As will be explained below, there are two different kinds of Yurupary rite amongst the Barasana. The first kind, Fruit House (*He rika sõria wi*), is held relatively often and I was able to observe a total of nine over a twenty-two-month period. At some, I devoted my time to writing

notes and making tape-recordings; at others, I endeavoured to observe them from the inside by dancing with the dancers, playing the
He instruments, chanting with the chanters and drinking hallucinogenic
drugs. The second kind of rite, *He* House (*He wi*), is held very in-
frequently, perhaps once in two or three years in some of the larger
longhouse communities. I was therefore extremely fortunate to see
it at all. I was allowed to participate on condition that I did *not*
play the role of the note-taking anthropologist and that I underwent
initiation in the mixed status of young man, elder and guest and
observed all the relevant prohibitions on diet and behaviour. My
wife remained secluded in the rear of the house together with the
other women who assisted her in taking notes. Her presence was
invaluable to me both for the data that she was able to record and
for the insights she brought into the role of women in this exclusive
men's cult.

2

The Barasana: land and people

The Barasana, numbering perhaps some three hundred individuals, are one of several small Tukanoan sub-groups who live in the area drained by the Pirá-paraná river in the Vaupés region of Colombia; other groups represented are the Bará, Karapana, Makuna, Taiwano, Tatuyo, Tuyuka and the Arawakan Kabiyerí. The river Pirá-paraná lies between 70 and 71 degrees W. and between one-half and one degree N. This area lies just inside the Colombian frontier with Brazil and forms the southern section of the Comisaría del Vaupés. Geologically, the area forms the southernmost extension of the Guiana shield and is known as the Vaupés Swell (Moser and Tayler 1963 : 440). The river Vaupés, rising to the south of the town of San José de Guaviare, flows east into Brazil crossing the frontier at Jauareté and entering the Río Negro above the town of Uaupés (São Gabriel); it lends its name, Vaupés in Colombia, Uaupés in Brazil, to the region that it bisects (see map 1). This region is one of flat river valleys and rolling uplands interspersed with isolated hills, outcrops of rock and low, flat-topped mountains with sheer sides. Most of the Pirá-paraná area lies between 600 and 700 feet above sea level, but hills of 1000 feet are not uncommon and the chain of mountains that divides the Pirá-paraná from the Cananarí rises in parts up to 2000 feet.

The vegetation of the area is characterised by tropical rain-forest with occasional stands of mirití palms (*Mauritia flexuosa*) and areas of savannah with xerophytic vegetation. The average annual rainfall is around 3500 mm but is subject to great variation both from year to year and from place to place (Instituto Geografico Agustín Codazzi 1969 : 67). There are four major seasons: a long dry period between December and March, a long wet season between March and August, a short dry season between August and September and a short period

18

of rains between September and December. The temperature usually varies between 20°C and 35°C, but may drop as low as 10°C during the *aru* or *friagem*, a cold period accompanied by fine drizzle that occurs around mid-June.

The river Pirá-paraná runs off the watershed that divides the river system of the Vaupés from that of the Apaporís–Caquetá. Its head-waters lie close to those of the Papurí, one of the major southern tributaries of the Vaupés, and the sources of two of its major affluents, Caño Colorado and Caño Lobo, lie close to the headwaters of the Tiquié, itself the major southern tributary of the Vaupés (see maps 2 and 3). The precise hydrological features of the Pirá-paraná have had, and continue to have, an important influence on the Indian groups that live in the area. As the only effective link, other than that of the Amazon river itself, between the river systems of the Vaupés– Río Negro on the one hand and the Apaporís–Caquetá–Japurá on the other, it is an important route of communication. In relation to this, it is significant that the Arawakan Yukuna of the river Mirití-paraná, an affluent of the Apaporís, share a number of cultural features, notably in the area of mythology and ritual practice, in common with the Indians of the Pirá-paraná drainage (Jacopin : personal communication). Some of these features are common to all the Indians of the Vaupés region and suggest Tukanoan influence spreading from the north and east; others, like the masked dances associated with pupunha palm (*Gulielma gasipaes*) fruit are found only amongst the southernmost Tukanoan groups (Makuna, Tani-muka, Letuama) of the lower Pirá-paraná and Apaporís, and suggest Arawakan influence from the south. In certain respects, the Indians of the Pirá-paraná and Apaporís, the only Eastern Tukanoan-speakers not living within the area of the Vaupés river drainage, are marginal to the main bloc of Tukanoan culture and display certain features transitional between Tukanoan and Arawakan culture.[1]

The strategic location of the Pirá-paraná has also had an important influence on the nature and extent of Indian contact with white people. On the one hand, as an important communication route

1 This is most true of the groups furthest to the south, but without more data than is at present available for the Tukanoan-speakers as a whole, the significance and magnitude of the cultural differences between different Tukanoan groups are difficult to estimate. The Cubeo, the northernmost Tukanoan-speakers, also have certain cultural features that appear to be atypical of the main bloc of Tukano culture. This may well be related to their marginal geographic location and to their relative proximity to the Arawakan Baniwa to the north and east. From the rather sparse ethnographic descriptions, it is clear that the Baniwa share many cultural features with the Tukanoans.

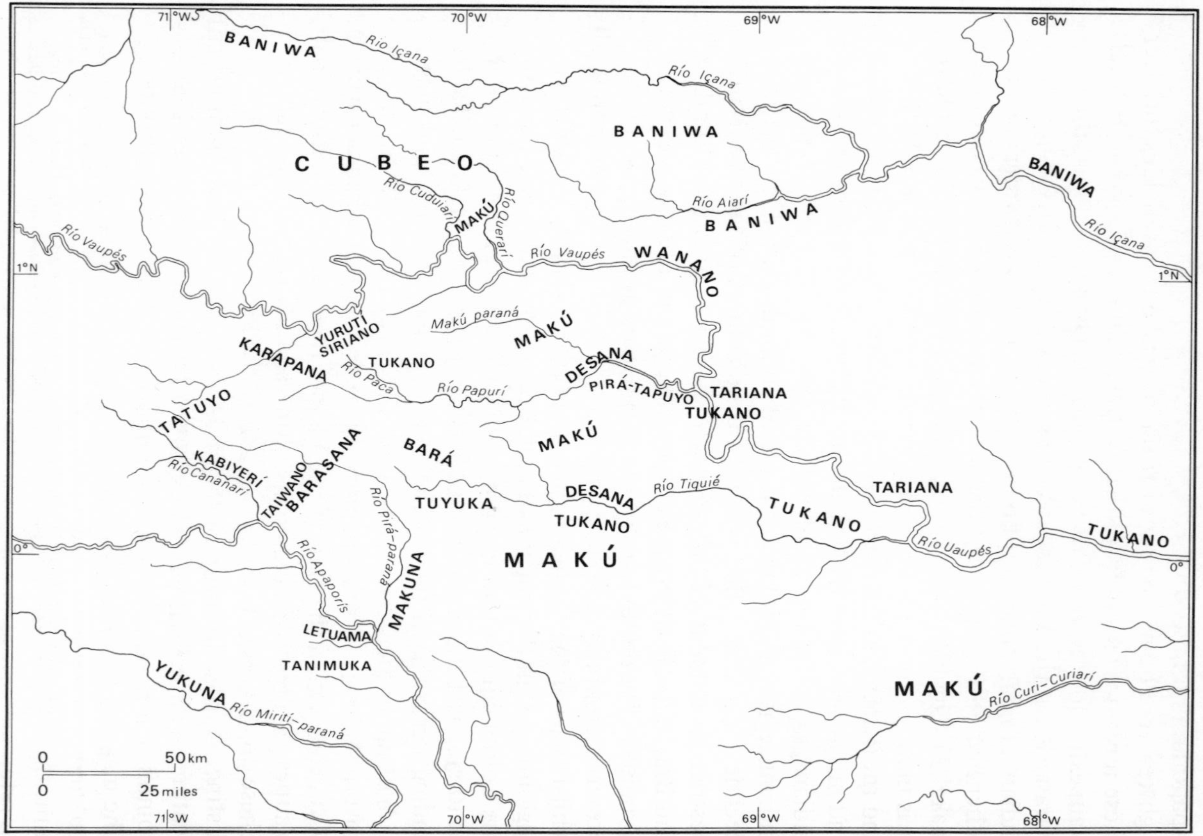

Map 2 The Vaupés region showing distribution of major Indian groups

between two major river systems, it has been an avenue of white exploration and penetration into the area. It is first mentioned, as a
route connecting the Vaupés with the Caqueta—Japurá via the
Apaporís, in reports of exploration from the latter half of the
eighteenth century (Brüzzi da Silva 1962 : 22). Also mentioned in
these reports is an Indian tribe called Panenua, living on the 'upper
Vaupés': the Panenua are probably identifiable with the contemporary
Barasana, known as Panenua or Pareroa in Tukano, the dominant
Indian language used as a lingua franca in the Vaupés region. On the
other hand, the Pirá-paraná is blocked by numerous rapids and falls that
make travel hazardous and dangerous even for the Indians themselves.
It is marginal to the Vaupés, the main avenue of white penetration,
and therefore has remained relatively isolated from the commercial
and missionary activity that has so radically altered the traditional
Indian culture of the main Vaupés region. Although the Pirá-paraná
Indians have suffered from the forced labour, disease and population
decline associated with the extraction of natural rubber and from the
destructive effects of missionaries operating from both Colombia
and Brazil, their relative isolation combined, in the past, with a
ferocious reputation, has meant that they alone have managed to
preserve the greater part of their traditional culture. Furthermore,
whilst the Protestant and Catholic mission posts in the Pirá-paraná
region were only established in the late 1960s, those in the rest of
the Colombian Vaupés were established around the beginning of the
century, and some in the Brazilian Vaupés date back as far as 1850
and beyond.

  With the exception of rubber gatherers, traders, missionaries and
government personnel, the majority of whom are concentrated in
Mitu, the administrative centre and capital of the Comisaría del
Vaupés, the inhabitants of the Colombian Vaupés are all Indians.
These people speak a variety of languages belonging to at least three
distinct language families, and one of the most striking cultural
features of the Vaupés area is that of extreme linguistic diversity
combined with widespread multilingualism (see Sorensen 1967).
The majority of these languages or dialects belong to the Eastern
Tukanoan family, named after one particular linguistic and social
unit, the Tukano; the name Tukano is also used in a loose fashion
to refer collectively to all the different Tukanoan-speaking groups in
the area. Arawakan languages are spoken by the various Baniwa
groups living in the area of the Guainía and Içana to the north of

the Vaupés, by the Tariana around the area of Jauareté, by the
Kabiyerí living between the Pirá-paraná and the Cananarí and by
the Yukuna along the Mirití-paraná to the south. The Carib language
family is represented by a remnant population of Karihona on the
upper Vaupés, and the semi-nomadic Makú speak at least two
languages or dialects, as yet of uncertain affiliation, which bear no
close relationship to any of the other languages spoken in the area.

Besides speaking languages or dialects of a common family, the
Tukanoan Indians of the Vaupés share a large number of basic cultural
features in common. This is true of fundamental patterns of subsistence: extensive cultivation of bitter manioc combined with
hunting, fishing and gathering; of traditional habitation and settlement
patterns: large communal longhouses built near the rivers and separated by one or more hours of travel; of kinship and social structure:
Dravidian kinship terminology combined with bilateral cross-cousin
marriage between groups of hierarchically ordered patrilineal sibs; and
of shared patterns of ritual organisation and a common mythological
tradition. At the same time, within this common cultural framework,
the Tukanoans are divided into a large number of discrete groups
differentiated by territorial location, language, rules of exogamy,
traditions of origin, versions and interpretations of myth, ecological
adaptation, etc. This has led to two diverging tendencies in the ethnographic literature: one, most apparent in Brüzzi da Silva (1962),
to emphasise the unity and similarity of the different groups; the
other, to lay stress on their diversity and specialisation (see Reichel-
Dolmatoff 1971). An extended discussion of the social structure of
the Vaupés region as a whole, in terms of the relationship between
language groups on the one hand, and social and ethnic groups on
the other, is beyond the scope of this book and would also, I believe,
require more complete data than is at present available.[2] But I shall
attempt to summarise some of the more salient points in order to
place the Barasana in a wider context.

In previous ethnographic accounts of the Indians of the Vaupés
region, the concept of 'tribe' has been used in at least three distinct

---

2 To date, the only attempts to discuss the social structure of the Tukanoans as a whole
are those of Brüzzi da Silva (1962, 1966) and Fulop (1955). On a more limited scale,
Jean Jackson has discussed the relation between social structure, language-group
affiliation and exogamy, with particular reference to the Bará of the Papurí region
(Jackson 1972, 1974, 1976). Christine Hugh-Jones discusses this same topic in relation
to the Indian groups of the Pirá-paraná area (1979). My own account is intended as no
more than a brief sketch.

ways: (1) to refer collectively to all Tukanoan-speakers, the 'Tukano tribe', that live in the area. Used in this sense, the term 'tribe' refers to a large group of people who share a common cultural tradition, who speak a number of related languages or dialects and who live in a more or less continuous geographic area. Used in this way, the term does not imply political unity under a single headman or chief and, perhaps unfortunately, it emphasises a common culture rather than the structural features that unite the Vaupés Indians, including non-Tukanoan-speakers, into an open-ended social system bound together by relations of marriage, economic exchange, reciprocal ritual interaction, etc. (2) With particular reference to the Cubeo, to refer to a largely, but not exclusively endogamous unit made up of three intermarrying sub-groups who claim common ancestry and who speak a single, common language (Goldman 1963). As will be seen below, the Cubeo are atypical of Tukanoan-speakers in their emphasis on linguistic endogamy rather than linguistic exogamy. (3) To refer to an exogamous patrilineal descent group, internally sub-divided into a number of hierarchically ranked patrilineal sibs whose members speak a common language or dialect (see e.g. Reichel-Dolmatoff 1971). The Desana, Tukano, Bará, Pirá-Tapuyo, Wanano, Karapana, Tuyuka, Tatuyo, Taiwano, etc. are all 'tribes' in this sense. Whether or not they did so prior to the influx of white people into the Vaupés, today none of these 'tribes' occupies a continuous stretch of territory although, in most cases, they are concentrated in one or more specific areas.

Amongst the Tukanoan Indians, with the exception of the Cubeo, there is an ideal that the boundaries of exogamous descent groups and those of language or dialect units are coterminous and to a considerable extent this is true in practice. For this reason, both Indians and ethnographers make use of language as a criterion for defining units of social structure. The ideal coincidence of language unit and exogamous group boundaries leads the Indians to use language as a way of talking about descent. Group membership is often indicated by saying that an individual 'says . . . ' and repeating a stock phrase in the language concerned. Sometimes, as for example amongst the Barasana and Taiwano, Indians will state that the languages of two intermarrying groups are entirely different whilst an outside observer can only detect minute dialectical variation and Indians will often claim that even the different sibs of one exogamous language unit speak in different ways. For similar reasons, ethno-

23

graphers frequently divide Tukanoan Indians into 'tribes' based on both language and descent-group criteria.

However, there are important exceptions to the ideal that units of language are also exogamous descent groups. As mentioned above, the Cubeo 'tribe' consists of three intermarrying sub-groups who share a common language. The Barasana and Taiwano, who share a common language and intermarry with other language units, also intermarry amongst themselves as distinct patrilineal descent groups. The Makuna, who share a common language (Makuna), are made up of one exogamic descent group intermarried with a segment of another that includes all the Barasana. Thus, by the criterion of language alone, the Makuna form a single 'tribe'. But the term Makuna may also be applied exclusively to the first-mentioned exogamic descent group who share their language with some Barasana. The Makuna in this latter sense marry both Barasana who speak Barasana and Barasana who speak Makuna. Finally, as mentioned below, the maximal exogamous descent group, or phratry, generally includes at least two distinct language groups. For these reasons, I do not consider the 'tribe' to be a useful concept in discussing Tukanoan social structure, nor do I consider that language alone is a useful criterion for the definition of the units of social structure. By concentrating on descent and exogamy rather than on language, the similarities and common structural features of all Tukanoan groups can be emphasised, rather than the differences between them. In this book, where the evidence makes it possible. I attempt to show these similarities at the level of ritual and myth.

In the Pirá-paraná region, the most inclusive social units that can be identified embrace the members of two or more language-bearing descent groups. These un-named phratries are defined partly in terms of exogamy, their members considering each other to be like brothers who should not intermarry, and partly in terms of common descent and origin from either the same anaconda ancestor or from two or more such ancestors who can be identified together. One such group includes the Bará, the Arawakan Kabiyerí, and those members of the Makuna 'tribe' who are not Barasana (see above). The anaconda ancestor of the Bará, Fish Anaconda, is said to be the same as Water Anaconda, the ancestor of the Makuna. In theory, the Bará and Makuna should not intermarry, but in practice a few marriages do take place between them. The component sub-groups of a phratry are identifiable by name, by a tradition of common ancestry, by strict rules of exogamy and in most cases by the possession of a common language.

The Barasana, as a patrilineal descent group, are internally sub-divided into a number of hierarchically ranked, named sibs. During our fieldwork, we were based in a longhouse or maloca of the *Meni Masa* sib, situated on Caño Colorado, an affluent of the middle Pirá-paraná (see map 3 below). When I refer to the 'Barasana' in this book, I refer in particular to this sib. The *Meni Masa* see themselves as one of an un-named group of five sibs, ranked according to a model of five male siblings. Terms used between siblings are never reciprocal as one is always older or younger than the other and the terms imply relative age. Likewise, relationships between patrilineal sibs are phrased in terms of relative seniority. The *Meni Masa* come in the middle of the group of five sibs; those above are referred to as 'our elder brothers' and those below as 'our younger brothers'. The five sibs, in decreasing order of seniority, are called *Koamona, Rasegana, Meni Masa, Daria* and *Wabea*. Each sib is in turn associated with a specialist ritual role: the *Koamona* are chiefs (*uhara*), the *Rasegana* are dancers and chanters (*bayaroa, keti masa*), the *Meni Masa* are warriors (*guamarã*), the *Daria* are shamans (*kumua*) and the *Wabea* are cigar lighters (*muno yori masa*) and are likened to the Makú who in other parts of the Vaupés region act as servants to riverine Tukanoan groups.[3] According to one informant, three generations ago the sibs listed above all lived together in one place but each in their own separate maloca. At that time there was actual specialisation during rituals so that, for example, only the *Rasegana* danced and chanted and only the *Daria* acted as shamans. Whether this is true or not I cannot say, but it is true that early travellers in the Vaupés region saw both conglomerations of malocas and also huge malocas containing upwards of seventy-five people. There is also good evidence that chiefs were of greater importance in the last century than they are now. But today this ritual specialisation is largely a matter of ideology and, as will be shown later, is only apparent, in disguised form, during major rituals.

Beyond this group of five, the *Meni Masa* recognise many other

---

3 The Makú are semi-nomadic hunter—gatherers living in the interfluvial areas of the Vaupés. They maintain a symbiotic relationship with the sedentary Tukanoan groups of the region, exchanging meat and other forest produce for tobacco, manioc products and merchandise of white origin. The sedentary agriculturalists view the Makú as their servants. For more details, see Silverwood-Cope (1972) and Jackson (1973). There are no Makú living in the Pirá-paraná area.

sibs related to them as elder or younger brothers and all of them are considered to be the common descendants of *Yeba Meni* Anaconda. These other sibs are also said to be arranged into ranked sets of five, each with its specialist role, though the *Meni Masa* are often unsure of the details of ranking and of role specialisation; one such set speaks the Makuna language, the rest all speak Barasana. In theory, these sets of sibs are also ranked in order of seniority as elder and younger brothers; in practice, whilst there is little disagreement as to ranking within a set, ranking between sets is open to dispute and sections of origin myths are cited and interpreted to provide evidence that a particular sib or group of sibs claiming senior status over another are, in fact, junior to them. To some extent, both the divisions of sibs into sets and their relative internal ranking is correlated with spatial distribution. The Barasana as a whole occupy a more or less continuous area of territory, surrounded on all sides by affinal groups. Within this territory, different sets of sibs are distributed in different areas and top-ranking sibs live, or should live, at river mouths whilst lower-ranking sibs are ideally arranged in descending order towards the headwaters. Today, the spatial distribution of sibs only very imperfectly reflects their hierarchical order, though this may in part be due to the disruptive effects of contact with white people. Though the internal division of language-bearing descent groups into hierarchically ranked sibs appears to be a feature common to all Tukanoan-speakers of the Vaupés, the division of these sibs into groups of five with specialist ritual occupations has not previously been reported in the ethnographic literature.

Local groups live in malocas or longhouses, each one generally separated from its neighbours by two or more hours of travel by canoe or trail. Prior to the effects of contact with white people, there were no villages in the Vaupés region and there are still none in the Pirá-paraná area. Ideally, all the members of one sib should live together in one maloca and there is some evidence that they did so in the past. Today, sib members are usually dispersed in a number of different malocas situated within the same general area. The household generally consists of a group of brothers or close patrilateral parallel cousins reckoned as brothers, sometimes with one or more of their parents, together with their children and in-married wives. Local groups vary in size from single nuclear families living alone, to large malocas containing upwards of thirty individuals. Residence after marriage is virilocal so that wives come in from other malocas and

daughters move out to them. The Barasana (*Meni Masa*) intermarry
with their neighbours, the Bará and Tatuyo; other Barasana sibs intermarry with the Taiwano, Kabiyerí and Makuna as well. In any particular longhouse, the men and their unmarried sisters will all speak
a common language whilst their wives may speak up to three other
languages. Children grow up to speak the language of their father
and though they will understand several languages, they will normally
only use their father's language in conversation.

The Barasana have a prescriptive marriage rule. They have a
Dravidian-type kinship terminology and would express their marriage
rule by saying that a man must marry a woman of the category
tenyo, a category that includes bilateral cross-cousins but covers
all women of the same genealogical level as ego who belong to
different exogamic groups. Within this category, preference is expressed for the exchange of true sisters and for marriage with the
true father's sister's daughter (*mekaho mako*).[4] The Barasana deny
that the ranked sibs of one group should intermarry with sibs of
equivalent rank in other groups, and an examination of actual marriage patterns shows no evidence that this happens. In the arrangement of marriage, each maloca community acts as a more or less
independent unit. Most marriages take place between malocas
separated by less than half a day's travel from one another; marriages between more distant communities are sometimes accomplished
by the forcible abduction of women. Marriages are relatively unstable,
especially prior to the birth of children, and it is common for a man
to have had a succession of two or more wives in his lifetime. Polygyny
occurs but is not widespread; many instances of apparent polygyny
in fact represent a transitional stage between two marriages. Men
who have stable unions with more than one wife are often also
maloca headmen or powerful shamans.

The maloca is always located near running water, usually with a
river running near the front of the house and a small stream behind.
The river is used for bathing, fishing and as a means of communication;
travel by canoe is often preferred to walking in the forest. The largest
houses are impressive structures, sometimes 80 feet long and 40
feet wide, with tent-like gabled roofs coming almost to the ground
on each side (see plate 1). The very large houses, called dance houses
(*basaria wi*), used to hold communal rituals or dances, serve as
ceremonial centres for other smaller houses nearby.

4 Barasana kinship and marriage is fully discussed by Christine Hugh-Jones (1979).

The maloca has two doors, one at each end. The door at the front is used by the men whilst that at the rear is used by the women and children. The rear of the house, which may be either rectangular or semi-circular, is used as a kitchen area where manioc is processed and made into cassava bread. This area is very much the domain of women. Around the sides of the house, towards the rear, there are screened-off compartments for each nuclear family. The front end of the house, associated with men and with public, social life, has no compartments and it is along the side walls at the front that visitors sleep and cook their food. These side areas are also used by men to toast coca leaves and to prepare tobacco. During the daytime, the men often sit just inside the front door, talking and making baskets and other handicrafts. At night, the men sit together in the centre of the house smoking large cigars, chewing coca and talking quietly. During the day, this central space is not used except for the eating of communal meals. The middle of the house is used most as an area for dancing and for other ritual activities.

Houses usually last for about eight to ten years after which they are abandoned. The Barasana prefer to build a new house rather than rebuild an old one. Houses are also abandoned after the death of an important person, very often with the new house being built a few hundred yards from the old one. The house is surrounded by an area of cleared sandy earth called the *maka* — I shall refer to this area as the plaza (see fig. 1). This area is kept clean and is weeded frequently as its state reflects upon the prestige of the community. The edge of the plaza is usually planted with fruit trees, most typically with pupunha palms. The importance of these fruit trees is one reason why new houses are so often built close to old house sites.

The plaza is in turn surrounded by an area of manioc gardens and there are generally other manioc gardens further away in the surrounding forest. In order to make these gardens, the men fell and clear the forest at the beginning of the dry season; the dead trees are burned off whenever there has been an extended period of sunshine to dry out the vegetation. No secondary clearing is attempted after burning; instead it is carried out piecemeal throughout the year. After felling and burning the forest, the men take no further part in the cultivation of food crops with the exception of maize which they both plant and harvest. The main food crop is bitter manioc, but this is supplemented by bananas, plantains, yams, sweet potatoes, pineapples, sugar cane and a variety of other plants. The

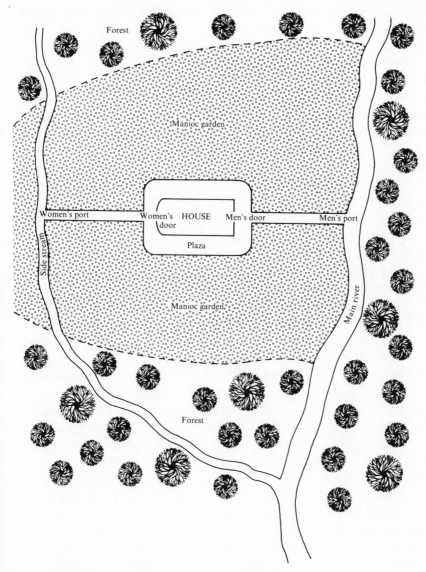

Fig. 1 The longhouse setting

manioc gardens are essentially the domain of the women but the men
plant coca, tobacco, fish-poisons and yagé (*Banisteriopsis* sp.) and make
almost daily visits to pick coca leaves. As a cultivation site for manioc,
the garden is abandoned after about three years, but fruit, drugs, fish-

29

poisons and a number of other crops are harvested for many years afterwards.

Most of an adult woman's time is spent in the cultivation of manioc and in the preparation of cassava bread. Much of a man's time is taken up in hunting and fishing. Though meat is highly valued and hunting carries great prestige, the bulk of the protein supply comes from fishing. The Barasana are expert fishermen and employ a wide variety of fishing techniques. Fish, in one form or another, is eaten nearly every day. There is not a great abundance of game in the Pirá-paraná region (the Indians relate this to the introduction of shotguns which have now completely replaced the traditional bow and arrow) and the Barasana rarely devote much time and effort to tracking game. Woolly monkeys and peccary are the most esteemed game but most of the animals killed are rodents and birds. In addition to shotguns, blowpipes are used to kill arboreal game. Dogs are also kept for use in hunting but most of them are somewhat ineffective. When the Barasana complain of hunger, they generally refer to the absence of fish or meat and not to manioc products which are in more or less constant supply; on the other hand, they will never eat meat or fish without cassava bread or fariña.

Gathering in the forest is of great importance both as a means of obtaining food and also as a source of raw materials. A considerable portion of the diet comes from insects and much time is devoted to obtaining these and other gathered foods. Large amounts of forest fruits are eaten and these fruits are of considerable ritual significance as will be shown later. Alongside fish and meat, gathered foods are also important as items of ceremonial exchange. Among other functions, these exchanges serve to redistribute certain food species that have a very localised distribution in the region. Collecting is done by both sexes, but when large quantities are collected and brought back to the house, this is generally done by men.

Almost all food preparation is done by the women. Men will prepare game animals for cooking but women also do this. Food is generally smoked and/or boiled; the only foods that are roasted are insects and small fish. Men hardly ever boil food, but when large quantities of fish or meat are to be smoked, this is done by the men. Ideally, each adult woman is expected to produce fresh cassava bread each day. Meat and fish are cooked individually by different families but should be served communally to the longhouse as a whole. Failure to share food at communal meals gives rise to a considerable amount of friction, and the extent to which this is done provides a fairly clear index of social cohesion within the maloca group.

Internally, the maloca community is divided in a number of different ways. A major division is along the lines of sex. In daily life, men and women spend much of their time apart, carrying out different subsistence activities in different places, using different spatial areas within the maloca, coming in and going out through different doors, often eating at separate times and in different groups, sitting in two conversational groups at night, etc. This division becomes even more strongly marked at dances, and especially when the *He* instruments are used, and women are totally excluded from a part or all of the rites. The group of male siblings or close parallel cousins who form the core of the community are ranked according to their order of birth, a ranking that is to some extent reflected in the distribution of family compartments along the walls of the house. Ideally, the eldest brother, who should marry first and be the headman, lives in a compartment nearest to the back of the house; his younger brothers live in compartments extending forwards towards the front and arranged in order of birth and marriage. The community is thus also divided into its component nuclear families, the primary units of economic production, a new unit being set up on the marriage of each young man.

The men are also divided into the age-grades of elders (*bukurã*), married men with children, young men (*mamarã*), initiated but not yet married, and children (*rĩa masa*), uninitiated and still closely attached to their mothers. Again, these divisions are spatially expressed: the elders sleep in family compartments along with their wives and young children whilst the young, unmarried men sleep in the open part of the house, in the middle towards the men's door where visitors also sleep. The elder married men play a dominant role both within the community and in its relations with other local groups. It is they who arrange the marriages of their sons and daughters, who initiate the communal rituals discussed below, and who act as an informal council that directs the affairs of the group, the headman acting as their spokesman. The younger, unmarried men are often called upon to carry out the more menial and less pleasant tasks in such activities as house building, felling the forest to make gardens, coca processing, etc. As will be shown below, the division of male society into age-grades plays an important role in ritual organisation.

Very often, one or more of the adult men in a maloca group will be recognised as a specialist in some aspect of ritual. Some men are specialist dancers (*baya*) who have a large repertoire of dance-songs and who know well the complicated steps and movements associated with each dance. Others are specialist chanters (*yoamʉ*) who can recite in detail the traditions of origin of the group. These men act as leaders for the long sessions of chanting, involving all adult men, that form an integral part of communal rituals. Very often these two roles overlap so that specialist dancers are also chanters and vice versa. A third specialist ritual occupation relates to shamanism. Amongst the Barasana, there is no absolute difference between those men recognised as shamans and those who are not. At the lowest level, most adult men have some abilities as shamans and will carry out some of the same functions as those men who have a widespread reputation for their powers and knowledge. The most common function that shamans perform involves the treatment of food and other things by blowing spells. The breath is believed to be the manifestation and seat of the soul or spirit (*ʉsʉ*). By controlled breathing, accompanied by muttered spells, the shaman can direct the power of his spirit or soul towards a specific end. Blowing not only has curative and protective power, but also imparts life force and can change the state of being of a person or an object.[5]

All foods are ranked into a graded series of relative danger; at one end are such things as mother's milk, at the other certain large species of animal and fish which are most dangerous of all. After birth, each new category of food that a person eats must first be rendered safe by a shaman who blows spells over a sample which is then given to the subject to eat. By about eight or nine years, a young boy or girl will be able to eat all but the most dangerous categories. After initiation or first menstruation, the person must start again from the beginning of the series and it may take three or four years before they can eat all the foods of a normal adult diet. Birth, menstruation, snake bite, illness, death in the community, participation in communal rituals and a number of other factors will all render specific categories of individual subject to danger from specific categories of food which must be treated by a shaman prior

5 The Barasana have a verb *base-* that covers the activities of shamans in general. I have translated this as 'blow, blowing' as this action is a common feature of these activities. In many respects this closely parallels the Akawaio concept of *taling* discussed by Butt (1956).

to consumption. Most adult men know the requisite spells for the
treatment of the less dangerous foods, but only a few, the most
powerful and knowledgeable, are able to treat the most dangerous
categories. In similar fashion, most adult men know something about
the curing of minor ailments, but very few know how to cure serious
illness. There is a graded series of curing techniques and only the most
widely known shamans know all of them.

Shamans are thus ranked according to their knowledge and abilities.
Their powers are founded upon their knowledge of myths. Most
adult men know a considerable number of myths but shamans differ
from the rest in two respects: first, they know more myths, and
secondly, they know and understand the esoteric meaning behind
them. In the hands of the shamans, myths are not merely sacred
tales or stories, but things with inherent power, and it is upon these
myths that shamanic spells are based.

As a counterpart to their highly dispersed settlement pattern, the
Indians of the Pirá-paraná region do a great deal of reciprocal visiting
between longhouse communities. Much of this visiting is informal
and involves individuals or families visiting their kinsmen or affines
in other houses. Sometimes these visits last only a few hours, sometimes individuals may stay in another house for a month or more. In
addition to this casual visiting, there are frequent occasions on which
individuals in one house formally invite the members of one or more
other houses to come and dance and to drink manioc beer. The scale of
these gatherings varies, from small groups of ten to twenty adults,
to grand occasions on which up to sixty or seventy adults are assembled under one roof. These communal rituals are divided into a
number of named categories; collectively they are referred to as
basa, a word meaning both dance and song. I shall refer to them as
'dances'.

Basaria wi, house of dancing, describes an occasion on which one
household invites those from other houses to drink and dance. The
dancing usually begins in the late afternoon of one day and continues
till nightfall of the next. These dances correspond to the Cubeo
drinking parties (*unkundye*) described by Goldman (1963 : 202–18)
but unlike their Cubeo counterparts, Barasana drinking parties involve
not only patrilineally related kinsmen but members of affinal sibs
as well. Also, unlike Cubeo parties, they do not generally end in
fighting. A special form of these dances, called *nahŭ kutiria wi*,
house containing cassava bread, involves the preparation of huge

quantities of cassava bread which the hosts distribute to their guests at the end of the dance. This dance is described in chapter 4.

Dances at which food is ceremonially exchanged between long-house communities are called *bare ekaria wi*, house where food is given. The food exchanged is always forest produce of some kind. Usually it consists of smoked fish or meat, but sometimes caterpillars and pupae, ants, termites, beetle larvae, or pulped mirití or pupunha palm fruit are exchanged, always in large quantities. For these dances, the donors travel to the recipients' house, usually arriving in the late afternoon. They do not enter their hosts' house that night, but sleep in shelters constructed a little distance off. After dark, they dance on the plaza in front of the house and chant there with their hosts. In the morning, they enter the house, carrying in the food amidst a great amount of noise. The food is then ceremonially presented to the hosts and dancing begins. The dancing continues all day and all night, ending at dawn. Exchanges of food are mostly, but not always, between affinally related local groups. A dance of this kind, involving the Barasana sib *Kome Masa* has been described by Torres (1969 : 145–52).

The other two categories of dance, *He rika sõria wi*, house into which tree-fruit are taken, and *He wi*, *He ĩaria wi*, *He* house, house where *He* are seen, form the subject of this book and will be described in detail in chapters 3 and 4. For convenience, I refer to these two rites as 'Fruit House' and '*He* House'. Both are distinguished by the use of sacred flutes and trumpets called *He*. Finally, according to informants, the Barasana used to perform masked dances similar to those of the Cubeo, described by Goldman (1963). These dances were held after the death of important people and a number of the older men can remember the songs, dances and organisational features of these rites. During Cubeo mourning ceremonies, large trumpets are used. The Barasana class these trumpets as *He* but deny that they were used at their own mourning rites. According to them, the Cubeo, Siriano and Tariana who use these instruments are endo-cannibals and they add cryptically that the men of these groups menstruate.

Dances not involving the use of *He* instruments will form the subject of a future publication. In most respects, the details of their organisation are very similar. Each has the same overall pattern of being divided into two sections, called the small dance and the big dance, the big following the small. Each section consists of periods of dancing interspersed with periods during which the men consume tobacco, coca, manioc beer and yagé (a hallucinogenic drink) and chant myths in unison. The most obvious differences between these categories of dance relate to the dances, songs and musical instruments involved. At *basaria wi*, songs and dance-steps are drawn from one particular set and accompanied by bamboo tubes thumped on the ground, or by seed-shell rattles held in the hand; at *bare ekaria wi* songs from a different set are sung and danced, accompanied by painted thumping tubes made of balsa wood; and at *nahu kutiria wi*, other songs are sung, accompanied by painted cane whistles. At Fruit House rites there is no singing during the first section of the dance; instead, the sacred flutes and trumpets are played. During the second section, a special set of songs are sung, accompanied either by maracas or by solid wooden staves thumped on the ground. Finally, during *He* House, the only 'songs' are those of the spirit people, represented by the *He* instruments themselves.

In the absence of permanent villages, and with a population dispersed in isolated maloca communities of usually less than fifteen adults, the dances provide the only occasions on which large numbers of people gather together. In this sense, these rituals serve to create what might be called temporary villages in which the relations of the local group to a wider community are created and maintained. Throughout the year, but especially during the long dry season, the inhabitants of each maloca take part in a succession of dances in their own and neighbouring houses. Dances are held on a variety of pretexts: to celebrate the building of a new maloca, the end of the hard work involved in felling forest to make gardens, the exit from puberty seclusion of a young girl or the various stages of the initiation process for young boys which will be described below. A series of Fruit House rites mark the seasons of the different wild and cultivated fruits which lend their names to the major calendrical divisions of the Barasana year. Food exchanges are seen as both repayments for previous gifts and as creating further obligations to exchange; a successful fish-poisoning expedition or hunt, itself motivated by exchange obligations, will provide a further pretext for a dance.

Aside from their importance as religious rituals, these dances provide the context for trading, for the exchange of news and gossip, for meeting friends and lovers, and for making and renewing social contacts more generally. The people of one community will usually attend the dances of their immediate neighbours, in any direction,

rarely travelling for more than a day at the most. This means that
the wider community of each maloca group is defined largely by
geographical propinquity. Within this wider local community, affinal
relations are equally important to those with agnatic kin. Beyond the
sib, members of the same exogamic group tend to be considered as
outsiders and strangers, and the closest relations of all are between
neighbouring malocas linked by marriage ties over several generations.

The holding of dances has significant political implications both
within and between local groups. The headman of the maloca is
described as the *umato moari masu* which can be glossed as 'the man
who initiates work projects', and this is a fairly accurate description
of his role. He achieves this status initially by being the man who
successfully initiates the building of a new maloca which is then
known as his house. Its size, in part a function of the number of
workers and therefore of the future group, is thus also an index of
his prestige and following. Each adult man within the group will
act as host for a number of dances which add to his standing; usually,
it is the headman who most often acts as host. Similarly, the number
of dances held in a particular house, and the number of other households that attend them, can be taken as an index of the standing
of that local group as a whole and of its sphere of influence over
others. Both the act of inviting to a dance on the one hand, and the
acceptance of the invitation on the other, indicate that two local
groups are on amicable terms.

The role of the shaman is also of great importance in intercommunity relations. In any one area, there are usually one or two
shamans whose reputation for curing and for blowing surpasses that
of all the rest. These men, known as *kumu*, generally live in very
large and important houses where numerous dances are held, and
people from neighbouring houses will request their services for curing
and for the treatment of food. Frequently, these shamans are also the
headmen of the house in which they live and the community of their
clients is closely related to that of the people who attend dances in
the house. Beyond this community, these same shamans are often
feared and hated as dangerous men who send sickness and other forms
of mystical attack. The other major function of the shaman is to
officiate at communal rituals or dances; he must blow over tobacco,
coca, yagé, and other substances that the participants consume, and
it is he who serves yagé to the men, who makes the contact established
with the spirit world during these rites safe for the participants, and

who generally conducts and organises the rites. These various activities are discussed in greater detail in the chapters that follow. Communal rituals, and the contact with supernatural forces that they imply, are considered to be beneficial for the participants both in the general sense of maintaining the cosmic order and, more specifically, in conferring protection on the people involved. Indeed, they are considered to be necessary for the well-being of the group. Potentially, they are also dangerous to the people involved and it is the shaman's responsibility to see that they come to no harm. *He* House, as the most important and elaborate of all Barasana rituals, is the most beneficial of all; paradoxically it is also the most dangerous. Unlike the other dances, these rites are held only very occasionally and very few shamans have the ability to conduct them. They are also the supreme expression of the shaman's power and influence over the wider community, for during the rites, the participants place their lives in his hands.

In daily life, the hierarchical ranking of sibs, and their association with the specialised ritual occupations described above, are of almost no practical significance. Difference in sib rank does not imply difference in wealth, power or life-style and although specific individuals do take on the specialist occupations of shaman, chanter and dancer, their choice of occupation is in no way determined by sib affiliation and each sib is self-sufficient in these respects. Indeed, it would be surprising if rank and specialist occupation were of importance in everyday life for, as mentioned above, the regular social contacts of a local group rarely go beyond the sib and involve members of affinally related sibs as much as they do agnatically related kinsmen. Social dances (*basaria wi*), food-exchange dances (*bare ekaria wi*) and Fruit House rites (*He rika sõria wi*), tend to involve relations between affinally related local groups and this is reflected in their associated myths (see e.g. M.7.H, I). As will be shown below, *He* House is more closely bound up with the structure and values of the descent group. During this rite, the unity of the sib, sib ranking within the wider descent group and specialised sib occupations, all receive expression, not by whole social groups but by individual male participants in the rites who, together with the *He* instruments they play, stand in a metonymic relation to the society as a whole.

At one level, *He* House is a rite of initiation for young boys into the secret men's cult centred on the instruments used. But it is much more than this. It provides a model for all communal rites amongst the Barasana; the other Barasana rituals are all structured according to a common pattern. This pattern reproduces, in a simplified and attenuated form that of *He* House itself. As the main expression of a secret men's cult, focussed on the *He* instruments that women are forbidden to see on pain of death, it establishes and maintains a fundamental division between the sexes. This division implies the power and dominance of men over women and a measure of antagonism between the sexes which is expressed in myth. The division relates also to the position of women who marry into a patrilineally based sib as outsiders from affinal groups. The *He* instruments represent the sib and descent-group ancestors who adopt each new generation of young men. *He* House thus serves to integrate young men into the sib and also underlines the alien position of their mothers. But the division expresses also the complementarity between the sexes in production and reproduction. Though women are excluded from the rites, female attributes and values form a major element of the ritual symbolism. Barasana rituals, and *He* House in particular, have also an ordering and life-giving role. Regular contact with the world of spirits and ancestors, described and made manifest in myth, imparts new life and energy to society and ensures that the human world is attuned to a wider and more embracing cosmic order. *He* House is intimately bound up with this order: its timing, at the interface of the two major seasons, is based upon the movements of the constellations and on changes in the natural environment. As the most important rite, it forms the keystone to a ritual cycle that punctuates the year. These themes, and others, will be taken up and explored in the chapters that follow.

PART II

The rites described

Here, Barasana rituals involving the use of the sacred flutes and trumpets called *He* are described and an account is given of the various dances, shamanic acts, taboos and other activities that are associated with them. In order to present as full and accurate a picture as possible, whilst at the same time avoiding overburdening the text, the rites are described with a minimum of analysis and explanatory detail. Part III will be devoted to an extended explanation and analysis of these rites, drawing both on the material presented here and on the myths presented in part V.

There are two different kinds of *He* ritual amongst the Barasana, one much more extended and elaborate than the other. One kind, called Fruit House (*He rika sõria wi*), lasting no more than a day and a night, centres on tree-fruit which is ceremonially brought into the house to the sound of the *He* instruments. Many of these rites are held throughout the year, usually as ends in themselves, but sometimes forming a phase or stage in the drawn-out process of male initiation, and sometimes forming a preliminary stage of the main initiation rite. The different aspects of these rites are described in chapter 3. The other kind, called *He* House (*He wi*), is the main initiation rite. The rite itself lasts for three days and nights, but it is followed by a period of restrictions on diet and behaviour, brought to a close in an elaborate dance. In chapter 4, *He* House and subsequent events are described and then compared with Fruit House.

I have avoided making a large number of forward references to the analysis in part III. References of the kind 'see M.6.A.17' relate to the myths, divided into numbered passages, that are presented in part V. The two kinds of *He* ritual are presented synoptically in tables 2 and 3. These tables show the two rituals as a series of events happening through time in a manner analogous to a musical score; the events are divided up according to the categories of actors involved. When informants described these and other rites to me, they did so with reference to a division of the day into dawn, midday, dusk and midnight. It is immediately apparent from the tables that the major events of the rites cluster around these points. The shamans are responsible for the proper conduct and ordering of rituals; after many conversations with them, it became clear that it is through a mental picture similar to these tables (i.e. of a string of events following each other in time and involving different categories of participant) that they are able to organise the rites so that each event occurs at the proper time and in the proper order.

1 Barasana longhouse

2 Fruit House

3 Men wearing feather crowns

4. Men wearing full head-dresses

3

Fruit House

Fruit House

In the Pirá-paraná region, the most frequently held communal dance or ritual involves bringing large quantities of wild or cultivated tree-fruit (*He rika*) into the house to the sound of the *He* instruments.[1] Some authors have tried to link such rites with particular species of fruit. Although there are preferences for some fruits over others, in the Pirá-paraná area any edible tree-fruit that can be gathered in sufficient quantity may be used, and generally two or three species will be gathered for a particular rite. One of these species will predominate and will lend its name to the occasion, so that Indians might say, 'They are bringing in mirití (or umari, or ingá, etc.) at Manuele's today.'

The Barasana say that each household should greet the ripening of each important fruit with Fruit House. In practice, the number of these rites that each house puts on depends on many factors, such as the number of inhabitants, their sex ratio, the amount of manioc available for beer-making, the ambitions of the male inhabitants, etc., all of which are interdependent. The large and relatively prestigious Barasana house in which we worked held twelve communal rituals over a twenty-month period between March 1969 and November 1970.

---

1 Though I never saw one, I was often told about rituals at which, instead of fruit, animal food collected in the forest is ceremonially brought into the house. Ants, termites, palm-grubs, caterpillars and small fish obtained with poison were all mentioned in this context. These foods were always raw, in contrast to dances at which food is ceremonially given away, where the food is always cooked or processed in some other way.

During rites involving raw animal food, small tubular flutes, fitted with a plunger and played according to the 'key principle', are used. These flutes, called *rika bʉ* (arm/ fruit/appendage, hollow tube) are not considered to be 'real' *He* though women must not see them; they are thrown away after use. Peter Silverwood-Cope (personal communication) states that similar flutes, called *Bisiw*'s Spittle, are used by the Makú of the Makú-paraná during a ritual at which raw eels are brought into the house.

41

Of these, seven were Fruit House, one was *He* House, the main initiation rite, three were social dances, including the dance following initiation, and one was a ceremonial exchange of food. In addition to this, the household attended a large number of other rituals in neighbouring houses.

The decision to hold Fruit House, as with any other dance, may be taken by any adult man of the house; this man then becomes the chief host. He discusses his decision with the other men as they sit together at night, smoking and chewing coca. If there is a shaman in the house, he will be asked to officiate at the dance, otherwise a guest from another house must be asked to do this. Also, a lead dancer must be appointed, again either from amongst the men of the house or from their neighbours and guests. Sometimes the host himself will act as either shaman or lead dancer. The chief host is also responsible for seeing that enough manioc beer is provided. Normally his wife will use her own manioc for the beer though this is often supplemented with that belonging to the other women of the house. Sometimes manioc must be brought in from other houses. The chief host will ask his wife (or an unmarried sister) to prepare the beer for him, and she will in turn ask other women to help her.

A man's social standing, and that of his maloca community, are intimately linked with the scale and number of dances that he hosts. A man without either a wife or unmarried sister will be severely handicapped in this respect as it is difficult for him to persuade other women to prepare beer for him. Similarly, a man with a lazy or inefficient wife is also handicapped as she is unlikely to have sufficient manioc to make large amounts of beer. The men of highest social standing generally live in large, spacious houses and have hardworking and efficient wives who cultivate large amounts of manioc; such women acquire considerable prestige in their own right.

Table 1 shows the participation, by household, at the nine Fruit House rituals and the single *He* House ritual that I observed. Each rite was held either in Mandu's house, or in a neighbouring house at which members of Mandu's house were present as guests (see map 3). This table represents a large proportion of those rites in which members of Mandu's household were involved (over a two-year period). The names along the top of the table refer to the headmen of the households involved; the dates are those on which the rites were held. The average number of men present at these rites was twenty-one; the unusually large number of people attending the ritual

Table 1. Attendance at the He rites (longhouse of Mandu, Caño Colorado, April 1969 – June 1970)

Longhouse

	Mandu (A)	Pedro (B)	Arturo (B)	Christo (A)	Luis (C)	Ignacio (B)	Julio (A)	Manecio (B)	Misele (B)	Pacho (A)	Mario (A)	Ugo (A)	Domingo (A)	Hernando (D)	No. of men present
April 1969	++	H	++	++	++	+	++								32
June 1969	H	++	+	++										++	15
July 1969[a]	++	H	++	++	+			++							27
November 1969	++	H		++		+									18
March 1970	++	++		++	+			H	++						12
March 1970	++	++								H	++	++	++		40
April 1970	H	++	++												14
May 1970	H	++	++	++											18
May 1970[b]	H	++		++											15
June 1970[c]	H	++		++	++	+				++					24

H = Hosts
++ = all or most of men of house
+ = only a few men of house

A = Barasana
B = Bará
C = Tatuyo
D = Makuna

a Fruit House as first stage of initiation
b Fruit House as prelude to He House
c He House

43

on 29 March 1970 can in part be explained by the fact that it was held in a maloca close to the Catholic Mission, from which people either working or visiting were invited.

It can be seen from the table that there are always guests at these rites and furthermore that these guests may be of the same sib as the hosts, or of a different sib within the same exogamous group, or members of sibs of one or more different exogamous groups. Invitations to these rites go out to a household as a unit and on really grand occasions people from all the categories mentioned above will attend. Even at very limited affairs, because households are invited as units, there are generally present representatives of yet more households who have been staying in the houses of the guests.

By relating the spatial distribution of the households (see map 3) to the table showing attendance, it can be seen that, in general, the participants in these rituals are people who live close to one another in neighbouring houses (up to about one day's travel apart). Households within this distance do a considerable amount of mutual visiting and usually invite each other to dances on a reciprocal basis. Thus, throughout the region, there are a series of overlapping 'social spheres', each one containing houses of both the same and of different exogamous groups and it is within these 'spheres' that most inter-marriage takes place. The households of Mandu, Pedro, Christo and Arturo form the core of one such sphere and this is reflected in table 1. However, it must be emphasised that geographical propinquity is not the only basis on which these spheres are formed: the current state of relations between individuals, especially between men of consequence, is another important factor and one which often partially explains the location of different houses. Although Ignacio's house is close to that of both Pedro and Mandu, relations between these households and that of Ignacio are strained and social contact is limited. Again, this is reflected in table 1. The attendance of people from Caño Tatú (Mario's, Domingo's and Ugo's households) at a ritual held at Pacho's house but not at any held in houses on upper Caño Colorado, reflects the fact that while they are within the social sphere of Pacho's household, they are outside those of the inhabitants of upper Canõ Colorado. Hernando's household from Caño Komeyaká came on a special visit to Mandu's house as part of an exchange of ritual property; normally there is no regular social contact between these houses. When guests come from a long way away it is generally

44

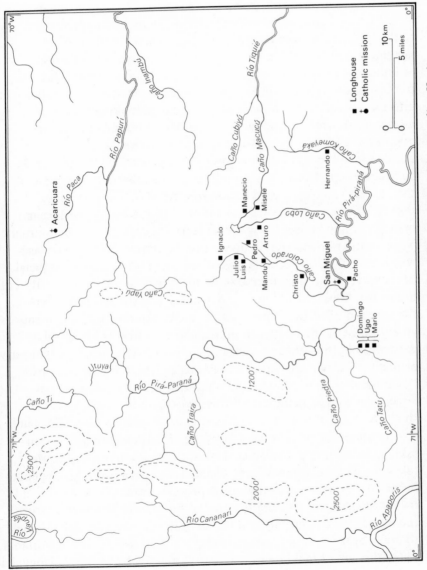

Map 3 The Pirá-paraná drainage showing location of longhouse communities attending *He* rites

part of an attempt to form new social alliances or to revitalise old ones. The social spheres are fixed neither geographically, for people may move house, nor socially, for political relations keep changing. The attendance at *He* House is discussed in chapter 4.

Invitations are sent out between one and two weeks in advance. The chief host and/or one or more people delegated by him travel to the different houses where they deliver the invitation to the headmen, first in the form of a ceremonial dialogue and then in ordinary speech. He counts off the days on his fingers until he gets to the day on which manioc is put down (*ki rohorirɯmɯ*), i.e. brought into the house. This is followed by the day of making beer (*idire moarirɯmɯ*), which is followed by the day of the small dance (*basa mɯtarɯmɯ*). In the case of Fruit House this is the day the *He* are brought into the house (see below). Having delivered the invitation he usually departs soon afterwards, sometimes asking the people of the house to convey the invitation to other more distant houses.

However, not all Fruit House rites take this form: sometimes a man, X, of one household will decide to give fruit to another man, Y, of another household. X may either take fruit to Y's house, in which case Y will be both recipient and chief host (who must provide beer and send out invitations) or he may invite Y to receive fruit in his own house, in which case X will be the host and donor and Y the recipient. But by no means all Fruit House rites take the form of an exchange of fruit between individuals of different households; very often both hosts and guests provide fruit without any exchange element. These details are naturally made clear in the invitations.

On the day on which manioc is put down, the women get up large quantities of manioc and other roots and the men, especially the host, often help them to carry the heavy baskets of manioc back to the house. The chief host acts as the director of the proceedings, asking, not ordering, the other men of the house to help him. He takes the men out to pick large quantities of coca, from his own coca bushes if possible, which they then process. Generally, the host and owner of the coca does the toasting of the leaves. The women spend the rest of the day grating manioc and preparing the other roots used to make beer.[2]

On the day of making beer the men go out early in the morning,

---

2 The processing and preparation of coca, manioc bread and beer are described by Christine Hugh-Jones (1979).

led by the host, to get firewood from the manioc gardens. They
return with huge logs on their shoulders and there is an atmosphere
of cooperative, friendly rivalry reminiscent of the log races of Central
Brazilian Indians. The wood is split and the men then pick and process
more coca while the women continue to prepare beer. During the day
fruit is gathered from the forest, generally by the younger men and
initiated boys; sometimes a pair of *He* trumpets is taken on these
expeditions and played in the forest. The fruit trees are felled with
axes and the fruit placed in palm-leaf baskets which are then left
near the house, usually on the path leading up from the port. Cultivated fruit may also be gathered from the gardens in which case
the trees are not felled.

After dusk the young men bring the *He* up from the river to the
front of the house where they are played until after midnight (see
table 2). Inside the house, the men process coca and the women
continue to prepare manioc beer. Once the coca has all been processed, the men assemble in the middle of the house where, after
eating the new coca, they are led in chanting by the chief host.
Later on, he leads another chant session, again involving all the men.

Throughout the evening the shaman (or shamans) sits by post 1
(see figure 2 for this and all subsequent references to precise locations
in the house), blowing spells into cigars and into gourds containing
tobacco snuff, coca, beer and lumps of beeswax mixed with coca.
When the blowing is completed, one gourd of coca and wax is
placed on a stand in the middle of the house and all the men come to
eat small pinches from it. One of the hosts then takes the lumps of
wax from the gourd and, putting them on burning embers in a
potsherd, he carries them twice round the dance path in a clockwise
direction, fanning the embers to produce aromatic smoke as he
goes. The wax is afterwards left smoking in the men's doorway.
Sometime later the women are also invited to eat small pinches of
the blown coca.

Later on one of the hosts blows large quantities of tobacco snuff,
blown over by the shamans, up the noses of the men, using a long
bone tube.[3] The snuff is then offered to the women who eat small
pinches. After midnight the *He* are taken back to the river by the
young men who play them till dawn. At the same time, they bathe

---

3 The administration of snuff as a prerequisite to seeing and touching sacred bark trumpets
is found also among Tikuna (Nimuendaju 1948 : 718)

Table 2. *Fruit House and dance*

	Shamans	Elders	Young men	Women	[Initiates]
Dusk	Blow on cigar, coca, snuff, beer, beeswax	Prepare coca PLAY LONG FLUTES (on plaza)	Prepare coca PLAY TRUMPETS (on plaza)	PREPARE BEER	Remain in house
	CHANT	CHANT	CHANT		
Midnight	CHANT [Blow on whips] ADMINISTER SNUFF	BURN BEESWAX CHANT RECEIVE SNUFF	CHANT RECEIVE SNUFF TAKE *HE* TO RIVER PLAY *HE*, BATHE, VOMIT	EAT BLOWN SNUFF	RECEIVE SNUFF
Dawn	[WASH INITIATES] Blow on coca, snuff, beer, yagé, cigar (& *kana*)	FLUTES INTO HOUSE PLAY FLUTES [BATHE]	TRUMPETS INTO HOUSE PLAY TRUMPETS [BATHE]	CONFINED IN REAR OF HOUSE	CONFINED IN REAR OF HOUSE WASHED & DRESSED LED INTO HOUSE PLAY SHORT FLUTES
	CHANT (giving coca) Serve yagé TIP OUT FRUIT	CHANT (giving coca) Drink yagé TIP OUT FRUIT PUT ON ORNAMENTS PLAY FLUTES	CHANT (giving coca) Drink yagé BLOW TRUMPETS ON FRUIT		EAT BLOWN *KANA* Drink yagé TIP OUT FRUIT
Midday	Blow on coca, wax	EAT BLOWN COCA BURN BEESWAX	EAT BLOWN COCA Follow elders		

48

				WHIPPED
	CHANT (pouring beer)	CHANT (pouring beer) [WHIPPED]	CHANT (pouring beer) [WHIPPED]	ENTER MAIN PART OF HOUSE
Dusk	[WHIP PARTICI-PANTS] LEAVE HOUSE	LEAVE HOUSE WITH FLUTES	LEAVE HOUSE WITH TRUMPETS	Eat Meal
	CHANT (ordering the dance)	PUT ON FULL ORNAMENT DANCE	PUT ON FULL ORNAMENT DANCE	DANCE
	CHANT	CHANT DANCE	CHANT DANCE	DANCE
	CHANT	CHANT DANCE	CHANT DANCE	DANCE
Midnight	CHANT (giving coca)	CHANT (giving coca) DANCE	CHANT (& play trumpets) DANCE	DANCE
			TAKE *HE* TO RIVER	
Dawn	CHANT (pouring beer)	CHANT (pouring beer) DANCE (ending the dance)	CHANT (pouring beer) DANCE (ending the dance)	DANCE
	REMOVE HEAD-DRESSES BATHE & VOMIT Blow on food	HEAD-DRESSES REMOVED BATHE & VOMIT DISTRIBUTE FRUIT	HEAD-DRESSES REMOVED BATHE & VOMIT	
Midday	Eat meal	Eat meal	Eat meal	

[ ] Involving iniates only.
- - - Division between small and big dance.

49

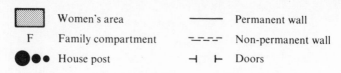

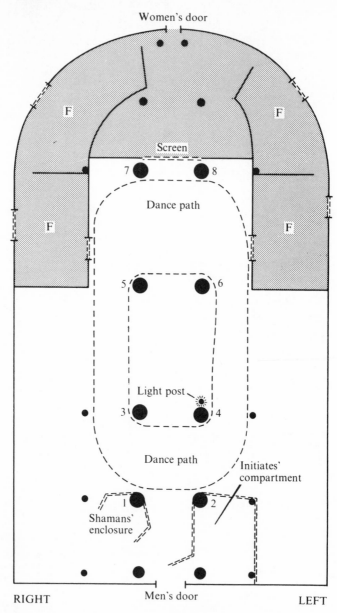

Fig. 2 Plan of the longhouse interior. The shamans' and initiates' compartments are only constructed for *He* House and for Fruit House as the first stage of initiation

in the river, thumping the water with their hands and vomiting, having drunk water mixed with the sap from the rind of a forest vine called foam vine (*somo misi*). The elder men sleep while the women finish making the manioc beer. In spite of the air of increased excitement and formality characteristic of these occasions, there is no marked separation between the sexes and the women show no apparent interest in the *He* being blown outside. If there are visitors present, the men sit in a group near the front door while their hosts sit in the middle of the house near the light-post. The visiting women help their hosts prepare beer.

Soon after first light, when the beer is all made, the women sweep the house clean and sprinkle water on the floor. A thick screen of woven palm leaves is moved across the house beyond posts 7 and 8, completely shutting off the rear end. Women, children and pets are then confined in this screened-off area whilst the *He* are played into the house. Later on the women may leave the house to go to the gardens.

The men bathe and prepare the instruments at the river and then walk back to the house playing as they come. They walk in pairs, usually with the trumpets in the lead, with short flutes and then long flutes behind them. The *He* players carry small bunches of fruits on their shoulders and more men walk behind carrying baskets loaded with fruit (see plate 2). The procession enters the door, goes twice (clockwise) round the dance path and then up the middle of the house to the screen where the baskets of fruit are deposited alongside other baskets already there. Generally, several different kinds of fruit are brought in. As the fruit is brought in there are shouts of 'hoo hoo hoo hoo' and much joking, often of a sexual nature and referring to mythical characters connected with forest fruits.[4] After this the trumpets and short flutes are played back and forth round the dance path while the long flutes are played up and down the middle of the house. For the rest of the day the instruments are played in this manner, always with the long flutes in the middle and the trumpets and short flutes round the edge (see appendix 3 for a detailed description of the movements associated with the playing of *He*). In general, the long flutes are played by the

---

4 I found it very hard both to hear properly and to understand these jokes. An example of one such joke is '*Kaheoua* (a small, black squirrel) has huge balls. The bastard has eaten all our fruit.' This was said to be an explicit reference to the squirrel in Myth 7.C.2.

older men, the trumpets by the younger men and the short flutes by the youngest boys present.

During the morning the men paint themselves with black paint called *we*, made from the macerated leaves of a cultivated shrub of unidentified species.[5] The rather crude designs, mostly on the upper and lower legs, are in marked contrast to the fine patterns applied during social dances (*basaria wi*) and dances at which food is ceremonially given away (*bare ekaria wi*). The men also paint their faces with red paint called *ngʉnanya* (caraiuru, an extract from the leaves of a cultivated vine, *Bignonia chica*). All morning the shaman(s) sits, either by post 1 or post 7 next to the baskets of fruit, blowing spells into gourds containing various substances which are consumed during the rite. He blows over beer which is then drunk off the ends of sticks from a gourd placed in the middle of the house, before being consumed from gourds in the usual way. He also blows over yagé (*Banisteriopsis*) bark which is afterwards added to the rest of the bark being pounded in preparation of the drink. He blows over coca, over a large ceremonial cigar and over a gourd of snuff from which the men eat small pinches when it is placed in the middle of the house.[6] Before the shaman blows over each of these substances, one of the host elders does a short chant with him.

In the late morning all the men assemble in the middle of the house between posts 1 and 2, sitting on ritual stools, and the senior host elder leads them all in chanting. During this chanting the coca and ritual cigar, blown over by the shaman, are handed round. At the same time yagé is served to all by the shaman. Following this the *He* are played again. By this stage the long flutes will have been decorated with a ruff of yellow and brown Oropendola (*japú*, *Icteridae* sp.) feathers tied round the lower ends and the engraved designs on them will have been filled with white manioc starch or chalk which stands out against the black palm wood (see fig. 8). Shortly after the end of the chanting, the elders playing the long flutes chant briefly with the shaman and then they, together with

5 The use of *we* in the Pirá-paraná area corresponds to the use of *Genipa americana* elsewhere in the Vaupés region.

6 These cigars, called *nykahua*, are made from *roe hʉ* leaves wound into a conical tube in the same way that the bark trumpets are constructed. The tube is then filled with tobacco chips, often mixed with aromatic resin and beeswax. In the past they were held in a carved hardwood holder. (See Koch-Grünberg 1909/10, vol. I : 281–2 for photographs.) They are lit at the narrow end and only a small amount is smoked at each rite, the rest being wrapped in white bast and stored away in a large box in which the feather ornaments are kept.

the other elders, go to the baskets of fruit at the screen. Then, as the long flutes are played up and down the middle of the house, the elders and shaman tip the fruit out on to flat basketwork trays, throwing the empty baskets over the screen into the rear of the house. This is done with shouts of 'hoo hoo hoo' and with exchanges of ritualised joking.[7] Once the fruit has been tipped into the trays, the trumpets are periodically played with their ends circling directly over the fruit, wafting it with their breath.

The tipping out of the fruit marks a distinct phase in the rite; up to this point the long flutes are played only sporadically by men wearing few or no ornaments. After this, the long flutes are played in relay more or less continuously by pairs of elders wearing diadem-like crowns on their heads. These crowns, made from woven palm leaf, have bright yellow Oropendola feathers radiating outwards like the rays of the sun, and with a single red macaw tail feather in the centre (see plate 3). They also wear monkey-fur bracelets on their right elbows and belts of jaguar or peccary teeth round their waists. As each pair starts and ends a session of playing they chant with the shaman. Their style of playing also changes: whereas before the players merely walked up and down, they now do a slow walking dance with rapid turns at each end (see appendix 3) and their playing becomes more refined and melodious. Overall, the rite becomes more formal and the focus of attention is fixed upon the men playing the flutes. It is to these men that most yagé is given, as it is to the main dancers during other dances. At the same time as this change in atmosphere, the shaman begins to blow spells over a gourd of coca mixed with lumps of beeswax.

The formal playing of the long flutes continues throughout the afternoon with three or four changes of players who each time salute the other men as they go out to play. The trumpets too are played continuously, every so often being blown over the piles of fruit. By mid-afternoon the playing of the long flutes reaches a climax: as they get to either end of the house, the players raise the ends of the flutes high in the air and then, playing 'toooo toooo toooo toooo too too to to ttt' on a descending scale, they run down the middle of the house with a short-stepped crouching run, accen-

---

7 This noise signifies approval and happiness. It is made also at the end of each session of chanting, at the end of sessions of playing the long flutes and during the last part of each dance set. The noise is specific to Fruit House; during ceremonial exchanges of food the noise 'ye ye ye ye ye ye' is made instead.

tuating the step of the right foot (see appendix 3). This action, called
encouraging the fruit, having the fruit (*He rika yohagu̶ He rika ku̶tigu̶*),
evokes cries of 'hoo, hoo, hoo' and ritual jokes from the audience.
When the shaman finishes blowing over the wax-coca mixture, it
is handed to an elder who places the gourd on a stand in the middle
of the space between posts 1, 2, 3 and 4. He then calls out, 'Come
and eat the blown stuff.' Everyone present, except the shamans and
the long-flute players, comes and eats a small pinch of coca. Then
they all line up clutching thin wooden staves in their hands like spears
and run up and down the edges of the house in a crouching position
making aggressive, grumbling noises.[8] At each end of the house they
spring into the air with loud cries of 'This is how I will kill you; now
I fear nothing; I will kill you; he killed my father by sorcery; I will
kill him,' etc. This action, called acting-out spearing (*besu̶u̶ kesose*),
is done with greatest enthusiasm by the younger men.

Immediately after this, one of the elders burns lumps of beeswax
in a potsherd, walking twice round the house clockwise, up the
middle to the fruit and then back down the house to the front door
where he leaves the smoking wax. As he does this he is followed
round by young men playing trumpets with the short flutes following
behind. From then on till dusk the *He* are played continuously. At
dusk, the feather ornaments used in dancing are prepared and the
main dancer and his partner put on the full complement of ritual
ornaments (see plate 4). On very formal occasions, the dancing may
start before the women enter the house; usually it starts afterwards.
At dusk, the short flutes and trumpets are played twice clockwise
round the dance path and then down the middle of the house and out
on to the plaza. At the same time the long flutes are played with
increased tempo and with the players now doing a fairly brisk walk.[9]
They are then played out of the house along the same route as the
trumpets. As the *He* are taken out, the men collect up the stools,
the yagé pot and the various gourds blown over by the shaman and,
taking them with them, go and sit out in front of the house on the
plaza. There the shaman blows spells over bundles of panpipes and
after each person has blown a short puff into the ends, they are
handed round and played. At the same time, other whistles of deer

8 These staves are used in place of bundles of poisoned javelins, the use of which has
  died out in the area. (See Koch-Grünberg 1909/10, vol. II : 271 for illustration.)
9 An increase in tempo marks the end of many different Barasana ritual acts: the end of
  each dance set, the end of each session of chanting and the final playing of the flutes
  and trumpets are all thus marked.

bone, cane and snail-shells are played — the first time since the start of the rite.

While the men sit outside, the screen shutting off the rear of the house is removed and the women once again re-enter the main part. After they have come in, the men return from the plaza and the dance begins.

In general, visitors arrive as household units, often accompanied by the guests who have been staying with them. They travel by canoe or on foot and often the men go ahead of the women. On arrival at the house, the men stop at the port, where they bathe, paint their faces and tuck sweet-smelling herbs under their bead arm-bands and G-strings. Sometimes they also put on feather crowns and other ritual ornaments. They they walk, in single file with the most senior men at the front, up to the house. If they have brought fruit and *He* instruments with them they enter the house in the manner described above, after which they reassemble at the men's door to be greeted. Otherwise they go straight to the men's door and stand in line in order of seniority.

The greetings start with the senior guest chanting a greeting which is repeated in chorus by those with him. The chief host receives this greeting, repeating the last phrase of each line of the chant. Then the chief host greets each man, in order of seniority, addressing him by the appropriate kinship term and talking in normal speech. He is followed by all the men present in the house who stand in line in order of seniority and greet each guest individually. The men then go off and greet the visiting women, in much less formal manner, while the women of the house greet the arriving men. Finally the host women greet their female guests. The men always enter through the men's door at the front of the house and usually the women come in through the women's door at the back.

Once the greetings are over, the visiting men are given beer to drink and then they move as a group and sit to one side of the men's door. The most senior men sit on stools which they either bring with them or which the hosts bring to them; the rest sit on long, low benches placed on either side of the door along the front walls of the house. There they are led in chanting (called *ehakoadiaha mani* — we have arrived) by a member of their own group. After a short interval, the chief host comes and sits in front of them and after an exchange of coca and cigars, he leads them in another chant, telling them to rest (*usuhea rotigu*). Once this is over, the guests begin to take part in the proceedings, though initially they tend to behave as a discrete unit. As time passes, the divisions between guests and hosts and between the different arrival groups become less and less marked.

Guests always arrive before the *He* are taken out of the house and usually before the burning of beeswax (see above). If they are bringing large amounts of fruit to present to their hosts they will arrive either early in the morning before the tipping out of the fruit (see above) or more usually on the evening of the start of the rite. When they arrive at this time, the greetings tend to be less formal and the fruit which they bring is left at the port, together with their *He*.

The dance

The overall pattern of the dance, consisting of a series of dance sets interspersed with sessions of chanting, is set out in table 2. What follows is a short account of the dance taken as an event through time.

Before going out to dance, the lead dancer does a short chant ordering the dance (*basa rotigɨ*), with the officiating shaman and the other elders. He then starts to dance back and forth between posts 1, 2, 3 and 4 and is gradually joined by other dancers. Each man dances with his left hand on the right shoulder of the one next to him so that a long line, facing in towards the centre of the house, is formed. In their right hands the dancers carry rattles or wooden staves, depending on the particular dance being performed. The dance line then moves off round and round the dance path, oscillating back and forth. As the dancing starts, the women partake of a communal meal in the centre of the house. Soon after they are offered the gourds containing snuff and wax—coca mixture from which the men ate whilst the *He* were still inside the house.

The dancing as a whole is divided into a number of sets interspersed with periods of chanting. One named dance is danced and sung throughout the entire night, but the words change for each set though they centre on a common theme,[10] Each dance set is in turn divided into a seemingly variable number of sequences with periods

---

10 Each exogamic language group owns a different set of dances and songs.
　　Most of the words of these songs are incomprehensible to the *Barasana* themselves, though they can generally pick out certain words in each phrase associated with a particular dance set, to which they can give meaning.

of rest, drinking and talking in between. The final sequence of each set, called ending, breaking the dance (*basa tadi yigu*) is marked by a change in tempo and by different movements, both of the dance line as a whole and of the steps employed. At the start of the dance, the main dancers represent a more or less clearly defined group of people who are essentially members of one particular household. In some cases it is the hosts who dance, in others the dancers comprise members of one or more visiting households who arrive in a discrete group; in yet other cases, one visiting group may dance together with the hosts while another plays an essentially passive role. There is no clear correlation between the role of dancers and the role of providers of fruit: sometimes it is the hosts who provide the bulk of the fruit and who dance in their own house; sometimes the hosts provide the fruit while the guests dance and sometimes it is the guests who both dance and provide the fruit. This is in marked contrast to dances at which the food is ceremonially presented by one or more households to another, at which, whether the dance is held in the house of the donors or the recipients, it is always the donors who do the main dancing.

The main dancers are distinguished from the rest by wearing the total complement of feathers, teeth belts, bark-cloth aprons, etc., which make up their dress (see plate 4); the others wear small woven palm-leaf crowns decorated with feathers like the rays of the sun (see plate 3). In Barasana categories the dancers wear *maha hoa*, while the rest wear *buya buku bedo*. When not dancing, the dancers sit on a row of stools between posts 1 and 2, facing into the middle of the house. The others sit in two groups, roughly defined by household or arrival group, along the front wall of the house on either side of the male door; those on the left are generally more distant and somewhat less active in the dance. As the dance progresses throughout the night, more and more people join in the main dancing and the discrete seating groups become intermingled so that by morning they are no longer easily discernible.

While the main dancers dance and chant, the other men sit talking and laughing and playing panpipes. Periodically groups of them, especially the younger men, go out into the middle of the house and dance with their panpipes. These dances are relaxed, individualistic and with an erotic and exciting air which contrasts with the more sacred and formal atmosphere of the main dance. As the night wears on, the main dancers take a more active part in these panpipe dances which reach a climax in the morning and often continue long after the formal dance is ended. On more formal occasions when there are large numbers (forty plus) of people present, those not involved in the main dance may form up into a separate dancing unit. They dance a special category of dances called *hia basa* using very small rattles and holding thin peeled wands high in their right hands. The overall form of these dances is similar to the main dance but the dancing starts and ends outside the house on the plaza. The tempo of these dances is also faster than that of the main dance.

The women sit, apart from the men, in small groups along the sides of the dance path and in the rear end of the house. After each dancing session has started, they come up behind the dance line and, tucking their heads and shoulders under the men's arms and holding on to their waists, they join in. They must leave the line again before the end of each session, their exit being signalled by a slight change in rhythm from the rattles or staves. When dancing in the formal dances, a woman must dance each time with the same man and enter through the same 'slot'.[11] In panpipe dancing, the men start to dance alone and the women then come out and choose their partners. There is often an air of friendly rivalry in these dances with the young men of one household trying to outdo those of another. Often there are three or more groups dancing at the same time, each playing a different melody against the rest.

The main chanting sessions (see table 2) are held between posts 1 and 2 and essentially involve the main dance line. One man, a specialist chanter, and often also the lead dancer, leads the chanting while the rest, seated in an oval round him, repeat each phrase in chorus. Each session is preceded by a long period during which each man receives coca, cigars and snuff from every other, starting with the chanter who hands round coca and snuff and a cigar, all of which have had spells blown over them by the shaman. Each session of chanting is named and the verbal content of each is different[12] The

---

11 Dancing in different 'slots' is considered to be, in some ways, analogous to promiscuous sexual behaviour. See M.4.D for the consequences of such behaviour in myth.

12 Limitations of space and of my own fieldwork data make it impossible to discuss the content of these chants in detail. The language employed in chanting differs from that of normal speech both in terms of syntax and in terms of the words used, many of which represent archaic or special forms. It was only at the very end of my fieldwork that I began to understand these chants.

The chants are based on myth but do not consist of simply chanting myth as a connected narrative. Much of each chant concerns various kinds of ritual possessions, coca, tobacco, yagé and manioc, and, in particular, how they were obtained and distributed amongst the different sibs and exogamic groups in mythic times.

58

two longest and most important sessions, giving coca (*kahi ekagu*) and pouring out beer (*idire iogu*) are held around midnight and dawn respectively. The former chant refers largely to the mythical origins of the various varieties of coca and how these were obtained from the group's ancestors, whilst the latter refers to the origins of beer and the manioc used to make it. During these chant sessions yagé is served by the shaman. Once the dancer/chanters have been served the rest of the people are given yagé, but it is always the former who receive most. Yagé is also served to the dancers during the pauses between sequences of dancing. At big dances with many visitors present, there are many subsidiary chant sessions involving the visiting households as discrete units, sometimes led in chanting by their hosts and sometimes by their own headmen or chanters. The *He*, which remain outside the house until first light, are played occasionally throughout the night. They are always played during the chant session 'giving coca'. At first light they are taken back to the river and hidden.

Throughout the whole dance, the officiating shaman remains more or less permanently seated by post 1, except when serving yagé or chanting with the dancers. He does not dance with the main dance line but may occasionally take part in panpipe dancing. He wears a palm-leaf crown often topped by dollops of white duck down. Most of his time is spent blowing spells on to various substances which are later distributed to the assembled company. Very often red paint is blown and each man and woman then wipes it on the

Most of the chants are based around the journeys of the first ancestors, the *He* people, from their place of origin in the east to the areas in which their descendants now live. The chants list off the named geographical locations where the first people stopped on their journeys, describing how they danced and obtained various cultural items, especially those used in ritual. Barasana myths, like many of their Australian aborigine counterparts, are precisely located in topographical space. For the sake of brevity, I have left out the geographical referents of the various incidents related in the myths. In practice, each incident is tied to a precise, named location, and each time a character passes from one place to another, all the places through which he travels are listed in detail. This geographical framework forms the major articulation between myths and chants.

During the chants, the specialist chanter, under the influence of yagé, is able to make his soul leave his body so that it repeats the mythical journeys of the first ancestors. He starts at Manao Lake (*Manao Utara*), identified with present-day Manaus in Brazil, and lists off all the named locations between there and the Pirá-paraná. The time sequence of this journey corresponds, in part, to the sequence of the ritual so that, by the end, the chanter will have 'arrived' back in the Pirá-paraná region, and, at different times during the rites, informants will say, 'Now he has got to such and such a place.'

Without first knowing well the myths that underlie them, it would be impossible to fully understand the chants. During my fieldwork, I concentrated on knowing the myths. I hope, in the future, to return and to work on the chants.

legs as a protection against snake bite. At the end of the dance, after the chanting called ending the dance (*basa gahanongu*), the shaman removes the feather head-dresses from the head of each dancer, starting with the leader, and then wipes away the harmful effects of wearing feathers with his hands, ending each wipe with a flick and clap accompanied by loud blowings.[13] This marks the end of the dance proper, though panpipe dancing and beer drinking usually continue until nightfall.

In cases where the hosts are the main providers of fruit of a kind that can be eaten without further elaboration, there is very often an informal distribution of fruit immediately following the dance. (This distribution may also take place just before the start of the dance when the sacred horns are removed from the house.) The recipients, who are called up by name to receive the fruit from the senior host, are generally those of a visiting household group who did not provide any of the fruit at the start of the rite. If the fruit requires further processing (cooking, maceration in water, etc.) it is given to the host women who make it up into food or drink which is later distributed to all present in the form of a communal meal.

Shortly after the end of the dance, all the men go down to the river to bathe and vomit, having previously wiped snuff, blown by the shaman, on their knees and legs to prevent aches and pains caused by contact with water after dancing and wearing feathers. On their return, the men are each given a small quantity of cassava bread and *meka* (large ground-living termites), blown over by the shaman, to eat. This is followed by a meal of the same. Soon after, fruit, smoked chilli pepper, salt and small fish called fish children (*wai ría*), cooked with manioc leaves or 'spinach' (*au, Phytolacca iconsandra*), are all blown over by the shaman and distributed to each man, after which a communal meal, of fish and 'spinach', is held. On the following day the shaman blows spells over various species of larger fish (the category big fish, *wai hakarã*), over meat (*wai bukurã*, meaning literally old mature fish) and over raw chilli pepper; and in the days that follow, other categories of food will be blown as and when they are available, each time preceding a meal.

On the day following the end of the dance it is customary for the host men to take their guests to pick coca and then to process it so

13 A filmed sequence of this action can be seen in *War of the Gods*, a film made by Brian Moser of Granada Television with the assistance of myself and Christine Hugh-Jones.

that, when they leave the next day, their coca pots will be full. It is
during this coca picking that some of the host men are sent to the
forest to catch certain categories of fish and game so that they can
be blown over by the shaman.

Fruit House as the first stage of initiation

For the Barasana and their neighbours, male initiation is a long-drawn-
out affair.[14] For a young boy, the process starts around the age of
eight years and continues often until he has reached the age of fifteen.
(These ages are approximate; the Barasana do not reckon age in years.)
The process can be divided into two stages which correspond to
Barasana categories. The first stage involves the initiates (generally
between two and ten of them, hence the difference in ages of the
candidates) taking part in a Fruit House rite for the first time in
their lives. Between this and the next stage they will take part in
a number of these rites as they are held regularly, outside the context
of initiation, as each fruit comes into season. The second stage involves showing the initiates a different set of sacred musical instruments, the true *He*, during a longer ritual, *He* House, followed by a
period of two months fasting and other restrictions.

Two other writers on the Vaupés region, Amorim (1926/8 : 52–5)
for the Wanano and Coudreau (1887 : 198) for the Tariana, have
reported two stages in the process of initiation; I suspect that lack of
such reports from other authors on this region may reflect inadequate
data and that it cannot be taken to indicate that the same pattern is
not found among the other groups. Among the Tariana, the first
stage, for boys between ten and twelve years old, involves fasting and
seeing the Yurupary instruments. At the second stage, between
thirteen and fourteen years old, the initiates are shown the sacred
Yurupary masks called *Macacaraua*.

Among the Wanano, the first stage, for eight-year-olds, consists
of a month of fasting in a special compartment followed by whipping,
teaching by the elders and the showing of Yurupary. The second
stage, for those 'who have shown the ability to impregnate' involves
two months of fasting followed by the showing of the more sacred
Yurupary called *Mahsankero*.

---

14 Among the Barasana, a girl's first menstruation is marked by ritual but there are no
female initiation rites.

For the Barasana, the decision to hold the first stage of initiation rests primarily with the fathers of the boys concerned and also with the shaman(s) who live with them or are most closely related to them. The rite is usually held in the house of the father of one or more of the initiates, usually the most senior, but may also be held in the house of the officiating shaman if he lives elsewhere. One of the fathers becomes the chief host, helped by the other fathers; often boys from several houses, not necessarily of the same exogamous group, are initiated at the same time. The details of the preparations are otherwise the same as those described above for a normal Fruit House rite.

I am not entirely sure how often Fruit House as the first stage of initiation is held. Informants state that, in the past, large numbers of (up to about ten) boys were initiated at the same time. In saying this, they are generally referring to the second stage of initiation, *He* house. Today, the first stage appears to take place as and when there are one or more boys of the appropriate age. Neither stage of initiation is exclusive to one sib or even to one exogamous group and it often happens that boys from different groups are initiated all together in one house.

The details concerning the arrival of guests are much the same as those given above except for the fact that when boys are being initiated outside their own home, they must be brought to the house where the initiation is held before the rite begins so that they can be prepared. Apart from being rather more formal and elaborate, the ritual and the preparatory activities are essentially the same as those described above. That description is based upon observations of several different rites; here my description is based on the observation of one particular case. Reference should be made to the column headed 'Initiates' of table 2.

Both on the eve of the rite and during the rite itself, each time that blown snuff, coca, etc. was eaten, the young boys ate first. When blown tobacco snuff was administered through the bone tube on the eve of the rite, the boys were given such large doses that they choked and vomited and had to be forcibly restrained from running away. The other men were also given unusually large quantities of snuff.[15] In addition to the usual round of shamanism preceding the rite, the

---

15 See M.5.A for a mythical account of the rites of initiation and, in particular, for the effects of this snuff in a mythic context.

shamans blew spells over whips made from peeled saplings with the twigs left on.

On the morning of the ritual, while the other men bathed at the river, the three boys were given a special wash outside on the plaza. The two shamans blew tobacco smoke over the heads and hands of the boys who then washed their faces and hands from a bowl of water. This was the only occasion I witnessed on which the men bathed *after* the fruit had been taken into the house. Once washed the boys painted their legs with black *we* paint, and were dressed with newly ochred garters below their knees, clean white handkerchiefs round their necks and palm-leaf crowns on their heads. They were afterwards led inside the house where they were sat down in a group on a woven palm-leaf mat placed directly on the floor to the right of the men's door.[16] Soon after this the senior host elder and the officiating shaman came and handed the boys the ceremonial cigar and the gourd of coca, blown over by the shaman. These were then offered round to everyone else. There was a definite sense in which the boys were being treated as honoured guests.[17] The boys came from two neighbouring houses, one of the same sib as the hosts, the other of a junior sib within the same exogamous language group.

Before the tipping out of the fruit, the initiates were each given small pink berries of the *kana* (*Sabicea amazonensis*) vine to eat which had previously been blown over by the shaman. They were then called up to help tip out the fruit, but apart from this and when they were playing the short flutes or taking substances blown by the shaman, they sat silent and motionless on their mat. During the rite the boys were given large quantities of yagé, each time served to them in a very ritualised and formal manner. This was the first time they had ever taken yagé. The yagé used was also much stronger than usual — a larger-than-usual amount of leaf yagé (*kahi uko*) being used.[18] Each time it was the initiates who were served first. Whenever

16 In accordance with Barasana practice, the right- and left-hand sides of the house are reckoned from the point of view of a person looking out from the front door.
17 The same is true for initiates among the Cubeo (Goldman 1963 : 196).
18 Most named varieties of Barasana yagé correspond to the species *Banisteriopsis inebrians* Morton. One variety at least corresponds to the species *B. Rusbyana* (Ndz.) Morton. The active principle of *B. inebrians* is harmine; *B. Rusbyana* also contains dimethyl triptamine. It is probable that leaf yagé (*kahi uko*) belongs to this latter species, hence its use to make the drink stronger (Schultes 1972 : 141—4 and personal communication). Even more leaf yagé is added to the drink consumed at *He* House.

the trumpets were played, the three initiates walked behind them playing the short flutes.

The main difference between this and other Fruit House rites observed by me came after the burning of the beeswax. All afternoon the shamans had flicked their whips making a loud swishing noise and once the wax had been burned this noise reached a crescendo. A young man of about twenty went out to the middle of the house near the screen where he was whipped by the two shamans.[19] He then ran up and down the house acting-out spearing. Then the two shamans were whipped by two host elders, again followed by acting-out spearing. Finally the two elders ran twice round the dance path in an aggressive manner, down the middle of the house towards the men's door, and then hurled the bundles of whips against the end wall with an angry shout. The younger men rushed forward and grabbed the whips which they carried with them until the end of the dance. While this went on, one of the host elders went to the rear of the house where the women and children were, and there whipped his two-year-old son gently across the legs and body. On the eve of the rite, I had been told that the young boys were to be whipped but in fact this never happened. This may have been because by the time the whipping started, one of the boys had collapsed from the effects of the yagé and the other two were suffering from extreme nausea and looked frightened and confused. Other boys who had recently undergone this rite assured me that they had been whipped.

The dance that followed was in no way different from any other that I saw except that, because whipping must always take place after dark, the dancing started later and the women were allowed back into the house much later.[20] Informants' descriptions of this rite correspond closely to what I observed, except that the informants state that usually a special compartment of palm leaves is constructed next to the men's door (see fig. 2). The *He* are placed inside this enclosure and are not seen by the initiates until they are taken out and blown in the middle of the house at midday. The initiates are then confined in this compartment, together with the *He*, until the end of the dance.

---

19 See p. 80 for a description of whipping.
20 Among the Cubeo, the men whip the women during the dance that follows the main rite (Goldman 1963 : 200). I did not observe this to happen among the Barasana or their neighbours.

Fruit House rites preceding *He* House

Fruit House in preparation for He House

The cultivated tree-fruit *mene* (*Ingá dulcis*) has two seasons, a major one in February, March and April and a minor one in October and November. During this latter season, a Fruit House rite is held at which ingá (*mene*) fruit are brought into the house and form its focus. The purpose of this rite is to enable the shamans to carry out protective shamanism (*wanose*) so that no ill befalls the participants at *He* House, the main initiation rite. Unfortunately, I never witnessed this rite and it was only when I had left the field that I realised its potential significance.

According to informants, the shamans blow spells over tobacco, tobacco snuff, coca, coca mixed with beeswax, red paint, manioc beer and yagé which the participants then consume or wipe over their bodies. This protects them from a series of harmful spirit encounters through dreaming, as follows: (1) Dreams of beautiful women who come to the sleeper's hammock to make love. These women are sickness women (*nyase romia*), women who fill one with fat (*ɯye sõria romia*), and who thus make the person ill or liable to attack from jaguars or snakes. (2) Dreams of small girls being carried on the sleeper's shoulders. These dreams cause illness (*nyase*), and cause pains in the back of the neck. (3) Dreams of a spirit (*wãti*) who clings to the back causing illness and backache. (4) Dreams of eating an abundance of fish. These fish are Pleiades fish (*nyokoaro wai*), illness fish (*nyase wai*), death fish (*bohori wai*), and sky-lake fish (*ɯmɯa ɯtarã wai*) (see M.6.A.17) which cause sickness; the shamans must send them back to the Water Door (*Oko Sohe*) in the east from whence they came.

The major features of this rite are said to be much like any other Fruit House.

Fruit House as a prelude to He House

The timing of *He* House is intimately connected with the movements of the Pleiades (*nyokoaro*) across the skies. In November, when the ingá fruit are ripe and when the preliminary Fruit House rite is held (see above), the Pleiades begin to appear on the eastern horizon at dusk.[21]

21 Virtually all observations of stars are done at dusk; relatively little attention is paid to the position of the stars at other times of the night.

In April, when the ingá fruit are again ripe, the Pleiades are setting on the western horizon at dusk. The Barasana say that *He* House should be held when the pupunha (*Gulielma gasipaes*) are ripe (February to March), when the umari fruit (*wamʉ*, *Poraqueiba sericea*) are ripe (February to April) and when the ingá fruit are ripe (February to April). They also say that it should happen just before the Pleiades rains (*nyokoaro hue*), the heavy rains that begin the major rainy season and cause a dramatic rise in the rivers (see fig. 3).

Among the Wanano, the main initiation rite (*kamoano ninde*) was preceded by the initiates having to spend two months secluded in a specially painted compartment.[22] There they lived on a diet, first

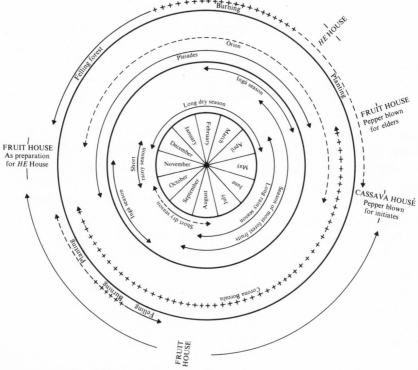

Fig. 3 *He* rites and the seasonal cycle

22 Such painted enclosures were also used by the Tariana to isolate young girls at first menstruation (see M.8.10). They are also used for the same purpose among the Tikuna (Nimuendaju 1948 : 718). Today the Barasana make the male initiates' compartment of woven palm leaves, though it may have been made of painted materials in the past.

of wasp eggs and cassava bread, then of sauba ants (*Atta* sp.). During this time they were forbidden to see or talk with women (Amorim 1926/8 : 54). The Iurupixuna-Tukano at the mouth of the Vaupés river also have a period of fasting prior to initiation but this time out on the savannah (Ypiranga Monteiro 1960 : 38). There does not appear to be any equivalent preliminary period of fasting or isolation amongst the contemporary Barasana.

The stated purpose of the Fruit House rite immediately preceding *He* House is for the shamans to carry out the necessary preparations. In broad terms it is no different from the rites described above, but certain specific features should be mentioned.

During the morning, the shamans construct a compartment of woven palm leaves next to post 1 (see fig. 2). This compartment is the shield and protection (*kʉni oka*) of the shamans and in the past it was made of painted tapir hide.[23] The shamans spend the afternoon inside this enclosure, chanting together and blowing spells over substances contained in gourds. They are surrounded by all their ritual paraphernalia: gourds on stands, bundles of whips, boxes of feather ornaments, lumps of beeswax, yagé vines, etc.

The other important difference between this and other like rituals is that different and more sacred flutes, trumpets and other ritual gear are used. Before the start of the formal playing of the long flutes (the ones used are called *Maha Bʉkʉ*, Old Macaw), tobacco snuff is blown into the sound holes by one of the shamans; this is food that the flutes eat.[24] Snuff is then administered through a bone tube to all present. While the long flutes are played, all the younger people must sit absolutely still and not look at the players.

The dance that followed was not observably different from any other that followed Fruit House except that it started somewhat later than usual. Between this rite and the start of *He* House there was a three-day interval. During this time the initiates and younger men ate only cassava, sauba ants and ground termites — they had already seen the sacred *He*. Each day they were woken before dawn by the shamans and taken down to the river to bathe and vomit. On

---

23 The words *wekʉ gase* ('tapir skin') apply both to this enclosure and to the shields made from woven vine (see Koch-Grünberg 1909/10. vol. I : 346). It may be that such shields were once made from tapir skin.

    In relation to the use, by shamans, of tapir-skin protection, it is of interest that shamans of the Orahone tribe (south of the Vaupés) used tapir-skin clothing (Whiffen 1915 : 73).

24 The Tariana also blew tobacco smoke into their Yurupary flutes (Coudreau 1887 : 167).

the day before the start of *He* House, a young man was sent to the forest to cut the tree bark used in the construction of the *He* trumpets. In the afternoon of the final day, all the men painted themselves with black paint. The initiates painted themselves from toes to chin, the younger men painted up as far as their hips and the elders as far as their thighs. Unlike that for Fruit House and other dances, the painting was uniform, with no patterns or designs, and it was stated that the more times a man has seen the *He*, the smaller the area of his body that he paints.[25]

25 Under normal circumstances only the young men and elders would have painted them-selves at this point. The initiates would have been painted just prior to their entry into the house during *He* House. It may be however that people seeing *He* for the second time in the status of initiate (as was the case for two of the four initiates) are painted at this point.

4

He House: the main initiation rite

Introduction

In the Pirá-paraná region, the rite of Fruit House, described in the last chapter, is held quite often by any moderately large maloca community. Most of these rites are not directly associated with the initiation of young men, but as already shown, they sometimes form the first stage of the initiation process and sometimes form a prelude to the main initiation rite of *He* House. Relative to Fruit House, this latter rite is held only very rarely. Together with the secrecy that surrounds it, this may well explain why it is that, with the possible exceptions of the Wanano (Amorim 1926/8 : 52–5) and Tariana (Coudreau 1887 : 198), no ritual equivalent to *He* House has been described from elsewhere in the Vaupés region whilst being common to all the Indian groups (Barasana, Tatuyo, Taiwano, Makuna and Bará) of the Pirá-paraná drainage. Just how frequently it is held is hard to say: one informant said that the rite could be held without the presence of initiates in the same way as Fruit House, and that when this happened it was referred to as house where shamanism is done (*baseria wi*). He added that in theory it should be held each year but that in practice this rarely happens. Today it seems that the rite is held only when there are young boys ready for initiation. The rite is normally referred to as *He wi*, *He* House, but may also be called house at which *He* are seen (*He ĩaria wi*) or house of initiate boys (*ngamʉa wi*).

As I have only seen one example of this rite, I present the description that follows in the form of an extended case. The account has been supplemented at certain points by informants' descriptions of similar rites partly because the rite that I witnessed was atypical in certain respects and partly because certain parts of the rite are no

longer carried out.[1] I indicate, either in the text or in notes, where
the description differs from what I actually saw. I have no concrete
data on who it is that decides when *He* House should be held though
I would guess that the decision is taken by the shamans in conjunction with the fathers of the candidates for initiation. There are
relatively few shamans of sufficient power, knowledge and standing
who can officiate at *He* House which means that very often young
boys are initiated away from their natal longhouse community or
that shamans from other communities must be brought in to officiate.
In addition, a specialist chanter must be present and he too may have
to come from outside. Once it has been decided to hold *He* House in
a particular community, the full cooperation of all the inhabitants
is needed.

The *He* House that I observed was held in Mandu's house on Caño
Colorado, an affluent of the Pirá-paraná (see map 3) on 2 June 1970.
(This was the only ritual of this kind that I observed over a twenty-
two-month period but I collected a number of different accounts of
these rites from informants both before and after the proceedings.)
The attendance by household is set out on the bottom line of table 1.
Essentially, the participants were made up of people from the houses
of Mandu, Pedro, Luis, Christo and Pacho. Though only two young
people from Ignacio's house attended, as one of them was one of the
two youngest initiates (both seeing the *He* for the *second* time in
their lives), that household is included in the table. The names and
kinship relations of the people involved are set out in fig. 4. The
dotted lines indicate a classificatory sibling tie (thus, Miguel is Mandu's
classificatory FEB). The plus signs indicate a person living or staying
in the host maloca but of a different exogamic group. Thus Simon

1 The description of the main initiation rite and its prelude is based on my observation of
a rite which took place in a Barasana maloca at the beginning of June 1970. The officiating
shamans stressed that the rite was atypical in two respects: first, it took place at the
wrong time of year (too late), and secondly, the two main candidates for initiation,
instead of being young boys, were young men in their late teens or early twenties. They
had been away working rubber and for this reason had not previously undergone the
rite, even though one of them was already married. The other two candidates were boys
undergoing the rite for the second time – each person must undergo the rite two or
three times in the status of initiate. For these reasons, parts of the rite were either
shortened or omitted completely. There are also certain parts of the rite that are no
longer carried out today but which even quite young men had undergone and could
describe.

  The description of the initial phases of the rite that concern the initiates is based on
my own observations together with informants' accounts. I am also indebted to Tom
Langdon, who carried out fieldwork with the Barasana of Caño Tatu, for an independent
description, based on informants' accounts, of the major features of *He* House.

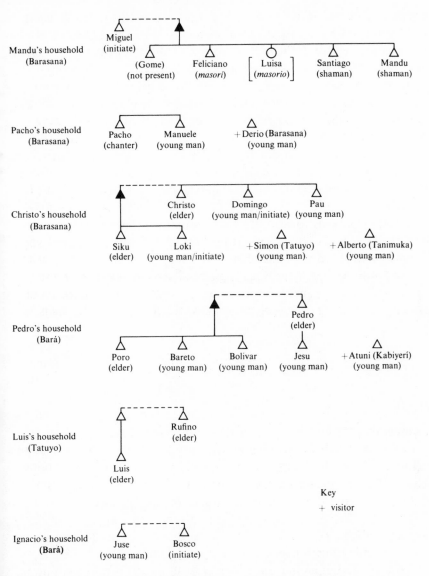

Fig. 4 Kinship relations and household affiliation of men present at *He* House (Caño Colorado, June 1970)

lives in Christo's house, Alberto was on a visit from the Popeyaká, an affluent of the Apaporís, Derio was visiting Pacho's house and Atuni lives in Pedro's house. Pacho and Christo are both related to Mandu as classificatory FYB. Pedro is related to Mandu as MB

71

and Jusé is Pedro's classificatory YB. Lius is related to Mandu as MB.

The two youngest initiates were Miguel and Bosco; Loki and Domingo were also in the status of initiate but older than they should have been and one of them was already married. The officiating shamans were Mandu and Santiago and the ritual guardian of the initiates (*masori* – see below) was Feliciano, the elder brother of the two shamans. Luisa, their sister, was the woman who provided the special food for the initiates after the rites (*masorio* – see below). All the guests arrived on the day of sitting out on the plaza, the day the rite begins and the equivalent of the day of making beer at Fruit House rites, except Pacho, Manuele and Derio who arrived the day after.

The preparations for the rite were much the same as those already described for Fruit House except that during the preceding two weeks, the men went to great pains to stop up every single hole in the walls of the house so that there was no possibility of the women seeing the sacred *He* instruments. For the same purpose, a new, extra-thick screen for shutting off the female end of the house was also made.

The rite
(Reference should be made to table 3.)

Day 1

From early morning there is a marked and increasing separation between the sexes; the women remain in the rear of the house making manioc beer whilst the men sit out on the plaza in front of the house. The initiates remain with the women in the rear of the house.[2] Early in the afternoon, the young men are sent to the forest to prepare the flutes and trumpets. In the late afternoon the shamans send the women and children out of the house so that they can blow spells over coca mixed with beeswax and over red paint. This blowing is to protect the participants from a variety of illnesses (shaking, vomiting, worms, coughing, flu, etc.). Later the women are called back to eat pinches of blown coca and to wipe the red paint on their bodies.

At dusk the younger men play the *He* up from the river and arrive outside the front of the house. Immediately, the women and children

2 They stayed with the men on the occasion seen by me. Informants said that, had they been younger boys, they would have remained with their mothers.

rush from the house to the surrounding scrub. For the rest of the night till first light the flutes and trumpets are played round and round the outside of the house. The flute Old Macaw (*Maha Buku*) dances on the plaza singing, 'Can you hear me? Are you well? Are you free from sickness? Is the beer good? Don't let the women see me.'

As the *He* arrive the shamans chant together and flick their whips aggressively, making a loud swishing noise. One of them then carries smoking beeswax on a potsherd out to the plaza. There he fans the smoke in the four cardinal directions to send away illness, disease and shamanic attack. As soon as the *He* are present, all communication is done in whispers and is kept to a minimum. The shamans then lead the elders inside the house in chanting and then go and lead the younger men in another session outside. Apart from the shamans, there is no movement between the groups inside and outside the house. During the night the shamans blow spells over beeswax, coca, beer and tobacco to ward off illnesses that would otherwise come with their consumption. The shamans also blow on tobacco snuff which is then blown in large quantities up the noses of the men, causing them to vomit.

Day 2

At first light the *He* are played into the house by those who have spent the night sitting outside.[3] They walk into the house, round the dance path twice in a clockwise direction, down the middle and out of the door again, right round the outside of the house, back in through the door, twice round the dance path and then down the middle of the house, stopping as the leader reaches the men's door. They then put the *He* down on the right-hand side of the house at the edge of the dance path and go and sit in a group in front of the shaman's enclosure. The elders sit in two groups on either side of the men's door with the two shamans sitting inside their enclosure. Only the shamans, and later the elders, sit on stools; the rest all sit on mats on the floor.

As the *He* enter the house, the women again rush out and into the scrub surrounding the house. If they failed to do this, when they became pregnant they would be unable to give birth. The children would remain in their wombs and they would die.

3 Which included the four initiates on the occasion I witnessed.

Table 3. *He House*

	Shamans	Elders	Young men	Initiates	Women & children
	Blow on wax, coca, red paint		Leave house	Leave house	Leave house
Dusk	CHANT	PLAY LONG FLUTES (on plaza)	BRING HE TO HOUSE PLAY TRUMPETS (round outside of house)	FLEE FROM HOUSE Confined in house	FLEE FROM HOUSE Confined in house
	Burn wax on plaza				
	CHANT CHANT Blow on snuff, beer, cigar, wax, coca	CHANT	CHANT		
Midnight	ADMINISTER SNUFF	RECEIVE SNUFF	RECEIVE SNUFF		
Dawn	CHANT	FLUTES INTO HOUSE	TRUMPETS INTO HOUSE	FLEE FROM HOUSE	FLEE FROM HOUSE
	CHANT (giving coca)	CHANT (giving coca) PLAY FLUTES (middle of house)	CHANT (giving coca) PLAY TRUMPETS (edge of house)		
	BATHE	BATHE	WASH HANDS & FACES		
Midday	CHANT (pouring beer)	CHANT (pouring beer) PUT ON FULL ORNAMENT	CHANT (pouring beer)		
				Hair cut, painted CARRIED INTO HOUSE Drink yagé SHOWN HE CHANT	
Dusk	Serve coca, yagé, *kana* to initiates	CARRY BOYS INTO HOUSE			LEAVE HOUSE
	CHANT BLOW ON SNUFF + COCA + WAX	SHOW HE TO BOYS CHANT	SHOW HE TO BOYS CHANT		
	Serve yagé	Drink yagé	Drink yagé	Drink yagé	

Midnight	→				
Dawn	WHIP PARTICIPANTS CHANT (giving coca) Blow on black paint	APPEAR AS *HE* SPIRITS EAT BLOWN SNUFF + COCA WHIPPED CHANT (giving coca) Play long flutes →	EAT BLOWN SNUFF + COCA WHIPPED CHANT (giving coca) MUTUAL PAINTING Play trumpets	EAT BLOWN SNUFF + COCA WHIPPED CHANT (giving coca) MUTUAL PAINTING	Return to house
Midday	CHANT (pouring beer) Play Old Callicebus trumpets Blow on snuff Administer snuff to flutes	CHANT (pouring beer)	CHANT (pouring beer)	CHANT (pouring beer)	
Dusk	Blow on stools SLEEP →	Take snuff Flutes out of house SLEEP →	Take snuff Trumpets out of house SLEEP →	Take snuff SLEEP →	Take snuff SLEEP →
Midnight		FLUTES INTO HOUSE	TRUMPETS INTO HOUSE Play trumpets		
Dawn	BATHE & VOMIT RETURN TO HOUSE	BATHE & VOMIT RETURN TO HOUSE Play flutes	BATHE & VOMIT RETURN TO HOUSE	BATHE & VOMIT RETURN TO HOUSE	
Midday	REMOVE HEAD-DRESSES Blow on cassava, termites	HEAD-DRESSES REMOVED →	Eat meal SLEEP	Eat meal SLEEP	REMOVE GOODS FROM HOUSE
Dusk	Eat meal SLEEP	Eat meal SLEEP			Remove dividing screen

– – – Division between small and big dance.

Soon after entry of the *He*, the younger men are led in chanting
by the shamans who come and sit in front of their enclosure. After
this, the long flutes are played up and down the middle of the house
by relays of players and the trumpets and short flutes, played by the
young men, are periodically played round and round the inside and
outside of the house in a kind of ceremonial parade (see appendix 3).

Around 9.0 a.m. the shaman hands round a ceremonial cigar over
which he has blown spells, together with a gourd of blown coca. He
serves people in order of seniority, the youngest being served first.
Then two gourds are placed in the middle of the house. The first
contains blown snuff and the second red paint, both taken from small
sealed gourds kept in the feather box (see M.6.A.64). The snuff,
mixed with beeswax, is wiped on the legs and knees using a stick. If
it gets under the fingernails it causes intense pain. It is applied so that
when the men bathe, they will not suffer stabbing pains caused by
the water spear (*oko besuu*). Apart from ritual bathing all contact
with water during the rite is taboo. The red paint is described as the
blood or flesh of the *He* (*He rĩ, He ruhu oko*) and as that which
makes us live (*mani katise*). It is wiped over the body, especially on
the navel and temples to replenish one's blood and make one strong.
If a woman has contact with this paint she will immediately start to
menstruate; the blood that flows is this paint.

Following this, everyone, including the shamans, goes to bathe
in the stream at the back of the house. The *He* are taken too and
played as far as the edge of the clearing round the house. At the
stream, the *He* are put into the water to make them sound well,
and the elders bathe. The younger men wash only their hands and
faces. Throughout the bathing, total silence is enjoined to avoid
attack from the *He* jaguars. On the way to and from the stream, the
shamans lead and take up the rear of the procession flicking their
whips aggressively. This bathing is called washing the tree bark from
the hands (*hea gase amo koera*). After more playing of the *He*, a
special form of playing, called going to make the tree bark low
(*hea gase bohoa wana*), is due (see appendix 3).

After this each person drinks beer blown by the shamans from the
end of a stick and beer is then served in large gourds throughout the
rest of the rite. Before this time no one must touch the beer. Then
a long chanting session is held. During the afternoon the long flutes,
Old Macaw, are decorated with feather ruffs and the engraved designs
on them are filled with manioc starch. Two elders put on jaguar-

teeth belts, feather crowns and elbow ornaments and then go out and
dance the Old Macaw flutes up and down the middle of the house.
Up to this point, those playing the flutes wear no ornament at all.
These flutes are now played continuously by a relay of players,
all elder men. Every so often the mouth-ends of the flutes are
dipped into a pot of water; this is to improve the sound quality and
also 'to give them a drink'. The players must never walk in the middle
of the house except when actually playing the flutes; at all other
times they walk along the dance path to one side.

   Towards dusk the initiates are brought into the house.[4] The
shamans and elders go outside and call them. Their hair is cut by the
women who also paint them from head to toe with black paint.
Once their hair has been cut, the initiates are carried into the house
on the shoulders of the elders. This act establishes a pseudo-kinship
link between carrier and carried: each calls the other '*yu umari*' (my
carrier/carried), terms which replace the kinship terms that were
previously used between them.[5] The initiates are placed standing in
a line by the men's door with their little fingers linked together.
Then they are given shamanised *kana* (*Sabicea amazonensis*) berries
to eat which makes them strong enough to withstand the rite.

   Throughout the rite, the initiates are looked after by an elder
man who is called their *masori* (the root *maso-* means to make human,
to adopt or to bring up). During the rite and thereafter, this man
addresses the initiates as *yu masori* (my *masori*) and they address him
in the same way. Those Barasana who know Spanish translate *masori*
as *padrino* (godfather) and people who are related as *masori* to each
other are expected to be firm friends. The same term is used also
between an adopted child and its parents. The female form *masorio*
is applied to the woman who cooks special food for the initiates after
the rite.

   When the initiates have eaten the *kana* berries their *masori* leads
them very slowly by the hand to a mat placed in front of the shaman's
enclosure. They are sat down slowly and their bodies arranged in a
foetal position with their knees drawn up to their chests and their
arms clasped round them. They are instructed to remain absolutely
motionless and not to glance from side to side. If they move it is said
that their backs will break.

4 This is what should happen when young initiates see *He* for the first time. This paragraph
  is based on informants' accounts.
5 This carrying of the initiates was also done among the Wanano, and as with the Barasana
  it gave rise to a pseudo-kinship link. Amorim (1926/8 : 53)

Once they are seated, the initiates are served the ceremonial cigar and blown coca. Outside the house, the shaman prepares the yagé. When he has finished, he draws a figure (Yagé Mother) in the doorway of the house using the pounded yagé bark (see fig. 5), throwing the rest of the poundings up on to the roof of the house. Then he comes in and serves each initiate a small sip of yagé.

(A)   (B)

Fig. 5 Yagé Mother (A) figure drawn on longhouse floor with pounded yagé bark; compare with (B) petroglyph on rock in Vaupés river above Jauareté (after Stradelli 1900: 476)

All the men take up the *He* instruments and move very slowly in front of the initiates, blowing the *He* with their ends held very close to the ground.[6] They parade in front of the initiates showing them each instrument in turn and then circle slowly round and round the house. This is the first time that the initiates see the *He*. Following this a long session of chanting is held. After this, apart from the playing of the flutes and trumpets and the chanting, almost total silence reigns in the house. Towards midnight, the shaman takes the pot of yagé and walks with it to the female end of the house, standing between posts 5 and 6 and facing the men's end. He calls the people to come and drink. They go up to him, youngest first, clutching staves in their hands and acting-out spearing up the side aisles of the house as they go. Each is then given yagé and blown coca after which

6 This was not done on the occasion witnessed by me.

they go back to their places, again acting-out spearing down the side aisles. There then follows another parade of the *He* (see appendix 3).

Soon after midnight, the two shamans chant together inside their enclosure while the guardian of the initiates burns beeswax, taken from the gourd of beeswax, in a potsherd round the house, taking the same path as during Fruit House. As he does this he is followed round by the younger men playing on the trumpets and the initiates playing behind them on the short flutes. They walk very slowly, crouching low to the ground with the ends of the trumpets almost touching the floor. If the trumpets were held high, the players' knees would break and the *He* jaguars would be angry.

The burning of the wax is considered to be the climax of the rite and during it the women must not be in the house for if they smelt the smoke they would die. The women go out to the edge of the clearing in the forest and listen for trees falling. The noise of falling trees is an evil omen (*yokero*) which foretells the death of the participants who will waste away and die. The women are sent as sentries and they report back in the morning.[7]

After the burning of the beeswax, two elders put on the full complement of ritual ornament — full head-dresses of macaw and egret feathers (*maha hoa* and *uga*), the sacred elbow ornaments (*rika sãria yasi*) (see M.7.I.3—4 and M.6.A.64), hanks of monkey-fur string worn on the back (*umaria yasi*), bark-cloth aprons (*waso boti*), belts of carved rose-coloured shell (*wai waruka*), etc., and then go out to play the long flutes called Old Macaw. These two are the *He* spirits (*He wãtia*), fierce spirits (*guari wãtia*), the ancestors of the living, and are very frightening and dangerous. Everyone, especially the initiates, must sit absolutely still and on no account look at them (see M.8.32). As the flutes play, everyone but the two shamans forms up into two groups on either side of the house carrying staves and whips. The flutes are then played with their ends raised in the air (see appendix 3) while the others run up and down the side aisles, in the opposite direction from the flutes, acting-out spearing. The flutes are threatening to kill; they say, 'I will kill you, I will kill you.' They are being fierce and teaching the initiates to be the same.

Immediately after this, two gourds are placed between posts 1 and

---

7 Brüzzi da Silva (1962 : 330 n. 26) mentions that *Wax-ti* (one of his names for Yurupary) is held responsible for falling trees by the Tukano.

Among the Makú of the Paraná Boá-Boá, if women should see the sacred flutes and trumpets (*Baritxai*) there would be much thunder and lightning, lots of rain would fall and many trees would come down (Schultz 1959 : 125).

2. One, the *werea koa*, contains beeswax mixed with coca, the other, the *muno koa*, snuff gourd, contains snuff. In order of seniority, initiates first, the people come up and wipe snuff on their knees and eat small pinches of coca. On no account must they look at the gourds which are covered with brown bark-cloth wrappings. Then the sequence of the flutes played with raised ends and the acting-out spearing is repeated. Following this the two elders playing the Old Macaw flutes chant with the shamans and then go back to playing the flutes. During their playing, the blown coca, taken from the beeswax gourd, is passed through to the older women behind the screen. They eat the coca and apply blown red paint to their bodies.

Then, as the pair playing the long flutes chant with one of the shamans, the other goes to the female end of the house carrying a bundle of whips. All present run up the side aisles, acting-out spearing, and stand in two groups by the shaman. One by one, starting with the youngest, they go forward and, standing with their legs apart and with their arms held above their heads clutching a staff hori-zontally in their hands, they are whipped on the leg, thigh, abdomen and chest. Holding their arms out in front of them, these are whipped too. After each person has been whipped, he runs back to his place, acting-out spearing as he goes. Finally the shaman comes back to the men's end of the house where he too is whipped by another elder. After this, more yagé is served, the long-flute players being given extra large amounts. This is followed by a very long chant session, giving coca, held by the screen at the female end of the house, which goes on till dawn.

Following the chanting, the shaman takes a pot of blown black paint to the screen at the female end of the house. There the initiates and younger men paint each other on the legs and body. Two men should do the painting, one for the lower body, one for the upper body. The people who paint each other call one another my painter/ painted (*yu suori*) a term which replaces the normal kinship terms between them from then on. People related in this way are seen as being 'like brothers' and the relationship is seen as being the male equivalent of the *henyeri—henyerio* relationship. I was told by one informant that, in the past, at this point the initiates were then made to stand in a row with their hands behind their backs. Their G-strings were cut so that their penis coverings fell to the ground. The *He* instruments were blown over their penises after which they went out

and played the short flutes in the nude. Then new G-strings would
be blown for them to avoid rashes round the groin.

This mutual painting is followed by a parade of the trumpets
and short flutes. Apart from during the burning of the beeswax,
the trumpets and short flutes are hardly played at all during the
night. The focus of attention is on the flutes, Old Macaw. For the
rest of the day the flutes and trumpets are played rather sporadically.
At mid-morning there is another long chant session, pouring out
the beer, during and after which much beer is served. Many people
begin to go to sleep at around this point. For the elders it is tolerated,
but each time a young man shows signs of sleep, the shamans come
up to him and angrily flick their whips and shout to wake him.

Around midday there is a parade of all the flutes and trumpets
round and round the house. During this parade a pair of trumpets
called Old Callicebus Monkey (*Wau Bʉkʉ*) are played by the two
shamans. This is the only time that these two trumpets are played.
All through the rite they are kept inside the shamans' enclosure,
apart from the other *He* instruments. Then the shamans blow over
snuff and place it in the mouthpieces of the flutes 'for them to eat'.
Following this, everyone, women too, is served the snuff to prevent
illness. Finally, just before dark, the flutes and trumpets are taken
on parade round and round the house and then the action of going
to remove the bark wrappings from the *He* is done (see appendix 3).
This is called ending the dance (*basa tadiyigʉ*). After this the *He* are
taken outside the house and the feather ruffs are removed from the
flutes. Then the shamans blow spells over their stools and invite
each person to sit momentarily upon them. This removes the prohibition on sitting on stools but it is only the elder people who in
fact sit on them. The younger people continue to sit on the ground.

Mats covered in white, plume-like grass (*ta boti*) are laid at the
end of the house near the screen and everyone but a few of the
elders goes to sleep on them. They must not sleep at the male end of
the house for the old *He* People (*He bʉkʉrã*) sleep there. If anyone
sleeps there they will dream that the *He* People give them large
quantities of fish at a food-exchange dance. The fish would cause
one to waste away and die. The male end of the house is ideologically
(though not always actually) the east end and is identified with the east,
the Water Door (*Oko Sohe*) where the shamans send these fish.
The Sun and the *He* People want the participants, especially the

initiates, to remain with them for ever so they give them fish to kill them.

Day 3

At dawn the flutes are again played up and down the inside of the house and the trumpets round and round the outside. While this goes on the shamans blow spells over gourds containing snuff and water. The snuff is then applied to the knees and the water is drunk in small quantities by each person. This is to prevent harm coming from contact with water, both in the form of dew at night and also during the bathing to follow. Without this, the initiates' joints would ache, and they would get fever and stabbing pains caused by the water spear (*oko besuu*). Then everyone goes down to the main river in front of the house to bathe, taking the *He* with them. Once the instruments have been immersed, all, including the initiates and young men, get right into the water and bathe. Then the shamans fill the Old Macaw flutes and a trumpet with water. They do this in such a way that water spurts out of the sound holes in the flutes; this is the flutes drinking and vomiting. The initiates must drink water from the flutes and trumpet, after which the rest of the water is poured over them. This is to make them fierce. Each person is handed leaves of the plant *sioro hũ* (meaning literally adze leaves, sp. un-identified) which are used as soap. The leaves are crushed up in water which is afterwards drunk, causing vomiting. The consumption of these leaves makes the initiates and young men into good dancers and singers. The vomiting is to clean out the *He* poison (*He rima*), the effects of seeing *He*, from the body and to remove the residual yagé which would otherwise cause the body to heat up and become sick. While the initiates bathe, two elders play the Old Macaw flutes.

Before the men return to the house, the women take all the food and goods in the house out on to the plaza.[8] If they were left in the house the initiates (and others) would suffer aches and pains. The men come into the house. The feather ruffs are put back on the flutes which are played by various elders, ending with the two who were the *He* spirits earlier in the rite. When the last two have finished playing, the shaman comes up and takes off their feather head-dresses.

8 This information comes from informants' descriptions. The goods were not taken out of the house on the occasion observed by me but I was assured that this would have been done if there had been young initiates seeing the *He* for the first time.

He blows spells on their heads and wipes his hands lightly over the surface, flicking off invisible but harmful substances. He does the same for each person who wore a full head-dress during the rite. If this is not done, the men are in danger of attack from jaguars and are also liable to suffer headaches caused by the silverfish that eat the feathers.

Then the young men take the trumpets for a final blow round the house while the shamans sit on stools blowing spells over small portions of food in little gourds. They treat sauba ants, ground termites and special cassava bread (*sireria*) made entirely out of manioc starch, in this way. Each person, starting with the initiates, eats a tiny portion of each of the blown foods after which a meal of the same foods is held. This meal must take place outside the house. The initiates and younger men eat their cassava bread from the ends of ritual whips so that their hands do not heat the food. They must also cover their mouths as they eat so that *He* jaguars do not see them eating and become angry. Whilst they eat they throw little pieces of cassava bread at the Old Macaw flutes as a kind of augury — a hit foretells that the person will find a wife soon.[9]

Following the meal, the bark wrappings are removed from the trumpets and after all the *He* instruments have been wrapped in fresh leaves they are taken down to the river to be hidden once again in the mud under water.[10] The house is then swept out very thoroughly so that no traces of the materials used to make the *He* remain. Small fires are lit outside the doors of the house and leaves of an unidentified shrub (*kawia beu hũ*) are burned on them. The smoke removes the smell of the *He* from the house. The whole house is saturated with *He* poison, and this must be removed by shamanism to prevent the women from becoming ill. In the past, the initiates used to be held by the feet and shoulders and swung bodily over the fires so that they were bathed in smoke. Their penises were stuck into cecropia (*wakubu*) wood tubes so that they would find wives quickly. Today the initiates simply bathe in the smoke to remove the ill-making effects of the *He*.

The shamans then construct a compartment of woven leaves just

9 The Makuna see the period following *He* House as a marriage season during which they set out to get wives (Kaj Århem, personal communication).
10 Informants said that properly the *He* should be left with the initiates inside their compartment for some time after the end of the rite and that the initiates took the *He* with them when they went bathing and gathering food in the forest. Others said that the *He* used after the end of *He* House were not the true *He* but those used at Fruit House.

inside the men's door on the left (see fig. 2) and there the initiates sling their hammocks. The shamans blow spells on to one of the hammocks and wipe harmful substances from it. Each person lies momentarily in the hammock which makes it safe for him to sleep in hammocks once again. Since the start of the rite everyone but the shamans and elders has remained sitting on the ground. Once the initiates are installed inside their enclosure, the screen shutting off the rear of the house is removed. The women still remain at the rear end of the house and the initiates must be protected from their gaze. Later on the initiates are sent to the forest to collect sauba ants and ground termites as food. They go to sleep early and are woken by the shamans well before dawn and taken to the port to bathe and vomit water.

The marginal period

Immediately following *He* House, all the participants and especially the initiates spend a period during which they are subject to rigid restrictions on their diet and on other activities. For the initiates the end of this period is signalled by the total disappearance of the black paint applied to their bodies at the start of the rite. The end of the period is marked by the eating of capsicum pepper, blown over by the shamans. On seeing the *He*, the participants become *He* People (*He masa*), and *He* enters their bodies. This gradually leaves the body as the paint fades from the skin. For the elders, the period lasts one month; for the initiates and younger men it lasts for two months. Pepper is thus blown twice, once for the elders and once for the initiates. During the period of restrictions, the men are described as *bedira*, a state when people fast and undergo restrictions. The same word also applies to menstruating women.

Throughout the period the initiates sleep and spend much of their time secluded in their compartment. The compartment is built in such a way that they can go in and out without seeing or being seen by the women at the other end of the house. The women fear the initiates for if they have any contact with them, *He*, in the form of an anaconda, enters their bodies and they die. If they touch one of the men, they become sick and waste away (*wisi-*); the man's body water (*ruhu oko*) would enter the woman's body and she would get stabbing sickness (*sarese*) and die. The men are harmful and poisonous 'like menstruating women' and they too are harmed by

84

contact with women. Sexual intercourse is absolutely forbidden as it would cause a broken back and the men fear possible contact with poisonous menstrual blood.

The avoidance of women is reflected in the use of house space. The adult men sleep in the middle front of the house (as do unmarried men at all times) and not in their family compartments. During the day the men must remain outside the front of the house on the plaza; the women must stay at the rear of the house. At first all the men must eat meals outside the house; later the elders eat just inside the front door whilst the initiates remain outside. Each day, one woman, the *masorio* or guardian of the initiates, brings food and water and leaves them outside the initiates' compartment. The containers used by the men must be kept separate from those used by the women so that indirect contact with prohibited foods is avoided, and again the initiates use separate containers from those used by the elders. In general, the restrictions apply with less force and for a shorter period for the elders.

The diet of the men consists essentially of cassava bread made entirely of manioc starch (*sireria*), toasted manioc starch (*nahū sūhu*), sauba ants, ground termites, forest fruit, especially umari — cultivated roots (*ote*) and bananas. The food eaten by the initiates must be especially pure and free from all traces of pepper, meat juices, etc. This food is prepared by the *masorio* who must carefully wash her hands and all the utensils she uses. She is also responsible for providing ants and termites for the initiates' diet. At the end of the period of fasting, this woman is given lots of basketry in payment for her services. Not only is the initiates' diet severely limited; they must also eat in a way that displays great control. They eat only very small mouthfuls at a time and must cover their mouths with their hands as they eat.

Each day the initiates are expected to get up before dawn and bathe at the port.[11] They must wash their faces with leaves that produce suds so that the facial skin is changed and becomes white.[12] These same leaves are mixed with water which is then drunk so as to produce vomiting. The vomiting (and also the fasting) cleans out the dirt (*ueri*) from the body; this dirt would otherwise cause list-

11 According to informants, the initiates should bathe to the sound of the *He* which they take with them to the port (see n. 10 above).
12 This washing of the face to make it white is even more marked during the period of restrictions that follows the rite of first menstruation for a girl.

lessness and lack of strength (*gaha huase*). The bathing and vomiting is also said to make the initiates grow faster.

For the initiates, the marginal period is a time of education. Immediately after the end of *He* House they are sent to the forest to collect large quantities of weaving cane (*Ichnosiphon*, a species of Marantaceae). The pith from the middle is blown over by a shaman and then eaten by all to prevent worms from eating the teeth and also to prevent splints of cane, sent by enemy shamans (*kumuanye waka*), from piercing the gums and causing inflammation. Then the elders systematically teach the initiates to make all the different kinds of basketry (carrying baskets, sieves, flat trays, cassava squeezers, etc.). By the end of this period the initiates amass considerable quantities of basketwork which they give away to the women at the dance following the blowing of pepper. Basket making is seen as a prerequisite of adult male status and the Barasana say that men give their women baskets in exchange for the manioc bread that this basketry helps to produce.[13]

In addition to basketry, the initiates are taught how to make the feather head-dresses and other ritual ornaments used in dances — ankle rattles, painted bark-cloth aprons, palm-leaf crowns, egret plumes, frontal crowns of yellow macaw feathers, etc. (see M.6.A.46). A considerable quantity of ornaments is made and used at the dance following the blowing of pepper. Though the learning of hunting and fishing skills is a never-ending process, there is a period of fairly intense education in these matters after initiation; once boys have been initiated their hunting and fishing becomes a serious matter. Just before the blowing of pepper, the initiates are taught to weave conical fish traps which they go and set in streams in the forest, accompanied by their *masori*. The small fish that are caught are afterwards blown over by a shaman and eaten after the blowing of pepper; this is the first fish that the initiates eat. In the past the initiates were also taught to use the weapons of war, especially the throwing lance. They had their arms cut and the blood was mixed with red paint and with yagé and then drunk. This made them so fierce that 'they saw their enemies as game animals'. As well as this practical education, the initiates are taught more esoteric knowledge by the shamans and elders. Again, though such education is part of

13 Ypiranga Monteiro (1960 : 38–9) describes this post-initiation basket making among the Iuripixuna-Tukano and Galvão (1959 : 50) mentions the same thing among the Baniwa of the Içana.

an ongoing process, after *He* House the initiates are taught the names and significance of the *He* instruments and the mythology associated with them, as well as much other knowledge. They are also given talks of the expected behaviour, etc., of adult men. Unfortunately, my information on this aspect of their education is rather limited.

People who have seen *He* and are under restrictions are believed to be inherently weak, lazy and soft; a Cubeo myth describes how when the women had the Yurupary instruments 'they danced all the time and did no work' (Goldman 1963 : 193).[14] There is in fact a real sense in which the men are lazy for after *He* House they are forbidden to carry out the normal masculine tasks of hunting and fishing and must do no strenuous work. The women fend for themselves by fishing and will even hunt small rodents with dogs – they thus become almost totally independent of the men. According to Barasana myth (M.1.D), when the women stole the *He* from the men, the women become dominant and the men began to menstruate. The temporary independence of women after *He* House is reminiscent of the matriarchal situation described in the myth and in accordance with this men who are under restrictions are explicitly compared to menstruating women. The Barasana say that a woman's hair is the seat of laziness; they also say that hair is the women's equivalent of *He* and that when they see it they begin to menstruate (*bedi-*), just as when men see *He* they undergo restrictions (*bedira*) (see M.1.B.5). Similarly, if a man copulates with a menstruating woman he will become lazy.[15]

The relation between *He* and menstruation will be fully explored in part III. For the moment I wish merely to draw attention to the fact that much of what goes on during the marginal period is designed to prevent the men, especially the initiates, from becoming permanently soft and lazy and instead to make them strong and fierce. Bathing and vomiting early in the morning when the water is cold make a man hard and fierce (*guamu*).[16] The initiates burn scars on their arms to show their endurance of pain and get up early so that they can do without sleep. They must keep the restrictions and behave properly otherwise they will become listless and lazy till they waste away and

14 The Puinave share this belief (Rozo 1945 : 245).
15 The Cubeo believe the same (Goldman 1963 : 181).
16 Barasana informants drew attention to the fact that *gua*, to bathe, 'sounds the same as' *guamu*, a fierce man. They describe how, in the past, 'when men were really men', a man worthy of respect would bathe early each day and how, in the summer when the water was warm, he would bathe in cold dew instead.

die. But above all, they must be industrious and make lots of basketry and feather ornaments, just as menstruating women must make string from silk grass (a cultivated Bromeliad) and then knot it into garters.[17]

Prohibitions during and after seeing He

All the prohibitions described below are the direct outcome of seeing or touching the *He* used at *He* House. They apply also, but in a very much milder way, to people who have seen the *He* used at Fruit House. None of the restrictions apply to the women or children though they must avoid exposing the men to indirect contact with forbidden foods, etc. The restrictions apply with most force to the initiates; the older a man is and the more times he has seen *He*, the less constrained he feels to keep the taboos. I shall therefore write with particular reference to the initiates.

From the time that the *He* are first seen at the beginning of the rite until the time that pepper is blown, all contact with heat in any form whatsoever must be stringently avoided. During the rite, the initiates must not see, smell or have any contact with fire. The men must not warm themselves by fires for fear of the fire women (*hea romia*) who would enter their penises and cause them to have exclusively female children. Fire would also cause them to waste away and die. The initiates must not smoke any tobacco except the ritual cigars that have been treated by the shamans (the elders do smoke however). Similarly, termites caught by blowing smoke down their holes must be blown before the initiates eat them so that the smoke does not harm them.

During the rite, the initiates must not expose themselves to the heat of the sun and must therefore not go beyond the eaves of the house, even to urinate. After the rite they are supposed to use big leaves as sun-shades. The Sun's heat would burn them to death just as Manioc-stick Anaconda burned his brother Macaw to death (see M.6.A.59–60). The Sun would also poison and ensorcell the initiates; their skin would become blotched with white patches and various small creatures would harm them by tying up their hearts with fibre or shooting darts at them.

---

17 The association between puberty- and initiation-rituals and a stress on the making of handicrafts appears to be widespread throughout Amazonia and merits a comparative study, especially in relation to the theme of laziness.

He House: the main initiation rite

The initiates must also avoid eating any food that is either physically hot or classified as hot — capsicum pepper is most taboo of all. Immediately after the end of *He* House they must eat their cassava bread from the twigs on their whips so that it is not made warm by their hands. They must also avoid any food on which sunlight has fallen for the Sun would put his sick-making fish into this food (see M.6.A.17). These restrictions on heat and fire remain in force throughout the marginal period and in general the initiates must remain as cold as possible.

Another set of prohibitions relates to being raised above the ground. During the rite, only the shamans (and later the elders) can sit on stools; everyone else must sit on mats on the ground. After the rite, the initiates must not climb up trees or sit raised above the ground on logs — jaguars would eat tree climbers and sitting on logs would cause aches and pains. In the past, the initiates would sleep on the ground on mats right up until pepper was blown; today they do so only during the rite itself, after which their hammocks are made safe again by the shamans.

During the rite, the initiates must try to avoid moving at all and if they have to move they should do so as slowly as possible.[18] Fast movement would cause their joints to make cracking noises and become weak. If they wish to urinate during the rite, they must be lifted up by their *masori* or another elder, led by the hand out to the eaves of the house and then gently replaced in their original sitting position. After the rite they must not make any strenuous movements with their bodies and such actions as throwing objects are forbidden.

With the exception of the *He*, no musical instruments may be played either during the rite or afterwards until pepper has been blown. If panpipes were played during the marginal period, grubs (*hikõroa*) would eat the teeth of the player. The use of deer- and jaguar-bone whistles, snail-shell whistles and leg rattles would all cause the player to become prone to attack by jaguars and snakes. All these instruments must be blown over by a shaman before they are used at the dance which follows the blowing of pepper.[19]

During the rite, all unnecessary noise and especially all laughter

18 The other occasion on which slow movement is enjoined is whilst lowering a coffin into the grave.
19 In general the Barasana appear to associate high-pitched, fast music with frivolous connotations while lower-pitched, slow music is sacred and solemn. The same is true of the Cubeo (Goldman 1963 : 214).

is forbidden; only the sacred sounds of chanting and of *He* , the sound of the *He* People or first ancestors, is allowed. The making of loud noises such as banging objects together is forbidden till after pepper has been blown. Sexual intercourse is also forbidden. All contact with human or animal blood would cause wasting away (*wisiose*) and must be avoided at all costs. Looking in mirrors would cause *He* jaguars to eat one's heart/soul (*ʉsʉ*).

Finally, contact with water is also dangerous: during the rite, when the men go to bathe (see above) the contact with water must be mediated with snuff blown over by the shamans. At the end of the rite the shamans blow spells on water in a gourd which is then drunk by everyone present. Contact with rain or dew must also be avoided both during and after the rite.

Prohibitions on food

Once the participants at *He* House have seen the flutes and trumpets they must not take any substance into their bodies until it has first had spells blown into it by a shaman. During *He* House itself, all the substances consumed (coca, tobacco, tobacco snuff, yagé and beer) are those that the Barasana treat as 'anti-food', i.e. substances which must not be consumed at the same time as ordinary food. All of these substances, except beer, are produced and consumed only by men (and old women) and all except beer are specifically associated with night-time, the sacred time when men do not consume normal food. The ancestors of humanity, the *He* People and the souls of the dead eat no normal food at all; they live entirely on coca and tobacco as did Yurupary in the myths of the Vaupés-Içana region.[20]

After *He* House is over, every single category of food, and in some cases individual species of animals and plants, must be blown on by a shaman before it is eaten. Immediately after the end of the rite, manioc starch bread (*sireria*), water, sauba ants, ground termites and toasted manioc starch are all blown. Freshly made coca is also blown to remove the harmful effects of the heat employed in toasting the leaves. The following day, termites caught by blowing smoke down their holes are blown — again the blowing is to remove the harmful effects of fire and heat; on this day tree-fruits are also blown. About a week later maize and some kind of cultivated root (yams, sweet

20 See Bolens (1967) for a useful summary of these myths.

potatoes, etc.) are blown so that the category cultivated roots (*ote*) are safe to eat. This list then forms the total diet of the initiates and elders until pepper has been blown. (Just before the blowing of pepper, salt and boiled manioc juice are added to the list of permitted foods.)[21]

The blowing of pepper and the drinking of boiling-hot manioc juice (see below) removes the prohibition on taking foods that are hot and at the same time frees people from the prohibition on contact with fire and other sources of heat. Immediately after the blowing of pepper, small fish (*wai rĩa*) caught by the initiates in funnel-traps (see above) are cooked with manioc leaves and then blown. This dish, together with the foods mentioned above, then forms the basis of the initiates' diet for the next month, being gradually supplemented by other categories of food.

At the end of the third month for the initiates, and at the end of the second month for the elders, fish caught with poison (*huari wai*) are blown, followed by each of the species of fish that belong to the category of large fish (*wai hakarã*). At the end of the fourth month (third month for the elders), the food category game animals (*wai bukurã*) is blown, each species being done separately in order of increasing size and ending with tapir meat. Roughly the same pattern of food blowing occurs after Fruit House but in this case it is done over a much shorter period of time and the list of foods treated is very much reduced. An even more reduced version is done after other kinds of dances.

The order in which the categories of food are blown after initiation corresponds more or less exactly to the order in which food is blown for a new-born baby. The first food that it eats, its own mother's milk, must have spells blown into it by a shaman and from then on, every new category of food to which it is introduced must first be treated in this way. As a child grows up, the range of food that it can consume gradually increases and there are some foods that only old people can eat. However, after initiation, the period of time between the blowing of each category of food is much less than that for a young child.

21 These foods, in the order in which they are blown, are as follows: *wasia wai* − fish caught with worms as bait; *wisiose wai* species of fish that cause wasting away of the body, especially the species *ewu wani* (*Chichlid* sp.); *oko kamo* − mingao, boiled tapioca drink; *au* − calaloo leaves; *soeri wai* − small fish roasted by the fire; *besuu wai* − fish which possess spears (erectile spines?); *wadoa* and *hikõroa* − insect grubs; *sãi* − a species of catfish; *osoa* − a species of fungus; *bia kati* − raw capsicum pepper; and a few others.

The blowing of food is done as follows: a small portion of the food is placed in a gourd and given to the shaman. He sits on a stool, sometimes for up to an hour, muttering spells which he blows into the food with short puffs of air. He then hands the gourd round to all the people present who each eat a minute portion of the food. The food eaten stands in a metonymic relation to all the food of a particular category; once eaten it is safe to eat all foods of the category until the individual in once again placed in danger from such food. After *He* House, the initiates are served this blown food first and are then followed by the other men in rough order of seniority, based on the number of times that they have been through the rite. After *He* House, women do not keep to the same dietary regime as the men (though some informants state that they should), but generally they too eat the blown food after it has been handed to the men.

Eating food that has not previously been rendered safe by blowing causes sickness and death. Each category of food, each edible animal and plant, has its own associated set of symptoms (sores on different parts of the body, swellings, aches, boils, fevers, worms, etc.) to which it gives rise. Most important after *He* House are the dangers from wasting away (*wisiose*) and from being filled with grease or fat (*uye sãhase*). The symptoms of wasting away are general listlessness, lack of breath, and a general debilitation of the body, the sufferer is said to have an enormous anus through which he literally drains away. Also mentioned as symptoms are madness, indecent sexual behaviour, loss of hair, vomiting and eating large amounts of earth. This illness is especially associated with contact with sources of heat, with capsicum peppers, and with the eating of large fish and game animals that have not been blown prior to consumption.

With fat filling the body becomes filled with fat or grease so that jaguars and snakes, attracted by the fat, see the sufferer as a suitable object of prey and attack him. In general, all fatty foods, especially food from which fat runs whilst being cooked, cause this condition. Foods such as toasted ants and termites, toasted palm-grubs, fish cooked in leaf packets and raw pepper (which causes a layer of grease to form when applied to the face) are particularly dangerous in this respect.

Breaches of these food prohibitions affect only the individuals concerned; other people, crops, weather conditions, etc. are not affected. In most instances, the Barasana emphasise that illness caused by the breach of these taboos cannot be cured by the action of the shamans and a considerable number of deaths in genealogies, especially of younger men, are attributed to breaches of food taboos following *He* House.

A full account of these taboos would involve a discussion of Barasana animal and plant taxonomy and also a knowledge of matters that my shaman informants were unwilling to divulge. However, certain general features can be seen from the data given above. The first animal foods that are eaten after *He* House are very small insects that live in the ground and are said to have no blood in their bodies. Then, following the blowing of pepper, the smallest kinds of fish are eaten, followed progressively by larger species culminating in the category of large fish. Then the smallest game animals are eaten, followed by progressively larger species culminating in the largest of all, the tapir. Thus there is a progression from low to high, from water to land, and from small to large. In view of this, the fact that the Barasana call game animals old mature fish (*wai bʉkʉra*) seems less surprising.

Foods are also categorised and blown according to the manner in which they are obtained. Thus fish caught in funnel-traps, in large traps, with worms as bait, in hollow logs, with sieves, with nets, with poison and with bow and arrow are all shamanised as separate categories. The manner in which food is cooked is also important so that boiled food, smoked food, food cooked in ashes and roast food must all be blown separately.

I have not attempted a full analysis of the food taboos that follow initiation, partly because my data on this subject is not sufficient and partly because these taboos form part of a much wider and more complex set that would require extended treatment in a separate work. The topic of the different shamanic categories of food, their effects in terms of illness and disease, and the preventative and curative treatment of illness through spells blown by shamans has been extensively treated by T. Langdon (1975) with reference to the Barasana of Caño Tatú. In almost all respects, his work applies with equal force to the Barasana of Caño Colorado.

The terminal rites

The blowing of pepper for the elders

At the initiation rite observed by me, pepper was blown for both the initiates and elders at the same time and the blowing was done only one month after the end of *He*. It was emphasised by everybody concerned that under normal circumstances when there are lots of initiates seeing *He* for the first time, pepper is blown twice, once for the elders and again for the younger men and initiates. This account of pepper blowing for the elders is based entirely on informants' descriptions.

One month after *He* House, smoked capsicum pepper is blown for the older participants. The purpose of this blowing is to cool down the pepper so that it is once again safe to eat; the blowing is called cooling the pepper. A rite of Fruit House is held at which green, unripe assai palm (*Euterpe oleracea*) fruit is brought into the house. Lots of cassava bread made entirely of manioc starch is prepared beforehand. The initiates tie pieces of this bread on to either end of strips of bark string and at midday they bring this and the assai fruit into the house to the sound of the *He* trumpets. They throw the pieces of cassava up into the roof of the house so that it hangs down from the roof beams 'until the house is white all over'. They then leave the house again while the shamans blow over smoked pepper which they distribute to the elders who eat it. As this goes on, the initiates and younger men outside the house pelt the roof with green assai fruit so that it sounds 'boro boro boro'.

The dance that follows the playing of the *He* in the house is not attended by the initiates who must remain outside the house separated from the women inside. They walk round and round the outside of the house blowing the *He* trumpets. They do not see the dancing in the house but the elders periodically come out to dance on the plaza in front of them. The dance that is danced and sung is called *He daroa mʉnganyaro* and is danced using gourd rattles. During the dance the shamans do protective blowing for the initiates and following it, they blow spells over fish caught with poison, big fish and game animals. These foods are eaten only by the elders; the initiates must wait till after pepper has been blown for them before they can eat these foods.

The blowing of pepper for the initiates and the dance that follows

According to the Barasana, though many people are invited to attend *He* House, very few in fact do so as they do not want to be burdened by the taboos and restrictions that follow it. They say however that

house containing cassava bread (*nahũ kutiria wi*) is the most popular
kind of dance there is and that everyone who can likes to attend.
They compare this dance to the fiestas that are put on in the Catholic
mission stations. During the period that follows *He* House the women
of the house make large quantities of cassava bread made entirely of
starch (thicker than the *sireria* mentioned above) which they then
store away. One woman is responsible for seeing that this bread is
made and she must keep a variety of alimentary and other restrictions
'as if she was menstruating'. Invitations are then sent out for the
dance and in particular the guests who attended *He* House are invited
as it is at this dance that they receive the shamanised foods that end
their period of fasting.

Pepper is blown for the initiates two months after the end of *He*
House. Before dawn on the day before this is done, the shamans take
the initiates and younger men to the port to bathe and vomit in
preparation for the rite. That evening, the two shamans sit in their
enclosure blowing spells into gourds containing smoked capsicum
peppers mixed with coca, placed on hourglass-shaped stands. They
both dress ceremonially with their legs and thighs covered in intricate
patterns of black paint (in contrast to the uniform paint applied prior
to *He* House), feather crowns on their heads, necklaces of jaguar
incisors round their necks, garters below their knees, etc. This time,
rather than muttering their spells they chant them together and as
they do so they enter a trance-like state. They become *He* People.
Manioc-stick Anaconda and Old Callicebus Monkey, the ancestral
shamans. Their chants refer to the origins of all the different varieties
of pepper. The pepper is referred to as the 'sun's plant' and they
describe how *Romi Kumu*, the creatress (see M.1), gave it to the first
shaman, *He* Jaguar (*He Yai*), Old Callicebus Monkey (*Wau Buku*),
who gave it to all people. When the shamans have finished, the initiates are called up to eat the pepper. They must chew a small quantity
of pepper and at the same time drink very hot boiled manioc juice
(manicuera, *nyuka*).[22] When the initiates have finished, the other
men, in rough order of seniority, come up and do the same.

In the morning of the next day the shamans again dress themselves
and blow spells into pepper but this time without the admixture of
coca. While they do this the initiates are taken to the forest by their
masori to collect small fish called *hoa* (unidentified sp.) from the

22 Tukano initiates are also made to chew peppers (see Brüzzi da Silva 1962 : 438).

traps that they have set in small streams. The elders go off to pick coca in the manioc gardens, accompanied by visiting men who have arrived for the dance. While they are away from the house, the shamans destroy the initiates' compartment and place their hammocks in the middle front of the house where they will sleep from now on. They also remove the baskets of special food and generally reorder the house. At midday, when the initiates return, they are once again made to eat pepper and drink hot drink, this time in much larger quantities. The women cook the small fish brought in by the initiates with manioc leaves and the shamans then distribute portions of this food, into which they have blown spells. When each person has eaten the blown food, a meal is served of these fish; two different pots are used, one for the initiates and young men and one for the elders.[23]

After this the initiates go to the men's port to bathe. When they return to the house they paint their legs with black paint, this time with the intricate designs used at dances, and put feather crowns on their heads. (The following section, not done at the rite seen by me, is based on informants' accounts.) The initiates and other men then enter the house where they form a circle in the middle, holding hands. The shamans call out, 'Here are the ones we have blown, see how their dirt (the black paint applied at the start of *He* House) has washed away, who wants them? Come *gahe masa romiri* (brother's daughters), come *buhibana romiri* (brother's wives and their sisters), come and make them beautiful.' The women come forward and paint each boy and man from head to foot with red paint, paying special attention to the initiates. They put strings of beads round their necks and new garters round their legs below the knees and give them gourds and packets of red paint. Then the initiates and other men go off to fetch all the baskets that they have made during the period following *He* House. Calling out 'Here my *henyerio*', they give the baskets to the particular women who have painted them. This rite, called taking a *henyerio*, establishes a special ceremonial friendship and trading partnership between the man and the woman who paints him. From then on the man calls the women my *henyerio* and the woman calls him my *henyeri*. The significance of this relationship is discussed below. In addition to giving basketry to these women, the initiates also give

23 One informant told me that in the past the initiates would have their ears and nasal septa pierced on this day, but others said that ear piercing took place when children were around three years old.

baskets to their *masori* and *masorio* and to the two shamans who officiated at *He* House. These gifts of basketry are seen as payments by the initiates for the services of these people. As the initiates give baskets to the shamans, they call they *yʉ gu*, my tortoise. (End of section based on informants' accounts.)

Once this is over, the initiates begin to dance. They dance *oko wewo* dance, holding small whistles in their hands. These whistles, called *oko wewo*, are made from pieces of hollow cane painted with geometrical designs in red and yellow and with conical basket-like structures attached to the ends and decorated with white down. From the end of these 'baskets' hang streamers, also decorated with down and ending in tassels of yellow feathers. As the initiates and younger men dance, more and more guests arrive. As each party arrives, the hosts chant greetings with them and then join them for longer sessions of chanting. The shamans blow spells into bundles of panpipes which are then handed round so that each man present can blow into them (compare p. 54 when the *He* are removed from the house at Fruit House). Then the men begin to play and dance with the panpipes, the first time that they are used after the end of *He* House. The younger men dance on through the night whilst the others chant, talk and prepare coca and the women prepare beer. Maize to make beer is also prepared by the men who are assisted in this by the women; this is the first joint activity since the start of *He* House. The initiates sleep early to be woken the next morning to bathe and vomit before dawn.

In the morning the shamans' compartment is demolished and the sacred equipment that was kept there is put away. Throughout the day of the small dance, *oko wewo* dance is danced. A full set of dances is danced, each interspersed with sessions of chanting as described in chapter 3. The dancers, mostly the initiates and young men, wear feather crowns (*buya bʉkʉ bedo*) and no yagé is served. In the middle of the house, inside the dance path next to post 6, there stands a huge round pile of cassava bread about three feet in diameter and more than four feet high. The whole pile is wrapped in brilliant white leaves bound with bark string and into the top are stuck red macaw tail feathers.

After dark, the shaman goes out to prepare yagé on the plaza in front of the house. As he does this, men begin to prepare themselves for dancing. These men, mostly elders who have not so far been dancing, will dance cassava dance (*nahʉ basa*) which forms the second section (the big dance) of the rite. They wear full feather head-dresses (*maha hoa*) and the full complement of ritual ornaments. As the dance changes from the small dance to the big dance, so also does the kind of beer being served. During the small dance beer made from manioc and other roots is served but this now changes to beer made from maize.

At around midnight, when the yagé is ready to be served, the dancers in full dress go out of the house where they form a long line, each man with both hands on the shoulders of the one in front. The leader of the line, the main dancer, plays on a whistle made from a deer skull covered in resin. To the sound of 'peeee-ru, peeee-ru, peeee-ru' from this whistle, the dance line moves slowly into the house crouching and rocking in unison from one foot to the other in imitation of the movements of a deer. As they advance, the shaman walks slowly backwards in front of them down the middle of the house to the female end, carrying the pot of yagé. He stops just beyond posts 5 and 6 and claps his hands, upon which the dance line stands up. He hands yagé to the first pair in the line who drink and then shuffle with quick steps round the dance path to the middle right of the house. The line slowly forms up as each pair is served. When the line is complete, the shaman hands a gourd of coca and the ceremonial cigar to each dancer. Then the line dances round post 5 and up the middle of the house, driving the shaman backwards in front of them as they go. When they reach the male end of the house, the line breaks up. This dance, called deer dance, is done only at house containing cassava bread following *He* House. The initiates must dance on the very end of the line. They must keep their heads down and must not look in front or to either side, nor must they rock from side to side as the other dancers do. If they look up they would be eaten by jaguars in the same way that jaguars eat deer.

Immediately after this, the second section of the dance, the big dance, begins. The cassava dance (*nahū basa*) is danced and sung by dancers wearing full head-dresses — those who did the deer dance. They hold *oko wewo* whistles in their hands which they blow in unison from time to time. At the end of the dance line dance two initiates, each holding a jaguar leg bone in his hand. These bones are wound with ruffs of brilliant yellow Oropendola feathers (the same ruffs that are placed on the *He* flutes) and look like sunbursts. The dancers who earlier danced *oko wewo* dance now go out and dance *hia basa* which starts and ends outside the house on the plaza.

The dancing goes on through the night and into the next day. At midday, the chant session, pouring out the beer, is held. The senior hosts and guests walk to the female end of the house. The chanter carries a long rattle-lance (*murucu, besuɨ*). This lance is decorated at one end with engraved designs, white down and feather streamers. At the other end there is a swelling filled with small quartz pebbles.[24] Standing between the two shamans, the chanter holds the lance in one hand and hits it with the other causing it to rattle with a rapidly increasing tempo 't t t t t t tttt'. At the same time, the young men of the dance line go to the long canoe-like trough of beer in the middle of the house and pound it with their fists in unison with the noise of the rattle-lance. They take beer from the trough and hand it round to the elders gathered at the female end of the house. There is then a short chant session after which everyone returns to the male end. There they sit between posts 1 and 2 and a much longer session of chanting is held. After chanting for more than an hour, the elders again return to the female end with the chanter hitting the lance against his shoulder as he walks. Another chant session is held there after which the elders return to the male end of the house and dancing starts once more. After a short period, the shamans call the initiates to give away their remaining basketry to the women. This time different women paint different initiates and give them more paint, beads and garters.

The dance ends just before dusk. After the shamans have removed the feather head-dresses from the heads of the dancers, the pile of cassava bread is distributed. The senior host calls up each person in the house, starting with the most important elders, and gives them a batch of cassava bread. Apart from the senior men, everyone receives roughly the same quantity of cassava bread, even quite small children. Soon after this everyone goes to sleep.

The shamans spend the following day blowing spells into gourds of different kinds of food and then distributing them to the men. For the elders, almost all of the remaining prohibited foods are made safe to eat at this point but the initiates must wait considerably longer until all food has been shamanised for them. The last food to be blown is tapir meat; I have no data on what happens when this food is blown among the Barasana but among the Tukano this occasion was marked by a dance festival. During this dance, the dancers would

24 See Koch-Grünberg (1909/10, vol. I : 345) for an illustration of this lance.

imitate the movements of the tapir. At midnight, the shaman blew
spells over tapir meat and then distributed it to the initiates. As they
ate, the other men again danced in imitation of the tapir while
outside the house the Yurupary were played (Stradelli 1890a : 450).

Fruit House and *He* House compared

The Barasana say that all the items of ceremonial equipment used at
Fruit House are simply man-made imitations of sacred objects, created
in mythic times together with the universe itself, that are used exclusively during *He* House. These sacred objects each have their own
myth of origin whilst their man-made counterparts have none. Thus,
for example, the sacred elbow ornaments used during *He* House are
the ones made by the Red Squirrel *Timoka* during the dance at which
Yeba, the ancestor of the Barasana, gave fruit to his father-in-law Fish
Anaconda (*Wai Hino*) (see M.7.I.4); those used at Fruit House were
mostly made no more than two generations ago. The relationship
between the ceremonial equipment used at the two rites will be further
discussed in part III.

Informants also state that the rite of Fruit House is itself simply a
reduced and attenuated imitation of *He* House. Limitations of space
make a point-by-point comparison of the rites impossible, but I
think it is safe to say that if the reader compares the descriptions
given above or compares table 2 with table 3, he will see that what
the Barasana say is indeed true. The parallel is most obvious between
the rites themselves; it is less obvious between the subsequent events
in each case. I shall therefore attempt to make this more explicit.

At the end of *He* House, the screen separating the men from the
women is removed and the women once again enter the main part of
the house. Their contact with the men is however very limited and
as soon as they enter, the men retire to the plaza in front of the house.
For the rest of the marginal period that follows *He* House the men
remain at the extreme front end of the house and spend most of
their time out on the plaza. During the whole of this period it is
forbidden to play panpipes or any other musical instruments except
the *He*. At the dance of house containing cassava bread that marks
the end of the marginal period, the men and women are once again
fully reintegrated, the men no longer spend their time at the front
of the house and the taboo on musical instruments is lifted.

During Fruit House, as soon as the *He* are removed from the house at dusk, the screen separating the men from the women is again removed and the women re-enter the main part of the house. As the women come in, the men leave the house to sit out on the plaza. After a short time, the shaman blows over panpipes thus making them safe to use, and then the men come back in again. This brief period out on the plaza between Fruit House and the dance that follows it corresponds to the period, also spent largely outside the house on the plaza between *He* House and the dance, house of cassava bread, that follows it.

The correspondence between the two rites can also be shown in another way: all Barasana dance rituals are divided into two sections called the small dance and the big dance. During the small dance, the dancers, mostly younger men, wear simple feather crowns; during the big dance, a different group of dancers, mostly older men, wear the full complement of ritual ornament, including elaborate feather head-dresses. The end of each section is marked by the chant session called pouring out the beer and by the change in dress and groups of dancers outlined above. The overall pattern of *He* House corresponds exactly to the division of a dance into these two sections: during the first part, young men dressed in feather crowns play trumpets; the end of this section is marked by the chant session pouring out the beer and after this elder men, wearing full head-dresses, play the long flutes.

In one sense, the whole period during which the *He* are in the house at Fruit House corresponds both to the small dance of ordinary dances and to the first section of *He* House during which young men play trumpets. Similarly, the dance which follows Fruit House corresponds both to the big dance of ordinary dances, and to the second, flute-playing, section of *He* House. This correspondence is in terms of the sequence of chant sessions. However, I have argued above that Fruit House as a whole corresponds to *He* House, also as a whole, and that the dance following Fruit House corresponds to the final dance that follows *He* House. If this is so, then one would expect to find that Fruit House would itself be divided into two sections, corresponding to those of *He* House. Here the correspondence is only partial: during Fruit House, the chant session pouring out the beer (which marks the ends of both the small dance and the big dance) is held only once, whilst at *He* House it is held twice. Thus, in terms of sessions of chanting, Fruit House is not divided into two sections. But in other terms it is so divided, for during the first part it is the

101

young men, wearing either feather crowns or no ornament at all, who play the trumpets, whilst in the second part it is the elders, wearing either feather crowns or full head-dresses, who play the flutes. Thus, the contrast between feather crown and feather head-dress that marks the transition between the small dance and the big dance, may be weakened to that between no ornament at all and feather crowns, but the contrast itself remains operative. During Fruit House, the transition between the two sections, marked at *He* House by the chant session called pouring out the beer, is marked instead by the tipping out of fruit.

This argument is somewhat condensed; to make it otherwise would require an extended description and analysis of Barasana dances not involving the use of *He* instruments. In itself, it is not of great significance for the discussion that follows; it merely sub-stantiates what the Barasana themselves say: that Fruit House is an attenuated replica of *He* House. I have gone into some detail in order to demonstrate that I am not being misleading when, in some sections of part III, I use arguments concerning *He* House to cover Fruit House as well. Whilst it is relatively easy to interpret certain features of Fruit House in the light of *He* House, it would be virtually impossible to work the other way round. Yet, assuming that a rite equivalent to *He* House occurs elsewhere in the Vaupés region, this is exactly what other writers have tried to do, for their analyses are based upon accounts of rites that correspond to the Barasana Fruit House. Many people have emphasised that the Yurupary cult is of central importance for an understanding of Tukanoan religion, but their analyses have not so far offered a convincing account of why this should be so. Having described these rites in detail, I shall now try to analyse them and to place them in the wider context of Barasana society, religion and cosmology.

PART III

Explanation and analysis

Here, the rites of Fruit House and *He* House, described in part II, are analysed from a number of different perspectives. I attempt to account for the details of the rites themselves, and having done so, to relate them to a wider picture of Barasana religious life. In order to do this, I make frequent reference both to the accounts of the rites given above, and also to a corpus of myth from the Barasana and their neighbours, presented in part V. In addition, I introduce a considerable amount of explanatory detail, some derived from informants' statements relating to the myths, the rites and to Indian society in the Vaupés more generally, and some from observations made in the field.

My basic argument is first, that many features of the rites only become fully comprehensible when related to myth, a view shared by the Barasana, and secondly, that it is through ritual that the myths, held to be of such central importance by the Barasana, are articulated with social structure and action 'on the ground'. Thus, by focussing selectively on a particular ritual complex rather than attempting to describe and analyse mythology and religion in general, important insights can be gained about the Barasana religious system and its place in the society at large. In chapter 5, I show how the different categories of participants attending the rites relate to the wider structure of Barasana society. Chapters 6, 7 and 8 are devoted to an extended analysis of the significance of certain material objects used in the rites. Certain themes, such as the role of the shaman, the relation between the sexes, symbolic menstruation, the relation between ritual organisation and social structure, the role of the *He* instruments as representatives of sib and descent-group ancestors, etc., raised in chapter 5, are taken up again and expanded in the light of this analysis. In chapter 9, the spatio-temporal structure of the rites is examined in relation to that of their associated myths, and the theme of symbolic death and rebirth is discussed. Chapter 10 is exploratory in nature; in it, I try to show how the rite of *He* House relates to wider aspects of Barasana cosmology, and how some of my conclusions concerning the significance of the objects used in the rites relate to some of the arguments presented by Lévi-Strauss in his analysis of South American Indian mythology (1968, 1970, 1971, 1973).

5

The participants

During the rites of *He* House and Fruit House, five major categories
of people are involved: initiates, young men, elders, shamans and
women. These categories, recognised by the Barasana themselves,
are the same as those employed in tables 2 and 3 which summarise
the two rites in synoptic form. The object of this chapter is to
describe the attributes of these different categories of people and to
show their significance in relation to their different activities during
the rites.

Initiates

The initiates are referred to as *rĩa masa*, an expression that more
generally means children of either sex. Children live in an undifferentiated, asexual world: both sexes play together and spend most of their
time with their mothers and with other adult women. They are tied
to their immediate nuclear family and to the female world in general.
They sleep next to their mothers and fathers inside the family compartments situated along the side walls of the house towards its rear
end (see fig. 2). They are not expected to take part in productive
activities and most of their time is spent in playing. They are called
by their proper names (*basere wame*, shamanism name) or by nicknames (*ahari wame*). They are not expected to know, to have knowledge (*masi-*), and frequently make incorrect use of kinship terminology,
especially when applied to outsiders. In general, they are considered
to be young and irresponsible.

Around the age of six or seven, female children are increasingly
expected to take an active part in the productive work of women,
especially with regard to the cultivation and processing of manioc.
At the same time boys begin to devote more time to playing at the

masculine pursuits of hunting and fishing; these activities are encouraged by the men who begin to take them on hunting and fishing trips to the forest. They also begin to teach the boys skills and techniques and knowledge about their environment. An integral part of this teaching is the telling of myths. Fathers begin to watch their sons for signs of increasing maturity and the decision to start the process of initiation is taken when the child is deemed ready. One of the reasons given for initiation is that it starts the process of growing up and that if it were not done the boys would not become adult.

Fruit House, as the first stage of initiation, does not bring about any dramatic change in the life of a young boy. Around the age of eight or nine, when boys undergo this rite, they will already have begun to show signs of maturity. This gradual process of growing up continues as the boys repeatedly take part in Fruit House rites. They remain classed as *rĩa masa* but there is a gradual incorporation into adult male society with a corresponding break in ties with the women. The boys play less and less with girls and begin to attach themselves to the company of older boys.[1] They hunt and fish in a more serious manner but instead of contributing to the communal supply of food, they give their catch to their mothers to cook and then eat it on their own. Increasingly they spend time in the company of adult men and continue the informal process of education. They begin also to take an active part in ritual, playing the short flutes during Fruit House and dancing, half jokingly, on the ends of the dance line at this and other dances.

As they get older, boys begin to resent being addressed in public by their proper names or nicknames and begin to demand that they be called either by their Colombian names or, more usually, by the appropriate kinship terms. Correspondingly, they themselves begin to apply correct kinship terminology to a wider social universe. They are however still basically tied to their nuclear families and continue to sleep in their family compartments.

For Barasana men, the process of education and learning, especially in matters related to religion and ritual, continues throughout their lives. However *He* House, the main initiation rite is considered to be

---

1 Among the Cubeo, boys of between about eight and fourteen years old form discrete play-packs (Goldman 1963 : 177). The small size and scattered distribution of longhouses in the Pirá-paraná area probably preclude the formation of such play-packs, but the kind of semi-isolated young boys' society described by Goldman does tend to form whenever many households gather together for dances or other communal activities.

both the climax and end of a more intensive period of education. It also marks a fairly abrupt change in the life of a boy. The candidates for *He* House, aged between twelve and fourteen, are still referred to as children. Immediately after the rite they are referred to as *ngamꭤa* (sing. *ngamꭤ*). *Ngamo*, the feminine form of the word, is applied to a girl who menstruates for the first time and, in a general sense, from then on till she marries. It is also applied more generally to menstruating women. After their first Fruit House rite, the initiates are said to be 'a little bit *ngamꭤ*', but only after *He* House are they truly *ngamꭤ*. The initiates remain *ngamꭤ* until the end of the period of restrictions following *He* House. During this period they are said to be *bedirã*, in confinement and under taboos; menstruating women are also *bedirã*. At the end of their period of confinement the initiates are then classed as young men (*mamarã*).

Young men

The word *mamarã* (sing. *mamꭤ*), is applied to all initiated young men who are not yet married. The feminine *mamo* applies to nubile but unmarried women.

After *He* House, the final stage of initiation, the ties that a young man had to the world of women and children and to his nuclear family are realigned towards the wider society of adult men. At the same time he is initiated into a secret cult, exclusive to adult men and centred on the sacred flutes and trumpets. During the period following *He* House, the initiates sleep in a special compartment constructed at the extreme male end of the house next to the men's door (see fig. 2). This stands in opposition to the rear of the house, the women's section. After the initiates' compartment has been destroyed (during the shamanism of pepper) they must sleep in the middle of the men's end of the house. They continue to sleep in this area until they get married, whereupon they build new compartments, for themselves and their wives, along the side walls towards the rear of the house.

Schaden (1959 : 159) has suggested that the 'religion of Jurupari' should be studied in relation to the institution of the men's house across the whole South American continent and to its corresponding myths and rites. I think it can be argued that the unmarried Barasana men sleeping in the middle of the front part of the house are in a homologous position to the bachelors in the men's house located in the centre of the circular villages of Central Brazilian Indians. In these villages, the central area is associated with exclusive male society and with sacred, ritual life whereas the periphery is the domain of family life, women and profane activities such as cooking. The same is true of a Barasana longhouse: the central area is associated with sacred, ritual activities, dancing and extra-longhouse social life. At night the men sit between posts 3 and 4 (see fig. 2), conversing and taking coca and tobacco, both ritual 'non-foods'. The edge of the house is the area of domestic, family life and of women and it is here that cooking and other profane activities are carried out. At night, as the men sit in the middle of the house, the women sit towards posts 7 and 8, often eating snacks of food. The very centre of the house, the area between posts 3, 4, 5 and 6, is considered to be semi-sacred and is rarely used at all, except for the eating of communal meals. When very large amounts of meat or fish are served, and when there are no visitors present, the men and women eat together from a pot in the very middle of the house. At other times they usually eat from different pots, slightly apart and off centre, towards the rear of the house.

These oppositions can be summarised as follows:

Centre of house	/	*Periphery of house*
sacred	/	profane
men	/	women (and children)
social life	/	domestic life
ritual activity	/	non-ritual activity
consumption of food (daytime)	/	production of food (daytime)
cooked food	/	raw food
'non-food' (night-time)	/	food (night-time)

This system is homologous to another which opposes the front of the house to the back. The front is the men's domain where they sit, work and talk during the daytime and it is here that all ritual activity takes place. When visitors are staying in the house, their men do not normally go beyond posts 1 and 2 except when specifically invited to do so (usually to eat). At night, they sleep along the side walls of the front of the house if accompanied by women and children or in the middle front of the house if alone. The back of the house, the women's section, is the centre of domestic life. It is here that the family compartments are located, where the processing and cooking of manioc takes place and where women and children are confined during secret male rites involving *He*. The preparation of coca, tobacco and snuff, all 'non-foods', involves cooking which is done by men along the side walls towards the front of the house.

Thus:

Front of house		Back of house
sacred	/	profane
men	/	women (and children)
social life	/	domestic life
visitors (guests)	/	residents (hosts)
ritual activity	/	non-ritual activity
consumption of food	/	production of food
cooked food	/	raw food
'non-food'	/	food

This digression about the symbolic significance of spatial arrangement in a Barasana longhouse is required, in this context, to demonstrate that the difference between a child sleeping in a family compartment at the rear and side of the house and an initiated young man sleeping in the middle and front of the house is of more than simply practical significance. During *He* House this opposition is elaborated upon, for on the final night of the rite the initiates and younger men must sleep as far towards the rear of the house as possible, but when the rite is over the initiates must sleep as far to the front of the house as is possible, inside the initiates' compartment. From then on till the end of the marginal period they must remain at the front of the house at all times. Thus the break between the initiates and the female world is expressed in terms of space.

In sleeping in the front middle of the house, the young men are in a sense identified with visitors or outsiders. Young men are neither fully adult, as they are as yet unmarried, nor are they children. They are thus in a real sense in a liminal position and form a definite subgroup within Barasana society. The most notable feature of this is that they spend a considerable portion of their time travelling around and visiting other houses, often up to a week's journey away. Today, this travelling period is often spent working on mission stations or tapping rubber for Colombian rubber gatherers. Apart from seeing the world and widening their social universe, young men also travel to make contact with unmarried girls for sex and ultimately for marriage. In particular, they try to attend as many dances as possible

as it is at dances that most liaisons are made. A man must not marry
nor have sexual relations until he has been initiated. At initiation,
there is thus a passage from the asexual world of childhood to the
sexual world of adults. From an outsider's point of view, one of the
most noticeable manifestations of this is the incidence of joking
sexual play among initiated but unmarried men. Before initiation, a
boy's closest ties, to people of his own age group, will be those to
his brothers (own Bs and FBSs). After initiation these ties become
increasingly more formal and restrained while those with 'brothers-
in-law' (*tenyua*, male affines of the same genealogical level) become
increasingly close and familiar. A young man will often lie in a hammock with his 'brother-in-law', nuzzling him, fondling his penis and
talking quietly, often about sexual exploits with women.[2] True and
close classificatory brothers never indulge in such activities with
each other. In addition to this play, 'brothers-in-law' very often
assist each other in sexual escapades involving each other's true or
close classificatory sisters.

Young men are given over to personal display, bathing frequently
and encouraging the formation of a greasy covering on their faces
by anointing them with pepper juice and pouring this same juice into
their nostrils through leaf-funnels. They also paint their faces each
day with red paint, an activity called making new or fresh (*mamongu*)
and stick sweet-smelling herbs under their G-strings and under the
bracelets of black beads they wear on their biceps.[3] The handsome,
well-painted and sweet-smelling youth is one aspect of the Barasana
concept of the warrior (*guamu*). The other aspect is an emphasis on
the qualities of hardness, strength, endurance and the ability to do
without sleep. Each morning, the young men are expected to get up
before dawn and go to the river to bathe and vomit to clean out
their stomachs. They also thump the water with their hands and arms
producing a loud noise that can be heard in the house and which tells

2 Lévi-Strauss (1943) has described similar 'homosexual' play between 'brothers-in-law'
amongst the Nambikuara. Such play probably does not entail sexual satisfaction and
continues, as it does amongst the Barasana, after the partners are married. Nevertheless,
it appears to provide unmarried men with an outlet for sentimental effusions (Lévi-
Strauss, personal communication).
   Missionaries working in the Pirá-paraná area are frequently shocked by the apparent
homosexual behaviour of Indian men. However, the Barasana distinguish between this
playful sexual activity and serious male homosexuality, regarding the latter as repugnant.
This play, rather than coming from a frustration of 'normal' desires, is itself seen as
being normal behaviour between 'brothers-in-law' and expresses their close, affectionate
and supportive relationship.
3 The smell of these herbs is said to attract women.

the world how strong they are. Bathing makes the men strong and
hard in particular by making them cold. Coldness and hardness are
linked together and associated with men; heat and softness are
similarly linked and associated with women. Young men are expected to remain as cold as possible at all times.

Unlike uninitiated boys, young men hunt and fish in a serious
manner, putting their catch to the communal food supply; they devote
much time to these pursuits as they are keen to display their skills.
They also take an active part in such activities as house building and
felling the forest to make manioc gardens: a young man of sixteen or
seventeen will very often fell his own garden which is then used by
his mother or sister. People who have been initiated at the same
initiation rite call each other my *kamokuku*,[4] a term which replaces
the normal kinship terminology between them. They are expected
to be particularly close companions, and in a more general way,
young, unmarried men as a whole form a close and friendly group.
This is especially noticeable at dances where they are the ones who
play panpipes most of all, dancing with them in a stylised, prancing
manner in order to attract the attentions of the women. They drink
as much as they can, dance for as long as possible (often well after
the formal dancing is over) and behave generally in a boisterous,
energetic and slightly aggressive manner.

The wearing of ritual ornaments is reserved for initiated men.
After their first Fruit House, boys can wear feather crowns (*buya
buku bedo*) (see plate 3); during this rite these feather crowns are
placed on the boys' heads after the ritual washing outside the house.
After *He* House, fully initiated young men can wear the head-dresses
called *maha hoa* (see plate 4). Thus the contrast between feather
crowns and feather head-dresses signals the contrast between younger
and older. Finally, it is only after they have been initiated that
young men may begin to eat coca, smoke tobacco and take snuff
in a regular way, and at the same time, it is then that young men
begin to take part in the adult men's conversational circle where,
each night, these substances are consumed. At Fruit House boys
consume these substances, in a ritual context, for the first time.

The distinction between the category young men and elders is
essentially that between unmarried and married and it is not until
a man is married that he is considered to be fully adult.[5] The Barasana

4 I am unable to give a translation for this term.
5 This is true as a generalisation, though an obviously mature and elderly man would

111

do not have a marriage ceremony as such but during the dance of house containing cassava bread that marks the end of the initiate's period of confinement there is a ritualisation of adult relationships between men and women.[6] This is the rite of taking a *henyerio*, in which the women paint the initiates who give them basketry in return; though other men may be painted during this rite, the focus of attention is upon the initiates. This rite sets up an exchange partnership between the initiate and the woman who painted him which endures throughout his adult life. As described above, the man calls the woman my *henyerio* and she calls him my *henyeri*, terms which replace the usual kinship terms between them.[7] Men give their *henyerio* basketry (carrying baskets, sieves, manioc presses, etc.) and today, merchandise obtained from Colombians, especially salt, cloth and combs. In return, women give packets of red paint, gourds, garters and occasional gifts of food such as smoked ants or caterpillars. They also paint their *henyeri* with red and black paint before and during dances, and paint their garters with yellow ochre and red paint. In addition to this, men often give raw fish or meat to their *henyerio* to cook for them and they should make friendly conversation with, and tell news to, these women.

Certain comments should be made about the objects exchanged; first, women make garters at all times, but in particular they weave them during menstrual confinement. Similarly, men make baskets at all times, but in particular they make them during the marginal period following *He* House. This period is a period of confinement (as is menstruation) and the same term, *bedigu̶*, *bedigo* applies to both. Secondly, basketry is used as a gift between affines (see M.4.E.1) and in particular, men make basketry for their mothers-in-law. The Barasana also say that men give basketry to their wives in exchange for the labour involved in making cassava bread from manioc and that the ability to make basketry is a prerequisite of adult status – it is for this reason that basket making is systematically taught to the initiates after *He* House. Thirdly, the act of cooking food for an adult man is taken, in other contexts, to be one indicator of the fact that

certainly be considered to be adult. The restrictions on adult but unmarried men among the Waiwai (Fock 1963 : 138) do not apply among the Barasana.

6 Marriage among the Barasana is treated in full by Christine Hugh-Jones (1979).

7 Informants would not translate this term beyond saying that it is the name of a ceremonial trading partner. However, the verb root *heni-* means to catch alight (of a fire) and in *nyango heni-* means to talk together or converse. In both cases there is the connotation of something passing between objects or people.

the man and the woman who cooks for him are related as man and wife. It is for this reason that the refusal of Manioc-stick Anaconda's wife to cook fish for him (see M.6.A.56–9) was of such importance. Finally, at dances, men may be painted by one of three categories of women: their wives, their sisters or their *henyerio* partners.

In saying all this, I do not wish to imply that the rite of taking a *henyerio* is in any sense a marriage ceremony. The Barasana say that a man's *henyerio* is like his sister and that the relationship has no sexual connotations. Furthermore, a man's *henyerio* may be of an affinal group but may also belong to the same exogamous group or even the same sib as himself; his wife must always be from a different exogamous group. What I am saying is that the *henyerio* relationship introduces the initiates to a general form of socially approved and recognised relationship between men and women, of which marriage is a particular case.[8] In this light it is interesting to compare the Barasana to the Akwē-Shavante and Kayapó. At the end of Shavante initiation, by lying momentarily with young girls who later become their wives, the initiates enter into what Maybury-Lewis (1967 : 75–90) calls 'a communal state of wedlock'. At the end of Kayapó initiation, the initiates spend a night next to young girls but these girls rarely if ever become their actual wives. Turner (n.d.) describes this as 'a symbolic dramatization of the boy's assumption of affinal ties which has no binding implications for his marriage in real life'. The *henyerio* rite could be said to be the weakest form of a series, the strongest form of which is Shavante marriage and the intermediary form, the Kayapó rite. But unlike the Shavante and Kayapó who stress both affinity and a potential sexual relationship, the Barasana stress merely the aspect of exchange. Finally, it should be added that the *sŭori* relationship, created during *He* House when men paint men, is a ceremonial friendship, seen as equivalent to the *henyerio* relationship but one which does not involve institutionalised trading.[9]

8 Rivière (1971) argues that marriage as an isolable phenomenon of study is a misleading illusion and that it should be studied as *one* of the socially approved and recognised relationships between the conceptual roles of men and women.

9 The Cubeo *hiku–hiko* relationship is virtually identical to the *henyeri–henyerio* relationship of the Barasana. However, among the Cubeo the relationship is always between members of the same sib or phratry (i.e. the same exogamous group); this is not necessarily true of the Barasana. Nor do I have any evidence to suggest that *henyeri* and *henyerio* form a team in an exchange marriage and try to arrange the marriage of their children to one another, as they do among the Cubeo.

Among the Cubeo, the relationship is also formed by the women painting the man with red paint, referred to as 'blood'. This is done at a drinking party (what I call a social dance (*basaria wi*)), but there is no indication given as to which particular drinking party,

Explanation and analysis

Immediately after they have given basketry to the women who become their *henyerio*, the initiates call up the two officiating shamans and present them with basketry too. This is in payment for their services during initiation. At this point, they address the shamans as my tortoise (*yu̶gu*). From then on the initiates will use this term instead of kinship terms, each time they address these men. (The reference form is a *guga*.) In turn, the shamans now address the initiates as my pepper (*yu̶bia*: the reference form is *biaga* and the plural *biase batia*). Shamans who officiate at rites of birth and first menstruation are also called *gu*, *guga* by the people for whom they acted. In none of the cases recorded by me was either of the officiating shamans at *He* House the father of one of the initiates, though the Barasana say that he may be. In most cases the shaman was of the same sib as the initiate but of a different household, but in some instances he was of a different sib or of a different exogamic group. (This follows from the fact that young boys of different exogamic groups are often initiated together.)

It can now be seen that at initiation, as at birth and first menstruation rites, a set of ties of ritual kinship are established between the subject(s) of the rites and the most important actors, each one expressed by terms of reference and address which replace the usual kinship terms. For an initiate, these are as follows: between the initiates and the officiating shamans (*guga–biaga*); between the initiate and the ritual guardian (*masori–masori*) and between him and the woman who provides pure food after the rite (*masori–masorio*); between the initiate and the elder who carries him into the house at the start of *He* House (*umari–umari*); between the initiate and the woman who paints him and to whom he gives basketry (*henyeri–henyerio*); between the initiate and those who paint him with black paint during *He* House (*su̶ori–su̶ori*) and between all the initiates who go through *He* House together (*kamoku̶ku̶–kamoku̶ku̶*). The initiate's *guga*, *masori* and *umari* are all said to be like fathers or father's brothers and his *masorio* like a mother (Spanish speaking Indians say these relationships are like those between a child and his *padrino* and *madrina*, godfather and godmother). The *henyerio* is compared to a sister and the *su̶ori* and *kamoku̶ku̶* are both compared to brothers. It is as if, after initiation, the initiate is reborn with a new set of elementary kin. These ties of ritual kinship

if any, is involved, and no indication of a specific association with initiation, as there is among the Barasana (Goldman 1963 : 130–4).

114

cross-cut those between the initiate and his nuclear family and long-house community. This corresponds to the fact that, at initiation, a person's social universe is opened out to embrace people outside the local group.

Elders

I have translated the Barasana category *bukurã* as 'elders' to emphasise their distinction from the younger men. The word *buku* does indeed mean old as opposed to *mama*, young or new, but it also means adult, mature or big. Objectively quite young people, particularly white people with whom Indians are on familiar terms, are often addressed or referred to by their name with *buku* as a suffix. In this context *buku* is a mark of familiar respect. Long-dead ancestors and mythical heroes are also referred to as *bukurã* and myths are called *bukurã keti*, the tales of the ancients. But in general usage, the term *bukurã* is applied to adult, married men whatever their age may be.

The elders as a group are those who control Barasana society. They are the people with knowledge and experience (*masise*), especially with regard to matters of religion and ritual. The core of each long-house consists of a group of married brothers or parallel cousins, together with their wives and children. Often there will be one or both parents still alive who are referred to as *buku* (masculine) or *bukuo* (feminine) without further clarification. In each house, the adult men form a kind of informal council which arrives at decisions which are then expressed by one of their number, the headman (usually the eldest brother). These men are the ones who decide to hold dances and who decide that their sons are ready for initiation. In this sense they are the actors, the initia*tors*, which the boys are those acted upon, the initia*ted*. During Fruit House and *He* House, it is the elders (including the shamans who fall within this category) who are the main actors and who fulfil the most important roles. They are the lead dancers (*baya*) and the core of the dance line (*baya koderi masa*, the people who accompany the dancer), the chanters (*yoamarã*), the chief hosts and principal guests, it is they who burn the beeswax and distribute the substances blown over by the shamans, who carry the initiates into the house at *He* House and who look after them during initiation (see especially the role of *masori*, the ritual guardian or father) and it is they who play the long flutes which are the focus of attention throughout these rites.

115

Explanation and analysis

At *He* House, there are four main categories of participant who can be identified according to the different roles that they play. These are elders, young men, initiates and shamans. Also added to this list should be the non-participant women and children confined in the rear of the house. The initiates occupy an intermediary status: on the one hand they are identified with the women and children from whose world they have been removed, but on the other hand they are associated with the young men whom they will join. These categories of participant correspond to the age-grades of child, young man and elder through which each man must pass. The elders who play the long flutes are all older men, married and with children (*bukurã*); the young men who play the trumpets are initiated but unmarried (*mamarã*); and the uninitiated boys, confined in the rear of the house are the children (*rĩa masa*).[10] Though the shamans are technically married men belonging to the age-grade of elders, during *He* House they are in many ways identified with the initiates. Like the initiates, intermediary between children and young men and between the male and female worlds, the shamans also have intermediary characteristics. Thus we have:

Participants:	elders (shamans)	young men	initiates shamans	women and children

Age-grades:	elders	young men	(initiates)	children

In chapter 2, it was stated that the Barasana, as an exogamic descent group, are divided internally into a number of sub-groups, each one ideally comprising five sibs ranked in seniority according to a model of five brothers of decreasing age. Each sib is associated with a particular ritual occupation: the top sib, *Koamona*, are chiefs (*ũharã*), the next, *Rasegana*, are dancers and chanters (*bayaroa, keti masa*), the *Meni Masa* are warriors (*guamarã*), the *Daria* are shamans (*kumua*) and the *Wabea* are cigar lighters or servants (*muno yori masa*).

Sibs:	*Koamona*	*Rasegana*	*Meni Masa*	*Daria*	*Wabea*
Occupation:	chief	chanter/ dancer	warrior	shaman	servant

10 According to Biocca (cit. Schaden 1959 : 154), the Tukano of the Río Tiquié are divided into three categories (apart from women and children): (1) caciques and chiefs,

The participants

Within the local group, the men who form the core, as brothers
or parallel cousins, are also ranked according to order of birth. Patrilateral parallel cousins, treated as brothers, are ranked according to
the birth order of their fathers — so that a man's father's elder brother's
son is his own elder brother, regardless of who in fact was born first.
The Barasana say that a group of brothers should take on specialist
occupations according to the order of their birth and, during the
rites of birth and name giving, they are differently treated by the
shaman to ensure that this happens. The eldest should become the
headman of the maloca (equivalent to chief), the next should either be
a chanter (*yoamɨ*) or a dancer (*baya*), the next should be an exemplar
of the Barasana ideals of bravery and hardness and equivalent to a
warrior, and the last should be a shaman (*kumu*). In connection with
this last category, people usually cite the mythical precedent of
Kanea, the youngest of the *Ayawa* brothers, the Thunders, who was
their shaman (see M.2.A.4).[11] This ideal correspondence between
birth order and specialist occupation does not always work out in
practice, but when it does, the fact is commented upon with approval.

The correspondence between the age-grades of Barasana society
and the participants at *He* House can thus be extended to include
that between birth order and specialist occupation at both an individual and sib level:

Sibling order:	1	2	3	4	5
Sibs:	*Koamona*	*Rasegana*	*Meni Masa*	*Daria*	*Wabea*
Occupation:	chief	chanter/ dancer	warrior	shaman	servant
Participants:		elders (shamans)	young men	initiates shamans	women and children
Age grades		elders	young men	(initiates)	children

From this it can be seen that the structure of the male core of the
maloca community reproduces in miniature that of the wider descent

---

(2) the general population, (3) recently initiated young men, in ranked order. This strati-
fication can be observed during Yurupary dances.

11 The youngest Thunder of the Tariana Yurupary myth is called 'the Thunder that does
not give rise to hunger' (see M.8.6). It is reasonable to assume that he too is a shaman on
the basis that shamans are the ones who oblige others to fast, either during rites of
passage or during the curing of illness. See also M.8.9.

group, a theme that will be taken up again and amplified when the significance of the *He* instruments is discussed.

During *He* House and Fruit House, the age-categories of elders, young men and initiates are marked off from each other in terms of dress, in terms of the *He* instruments they play and in terms of vertical and horizontal space. During the first part of *He* House, the young men wear no feathers or other ritual ornaments at all whilst a few of the elders wear simple feather crowns, and during this section the predominant instruments are the trumpets played by the younger men. The elders then put on full feather head-dresses and other ritual ornaments while the younger men put on feather crowns, and from then onwards the predominant instruments are the long flutes played by the elders. Correspondingly, during the first section of *He* House, the long flutes are undecorated whilst during the second section, the engraved designs are filled with white paint and ruffs of yellow feathers are put round the ends. The same pattern can be observed at Fruit House, although, particularly on the less formal occasions, the contrasts may be weakened.

Throughout both *He* House and Fruit House, the initiates and shamans wear feather crowns. At other dances, the first section (the small dance) is danced by younger men wearing feather crowns whilst the second section (the big dance) is danced by elders wearing feather head-dresses. I have already stated that after their first Fruit House young initiates can wear feather crowns and that after *He* House they can wear feather head-dresses. The above information can now be summarised by saying that the contrast between feather crowns and feather head-dresses signals the contrast between small and big, younger and older, before and after, earlier and later.[12]

During *He* rituals, the long flutes are always played by the elders, the trumpets by the young men, and the short flutes by the initiates (or by the youngest boys present when Fruit House is not part of an initiation). Thus:

elders	:	young men	:	initiates (boys)
long flutes	:	trumpets	:	short flutes

In addition to this, further contrasts should be noted: the long flutes are played as a single pair at a time; the trumpets and short flutes are

---

12 According to Biocca, among the Tukano the difference in social position (see n. 10 above) was marked by a difference in dress.

played as many pairs in a group. The long flutes play melodically and harmonically with a slow, complex rhythm and with the players moving slowly; the trumpets and short flutes play a single note with a fast simple rhythm and with the players moving fast[13] (see appendix 3).

In terms of horizontal space, the long flutes are played in the middle of the house (except on entry and exit) while the trumpets and short flutes are played round the dance path on the edge of the house and during *He* House also round the outside of the house (see appendix 3). At rest, the long flutes are placed vertically in the middle of the house by post 3 while the trumpets and short flutes are placed horizontally on the ground on the edge of the dance path. (During *He* House there are certain exceptions: the short flutes are also placed upright in the middle of the house together with one pair of trumpets, Old Star (*Nyoko Bɨkɨ*).)

In terms of vertical space, the shamans and elders sit on stools during *He* House while the young men and initiates sit on mats on the floor. Similarly, on the final night of *He* House, some of the elders sleep in hammocks while all the young men and initiates sleep on mats on the ground. In addition to the contrast between vertical and horizontal when the *He* are not being used, during *He* House, when the beeswax is burned, the trumpets are played with their ends as low to the ground as possible, while during the acting-out of spearing, the long flutes are played with their ends raised high in the air.

All this can be summarised as follows:

Elders	*Young men and initiates*
feather head-dresses	feather crowns
long flutes	trumpets and short flutes
single pairs	many pairs
melodic—harmonic	unison
complex rhythm	simple rhythm
slow	fast
centre	periphery
high	low

13 The word for fast, *guaro*, contains the same root *gua-* as *guamɨ*, a fierce man. Fastness and fierceness are seen as being connected and it is therefore appropriate that the young men (warriors) should move fast.

119

In conclusion it can be said that the age-grades of elders, on the one hand, and young men and initiates, on the other, play distinct roles during *He* rites and are marked off from each other by a series of opposed attributes. The full significance of these oppositions will be discussed below after more explanatory data has been introduced.

Shamans

The role of the shaman in Barasana society was briefly discussed in chapter 2. Here, I shall confine my discussion to the attributes and role of the shamans who officiate at *He* House.

Very few shamans have the necessary power and knowledge to officiate at this rite. Those who do are known as *kumu* or as *werea koa baseri masa*, the people who blow over the gourd of beeswax. Officiating at *He* House is considered to be an onerous and dangerous task. The successful outcome depends on the shamans' abilities and if they fail the results are disastrous, causing the deaths of many people, in particular of the initiates. Objectively it is also a physically exhausting task. For these reasons, the two officiating shamans are paid in basketry and other goods by the other participants at the dance that follows the rite. The shamans are the ones who know the correct procedure and sequence of events for *He* House and they are in control, as 'masters of ceremony', throughout the rite and subsequent events. Their task is to bring about a change in state in the initiates, called changing the soul or spirit (*usu wasoase*), and also to protect them and the other participants from illness and other danger that may result from undergoing the rite. This danger comes partly from contact with the ritual objects themselves, and partly from mystical attack from enemy shamans and from the spirit world upon the initiates, who are in an especially vulnerable condition. This condition is compared to that of crabs and other animals that have shed their old shells or skins. This is both a simple analogy and also an allusion to the fact that *He* House is believed to bring about a change of skin.

As the shamans blow spells during the rites, their souls are said to leave their bodies and to travel between the different layers of the cosmos (basically those of sky, earth and water). This ability to mediate between different cosmic levels is seen as the key to the shaman's ability. Whilst telling the myth of Manioc-stick Anaconda (M.6.A), an informant explained,

120

The participants

The whole of this myth is about shamanism. This is how the shamans travel, as they see with their thoughts and cross between the levels of the world. At the point where Macaw dug a hole and got rid of Manioc-stick Anaconda and went away (M.6.A.5–7), the shaman goes down (to the Underworld) as he blows. They go down to the Underworld as Manioc-stick Anaconda went down; then again, as Manioc-stick Anaconda came up (after visiting the *Ka* People's (termites) house – M.6.A.41–2), so they come up again. This is the blowing and spell against disease, everything, the blowing for food, the blowing for coca. This is the real shaman's path.

Thus, as they blow the spells, the shaman in spirit form relives the myth.[14]

At *He* House, except when whipping the participants, serving the yagé, or accompanying the people as they bathe in the rivers, the shamans remain secluded inside the palm-leaf enclosure constructed during the Fruit House rite immediately before. The enclosure is by post 1; at other rites involving the *He* instruments, no enclosure is built but the shamans always sit in the same position (see fig. 2). Inside their enclosure, the shamans are surrounded by gourds placed on hourglass-shaped stands containing coca, snuff, beeswax, and *kana* berries, by large ceremonial cigars, boxes of feather ornaments, whips, bundles of yagé and by a pair of *He* instruments called Old Callicebus Monkey (*Wau Buku*). They wear feather crowns on their heads and necklaces of jaguar canines and large cylinders of polished white quartzite (called 'stones' but identified with jaguars) around their necks. They sit on special old stools reserved for use during this rite. The stools, called shamans' things (*kumuro*), are identified with mountains, the abodes of spirits and the houses of spirit humans and animals that are called people's waking-up houses (*masa yuhiri wi*). Sitting on such a stool is sitting high up and is an essential element of the shaman's visionary powers; blowing and other shamanic acts are always done sitting on a stool.

In the past, the shamans' enclosure was made of tapir skin; the enclosure is the shamans' protection, symbolised by the thick, protective hide. This in itself suggests that shamans and tapirs are associated together. This same identification of shaman with tapir is found in the myth of Manioc-stick Anaconda (M.6.A), one of the key myths behind the spells used at *He* House. In this myth, Tapir carries Manioc-

---

14 The same is true of the specialist chanter whose soul/spirit leaves his body as he chants and retraces the mythical journeys of the first *He* people from the Río Negro to the Vaupés and Pirá-paraná.

stick Anaconda across a wide river and, while so doing, teaches him the shamanic spells used to ensure a safe birth and to treat maternal milk before it is given to the newly born (M.6.A.28–30); this same Tapir is the shaman who then officiates at a dance in the termites' house which is explicitly compared to initiation (M.6.A.35). But if tapirs represent the good aspects of shamanism, they also represent the bad: Macaw, the brother of Manioc-stick Anaconda, and also a shaman, becomes a tapir in order to kill his brother and to steal his brother's wife; he thus represents the 'tapir seducer', incarnating the seductive power of nature, a theme widespread in South American Indian mythology and discussed extensively by Lévi-Strauss (1973). Again, in the myth of *He* Anaconda (M.5.A), the tapir that took the flute made from the top of the palm tree that sprang from *He* Anaconda's ashes, threatened to use it to suck new-born babies into his body and to kill them (M.5.A.18). The Barasana say that the tapir is a taking-in person (*sóri masu*) who is jealous of the baby's transition from the *He* or spirit state to the human state and who tries to suck it back into his anus. A Barasana myth (not presented in part V) centres on a tapir who sucks a menstruating girl into his anus, later to be killed by a tortoise that the girl kept as a pet. The wife of the Tapir shaman in the story of Manioc-stick Anaconda, whose farts are interpreted as a sexual invitation, is a 'tapir seducer' in the literal sense of the word (M.6.A.36–7). Finally, the Tatuyo, neighbours and affines of the Barasana, make the association between shamans and tapirs yet more explicit in having *Wekua kumu*, Tapir shaman, as their ancestor (Bidou 1976). The tapir in the instances mentioned above acts as a mediator: across a river, from land to water and back again (tapirs live near water and, according to the Barasana, can literally walk under water); between the termites in their under-ground house and those who fly off in this world (M.6.A.35); between this world and the Underworld in the 'death' of Manioc-stick Anaconda who falls to the Underworld through a pitfall trap for a tapir; and between the *He*, spirit state, and the human state, between nature and culture, as a taking-in person (see above). The shaman is also such a mediator.

Shamans are not only identified with tapirs; they are also identified with monkeys. Throughout *He* House, the trumpets called Old Callicebus Monkey remain with the shamans in their enclosure. During the rite, the souls of the shamans become the ancestor Old Callicebus Monkey, represented by the trumpets; they also become Manioc-stick

Anaconda. The link between shamans and monkeys is also illustrated in myth. The youngest of the *Ayawa* or Thunders, *Kanea* the shaman, became a callicebus monkey (*wau*) in order to steal fire from his grandmother and for this reason, the callicebus monkey is known as 'Fire Callicebus' (*Hea Wau*) (M.2.C.2). Fire Callicebus, together with Fire Howler Monkey (*Hea Ugʉ*), appears in another myth as one of the people who paddle the Sun's canoe up the Underworld River at night (M.6.A.16). Apart from their common association with fire in Barasana myth, there are good behavioural reasons why howler and callicebus monkeys should be linked together: both make very loud and similar-sounding noises during the early morning and at dusk. The howler monkey also figures in the myth about the tapir who threatens to suck new-born children into his anus. He tells the tapir that he is abusing his *He* instrument (= voice) and that far from being used to impede birth, it should be used to 'open the *He* People's doors to make men', i.e. to facilitate birth by making the vaginas (= doors) open. The monkeys then remove the tapir's deep and powerful voice and replace it with their own high-pitched squeak (M.5.A.19).

In this myth, the howler monkey and the tapir are being opposed in terms of low, loud voice and high, quiet voice or oral incontinence/ oral continence. In myth, the tapir uses its anus to ingest people, and in life the tapir marks its territory by defecating in the same place. This anal continence is opposed to the incontinence of the howler monkey whom the Barasana consider to be a proverbial shitter. In addition, whilst howler monkeys and callicebus monkeys are associated with fire (see above), the tapir, as an amphibious creature, is associated with water. Shamans are associated with both fire and water. Manioc-stick Anaconda, the prototype shaman with whom contemporary shamans are identified, is the master of the Sun's fire, obtained in the Underworld in the form of snuff and used to burn his brother Macaw to death (M.6.A). Today, this snuff plays a crucial role at *He* House. One method of curing serious illness, known only to the most powerful of shamans, involves throwing water over the patient. Men who know this treatment are known as water throwers (*oko yueri masa*) and are generally the shamans who officiate at *He* House. According to a Yurupary myth from the Baniwa, the two brothers of *Amaru*, Yurupary's mother, were called *Dzuri*, 'blow', and *Mariri*, 'suck' (Saake 1958a : 272). Both were shamans and their names are a neat summary of shamanic activity.

123

Explanation and analysis

Tentatively, I would suggest that the actions of blowing (of spells and of pathogenic agents to kill) and sucking (for the removal of pathogenic agents from the patient's body) correspond to the opposition between oral incontinence and oral continence mentioned above. Thus in the character of the shaman are combined a set of complementary but opposed attributes, represented by his identification with the tapir on the one hand and with the howler and callicebus monkey on the other. In different contexts, these attributes relate to different shamanic techniques, to the ambiguous moral position of the shaman as killer and curer, and to the different cosmic layers in which he operates.

shaman

monkey/tapir

(howler + callicebus)

oral incontinence/oral continence

anal incontinence/anal continence

fire/water

shaman

In addition to his association with tapirs and monkeys, the Barasana shaman is above all identified with the jaguar. Very powerful shamans of wide repute are sometimes referred to as 'jaguar' (*yai*), and are said to be able to change into jaguars at will, to keep jaguars like other men keep dogs, and to become jaguars on death. The Barasana word *yai*, which I translate as 'jaguar', has the wider connotation of 'predator'. Thus, from the point of view of termites, termite-eating birds are their 'jaguars' (see M.6.A.39). Within each of the three basic divisions of the Barasana cosmos, there is one large and dominant predator: the eagle in the sky, the jaguar on land and the anaconda in the water. Each of these animals is seen also as a mediator between cosmic domains: eagles come to land and fish in rivers, jaguars swim and climb trees, and anacondas come out of the water on to land. According to the Barasana, if an anaconda wants to eat birds, it sheds its skin and becomes an eagle. These animals, as predators, control the passage from life to death amongst the other animals in their domains. In myth, as the ancestors of humanity, they are also given creative powers. The Barasana and their immediate neighbours the Bará and Tatuyo are each descended from an anaconda ancestor: the Bará from Fish Anaconda, the Barasana from *Yeba Meni* Anaconda, and the Tatuyo from Sky Anaconda. The word *yeba* means 'earth' in Tukano and some other Vaupés languages; *Yeba*, the ancestor of the Barasana, was himself a jaguar (see M.6.A.62 and M.7). Sky Anaconda, the ancestor of the Tatuyos, is identified with *Rame*, the giant eagle of M.4.F,H who is also called Eagle Jaguar. Thus we have a 'totemic' system in which three intermarrying groups, Bará, Barasana and Tatuyo, are alike in having a large predator as ancestor, but are differentiated as sky, earth and water people by the appropriate domains of their respective ancestors. Jaguars are thus conceived of as mediators: between the three cosmic divisions of the world, between life and death, between the human world and spirit world of the ancestors, and between nature and culture. These are also the attributes of the shaman who travels between cosmic levels, who as killer and curer controls the passage between life and death in the human world, and who mediates beween the worlds of humans and spirit ancestors in ritual. Maniocstick Anaconda, ancestor of the Barasana, shaman and killer of his own brother, was also a jaguar (M.6.A).

In addition to being a mediator who combines opposed qualities, there is a sense in which shamans are also conceived of as sexually ambiguous. First, there is an ideal that they should remain celibate and unmarried as contact with women diminishes their powers. Secondly, whilst today all shamans are men, *Romi Kumu*, Woman Shaman, the female creatress identified with the sky (M.1), was the first shaman and it is from her that all shamans derive their powers. She herself is also sexually ambiguous and described as being like a man.

The Barasana see shamanism and the ability to menstruate as being mutually exclusive but also closely linked. In myth, *Romi Kumu* was called 'Vagina Woman' before she stole the *He* instruments from the men; after the theft, she became Woman Shaman and the men began to menstruate (M.1.D). According to Barasana shamans, the hair of women is their equivalent of the *He* instruments. When women see their hair falling in front of their faces they menstruate; when men see the *He* instruments they undergo a period of restrictions seen as equivalent to menstrual confinement; by controlling the *He* instruments, shamans thus control menstruation.

According to the Trio Indians of Surinam, shamans are like menstruating women (Riviére 1969a : 268); the Barasana would well understand this statement. At the onset of puberty, a girl becomes 'opened up' and from then on she is 'opened up' during each menstrual period.[15] Shamans are also 'opened up' in that the positive aspects of their activities are associated with oral and anal incontinence. Finally, shamans are also like menstruating women in that they are confined in special enclosures during *He* House just as women are so confined during menstruation; the painted enclosure in which Tariana women were enclosed at first menstruation (see M.8.10) sounds remarkably like those in which Barasana shamans used to be confined during initiation rites.

We are now in a position to explain in part why it is that initiates and shamans are associated together. During *He* House, shamans and initiates are identified together in the following respects: both wear feather crowns throughout the whole proceedings, and both are confined in enclosures situated symmetrically on either side of the front end of the house (see fig. 2).[16] Initiates, shamans and menstruating women are all confined in enclosures. It has been established that shamans are like menstruating women and some evidence for an association between initiates and these women has also been given. A full account of this latter association depends upon further explanatory data concerning the sacred objects used at *He* House which will be given below (pp. 178ff). Riviére (1969a : 268) argues that shamans and menstruating women are both in a betwixt-and-between state 'the one suffering from an excess of power and the other from an excess of fertility'. Shamans are also in a betwixt-and-between state as mediators characterised by complementary but opposed attributes. Finally, initiates are half-way between the age-grades of child and young man. Barasana myth provides evidence that shamans too are seen as being half-way between genealogical levels: *Kanea*, the youngest of the *Ayawa* brothers, the Thunders, was born after his elder brothers had impregnated their mother with their own semen hidden in a fruit. As a child of the same mother, *Kanea* is in the same genealogical level as his elder brothers, but as their son, he is in the one below (see M.2.A).

I shall return to the theme of open and closed bodily orifices and to that of the link between *He* House and menstruation below, each time presenting data that amplifies and substantiates the arguments presented above.

15 This is both objectively true and also corresponds to Barasana ideas concerning the physiology of menstruation.
16 A distinction in seniority is however maintained in that the right-hand side of the house, where the shamans' compartment is situated, is the side on which the headman of the

Women

According to a Barasana myth, the *He* instruments were originally the property of the men. *Romi Kumu* and the other women stole the *He* from the men, and when this happened the men became like women: they became the cultivators of manioc and they began to menstruate (M.1.D). The version of this myth given in part V is in some respects a 'weak' version; in most of the versions told to me it was stated that when the women were in possession of the *He*, the men did not merely cultivate manioc but were also subject to the political dominance of the women. This theme of social revolution in which women overthrow the power of men is common to all the versions of the Yurupary myth from the Vaupés–Içana region and is also widespread amongst the Indian groups of lowland South America. These 'myths of matriarchy' (Bamberger 1974) are generally associated with secret men's cults centred on the use of esoteric musical instruments, notably bull-roarers, flutes and trumpets. This same cultural complex, showing striking parallels with South America, is found also in New Guinea and Australia.

The theme of male menstruation, frequently associated with secret men's cults in New Guinea and implicit in variants of Yurupary myths from the Vaupés–Içana region, is made explicit in Barasana myth. In other Yurupary myths it is frequently explained that the reason why the women were able to steal the Yurupary instruments was that they heard young men being told by their father to get up early in the morning to bathe and play the instruments at the river. The men were lazy and remained in their hammocks so the women seized the opportunity to steal the flutes (see for example Fulop 1956 : 359 and compare with M.1.D.1). This refusal to bathe in the morning can be linked to menstruation in two respects: first, it has connotations of laziness, itself connected with confinement during menstruation and after *He* House, a confinement described by the same word *bedirã*. Secondly, amongst the Barasana at least, the most common way of describing a menstruating women is to say she is 'one who does not bathe', for such women are forbidden to bathe. Hence, by their refusal to bathe in the morning, the men in the myth were behaving as if they were menstruating.

house has his family compartment. The headman is, in theory, and usually in practice, the eldest brother.

Explanation and analysis

It should be noted, with regard to the social revolution of women, that two themes are expressed concurrently in Barasana mythology. One myth (M.1.C) presents a picture of an original state of matriarchy which was overthrown by the men: *Romi Kumu*, who controlled the *He* instruments and was thus dominant over the men, was going to initiate the first people by showing them the instruments. Another myth (M.1.D) implies that it was the men who originally controlled the *He*; the women stole the *He* and thus usurped male power but the 'normal' order was re-established when the men got back the possession of the instruments. In discussing such myths throughout South America, Schaden (1959 : 162) comes close to seeing the difference between original matriarchy and the usurption of power but fails to see its full significance. I shall show below that the theme of usurption stresses the political relations of dominance and submission between the sexes whilst that of an original state of matriarchy stresses also the distribution of creative power between them. Bamberger is probably right in seeing 'myths of matriarchy' as an ideological prop for the dominance of women by the men but is certainly incorrect when she states that the unique ability of women to conceive, bear and nurse the young of the species, so important to group survival, is celebrated in female puberty ritual but over-looked in myth (1974 : 279). Whilst there is no question as to who rules today in Barasana society, the question as to who creates remains unresolved and in private the men will admit that in this respect their victory over the women was at best double-edged.

In addition to being a rite of passage into adult life, Fruit House and *He* House also involve the initiation of young men into a secret men's cult from which women are systematically debarred. Women must never see the *He* instruments and are excluded from participating in rituals where these instruments are used. The *He* instruments are the symbols and means of the subjection of men and women and the Yurupary myths make this point quite explicit.[17] The Barasana do not say that if the women saw the instruments they would once again become dominant over the men, but they do say that there would be a period of chaos during which the men would fight amongst themselves and kill each other. It is concerning the Yurupary instru-ments as the means of male dominance that Schaden suggests that

17 Both Lévi-Strauss (1968 : 138) and Schaden (1959 : 157–9) make this fact a major part of their interpretations of the Yurupary cult.

128

the cult that surrounds them should be seen in relation to the institution of the men's house, and according to this author, myths concerning the rebellion against a primitive matriarchy form the background to male initiation rites over a wide area of South America. It is with this point in mind that I drew attention to the parallel between the Barasana maloca and the circular villages of Central Brazil.

In accordance with their use as the symbol and means of male dominance, many authors writing about secret men's cults have claimed that the musical instruments on which they focus are used to terrorise and frighten the women, and the impression is often given that the women are simply excluded from the proceedings and know nothing about what goes on. One of the problems involved in the interpretation of secret men's cults is that they are generally seen, described and analysed by male ethnographers who give little or no attention to the part played by women. Where information is available on this aspect, it frequently suggests that female ignorance is a fiction maintained by *both* sexes and that women often connive and collaborate with the men.[18] According to my wife, who remained with the women during the *He* rites described in part II and to whom I am indebted for much of the information that follows, young Barasana women are indeed afraid of the *He* instruments and it is they in particular who rush out from the house when they are brought to the outside from the river and when they are brought inside early the next day. But this fear is actively induced by a kind of mock hysteria from the elder women. To say that all Barasana women were afraid of the *He* would be to confuse ideal with practice. In fact, most Barasana women know in precise detail what the *He* look like and know more or less exactly what is going on on the other side of the palm-leaf screen that separates them from the men during the rites, even to the extent of being able to say which particular named instruments are being played by which individuals. The women say that they are not so much afraid of seeing the *He* themselves as of the reaction of the men if they do. Nor do they feel any desire to see the instruments even if they could, a reaction echoed by the fact that when missionaries have exposed the Yurupary

18 This point has also been made by Gourlay (1975) with reference to secret men's cults in New Guinea. His work presents a useful comparative survey of these cults and their associated mythology in this area.

Explanation and analysis

to women elsewhere in the Vaupés as part of a war against 'devil worship', these women have tried to resist seeing the instruments.

However, the fact that the women know about the *He* and express no desire to see them should not be taken to suggest that the women are therefore in any way contemptuous of the cult that surrounds them.[19] In fact the women are proud of the *He* instruments owned by their own and their husbands' groups and are positively committed both to the fact that these rites should be held and to their successful outcome, which is considered beneficial to the community as a whole. In a very real sense the women are also actively involved in the proceedings. When the *He* arrive outside the house at the start of *He* House, the women should begin to mourn because the initiates (their sons) are to be exposed to the *He* which, coming from the spirit world, may make them waste away and die. They also consume the magic substances that are given to the initiates so that they too should benefit from the protection that they confer, and during the rites they leave the house at certain crucial points. Finally, it should be noted that during and after *He* House, the women are supposed to keep to the same taboos as the men. Thus the women may be excluded from the rites but they are very definitely involved.

If the women do happen to see the *He*, it is said that they would die but that they may be saved by treatment from a shaman.[20] The *He* used at Fruit House are not considered to be the real *He*, and if women see these they merely become ill. According to other writers (Biocca 1965 : 23; Costa cit. Schaden 1959 : 151 n. 5.), if women should see the Yurupary they would be afflicted by the 'three major defects of women' – licentiousness (given as '*incontinencia*' in the Portuguese original), curiosity and a proneness to reveal secrets. These defects have the common feature of implying that the women would become excessively open in either a literal or figurative sense: their eyes and ears become too open (curiosity), their vaginas become too open (licentiousness) and their mouths become too open (talkativeness).[21] The belief, from other parts of the Vaupés area, that women become excessively open as the result of seeing Yurupary

19 An argument along these lines has been suggested for the Mundurucú men's trumpet cult (Murphy and Murphy 1974).
20 Ypiranga Monteiro (1960 : 37) describes the shamanism of a woman who had seen Yurupary among the Iurupixuna-Tukano.
21 Bolens (1967) bases a considerable portion of her interpretation of Yurupary myths on the opposition between open and closed bodily orifices. She uses some of the data that

130

is entirely in accord with the Barasana belief that women menstruate
(a condition in which their vaginas are open) as the result of seeing
their hair. Furthermore, this same theme is found in the punishments
that the men inflict on the women for stealing the Yurupary or *He*:
the women are gang-raped, have the flutes rammed up their vaginas
and are made to menstruate (see M.1.D.7). Again the women are
opened up and made to bleed from their vaginas. The above data
implies first, that the condition of having seen Yurupary is in some
sense the same as that of menstruation, and secondly, that this
condition involves an excessive openness of bodily orifices.

Yurupary, the hero of the myths, was a divine legislator and
among his laws the following were to be taught to girls: that they
should remain virgins until puberty, that they should remain faithful
to their husbands and not prostitute themselves, that they should
not see the Yurupary and that they should not be curious nor talk
too much and reveal secrets (Stradelli 1890b; Costa cit. Schaden
1959 : 151 n.5). All these laws imply the ability to control the
orifices of the body, especially the vagina, and it is significant that
it was during a period of intense education at rites of first menstruation that these laws were taught to young girls.[22] It would seem
therefore that women are thought of as in danger of becoming excessively opened up and that this danger becomes acute at puberty
when, in a very real sense, they become more open. This suggestion
receives confirmation from the fact that, in the Tariana Yurupary
myth recorded by Stradelli (1890b), the Sun sent *Izy* to the earth
to find a 'perfect woman'; one who was dumb, patient and who
lacked curiosity. Such a woman would be one who obeyed to the full
the laws of Yurupary mentioned above.

M.1.D makes it clear that the possession of *He* (instruments) and
the ability to menstruate are seen as being complementary but
mutually exclusive: when woman had the *He* (instruments), the men
menstruated and when the men regained the *He* they punished the
women by making them menstruate. Also implied is the fact that
the sex that controls the *He* (instruments) and which does not
menstruate will be the one that is politically dominant. But M.1.B

I have used but arrives at somewhat different conclusions. I do not entirely agree either
with her interpretation of the data being considered here (largely because she fails
totally to take into account the theme of menstruation) or with her more general conclusions (see also ch. 8). However, I have found that the way in which she has looked
at the data has helped me greatly in my own analysis.
22 See also Lévi-Strauss (1968 : 420–1) on the education of young girls at rites of first
menstruation.

implies that the women still have the *He* and that it is this that causes them to menstruate; the *He* is their hair. It is for this reason that when the men took back the *He* from the women, their victory over them was double-edged (see above). They regained only one kind of *He* (instruments) which implies political dominance but they lost another (women's hair) which implies menstruation and the power to create children.

It will be argued below that in some senses *He* House can perhaps be interpreted as a symbolic act in which adult men give birth to the initiates. In order to give birth, men must first be opened up and made to menstruate. I have already stated that people who see the *He* are in some sense in the same condition as menstruating women. It is entirely appropriate therefore that after *He* House, the initiates should be confined in a compartment, as are menstruating women, and referred to by expressions which, in their feminine form, refer to women in this condition. After the introduction of more evidence, it will be shown that, during *He* House, the initiates are symbolically opened up and that this is done in part by showing them women's hair. If, after *He* House, the men are in a condition equivalent to that of menstruation then, according to the argument above, the women should temporarily become dominant. In relation to this, it is significant that during the marginal period following *He* House, something very like the social revolution of women described in Yurupary myths occurs.

Finally, there is another possible interpretation of the mythical incident in which the women steal the Yurupary. In most of the Yurupary myths, immediately after he is born, Yurupary is stolen from his mother by the men. He is later burned on a fire and from his ashes grows the palm from which the Yurupary instruments are made. These instruments represent the bones of Yurupary (see e.g. M.8). By taking back the Yurupary instruments, the mother of Yurupary is effectively taking back her own son, represented by his bones. In this sense the story may be seen as an expression of tension between men and women, the women resenting the loss of their sons who are taken from them by the men at initiation.

Guests

The part played by *He* House, Fruit House and other communal rituals in intercommunity relations was discussed briefly in chapter 2, and information concerning the role of the guests at *He* rituals was presented in part II.

During Fruit House, the guests are distinguished from their hosts by their seating positions, though the importance of this should not be overstressed. They may also bring their own *He* instruments and if they do, they will tend to play these rather than those of their hosts. During *He* House, the distinction between hosts and guests is even less marked and in general, the guests act in terms of the ritual roles appropriate to their age-grades rather than in terms of their position *qua* guests. At the *He* House that I observed, the members of the most important visiting household (that of Pedro) brought their own *He* instruments with them, and also their own yagé vines which they prepared separately, and drank from their own yagé pot.

Perhaps the most significant thing that can be said about both these rituals in relation to the guests is that at all the rites I observed, guests from affinally related groups were present. This means that neither stage of initiation is exclusive to either one sib or to one exogamous group.[23] In addition, it has already been seen that a boy may be, and often is, initiated by being shown *He* instruments that belong to an affinal group. This point will be taken up again below.

23 Among the Cubeo also, the Yurupary cult is not an exclusive sib cult (Goldman 1963 : 195).

6

The flutes and trumpets

The musical instruments

From an observer's point of view, the *He* instruments may be divided
into two classes: flutes and trumpets (in fact large megaphones). This
division corresponds to one way in which the Barasana classify these
instruments: the flutes, called the form of a palm (*ruha nyo*) or the
form of a post (*ruha bota*), are distinguished in terms of shape from
the trumpets, called *hotiri* or *rĩhoa*, depending on the manner of their
construction.

According to Izikowitz (1934), the flutes are duct flutes with
deflectors, lacking stops but with a partially covered sound orifice.
They consist of a straight tube, about 50–100 mm thick and with an
internal diameter of between 5 and 7 cm, made of highly polished,
black wood – a section of a trunk of the paxiuba (*Iriartea exorrihiza*)
palm. This is the only permanent part of the instrument and when
not in use it is kept, wrapped in palm leaves, under water in the mud
at the bottom of a small stream or river. The rest of the instrument
(leaf vibrators, clay plug and vine bindings – see fig. 7) is made
freshly each time it is used. The length of the flutes, always in pairs
with one slightly shorter than the other, varies from approximately
60 cm to 160 cm. The long flutes are called long (*yoese*) in Barasana
also. Fig. 6 shows a flute of medium length.

Some of the longest flutes have incised geometric designs on the
lower end which are filled with chalk or manioc flour when in use
(see fig. 8). The extreme ends of the flutes are painted uniform
white. The shorter flutes do not have such designs but are also painted
white on the bottom end. During *He* House, and sometimes at Fruit
House, a string of yellow and brown feathers (from the tail of the
Oropendola bird) is tied in a ruff round the ends of the long flutes.

134

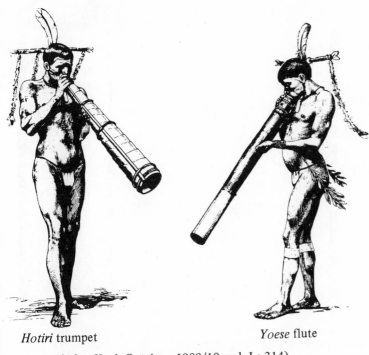

Hotiri trumpet   *Yoese* flute

(After Koch Grünberg 1909/10, vol. I : 314)

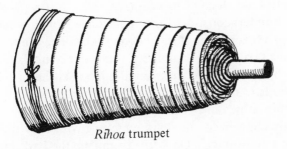

Rĩhoa trumpet

Fig. 6 Yurupary instruments

    The permanent part of the trumpets consists of a tube of black, polished paxiuba palm wood about 45 cm long and about 5 cm internal diameter. When not in use, this part, like the flutes, is kept under water. Before each ritual, strips of bark, from the trees *hau̶, rĩa hau̶* and *kahe rokou̶* are wound round the ends of these tubes to form an elongated cone.[1] The Barasana divide the trumpets into two cat-

1 According to Brüzzi da Silva (1962 : 306), the bark comes from the chibaru (*Eperua*

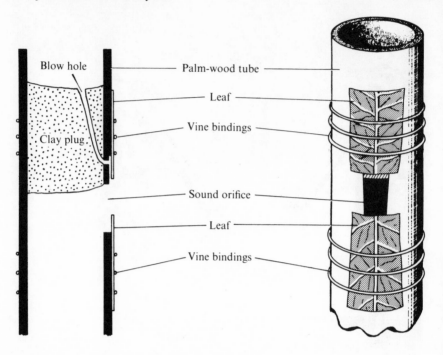

Fig. 7 The construction of a Barasana *He* flute

egories according to their shape. One category, called *hotiri* (*hoti* means a wrapped bundle) consists of trumpets made from a conical spiral of bark, expanding out from the wooden tube. The other category, called head (*rīhoa*), are trumpets of more rectangular appearance made by winding the bark round upon itself before extending it forwards to make the bell of the instrument. Both types of trumpet are shown in fig. 6. In both instruments, most of the wooden tube remains inside the bark wrapping with only the end protruding as a mouthpiece. On *hotiri* trumpets, the bark spiral

grandiflora) tree. Galvão (1959 : 47) gives the same identification and adds that this tree sprang up from the ashes in the place where Yurupary was burned, together with the first paxiuba palm (see M.8.63).

McGovern (1927 : 144) says that, among the Waikano (Pirá-Tapuyo), only old men may cut the bark from the trees and only after they have asked permission of the tree's spirit. They must also blow tobacco smoke over the wound they make. I was never present when this bark was cut by the Barasana so I cannot say if this is true of them also.

In general, the Barasana refer to the cut bark as tree covering (*hea gase*), or as cotton covering (*yuta gase*). This latter name is an allusion to the fact that the bark on the trumpets is seen as the equivalent of the garters (*yuta gasero*) worn by men below the knees.

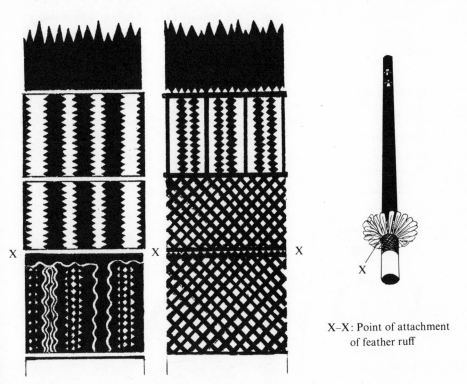

X–X: Point of attachment
of feather ruff

Fig. 8 Engraved designs on Barasana *He* flutes

is sometimes supported by two sticks running along the length of
the instrument.

The length of *hotiri* trumpets varies between about 60 cm and
250 cm. The very long trumpets are played with a man walking
in front supporting the ends and raising them up and down in alternation. The *rĩhoa* trumpets are generally about 100 cm long or less.
Like the flutes, the trumpets are in pairs.

With the exception of some trumpets used in the Içana area,
which are made of basketwork with a resin covering, the descriptions
of the flutes and trumpets given above appear to apply to all Yurupary
instruments used in the Vaupés/Rio Negro/Içana region.[2] According
to Humboldt (1966, vol. V : 232, 273), the Indians of the Atabapo
and Inirida area (north of the Vaupés) used trumpets made of clay,

2 Photographs of Yurupary instruments may be found in the following sources: McGovern
  1927 : 152; Paes de Souza Brazil 1938 : 68; Allen 1947 : 572; Biocca 1965 : 220–1
  and Reichel-Dolmatoff 1971 : 168. This last photograph shows a Barasana *hotiri* trumpet.

called *botuto*. He states that these trumpets were exactly like those
illustrated by Gumilla (1963 : 162–7) and used by the Saliva further
to the north (see fig. 9).

The concept of *He*

The Barasana refer to these flutes and trumpets as *He*, a word probably
related to *hea*, meaning fire, firewood and by extension dead wood in
general. The association with fire and wood is suggested in part by
the material from which the instruments are constructed, and also
by the fact that the instruments were created by the burning of the

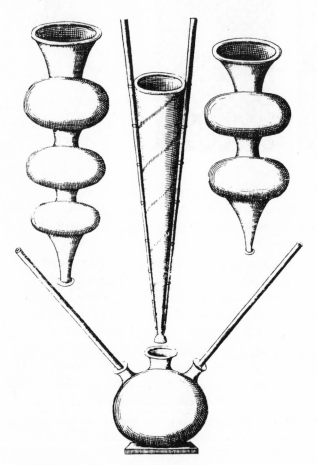

Fig. 9 Instruments used by the Saliva Indians during mortuary rites (after
Gumilla 1963 : 165)

138

body of a mythical hero (see M.5.A.12—17 and M.8.56—62) and that when Manioc-stick Anaconda was burned, his bones (identified with the *He* instruments) became the burned logs of a manioc garden created by felling and burning the forest (see M.6.B). In conversation with non-Indians, the Barasana refer to these instruments as Yurupary.

The word *He* is also used in a more general sense as a concept which covers such things as the sacred, the other world, the spirit world and the world of myth. Used in this latter sense, the word is often added as a prefix to other words. Thus *He* river (*He rīaga*), or *He* water path (*He oko ma*), is the river up which the ancestral anaconda *Yeba Meni* Anaconda swam to give birth to humanity (see below); *He* People (*He masa*) are either the first ancestors of humanity, represented by the *He* instruments, or the people who take part in *He* House; *He* possessions (*He gaheuni*) are the objects and items of ceremonial dress used at dances, etc.

He pertains to the world of myths. This world is timeless and changeless and persists as another aspect of everyday existence. All living creatures have their *He* counterparts which live in stone houses, the rapids in the rivers and the mountains and outcrops of rock. Human beings too have their *He* or spirit counterparts that live in stone houses called people's waking-up houses (*masa yuhiri wi*). The souls of new-born babies come from these houses and the souls of the dead return to them. The idea of waking-up house puts in mind the Australian aborigine concept of the Dreaming, and indeed Stanner's account of this concept among the Murinbata (1960 : 246—7) can be read, almost word for word, as an account of the Barasana concept of *He*.

The *He* world was created in the distant past but persists as another aspect of reality. As the generations succeed one another, or, as the Barasana view it, as they pile on top of one another like the leaves on the forest floor, human beings are in danger of losing touch with the beginning and source of life, the world of myth. According to one informant, the object of *He* House is literally to squash the pile so that the initiates, described as people of another layer (*gahe tutiana*), are brought into contact with, and adopted by, the first *He* People. Ordinary human beings enter into involuntary contact with the *He* world when sick and also when asleep. Such uncontrolled contact is potentially dangerous. Controlled contact is both desirable (though again potentially dangerous) and also necessary for the continuance of the world and human life. Shamans are able to perceive this other-world aspect of existence at all times and it is they who act as mediators for the rest of society. Adult men enter into voluntary contact with the *He* world by wearing ceremonial dress and by taking the hallucinogenic drug yagé. One informant summarised the use of this drug by saying that under its influence the house becomes the universe itself so that a man can see and know everything. At Fruit House, and more particularly at *He* House, young boys enter into controlled and voluntary contact with the *He* world for the first time.

In chanting, the *He* are referred to as *minia*, a word which means both birds and also pets. In Tukano, the Yurupary are called *miria pora* and in Desana, *minia poari*. According to both Brüzzi da Silva and Reichel-Dolmatoff, the root *mini-* (Pirá-Tapuyo) or *miriye-* (Tukano), means to submerge or to go under water. Brüzzi da Silva (1962 : 337) argues that this indicates that the Yurupary are secret, occult and hidden and therefore 'submerged'. A more obvious interpretation is that the Yurupary are 'submerged' precisely because they are kept hidden under water. According to Reichel-Dolmatoff, (1971 : 171) the Pirá-Tapuyo compare sexual intercourse to the act of 'submerging oneself in water' and he adds that *poari* means 'hair, pubic hair'. These facts are used as evidence in his argument that the flutes have a sexual character and that the men who play them 'represent those who are "drowned", those who committed the sin (of incest)', the cult of Yurupary being interpreted as a warning against the sin of incest and an exhortation to obey rules of exogamy. Again, a more obvious interpretation of the 'drowned' flutes is that they are kept under water.

Whilst I do not doubt for one moment that the root *mini-* or *miriye-* means to drown, I feel that Reichel-Dolmatoff and Brüzzi da Silva have both ignored overwhelming evidence in favour of translating *minia poari* and *miria pora* as 'children/descendants of birds'. The evidence is as follows: (1) the word *pura/pora*, in both Tukano and Desana, means children or descendants and it may well be that Reichel-Dolmatoff has confused *poari* with *pura/pora*. Significantly, in a later work, Reichel-Dolmatoff writes, 'In most of the Tukano dialects, *yuruparí* is called *miria-pora*, from *miriri* (to suffocate or drown oneself or to submerge oneself), and *pora* (children, descendants (1972 : 94). (2) To emphasise that *poari* means pubic hair is to beg the question, for it also means feathers which, by the same kind of argument, would redress the balance in favour of birds. (3) In every Tukanoan language spoken in the Vaupés region, *minia, miria* or something close to it (*memea* – Karapana; *miua* – Cubeo) means bird (Koch-Grünberg 1912–16). (4) the Baniwa, like the Barasana, identify the sound of the Yurupary with birdsong (Galvão 1959 : 49). (5) The Tukano Yurupary were originally birds kept in a cage (Fulop 1956 : 360). (6) The Tanimuka and Yahuna of the Apaporís called Yurupary *wekoa, Amazona* parrots. (7) A large proportion of the specific names of individual Yurupary instruments, published in the literature of the Vaupés–Içana region, are the names of species of birds. (8) Finally, the Iurupixuna-Tukano called their Yurupary *mimbaua*, tamed animals or pets (Ypiranga Monteiro 1960 : 37), the word for which, in Barasana, is *minia*.

The *He* world described in Barasana myth is one in which human beings and animals are not as yet differentiated from one another; the myths in fact describe a gradual process of differentiation. The Barasana would often start to tell a myth in this way, 'There was a man called X (the name of an animal); at that time there were no people . . . ' The *He* world is thus, in one sense, the world of the forest and of animals, nature. I say 'in one sense' because whilst the Barasana see human souls and spirit people as being like animals, they emphasise that they are not identical. The situation can be represented as in fig. 10.

The life cycle of each person repeats this process of differentiation between men and animals. At birth, a child's soul changes from the spirit, *He*, state to that of a human being. That an unborn soul is part of a world that includes animals is evidenced by the fact that tapirs and other Taking-in People (*sõria masa*) try to suck the child into their anus – a reversal of birth – as they are jealous of the loss of one of their number (see M.5.A.18). Birth is thus like a passage from the animal world (nature, *He*) to the human world (culture).

If new-born babies are on the side of animals and nature, adult men are on the side of spirits and the *He* world. By taking part in rituals, especially *He* rituals, the men are constantly entering into contact with the *He* world. It will be shown below that the *He* instruments are animals and birds. These instruments are kept in rivers in the forest so in this sense they are closely associated with human beings and, at Fruit House, they enter the house bearing gifts of fruit from the forest. This fruit, called *He* fruit, is the food of animals and birds (see M.7.I). The *He* are thus mediators between

141

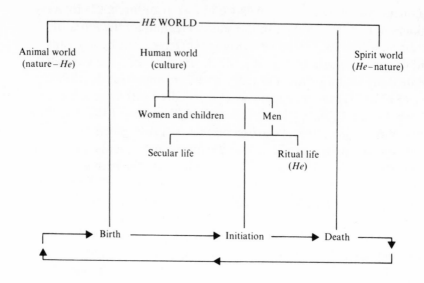

Fig. 10 The *He* world

nature and culture, between animals and men and between the forest
and the house. They are therefore exactly like pets or tamed animals
and it is entirely appropriate that the Barasana should call them
minia which means both birds and pets. The fact that the Tukano
and Iurupixuna-Tukano also identify their Yurupary with pets (or
caged birds) (see above) suggests that they also can be seen in this
light.

In addition to being identified with animals, the *He* are also
identified with characters in myth. Like pets, these characters are
neither fully human nor fully animal. They are *He* People belonging
to a world in which men and animals are as yet undifferentiated.
During *He* House, the participants become *He* People. They also
become like animals on the side of nature: they wear bird feathers,
bird beaks, animal fur, teeth, bones and claws. Thus when the *He*
are brought into the house, a passage from nature to culture, from
animal to human, the men in the house change from culture to
nature, from human to animal.

The true *He*: the instruments used at *He* House

At the *He* House I observed, a total of twelve pairs of *He* instruments

The flutes and trumpets

were used (see table 4). Two of the pairs, Old Parrot (*Weko Bʉkʉ*) and Old Deer (*Nyama Bʉkʉ*), were brought by Bará guests; all the rest belonged to the Barasana sib *Meni Masa* and were kept at the maloca where the rite was held. A pair of long flutes called Old Guan (*Kata Bʉkʉ*) should also have been used but had rotted away and no longer exist. As the *He* were created in the mythic past and are not man-made, the Barasana say that they cannot remake these instruments. All the flutes, together with the short trumpets called Old Star (*Nyoko Bʉkʉ*) were placed vertically over sticks stuck in the ground in a line stretching down the middle of the house from post 3. The other instruments, all trumpets, were laid on the ground, with their mouthpieces towards the middle, on the right-hand side of the house beyond the dance path.

Table 4. *The instruments used at He House (Caño Colorado, June 1970)*

Name of instrument	Barasana name	Type of instrument
Old Macaw	*Maha Bʉkʉ*	Long flute
Tree-Fruit Jaguar	*He Rika Yai*	Long flute
Old Sloth	*Kerea Bʉkʉ, Wʉnʉ Bʉkʉ*	Shorter flute
(unknown)	*Bosoro Huria*	Short flute
Old Amazona Parrot	*Weko Bʉkʉ*	Short flute
Old Deer, Old Muscovy Duck	*Nyama Bʉkʉ, Rĩa Kata Bʉkʉ*	Very long trumpet (*hotiri*)
Manioc-squeezing Woman	*Bʉhe Romio*	Long trumpet (*hotiri*)
Dance Anaconda	*Basa Hino*	Long trumpet (*hotiri*)
(unknown)	*Wenadurika*	Shorter trumpet (*rĩhoa*)
Sabicea Flower	*Kano Goro*	Shorter trumpet (*rĩhoa*)
Old Callicebus Monkey	*Wau Bʉkʉ*	Shorter trumpet (*rĩhoa*)
Old Star, White Star	*Nyoko Bʉkʉ, Nyoko Bokʉ*	Short trumpet (*hotiri*)

Explanation and analysis

These instruments are the *He* People, or ancestors, and their names are the names of the people created by *Romi Kumu* (see M.1.C), the ancestors of the Barasana sibs *Koamona, Rasegana, Meni Masa, Daria* and *Wabea*. According to the Barasana, the large communal houses in which they live represent the universe: the roof is the sky, the house posts are the mountains that support the sky, the men's door is the Water Door in the east where the sun rises and the women's door is the door in the west where the sun sets; the walls of the house are the edges of the world. Shamans see the house like this, as do other men when under the effects of yagé. At *He* House, all the animals in the world come to dance; they are *He* People, the *He* instruments and the other items of ritual equipment.

Old Macaw (*Maha Buku*) is Manioc-stick Anaconda's brother, the shorter of the pair of flutes being his ex-wife (see M.6.A). He is the lead dancer and he dances in the *middle* of the house, just as, in a normal dance, the lead dancer dances in the middle of the dance line with the other dancers, his helpers, on either side. The other long flutes are these other dancers. Likewise, the elders playing the long flutes are dancers. The melodies of the flutes, to which the shamans can put words are the songs that these dancers sing.

It will be noticed that during both Fruit House and *He* House, there is no singing by humans when the *He* are played in the house, but that during the second part of Fruit House, when the *He* are silent, the people sing. The sound of the flutes is also the sound of chanting, for, at dances, when the dancers are not dancing they chant. Old Macaw leads this chanting and is the specialist chanter.

The identity of the trumpet, Old Star, White Star, is problematic but there is circumstantial evidence that the star(s) in question may be part of the constellation Orion. Lévi-Strauss has shown that the Pleiades and Orion are diachronically related, since the Pleiades rise within a few days of Orion and announce the coming of the latter, but that they are also synchronically opposed, since the Pleiades are connected with the continuous and Orion with the discontinuous (in terms of the shape of the two constellations). He has further shown that in South American myth, Orion is frequently associated with either a man whose leg has been cut off or with the cut-off leg itself (Lévi-Strauss (1970 : 220–30; 1973 : 266–70). It has already been established that the Pleiades are used as a time-marker (i.e. announce *He* House and the use of the *He*). It can be shown also that the *He* are identified with bones (see M.5.A.11 and M.6.A.63), in particular with the paired long bones of the upper and lower leg. (The word for leg, *niku*, also means ancestor; the *He* are leg bones and also ancestors.) It will later be shown that the gourd of beeswax used at *He* rites is associated with viscera, the head and with the Pleiades. It is opposed to the *He* by the fact (among others) that it is round and continuous as opposed to long and discontinuous. Thus we have:

> Pleiades : Orion :: viscera (+ head) : long bone

and

> Gourd of wax : *He* instruments :: O : ———

The Barasana call part of the constellation Orion the Adze (*Sioruhu*). The part concerned is the belt together with the two shoulders (Bellatrix and Betelgeuse – see fig. 11).

The myth of origin of the Adze constellation is as follows: when the *Oa Suna*, Opossum Tatuyo People, saw *He* for the first time, there were three men standing in a line (the three stars of Orion's belt). The middle man was bitten in the leg by a snake. This is why the middle star is smaller than the other two. The man's leg became bent and shrivelled and became the ceremonial adze which the Tatuyo wear on their shoulders during dances, called dance adze (*basa sioro*). These adzes, originally used for wood-working, were used as a dance ornament during Yurupary rites among the Tukano, Tariana, Bará and Tatuyo. They were worn, slung over the left shoulder, by chiefs, shamans and lead dancers (Koch-Grünberg 1909–10, vol. I : 350; Brüzzi da Silva 1962 : 315).[3]

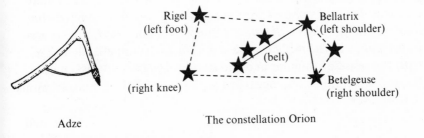

Adze   The constellation Orion

Fig. 11 The Adze (*Sioruhu*), part of the constellation Orion

---

3 Neither author seems aware that the ceremonial adze is identified with a constellation, though Brüzzi (1962 : 260) does mention a constellation called 'adze handle'.

Explanation and analysis

The theme of the shrivelled, atrophied leg is found also in the character of *Warimi* (see M.4.A–H). In part of the *Warimi* cycle, (not included in the myths in this book), *Warimi* is bitten by a snake which causes one leg to shrivel up. This would suggest that *Warimi* should be identified with Orion and, in fact, at the end of the myths, *Warimi* took leave of this world and went into the sky, hence his name *Warimi*, He-Who-Went-Away. Finally, *Warimi* is himself a variant of the character Yurupary of Vaupés mythology.[4] To summarise: it has been shown that there is evidence to link the *He* instruments as a whole with Orion; that the Adze constellation (= Orion) is identified with an adze used as an ornament in Yurupary rituals; that *Warimi's* shrivelled leg can be linked with both Orion and the Adze and that *Warimi* is a variant of Yurupary from whose bones, represented by the paxiuba palm, the Yurupary instruments were made (see M.8.62–3 and compare M.5.A.17 and M.6.A.63). It seems therefore reasonable to conclude that Old Star may also be Orion.

Old Star is called the fierce one, the fierce *He*, the fierce thunder jaguar. He is the jaguar at the dance and is the protector of the *He* People. The trumpets as a group are described as warriors (*guamarã*) and as the people who make others frightened. (Spanish-speaking Barasana say they are soldiers and policemen.) Old Star is the leader of the trumpets, their chief and, as a group, they accompany Old Macaw and the other long flutes (the dancers) to protect them. They walk round the edge of the house, both inside and out, forming a protective shield around the dancers and shamans in the middle. It is therefore appropriate that, during *He* House, it is the *younger men*, the warriors, possessed of the qualities of strength and courage, that play the *undecorated* trumpets *walking* round the *edge* of the house while the *elders*, *decorated* themselves and playing *decorated* flutes, *dance* in the *middle*. The sound of the trumpets, identified with the noise of thunder and the roar of jaguars, contrasts with the sound of the flutes, identified with birdsong. This contrast is part of a set:

Long flutes	Trumpets
birdsong	jaguar and thunder noise
high pitch	low pitch

4 See ch. 7 for further evidence for this assertion.

The flutes and trumpets

decorated	undecorated
players dance	players walk
centre	periphery
elders	young men

The pair of trumpets called Old Callicebus Monkey, identified in particular with Manioc-stick Anaconda (see M.6.A), are the shamans at the dance who sit inside their enclosure blowing spells, and at *He* House they remain inside the shamans' enclosure on top of an hourglass-shaped stand made from palm-wood splints. This stand is Old Callicebus's stool, and just as at the start of *He* House only the shamans sit on stools (later to be joined by the elders), so only Old Callicebus is placed raised above the ground on a stand; the flutes, representing the elders stand vertically with one end resting on the ground, whilst the trumpets, representing the young men, are laid on the floor. Old Callicebus Monkey represents Manioc-stick Anaconda sitting upon his stool.

I have no direct information as to whom the short flutes represent and am unable to fully translate the name *Bosoro Huria* (*huria* means 'piece of'). However, in line with the data presented above, it is not unreasonable to assume that they represent the initiates themselves. With the exception of the trumpets Old Star, they are the smallest *He* instruments and their sound is neither the melody of the long flutes nor the thunderous roar of the trumpets, but a single, quiet and high-pitched noise which would fit well with the qualities of the initiates. These flutes are always played by the initiates (or the youngest boys present) and always in conjunction with the trumpets. That the very youngest should be taken under the wing of the young men, represented by the trumpets, seems highly appropriate, for once the initiation is over, the initiates too will be young men.

In the last chapter, I showed that there is a correspondence between the Barasana sibs (*Koamona*, *Rasegana*, *Meni Masa*, *Daria* and *Wabea*), their specialist occupations (chiefs, chanters/dancers, warriors, shamans and servants), the participants (elders, young men, initiates and shamans, and women and children), and the age-grades (elder, young men, child). It is clear from the data presented above that the *He* instruments can also be fitted into this schema in the table on p. 148.

The correspondence between the ranking and specialisation of the sibs and that of the *He* instruments follows from the fact that the instruments are the dead ancestors of the sibs concerned. The cor-

Sibling order	1	2	3	4	5
Sibs	*Koamona*	*Rasegana*	*Meni-Masa*	*Daria*	*Wabea*
Occupations	chief	chanter/dancer	warrior	shaman	servants
He instruments		long flutes	trumpets	trumpet (Old Star)	short flutes (& other wives)
Participants		elders (shamans)	young men	initiates shamans	women & children (initiates)
Age-grades		elder	young man	(initiate)	child

respondence is only partial. The Barasana say that there are no true chiefs amongst the *He* instruments just as there are no true chiefs in human society, but they add that the flutes Old Macaw are 'like chiefs'. Again, there are no instruments that can be directly identified with servants. Amongst the Barasana, the servant sib *Wabea* are seen as equivalent to, but not the same as, the semi-nomadic Makú who act as servants to some other Tukanoan groups in the Vaupés region (Tukano, Desana, Cubeo and Pirá-Tapuyo), but who are not present in the Pirá-paraná area. Amongst the Tukano, who do have Makú servants, some of the Yurupary instruments are said to have wives and some of these wives are the Makú servants of the other instruments (Brüzzi da Silva 1962 : 307). According to Reichel-Dolmatoff (1971 : 19), the Desana also consider their Makú servants as representing a female element. Of the Barasana *He* instruments, women are represented by the trumpets called Manioc-squeezing Women (*Buhe Romio*), the daughter of *Romi Kumu*, by the shorter of the two Old Macaw flutes, Old Macaw's wife and by the short flutes played by the initiates, described as the wives of the other instruments in general. If servants or Makú are represented by the wives of the Yurupary instruments in other parts of the Vaupés, then the wives of the Barasana *He* instruments, notably the short flutes, can be identified as servants. Finally, the guests at *He* House are also represented by the *He* instruments they bring with them. At the *He* House I observed, the most important group of guests, members of Pedro's household and representatives of the Bará sib *Wai Masa*,

close affines of their hosts, brought with them the trumpets called
Old Deer or Old Muscovy Duck.

The division of sibs into a ranked series associated with specialist
ritual occupations and the corresponding division of the *He* instruments into the roles of chanter/dancers, warriors and shamans, is
found also amongst the Bará, Tatuyo and Taiwano. The only evidence
for such a system outside the Pirá-paraná area is as follows: the
Baniwa have a hierarchy of ranked patrilineal sibs and some at least
are associated with particular named Yurupary instruments; they also
recognise the category of cigar lighters or servants as corresponding
to the most junior sib (Galvão 1959 : 22, 42, 49). The ranking of
sibs into a hierarchical order appears to be common to all Tukanoan
groups in the Vaupés. The Tukano have Yurupary instruments which
are described as being the Makú of the others. The Cubeo Yurupary
instruments *bwu* and *onpwenda kudjuwe*, described by Goldman
(1963 : 193) as the 'strongest and fiercest', may correspond to the
Barasana category of fierce *He* and be represented by Old Star,
the warrior. It may well be that the very fact that throughout the
Vaupés—Içana region the Yurupary instruments are divided into
two classes, trumpets and flutes, can perhaps be taken as evidence of
a division into ritual occupations, for amongst the Barasana at least,
this division corresponds in broad terms to that between chanter/
dancers and warriors. Finally, according to Biocca (cit. Schaden 1959 :
154), the Tukano of the Río Tiquié are divided into three categories:
(1) caciques and chiefs, (2) the general population and (3) recently
initiated young men, in ranked order.

The significance of the true *He*

Romi Kumu is called the mother of *He*. The *He* are her children (also
her grandchildren) (see M.1.C.2). The Barasana say that the *He* are
ancestors (*nikua*). In theory at least, the different *He* are the different
ancestors of each of the five Barasana sibs mentioned above. In
practice, while informants repeatedly stressed that Old Star, the
warrior, was the particular ancestor of the *Meni Masa* sib, also warriors,
they were unwilling or unable to assign other individual instruments
to the other sibs. I was also unable to obtain data on this matter
from informants of sibs other than *Meni Masa*. However, there is no
doubt that, as a group, the *He* are the ancestors of the five sibs, also

as a group. This statement is true also of the other groups (Bará, Taiwano, Tatuyo and Makuna) in the Pirá-paraná area. It can be said, therefore, that one interpretation of *He* rituals in the Pirá-paraná area is that they represent an ancestor cult and that it is this cult into which young boys are initiated. Goldman reached this same conclusion concerning the Cubeo Yurupary cult, adding that no other ancestral cult had been reported for the entire Northwest Amazon. It is certainly true that Goldman has, till now, remained alone in associating Yurupary with such a cult (Goldman 1963 : 190ff).

According to the Barasana, the *He* instruments, the *He* People, are as if alive. They have names like ordinary people but are the living dead. As such they are very cold (like dead people) and this is one reason why they must be kept under water. They also smell strongly (my informants would not say of what they smelled but my guess is of rottenness). Because they are the living dead, ordinary people are very afraid of them and they themselves are very dangerous as they tend to make people waste away and die. The *He* People want the living to join them permanently so they encourage the people who see them to break the taboos so that they too will die. When people become ill after seeing *He*, they can hear the *He* People calling them to join them. One way in which the *He* try to kill the living is by giving them fish to eat – these are the fish that the shamans send away at the Fruit House in preparation for *He* House and the fish that people dream of if they sleep in front of the house on the last night of *He* House. The Barasana say that the *He* People give the fish at a ceremonial exchange-of-food dance which is *He* House itself and there are striking parallels between the overall pattern of the two rites: at ceremonial food exchanges the donors come to the recipients' house. On the day they arrive, they do not enter the house of their hosts but sit out all night on the plaza. At *He* House too, the *He* are brought to the house on the evening of the day of sitting on the plaza and there they remain till dawn. As they arrive, the people in the house say, 'The old people have arrived.' At food-exchange dances, the donors enter the recipients' house early in the morning, carrying bundles of food and blowing on clay trumpets; they walk twice round the dance path in a clockwise direction then up the middle of the house, depositing the food between posts 7 and 8. At *He* House, the *He* enter as real trumpets and walk in the same manner. The parallel is even more striking at Fruit House, for

again the *He* remain outside on the first night, but in the morning
they come in bringing food, but, unlike the cooked food at food-
exchange dances, this food is raw. The *He*, like food givers, are
outsiders and guests but from another world rather than another
house. The *He* represent the ancestors of the Barasana. These ancestors
were jaguars and the *He* too are jaguars as many of their names
suggest; as jaguars they are also shamans. The sound of the trumpets
is the roar of the jaguar and the Barasana say that when the *He*
are not in use, their souls wander in the forest in the form of jaguars.
The *He* are also anacondas: they have their origin in the burned bodies
of *He* Anaconda and Manioc-stick Anaconda (M.5.A., M.6.A); their
sound is that of the anaconda that makes a terrifying guttural roar
when provoked; lying hidden under water, they are the anacondas
that live in the rivers. I have already signalled the importance of
breath and blowing in the activities of Barasana shamans. Breath is
the manifestation of the soul (*usu*) and can be used to cure and
impart life and vigour. It is this same breath that imparts life to the
He instruments: they are blown, they make sound and they live.
Tobacco snuff is blown into the *He* by the shamans to feed their
souls and to impart life. The roar of the jaguar and the anaconda is
the sound of their breath; by blowing into megaphone trumpets,
the Barasana amplify their breath to a roar. They say that their house
is a person and that when there are people inside, its heart and soul
become alive. The *He* instruments, brought from the forest, breathe
life into the house. At Fruit House, this same life-giving ancestral
breath is blown from the trumpets over the piles of fruit so that its
soul is changed and becomes ripe and abundant, and at *He* House,
it is blown over the initiates themselves to change their souls and to
turn them into strong adults.

   As mentioned above, the Barasana maloca is a microcosm of the
universe itself: the roof is the sky, the house posts are the mountains
that support the sky, and the floor-space is the earth. Malocas are
conceptually, though not always actually, oriented along an east–
west axis so that the men's door represents the Water Door in the
east where the sun rises, and the women's door is the door in the
west; the centre of the house is the Pirá-paraná area, the centre of
the world. The earth is thought of as being bisected by a river running
from west to east and conceptually the house, as a microcosm of
the universe, is also bisected by a river. Thus, on a cosmic scale, there
is only one house, the universe itself. In the beginning, this universe–

house had no people inside. The anaconda ancestors of the Bará, Barasana, and Tatuyo were the sons of the Primal Sun, *Yeba Hakɨ*. *Yeba Meni* Anaconda entered the world through the Water Door in the east and from there swam upriver towards the west. He travelled up the Milk River (the Amazon?) to the Apaporís and thence to the Pirá-paraná, the middle of the world. Undifferentiated and as yet not human, the head of the anaconda represented the top-ranking sib and its tail represented the lowest sib; the head was towards the west, the tail towards the east. On arrival at the centre of the earth, the anaconda reversed its position so that its head now faced the east and its tail the west, and then it gave rise to human beings, its sons, either by vomiting them out of its mouth or by transforming its body. These human beings were the *He* People whose names are those of the *He* instruments, and their order of emergence, or creation, gave rise to the ranking of the different sibs. This explains why ideally the highest-ranking sibs live at the river mouth and the lowest at the headwaters for, in the Pirá-paraná region, the rivers flow east. The universe—house now contained people, the anaconda—father representing the unity of the group, and his sons its internally segmented and ranked parts.

Myths from elsewhere in the Vaupés region (see e.g. M.8.25) tell much the same story but in some, rather than giving rise to different sibs within one exogamic group, the anaconda ancestor gives rise to all the different exogamic groups in the region. These myths, like the Barasana origin myth mentioned above and like the myth in which *Romi Kumu* creates the *He* People from Her own body (M.1.C), all describe a process of differentiation and generalisation from a common source. The Primal Sun, *Yeba Hakɨ*, the creator of the universe, gives rise to three anacondas, his sons, associated respectively with sky, earth and water, the ancestors of three intermarrying descent groups. These ancestors give rise in turn to their sons, the ancestors of the ranked sibs of each descent group. *Romi Kumu*, the sky, and creatress of the universe, gives rise to the *He* People, the ancestors of the Barasana sibs. Exactly the same process of differentiation from a common source is described in the myths of origin of the Yurupary instruments. In each case, one individual dies or is killed, after which his bones become the instruments, sometimes directly as in M.6.A, sometimes by way of the paxiuba palm that springs from his ashes as in M.8 or M.5.A. Some versions concern the origin of the instruments belonging to one descent group (M.6.A,

M.4.H), others explain how all the different groups obtained their Yurupary (M.5.B), just as some of the origin myths cited above concern the origin of a specific descent group and its component sibs, whilst others concern the origin of all such groups.

The journey of the ancestor anaconda and its subsequent division into sons, the apical ancestors of the different sibs, is paralleled by the sequence of events at *He* House where, through the powers of the shamans, hallucinogenic drugs and contact with sacred ritual objects, the maloca becomes the universe and the people inside become the *He* People or first ancestors. The *He* instruments are taken from their hiding-places under water in the forest. They are inert (dead), and outside the house and thus outside the world. The women and children are confined in the rear of the house so that an exclusively male society is brought about, just as in ancestral times there were no women. As the *He* enter the house, they are played by a column of men, walking two abreast, the front of the column representing the head of the anaconda and the rear, its tail. They enter through the men's door, equivalent to the Water Door in the east through which the anaconda ancestor entered the world. The column proceeds from the men's door towards the women's door, from east to west, as the anaconda swam upriver from the east. Once inside, the column goes around the edge of the house and then comes down the middle from the rear end, stopping as the head reaches the men's door. The men then put their instruments down on the floor in two parallel rows lying end to end up the middle of the house and representing the anaconda lying along the middle of the earth. The head of the column now faces east with its tail to the west, as did the anaconda at the end of its journey. Then the column is broken up and the instruments dispersed, just as the anaconda's body was divided into its component sib ancestors or sons.

If *Yeba Meni* Anaconda's body gave rise to the different Barasana sib ancestors and if Manioc-stick Anaconda's body gave rise to the different Barasana *He* instruments, then this would suggest that *Yeba Meni* Anaconda and Manioc-stick Anadonda are the same person, for the *He* instruments represent the *He* People and bear their names. Informants agreed with this mutual identity, stating that both are the sons of *Yeba Haku*, the Primal Sun. The *He* instruments are the bones, especially the paired long bones of the legs and arms, of Manioc-stick Anaconda (M.6.A.62–5). They are also said to be the bones of the Sun. The other items of ritual equipment are also parts of

Manioc-stick Anaconda's body: the gourd of beeswax is the lower half of his skull; the snuff gourd is his skull cap; the beeswax is his liver and tongue; the snuff is his brain; the ceremonial cigar is his penis; the small gourds used to contain the snuff used at *He* House are his testicles; the elbow ornaments are his elbows; the metal ear ornaments that hang from the ears of the dancers are his eyes; the black colour of the *He* instruments is the paint on his legs; the engraved designs on the flutes are the patterns of the paint on his body, and the feather ruffs around the ends of the flutes are the garters below his knees (see M.6.A.63–4). When all these items are assembled together at *He* House (the only time that this ever happens), then Manioc-stick Anaconda's body is once again complete. By blowing snuff down the blow holes of the flutes, the shamans bring Manioc-stick Anaconda back to life – snuff is the food of spirit people and makes their souls alive.

The two men, dressed in the maximal amount of ritual ornament, who play the Old Macaw flutes at the climax of *He* House immediately after the burning of beeswax, represent Manioc-stick Anaconda and his brother Macaw brought back to life. These are the *He* spirits, the fierce spirits (*He wãtia, guari wãtia*) who shine bright like the Sun and from whom the participants must avert their eyes. It is above all the presence of the *He* and these two spirits that makes *He* House so dangerous, for the participants are brought into direct contact with the living dead, the spirits of the first ancestors. Thus, the process of differentiation and generalisation mentioned above is reversed so that the initiates and other participants are brought into contact with, and adopted by, the anaconda ancestor as his sons. They are also brought into contact with the Sun and the sky, the common sources of all life, for the *He* are both the bones of the Sun and the children of *Romi Kumu*, the sky.

At *He* House, the macrostructure of the universe and its people is made coterminous with the microstructure of the maloca and the local group that it contains. In myth, the universe is presented as a single house; in it, the unity of the descent group is represented by the anaconda ancestor and the differentiation of its component parts by his sons, the *He* People. The core of a longhouse community consists of a group of male siblings united as the sons of one father. At *He* House, the maloca becomes the universe, and the anaconda–father *Yeba Meni* Anaconda is brought to life by assembling the parts of his body. This anaconda adopts the participants as his sons and they

become *He* People, equivalent to the first sib ancestors. Thus *He*
House can be considered as a symbolic statement of Barasana social
structure in its wider setting, a structure that is largely inoperative
in daily life. The different age-grades are represented by the participants themselves and by the differend kinds of *He* instrument they
play; and the sib structure and ranking is represented by the *He*
instruments and also by (at least some of) the ritual roles of the
participants which correspond both to the age-grades and to the sibs
with their specialist ritual occupations (see ch. 5). Women (both
sisters and wives) are represented by some of the *He* instruments and
by the women confined in the rear of the house. Affines are represented by the participating affinal groups, by the *He* that they
bring with them and by the wives, external to the descent group and
excluded from the rites.

The instruments used at Fruit House

At most of the Fruit House rites that I observed, there were only
three pairs of *He* instruments used: one pair of long flutes, one pair
of short flutes and one pair of trumpets. These instruments belonged
to the hosts. When more instruments were present they were brought
by the guests; usually only trumpets were brought but at the Fruit
House held as the first stage of initiation the guests, from whose
households the initiates came, also brought a pair of long flutes.

The trumpets used at Fruit House, all *hotiri* trumpets, are collectively known as *sõri buku*, and do not have individual names like
the *He* used at *He* House. The long flutes are known collectively as
He rika samarã. The pair of long flutes used by the Barasana at these
rites is called Tree-Fruit Jaguar (*He Rika Yai*) (see table 4) and also
called Old Cotinga Bird (*Rasuu Baku*). Only at the Fruit House
immediately preceding *He* House were the long flutes Old Macaw
used. The short flutes used at Fruit House are called *Bosoro Hulia*
(see table 4).

According to the Barasana, the *He* used at Fruit House, like the
other ritual equipment, are not true *He* but imitations of them. The
whole rite is described as being 'a little bit an imitation' and is only
a rough approximation of *He* House, the real thing. It is for this
reason that I have concentrated my discussion on *He* House, for in
most respects Fruit House is simply an attenuated replica. This is not
only how the Barasana view it but is also apparent from a comparison

of the two rites. The *He* used at Fruit House are not true *He*, they are not bones nor are they jaguars. They are not people and are not alive and are therefore not very dangerous. Although women should not see these instruments, the Barasana are much less worried if they see these rather than the true *He* and say that the women would merely become ill rather than dying. Most of the instruments used are relatively new and people will freely admit to having made them; they deny strongly that the true *He* were made by men at all.

M.7.1 is the myth told to me by the Barasana to explain the meaning of Fruit House. The *He* instruments and the other items of ritual equipment used at Fruit House all represent the animals and birds, *Yeba*'s people, who went with him to give tree-fruit to Fish Anaconda, his father-in-law. The long flutes are specifically connected with small birds (*minia*), and in particular with the blue cotinga (*Cotinga nattererii*) and the musical wren (*Cyphorhinus aradus*). When the flutes are played with their ends raised in the air, this action, as well as being called having or encouraging the fruit, is also called seeing Old Cotinga, seeing Musician Wren (*Rasuʉ Bʉkʉ ĩangu, Bu Samʉ ĩangʉ*). These birds are called *He* birds, and the long flutes are called old tree-fruit birds (*He rika bʉkʉa minia*). The sound of these flutes is the sound of birdsong.

The trumpets, while not having specific names, in general represent the animals that carried the fruit to Fish Anaconda's house. In particular, they are associated with peccaries whose grunting is the noise of the trumpets. They are also associated with monkeys and again their noise is compared to the noise of these animals. Collectively, these animals are called the people who carry tree-fruit. The other animals are represented by different items of ritual equipment, the details of which can be found in M.7.I.3−6

Like the myths associated with *He* House, this myth is also concerned with differentiation for it explains how the birds got their colours and why it is that some animals have long tails and others not. But this differentiation occurs at a different level for it concerns animals *qua* animals and not the differentiation of one being into proto-human ancestors, the *He* People. Chronologically, myths about *Yeba* are later in time (and therefore 'younger') than myths about the *He* People: Manioc-stick Anaconda, a *He* person, is the son of the Sky People (*Ʉmʉari Masa*) but is the father of *Yeba* (see M.6.A.62). Much of the story of *Yeba* describes his progressive 'civilisation' by *Yawira*, his wife: he starts off like an *animal* − his manioc garden

was the forest, his manioc was a forest plant, etc. (see M.7.B).
Yawira 'civilises' him by introducing him to cultivation (M.7.C,
D, E) and also does the same at a physical level by transferring his
penis from his belly (see M.7.B.6) — an animal-like state, to its
proper place between his legs (see M.7.F) — the human state. This
mythic chronology suggests what the Barasana say explicitly: that
the development of true human beings starts with the Sky People,
then goes on to the *He* People, then to the animals and finally to
true human beings who become differentiated from animals. The
Barasana say that *Yeba* was the first true human being like you and
me. It is therefore appropriate that at Fruit House, when the initiates
are *youngest*, they are shown instruments that are *younger* in time
and which represent *animals* which are but one stage before humans,
while at *He* House, when the initiates are *older*, they are shown
instruments that are older in time and which represent spirits or
He people who are two stages before humans.

To summarise so far: initiation among the Barasana involves two
separate stages, Fruit House and *He* House, held one after the other
with a gap in between. These two rites are different in terms of the
times at which they are held and also in terms of the instruments
and other equipment used. The first rite is considered to be an
attenuated imitation of the second. This is true not only in terms of
the overall structure of the rites but also in terms of the equipment
used; the equipment used at Fruit House is said to be a man-made
imitation of the sacred equipment, created in mythical times, which
is used at *He* House. In another sense, however, the equipment is
different in kind, for the *He* used at Fruit House represent animals
whilst those used at *He* House represent the *He* People, proto-human
spirit ancestors. The process of transforming an uninitiated boy into an
adult man involves retracing the steps in the development of human
beings.

The *He* instruments as shamans

In chapter 5, I argued that shamans and jaguars, identified together,
share the common attribute of being mediators. The *He* instruments,
identified with shamans, jaguars and anacondas, are also mediators.

The instruments themselves are made from sections of the trunk of
a paxiuba palm, as are all Yurupary instruments. According to Yurupary
myths, this palm grew up from the ashes of Yurupary's burned body
(see M.5.A.12 and M.8.63). The soul of Yurupary (or of *He* Anaconda

in the Barasana myth) went up in this palm as it grew and from there went up into the sky. Thus the palm mediates between earth and sky. The paxiuba palm only grows in swamps and could thus be said to mediate between water, earth and sky. Though the Barasana did not draw specific attention to this, one cannot help being struck by the form of the aerial roots of this palm for they make it look as if it hangs between the sky and the ground (see fig. 12). The *He*

Fig. 12 The paxiuba palm (*Iriartea exorrhiza*) with detail of buttress roots (after Wallace 1853)

instruments also mediate between land and water for whilst they
are kept under water in rivers, they are brought out on to dry land
when in use. The passage from water on to land, and from the forest
in which they are kept to the house where they are used, also signals
a passage from a dead, inert state to an alive and active state. As the
living dead, they mediate between the human and spirit worlds,
between life and death. This in-between state is neatly summarised
by their being called pets, animals that come from the forest but
live in the house. Finally, like the shamans, they mediate between
the world of childhood and that of adults during rites of initiation.

As mediators, shamans combine in their characters attributes that
are complementary but opposed: they are associated with fire and
water, and they have the power to both create and destroy life.
These complementary but opposed attributes are shared by the
He instruments: they were created through fire (see M.5.A, M.6.A.
57–60, M.8.57–64) but are now kept cool in water. As anaconda
ancestors they have the power to create life, but in their fierce aspect
as jaguars (see especially the discussion of Old Star above) they are
associated with the life-destroying qualities of warriors and killers.
The Barasana call the paxiuba palm the *He* palm and also *besuᵾ*
palm: the word *besuᵾ* means spear or lance and more generally any
lethal weapon.[5] Unlike most other palms with large fruit, the fruit
of the paxiuba is poisonous and the sap from its roots causes violent
irritation of the skin.[6] The association of the paxiuba with poison
is found again in the Yurupary myths, for it grew from Yurupary's
ashes along with the first poisonous plants (see e.g. M.8.66). The
ambiguity between creation and destruction, between good and bad,
is found again throughout *He* House, for if the shamans are successful
and if everyone keeps the appropriate taboos, the outcome will
benefit the whole community, but if not, the whole thing will end
in disaster.

The significance of pairs

The above discussion of complementary but opposed attributes brings

5 The Barasaña word *besuᵾ* is very similar to the name *Bisiu*, the Tukano name for the
  character Yurupary (Brüzzi da Silva 1962 : 332). This is also close to *Bisiw* whose
  spittle is identified with the instruments the Makú use when they bring live eels into the
  house (see ch. 3 n. 1) and to *Bihuinoe*, the name given by the Puinave to their Yurupary
  rites (Rozo 1945 : 243).
6 The juice of this root is also said to be used as an 'aphrodisiac' for when applied to the
  penis it causes it to swell enormously.

me to a final point to be made about the *He* instruments: why they are in pairs. According to Brüzzi da Silva (1962 : 307) the Tukano say that the instruments are in husband—wife pairs, the wife being the shorter of the two. According to Fulop (1956 : 356), also for the Tukano, the pairs represent male and female, brother and sister. The Cubeo are also said to conceive of the pairs as brother and sister (Bolens 1967 : 65). Finally, Reichel-Dolmatoff says that the Desana also divide the flutes into male/female pairs (1971 : 168).

The Barasana repeatedly denied that, *in general*, the paired instruments were male and female but at the same time they mentioned two *particular* cases: the shorter of the two Old Macaw flutes is Old Macaw's wife and both the trumpets called Manioc-squeezing Woman are female (see table 4). The Bará (*Wai Masa*) also said that the trumpet Old Deer had a wife represented by a pair of flutes (not present at the *He* House I observed) and that the short flutes Old Parrot were the wives of the trumpets used at Fruit House. But, like the Barasana, they too denied that all the *He* instruments were in male/female pairs. According to the Barasana, the pairs were an elder and a younger brother. The elder brother (the longer instrument) is the dancer—singer and the younger (the shorter instrument) is the one that follows. I am in no position to criticise the data of the authors mentioned above but I suspect that in each case there is an element of oversimplification in what they say. For the Barasana at least, the *He* instruments are first and foremost a *male* symbol (with limited female associations) and as such they are opposed to the gourd of beeswax which is an essentially female symbol (again with limited male associations. According to them, the *He* are in pairs because they came from the paired long-bones of Manioc-stick Anaconda and Macaw. The paired *He* instruments should be considered in relation to other pairs: there are two shamans at *He* House, the Sun and Moon are two manifestations of the Primal Sun, the feather head-dresses are kept in pairs as are many other items of ritual equipment, etc. In many instances, these pairs represent opposed but complementary opposites; male and female is one such opposite but it is by no means the only one.

The *He* and mortality

I mentioned above that the word *He* may be related to the word *hea* meaning fire, firewood and dead wood in general. Lévi-Strauss (1970 :

147–95) has argued that the Gê myths about the origin of cooking fire are also myths about the origin of man's mortality and that to cook, which of necessity involves the use of dead wood, is to 'hear the call of rotten wood'; rotten wood signifies mortality. He also argues that myths of the origin of cultivated plants are also myths about man's loss of immortality for these plants must be cooked with fire. M.6.A, the story of Manioc-stick Anaconda, is a myth about the origin of destructive fire which Manioc-stick Anaconda obtains from the Sun in the underworld in the form of snuff. He uses this fire to kill his brother Macaw and thus to create the Old Macaw flutes. Manioc-stick Anaconda himself is then burned to death, giving rise to the *He* instruments in general. In M.6.B, this same fire (snuff) burns Manioc-stick Anaconda to death but this time his body gives rise to cultivated plants and his bones, instead of becoming *He* instruments as in M.6.A, become the charred logs of a manioc garden. M.8.57–61 unites these two themes for after Yurupary has been burned, the survivors plant seeds in the ashes of the fire. From these same ashes grows the paxiuba palm from which the Yurupary instruments are made (see also M.6.A). The association between the words *He* and *hea* seems thus to be confirmed and it can be further said that to take part in rites involving *He* instruments is in a very real sense 'to hear the call of rotten wood'. If this is so, then it implies that the participants at *He* House and Fruit House must die. They are killed by having large amounts of snuff (= destructive fire) blown up their noses prior to the rites. More details concerning this symbolic death (and the consequent rebirth) are given in chapter 9 below.

According to a Baniwa Yurupary myth, as Yurupary was burning to death on the fire he told the men that because he was being killed, from henceforth all men must die before they went to heaven like him (Saake 1958a : 274). A Tukano Yurupary myth states the opposite, that (in mythical times at least) the Yurupary instruments were going to make all people immortal (Fulop 1956 : 356). This ambiguity is combined in one Barasana myth, M.5.A, where the Howler Monkey and the Tapir, whose voices are equated with *He* instruments, signify life and death respectively.

I argued above that the creation of the Barasana sib ancestors, like the creation of the *He* instruments that bear their names, involved a process of differentiation and generalisation from a common source. In the case of Manioc-stick Anaconda, and, by extension, of *Yeba Meni* Anaconda, this differentiation only happens after the death of the character concerned. The *He* instruments and the Barasana sib ancestors, the *He* People, are the sons of Manioc-stick Anaconda and *Yeba Meni* Anaconda which would seem to imply that for men to have sons they must die. *Romi Kumu* also gives birth to sons who are both the *He* instruments and the Barasana sib ancestors, the *He* People, but there is nothing to suggest that she dies.

The death of Macaw and Manioc-stick Anaconda is a death only in one sense for they become living spirits in the sky, represented on this earth by the *He* instruments, the living dead, and at *He* House, by reassembling the *He* instruments and other ritual equipment, their bodies too are brought back to life. Their immortality is echoed in the constant reiteration of the words 'you won't disappear, you won't die' in M.6.A. This is, in effect, to say no more than that life and death are seen as an oscillation between opposite states and that souls are reborn as children, which is what the Barasana believe (Leach 1961 : 124–32). Although the passage of time is conceived of as an oscillation between two opposite states, day and night, dry season and wet season, life and death, the succession of generations is nevertheless irreversible. In a sense, it is women, and not men, who replace themselves with their children and hence have a kind of immortality. This theme will be more fully discussed in chapter 7 after the significence of the beeswax gourd has been explained.

7

The gourd of beeswax

The last chapter was devoted to a discussion of the significance of the *He* instruments, the dominant symbolic objects on which the rites focus. In this chapter I shall discuss the beeswax that is burned during the rites, and the gourd in which this wax is placed. I shall argue that although it is less likely to attract the attention of an observer, the beeswax gourd is no less important than the *He* instruments, and that it stands in a complementary relation to them.

Most South American Indians appear to have a passion for honey and many authors have described the often extraordinary lengths to which they will go to obtain it. The Barasana with whom we lived collected honey only twice in two years and then only at our insistence. It is as if the interest in honey has been replaced by an interest in beeswax, as the rest of this chapter will show.

The wax gourd as an object

When not in use, the gourd of beeswax (*werea koa*) is kept in the family compartment of the shaman – only the most powerful and knowledgeable shamans have these objects under their control. At all times it is kept wrapped in brown bark cloth. During *He* House, lumps of wax are placed inside the gourd together with coca powder. Throughout the rite, the gourd is kept inside the shamans' enclosure on top of an hourglass-shaped stand. At one point only, after the acting-out of spearing that follows the burning of beeswax, the gourd is placed between posts 1 and 2 so that the participants can eat pinches of the coca.

The gourd itself is hemispherical in shape and varnished black inside. It is made from the fruit of the calabash tree (*Crescentia cujete*). Gourds of this kind, called *tuga koa*, are grown by men and

163

are their exclusive property. They are used as containers for coca, snuff and beeswax and to make the maracas used in dancing. In each case the use is associated with ritual activities. These gourds are opposed to those made from the fruit of the *Lagenaria* vine, called *koa*, which are the property of women and are used in the preparation and consumption of food and drink, both secular activities.[1]

The wax *werea* inside the gourd is a hard, black, brittle substance called cerumen, a mixture of wax and tree resin. It is used by *Meliponae* bees to make the flight-hole leading to the nest, usually situated inside a hollow tree. These flight-holes consist of tubes, up to 38 cm long and often in expanded funnel form, which project outwards from the trunk of the tree containing the nest (Schwartz 1948).

The Barasana distinguish three classes of bees: *werea, berua* and *momia*, each distinguished from wasps (*utia*); wasps are like bees in that some of them make honey but only wasps sting. Only the class of bees called *werea* produce the wax—resin mixture of the same name; the wax produced by other bees is called bee sperm/brain (*beruabadi*). According to Schwartz (1948), with a few exceptions, only bees of the sub-genus *Trigona* produce cerumen; the other *Meliponae* make their flight-holes from a mixture of wax and mud. The Barasana class *werea* therefore appears to correspond roughly to the sub-genus *Trigona*. The characteristics that the Barasana attribute to *werea* bees, notably their fierce bite, also correspond to those described for *Trigona* (Schwartz 1948).

The shamans that officiate at *He* House are called the people who blow over the gourd of wax (*werea koa baseri masa*). Appropriately, a variety of *werea* bees called *daria* give their name to the Barasana sib who have the ritual role of shamans. The ancestors of the *Daria* clan were *werea* bees and today these bees are said to be shamans and *He* People.

The significance of the wax gourd

The wax gourd as Manioc-stick Anaconda

The gourd itself is the bottom half of Manioc-stick Anaconda's skull,

1 In general, the useful parts of the plants cultivated and owned by men come from *above* the ground (leaves and bark). The useful parts of the plants cultivated and owned by women tend to come from *below* the ground (roots and tubers). This same contrast

created when he was burned to death (see M.6.A.64);[2] Manioc-stick Anaconda is also called Old Gourd, which is appropriate to his connection with this object. The true wax gourd, used only at *He* House, is said to have been created together with the universe itself. As bone (a skull), it is associated with the qualities of hardness, permanence and durability; it is also said to be made of stone.[3] The gourd used at Fruit House is not identified with bone and is said to have been made by a shaman in historical times. Thus the contrast between true, sacred objects used at *He* House and man-made imitations of them used at Fruit House, already mentioned in connection with the *He* instruments, is found again in the wax gourd.

The gourd is also the Sun, the Primal Sun, *Yeba Haku*, the father of the earth. As the Sun, the gourd is so bright that it would hurt the eyes of those who looked at it; it is for this reason that it is kept wrapped in bark-cloth and for this reason also that, when coca is eaten from the gourd during *He* House, the people must avert their eyes. The Sun created the gourd and it is his head, with a feather crown, eyes, eyebrows, a tongue and a mouth (see fig. 13). It is more powerful and dangerous than the *He* instruments themselves and causes wasting-away illness (*wisiose*).

The gourd must never touch the ground which is why it is kept on a stand. One Barasana informant compared the gourd on its stand to the flat basketwork trays containing cassava bread which are placed on larger hourglass-shaped stands outside each family compartment in the house. Manioc-stick Anaconda, he said, was the cassava bread inside the trays, the bread being made from the manioc plants that sprang up from his ashes when he was burned (see M.6.B.4).

The wax gourd as viscera

The wax inside the gourd is Manioc-stick Anaconda's liver, created when he was burned to death (see M.6.A.64); it is also his tongue (the Barasana associate the liver with the tongue: the word *nyemeriti*, liver, is close to *nyemero*, tongue). This fact alone establishes a visceral association for the wax. However, the argument can be taken

is found in these two kinds of gourd: men's gourds come from trees, women's gourds come from vines that trail on the ground.
2 The wax gourd of the Tatuyo is the skullcap of *Rame* who was killed by *Warimi* (see M.4.H.6).
3 It may be significant that the Barasana word *koa*, gourd, is phonetically close to *ngoa*, bone, and also to *oa*, opossum.

Key
Black (red) = Sun
Dark tint (blue) = sky
Light tint (green)
    = sky powder

Rays of Sun – his feather crown

Yagé vine

Eye

Eye

Eyebrows
and
feather crown

Mouth

Tongue

Mouth

Lumps of beeswax

Designs on *He* instruments

Rays of Sun – his feather crown

Fig. 13 The beeswax gourd (bracketed colours in key refer to original
Barasana drawing)

further: the wax is also likened to children inside a womb, the wax
being the shadow (*wɨho*) of the children and the gourd itself being
the womb. This fact can, I think, be linked to the comparison the
Barasana make between the entrance to the flight-hole of the *werea*
bees' nest and a vulva.[4] If the entrance to the nest be compared to a
vulva, then it is reasonable to assume that the nest itself, located
inside a hollow tree, should be likened to a womb. The *werea* bees
that live in this nest should then be like children in a womb.[5] Further
evidence for this assumption comes from the fact that *Romi Kumu*,

4 Lévi-Strauss (1973 : 53) also states that the nests of some South American bees are
  called 'vagina'.
5 Though I have no data on this, it may be that the shamans (identified with *werea* bees)
  inside their enclosure during *He* House are also compared to *werea* bees inside a hollow
  tree.

166

who is herself identified with the wax gourd, is, at the time that she creates the *He* People, also compared to a hollow tree (see M.1.C.2). There is also a Barasana myth (not included here) which tells how *Romi Kumu*'s menstrual blood, the rain, fell into a hollow tree which then became 'pregnant'. This again establishes a connection between wombs and hollow trees.

If it is accepted that the gourd with wax inside is like a womb containing children, then the comparison between the wax gourd and trays containing cassava bread becomes even more appropriate: in shamanic language, women, the cultivators of manioc, are called food mothers. The manioc tubers are their children; the bread prepared from these tubers lies inside a container, compared to a gourd which is in turn compared to a womb.[6]

The wax gourd, Romi Kumu and the Pleiades

Romi Kumu, Woman Shaman, is the sky and the sky mother (see M.1.B.6). The sky itself is compared to a gourd. The Primal Sun, *Yeba Haku*, is the father of the sky (*umuari haku*: *umuari* means both sky and day and more generally the universe as a whole). According to a Barasana shaman, the sun and the sky are like a man and a woman and as men and women have children, so the sun and sky are responsible for the whole universe and all that exists within it.

Romi Kumu is closely identified with the wax gourd: she owns it and has it with her up in the sky (see M.1.B.1). At the time when the *He* people were created, she kept the wax gourd between her legs (see M.1.C.12) and when she offered it to the *He* People, Old Star, the fierce warrior, refused to eat from it on the grounds that it stank of her vagina (see M.1.C.11). This emphasises that, in particular, the wax gourd is identified with *Romi Kumu*'s genitals; *Romi Kumu* is herself a very 'genital' person for until she stole the *He* from the men she was called 'Vagina Woman'. When the wax is burned it releases smoke with a pungent, aromatic smell which, like the smell of musk and civet, has obvious sexual overtones. The Barasana consciously associate this smell with vaginal odour. This

---

6 The equivalence between cassava and beeswax would suggest that wax is thought of as a vegetable substance. The Barasana say that this wax is made from flowers and treesap, which suggests that this is so.

smell, together with the shape of the entrance to the *werea* bees' flight-hole further emphasises the connection between the wax gourd and the vagina.

Romi Kumu is the Pleiades (*Nyokoaro*) (see M.1.C.17), as is *Ceucy*, *Seucy*, the mother of Yurupary in the Tariana Yurupary myths (Stradelli 1890b). If *Romi Kumu* is identified with both the wax gourd and with the Pleiades, then it can be assumed that the wax gourd is itself directly identified with the Pleiades. This identification is confirmed by two pieces of indirect evidence: (1) bees (of an unspecified variety) are closely linked with *Ceucy* (identifiable with *Romi Kumu*) in Lingua Geral, the trade language once used throughout the Vaupés/Río Negro/Içana region and the language in which many of the Yurupary myths were recorded (Stradelli 1928–9 : 415). (2) The Cubeo call the Pleiades 'the swarm of wasps' (Koch-Grünberg 1906 : 62; 1912–16, vol X/XI : 116).[7] While wasps are distinguished from bees by the Barasana, it will be shown later that the wax is associated with all insects that bite or sting.[8] Finally it should be added that the Barasana have a myth about wasps in the sky that sting to death the Star People, though in this case the wasps are not specifically linked with the Pleiades.

Romi Kumu, Meneriyo and Yawira

Barasana myths are divided into a number of different cycles. Although not all the cycles are placed in a single, chronological order, stories about *Romi Kumu* and the other Sky People (*Umʉari Masa*) are seen as older and earlier than stories about Manioc-stick Anaconda, which in turn are earlier and older than stories about *Yeba*. While the Barasana definitely recognise this chronology and also stress that the stories of each cycle are different, this does not prevent a certain degree of fusion from taking place. One of the most striking aspects of this fusion is that a person will often start telling a myth with one character as the main protagonist and then, half-way through the story, he will switch and start talking about another character. The most frequent of such 'confusions' is that between *Warimi* and *Yeba*.

With a more extended analysis of the myths, it could be shown

---

7 Somewhere in the literature on the Vaupés area I have also read that the Tukano call the Pleiades 'the swarm of *bees*', but I am unable to retrace this reference.
8 Lévi-Strauss (1973) has also argued that bees and wasps are 'combinatory variants'.

that the different mythic cycles represent transformations of one another and furthermore that the main characters in each cycle can be shown analytically to be the 'same' as each other to a greater or lesser degree (this has already been suggested in chapter 6). In addition to this, it could be shown that there is a close correspondence between the classic Yurupary myths and the different Barasana myth cycles. The myth of Yurupary, the life history of a culture hero of the same name, is usually presented as a single, continuous story. Virtually every episode of this story has its counterpart in Barasana mythology, although the correspondence may be more or less exact. However in the Barasana myths, the sequence of events is often different and fragmented so that adjacent sections of the Yurupary myth may be found occurring in separate Barasana myth cycles. A comparison of the Barasana myths presented in this book with the Tariana Yurupary myth (M.8), a representative version, will show that this is so.

I have already argued that the wax gourd is identified with *Romi Kumu* and in particular with her vagina and womb. I shall now argue that, in some senses, *Romi Kumu, Meneriyo* and *Yawira* (see M.1, M.4 and M.7) are the 'same' person, by establishing that there is a web of interconnections between these women, the opossum and the Pleiades. In doing this I shall make frequent references to Lévi-Strauss's *Mythologiques* (vols. I and II), in part to show how my own data fits in with his, and in part as a rapid means of covering ground which would otherwise require an exhaustive structural analysis of Barasana myth. As the myths I am discussing are all close variants of myths analysed in *Mythologiques* I consider that my method is justifiable. My argument proceeds by establishing a series of equivalences, each one interconnected to the others. I shall use the symbol ≡ to indicate congruence, homology or correspondence.

Pleiades ≡ *Opossum*: The Baniwa sib *Siusi* (Siusi = Pleiades in Lingua Geral), call themselves *Oaliperi-dakeni* (Koch-Grünberg 1906 : 168; 1909–10, vol. I : 54); *oaliperi* means Pleiades[9] and *dakeni* means 'descendants of' (Galvão 1959 : 40). The Barasana call these people Star Opossum (People) (*Nyokoa Oa*), providing a direct link between the opossum and the Pleiades in Barasana thought. The Tatuyo sib called Opossum Tatuyo (*Oa Suna*) by the Barasana and Big Stars

---

9 I cannot find the Baniwa word for opossum. In Barasana the word is *oa*; it is possible that this is the same *oa* as in *Oa*liperi.

(*Nyokoa Pakara*) by the Tatuyo, have the ritual role of shamans in the sib hierarchy and are 'the people who blow over the wax gourd' (*werea koa baseri masa*). This provides a similar but less direct link between the Pleiades and the opossum, in that a group called Opossum are intimately linked with the wax gourd which is in turn identified with the Pleiades. Finally, when in M.7.K, Opossum is killed by Tinamou, he falls to the ground from a tree and it immediately starts to rain (see M.7.K.7). While, in the context of this myth, the Barasana do not draw an explicit connection between the opossum and the Pleiades, it is certainly striking that when the Pleiades set on the western horizon at dusk (as if coming *down* from heaven to earth) the rainy season begins with rains called *Nyokoaro Hue*, the Pleiades rains (see fig. 3).

As well as stating that the opossum has affinities with the dry season,[10] Lévi-Strauss has also drawn attention to the direct affinity of the opossum with the Pleiades (1970 : 218 n.8) and its indirect affinity with this constellation through honey (1973 : 288–9).

Meneriyo ≡ *Pleiades*: When *Meneriyo* went into the sky, bees came and buzzed round her (M.4.A.9); bees are identified with the Pleiades. The mother of Yurupary, herself identified with the Pleiades, was a virgin with no vagina so that when she became pregnant she was unable to give birth until a birth canal had been made in her body (by a variety of different agents in different versions of the myth: see e.g. M.8.21). In spite of the fact that *Meneriyo* was clearly no virgin and had a vagina, the birth of her son *Warimi* is strongly reminiscent of that of Yurupary: in both cases the mother must be opened up by an external agent (though for *Meneriyo* this opening up was more drastic – see M.4.D.14–15).[11] Nonetheless, the Thunders who open up *Coadidop*, the mother of Yurupary in M.8, are in fact the very same people who open up *Meneriyo* in M.4.D: the Thunders of M.8 are the ancestors of the Tariana; the jaguars who open up *Meneriyo* in M.4.D are *Bʉho Yaiya*, Thunder Jaguars who live at Jaguar Rapid, the Barasana name for the village of Jauareté (Jauareté = jaguar in Lingua Geral) on the Vaupés which is the home of the Tariana both in mythic times and also today.

10 'The burial of the opossum . . . must coincide with the end of the dry season' (Lévi-Strauss 1973 : 292–3).
11 By this I mean that, unlike Yurupary, *Warimi* was conceived as the result of normal sexual intercourse, either between *Meneriyo* and the Moon (M.4.A) or between her and Little Sticky Man (*ʉmʉaka Widaʉ*) (M.4.B); Little Sticky Man is, in fact, the Moon (see M.4.C).

The gourd of beeswax

Yurupary started life with no mouth at all and he grew very rapidly. Like him, *Warimi* grew very rapidly but rather than having no mouth at all, all he could say was 'we we we we' in a feeble, quiet voice which implies that in the figurative sense his mouth was much reduced. If it is accepted that *Warimi* be identified with Yurupary,[12] then his mother *Meneriyo* can in turn be identified with the mother of Yurupary who was herself the Pleiades (Stradelli 1928–9 : 415).

The name *Meneriyo* means Ingá Woman. Ingá (Ingá dulcis), called *mene* in Barasana, is a tree (mostly cultivated but there are also wild varieties) which bears long pods containing seeds, each one surrounded by a sweet, white, fluffy integument the appearance of which may well be directly associated with that of the Pleiades (though I have no direct evidence that this is so). It has already been shown that the two fruiting seasons of ingá coincide with the rising and setting of the Pleiades and that both ingá and the Pleiades are used as time-markers for Barasana *He* rituals (see fig. 3). This again confirms that *Meneriyo* and the Pleiades are linked.

In this context, two other points should be made about ingá trees: (1) in M.4.B and M.4.C, when *Meneriyo* returns from her visit to the sky, she lands on top of an ingá tree. If *Meneriyo*, Ingá Woman, is identified with the Pleiades, then her going up into the sky (when she is captured by Little Sticky Man – see M.4.B) should correspond to the rising of the Pleiades in November and her coming down again (when she escapes from Little Sticky Man – see M.4.B) should correspond to the setting of the Pleiades in April (see fig. 3). It is therefore entirely appropriate that she should land on a tree which bears fruit at this time and, furthermore, fruit which is in itself identified with her. The ingá tree is thus a mediator between heaven and earth, high and low, and also between the wet and dry seasons (for it fruits at the end of the rains and beginning of the dry season and again at the end of the dry season and the beginning of the rains). The Pleiades too have this double connotation of wet and dry season for their rising heralds the dry season and their setting heralds the wet. When Manioc-stick Anaconda falls to the Underworld through the trap dug

---

12 The identity between Yurupary and *Warimi* can be demonstrated in another way: *Warimi*, the name, means 'He-Who-Went-Away'. The Bara call *Warimi* Bone Son (*Koa Makʉ*). The Tukano have Yurupary myths about *Oa'kʉ*, a name that can be translated both as 'Bone Son' and as 'He-Who-Went-Away'. *Oa'kʉ* is identified with *Kowai* (who is the Cubeo Yurupary) and with Yurupary himself.

The reader can find many other instances in which *Warimi* is identifiable with Yurupary characters by comparing *Warimi* myths (M.4) with the Yurupary myths listed in appendix 2.

by his brother (see M.6.A.7) and, in other words, comes down from the Underworld sky, he too lands on an ingá tree, again a mediation between (Underworld) sky and (Underworld) earth.[13] (2) In M.8.52, Yurupary insists that the only way in which he can be killed is to be burned on the dry husks of ingá fruit. The resulting fire is a universal conflagration, a phenomenon closely linked with both *Romi Kumu* and the Pleiades.

Finally, Lévi-Strauss (1970 : 240–6) has shown that viscera, especially floating viscera, are closely linked with the Pleiades. I have already shown that the wax gourd (Pleiades) is identified with viscera; it is possible that the theme of the floating viscera identified with the Pleiades is also present in a disguised form in Barasana mythology. For *Warimi* to be born, *Meneriyo*'s womb had to be taken to the river (see M.4.D.15); though the Barasana do not actually say that the womb became the Pleiades, animals are always gutted in rivers and their viscera are allowed to float away with the current.

Meneriyo ≡ *Opossum*: M.4.A.12–15 in which *Meneriyo* visits Opossum's house and is (all but) seduced by him, is remarkably similar to the Tupí myth cited by Lévi-Strauss (1970 : 172, *M96*), in which a child who talks to his mother from the womb later becomes angry with her and refuses further communication. Because of this she loses her way and arrives at an opossum's house where she is raped. *Warimi* also talks to his mother *Meneriyo* from her womb but instead of later refusing to talk at all, he gives her wrong directions so that she too arrives at an opossum's house where she is (all but) raped by him. Lévi-Strauss (1970 : 170–1), in discussing 'opossum myths', comments on the lack of explicit reference to this animal's marsupial pouch, but argues that the woman's 'opossum function' becomes metaphorical: 'her child talks in her belly *as if* he had already been born and were using the maternal womb as a marsupial pouch' (1970 : 180). If this is true of the heroine of Lévi-Strauss's *M96*, it is true also of *Meneriyo* who must also be a 'metaphorical opossum'. Finally, in M.4.A.10–11, *Meneriyo* is shown to be closely associated with the japú bird. According to Lévi-Strauss (1970 : 185), this bird represents the 'opossum function' coded in ornithological terms, opossums and japú birds both being characterised by a strong smell.

Yawira ≡ *Opossum*: Like *Meneriyo*, *Yawira* also visits Opossum's

---

13 According to Barasana cosmology, the earth is like a cassava griddle (see M.1.A), the underneath of which is the sky of the Underworld.

house where she is actually seduced by him. Because of this, she stinks so much (from contact with a stinking opossum) that her next lover, Tinamou, initially refuses to sleep with her (see M.7.K). As a person who stinks, *Yawira* is homologous both with an opossum and with *Romi Kumu* (who also stinks). After being seduced by Opossum and Tinamou, *Yawira* goes off and marries the Chief of the Vultures. *Yeba,* her true husband, finally catches up with her only to drown her in honey inside a hollow tree because she refused to drink the honey modestly. When drowned, *Yawira* becomes the cunauaru frog (*ēhoka, Phyllomedusa bicolor*) which lives inside hollow trees (see M.7.L). *Yawira* is a 'girl mad about honey', a character extensively discussed by Lévi-Strauss, *Mythologiques II* (1973). One of the conclusions Lévi-Strauss reaches concerning such characters is that they are homologous with opossums. *Yawira* can also be linked directly to *Romi Kumu* because cunauaru frogs are referred to as *He* mother, the name applied to *Romi Kumu.*[14]

Finally, according to a Barasana myth, *Romi Kumu* ($\equiv$ Pleiades) created the rainbow to keep warm the child born of her menstrual blood (the rain) which fell into a hollow tree. Lévi-Strauss (1973) has shown that, in South American mythology, there is a direct affinity both between the Pleiades and the rainbow, and between the opossum and the rainbow.

To summarise so far: using a combination of data from my own fieldwork and from Lévi-Strauss's *Mythologiques* I have established the following links:

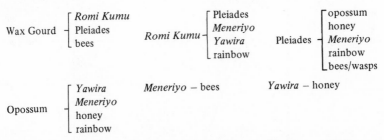

and I have also established possible links between *Yawira* and the wax gourd (through the resin collected by the cunauaru frog – see n. 14), and between the wax gourd and the opossum (through the Opossum

14 The cunauaru frog makes brood-cells from tree resin which it collects. In some parts of South America, this substance is used as a fumigant to relieve headaches (Lévi-Strauss 1970 : 264). Beeswax is also used as a medicinal fumigant which suggests a possible direct link between *Yawira* (= cunauaru frog) and beeswax.

Tatuyos who control the wax gourd). *Romi Kumu* can be linked with the opossum through shared associations with both the Pleiades and the rainbow. Like the opossum, she also stinks and shares with it the characteristic of giving birth to many children (the *He* people) all at once. The Barasana emphasise this characteristic of the opossum and one explanation they give for the name of the Opossum Tatuyos is that their ancestress had so many children all at once that she had to carry them around on her back, like an opossum. The wax gourd can be linked to honey through the bees that produce both honey and wax and *Romi Kumu* is linked with bees and wasps through their common association with the Pleiades, and she is further linked to the honey that bees produce. Fig. 14 is a summary of the links mentioned above; the main one that is missing is that between *Meneriyo* and *Yawira*. This link is implied by the obvious similarity between M.4.A.12–15 and M.7.K.1–5 but a full demonstration would require analysis of unwarranted length.

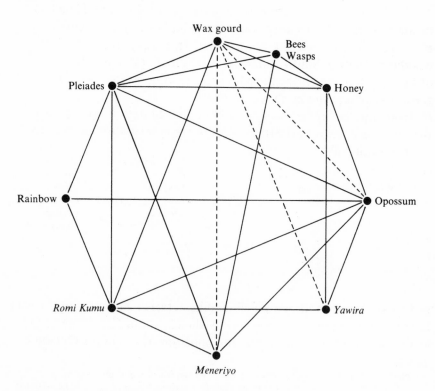

Fig. 14 Links between female characters in Barasana myth

The gourd of beeswax

From the above it can now be concluded that the wax gourd is an essentially female symbol for it subsumes virtually all the important female characters of Barasana mythology. As such it is opposed and complementary to the *He* instruments which are essentially male symbols and identified with male anaconda ancestors. But just as the *He* instruments have limited female associations — some of them represent women, and they represent *He* People created without male intervention by *Romi Kumu* (M.1.C) — so too does the wax gourd have limited male associations. It is identified with the Sun and with Manioc-stick Anaconda (who himself has female associations as the origin of manioc, a function shared with *Yawira*), and it is also identified with *Romi Kumu* who is herself sexually ambiguous (M.1.C.3) and who gave rise to the *He* People, a function shared with Manioc-stick Anaconda.

An 'instrument of darkness'

In the Vaupés region, the rising of the Pleiades on the western horizon at dusk heralds the coming of the long dry season. This is the time when the forest is felled to make gardens and when large quantities of fish are caught by poisoning the rivers and streams as their water gets lower, and it is the time for holding Fruit House to prepare for *He* House.[15] As the Pleiades set in the west, they herald the end of the dry season and the coming of the long rainy season (*hue buku* in Barasana); the dried-out trees in the gardens are fired and manioc is planted in the ashes ready to grow in the coming rains. This is the time that *He* House should be held, just before the first rains, the Pleiades rains, begin (see fig. 3). With the rains, the waters rise and fish ascend the rivers in huge numbers to spawn. Again there is an abundance of fish to eat, this time caught in traps. These fish, like those caught with poison, are Pleiades fish which are both a source of food and a potential source of sickness and death.

The first-ever dry season was a universal conflagration when the sun remained at its zenith and burned up the world; this was the time when *Romi Kumu* lit the fire to fire the clay griddle she had made which was the earth (see M.1.A). After this came the first

15 It is worth noting here that, according to Ypiranga Monteiro (1960 : 38), Yurupary instruments are used at meetings for communal land-clearing or cultivation. Among the Saliva, to the north of the Vaupés, young men were whipped and shown the instruments illustrated in fig. 9 to remove their laziness prior to communal clearing of the land (Gumilla 1963 : 160). See also Galvão 1959 : 21.

rainy season; rain-clouds blotted out the sun and all went dark like a long night. Heavy rain fell so that the rivers rose and caused a catastrophic flood (see M.1.A).

Thus the Pleiades stand both for the dry season and for the rainy season and for an abundance of food which is also potentially lethal. *Romi Kumu*, identified with the Pleiades, stands also for the dry season and the wet season, for fire and flood and for light and darkness. She is also a creative mother (see M.1.C) and a sexually voracious ogress (see M.4.F.17).[16] The wax gourd, identified with both the Pleiades and with *Romi Kumu*, also has these same meanings.

Lévi-Strauss devotes a considerable portion of *Mythologiques II* (1973) to a discussion of 'the instruments of darkness'. However, with the exception of the Bororo *parabara*, he is unable to demonstrate that, outside the realm of myth, such a thing exists in South America and most of his material about real 'instruments of darkness' is drawn from European and Chinese society. He argues, with reference to a myth from the Tupi of the Amazon (*M326a*), that a nut which, when opened by melting the resin that sealed it, gave rise to night is an instrument of darkness 'in the literal sense, whereas, the similar instruments in Western mythology can only be given the appellation in a figurative sense' (1973 : 416–7). He argues further that, in South America, instruments of darkness are linked with honey, with 'honey smoke', and that the use of such instruments is universally associated with a change of season (1973 : 423, 443, 469–70).

The Barasana myth of the *Ayawa* asking for night (see M.2.B) also describes a container which when opened releases night. Most versions of this myth (all very similar to Lévi-Strauss's *M326a*) emphasise the precise nature of this first, excessively long night: rain poured from the sky and the rain-clouds blotted out the sun. The association between heavy rain (and hence the rainy season) with the long night is found again in the story of the flood caused by *Romi Kumu* and it is notable that the detail concerning household objects which become dangerous animals (M.1.A.4) parallels exactly the same detail in Lévi-Strauss's *M326a*. In another Barasana myth (not included here) a packet is opened which releases vast clouds of ants called night ones (*nyamia*).[17] In variants of this myth from other

16 See also Lévi-Strauss 1973 : 268–9 for a discussion of the ambiguous significance of the Pleiades and *M277*, p. 273 for a portrayal of *Ceucy* (Pleiades) as a man-eater in the literal sense.
17 The flying forms of these sauba ants (*Atta* sp.) leave the nest in the early morning before dawn. The flying forms of other sauba ants leave the nest during the day.

parts of the Vaupés region, it is these same ants which, when released from a container, give rise to the first, catastrophic night (Reichel-Dolmatoff 1971 : 26). This container was a 'sound instrument' in that it also contained frogs, crickets and ants (called *roe* in Barasana) which makes a 'ti ti ti ti ti' sound. Collectively, these animals are called old ones of night.

The manner in which the nut of Lévi-Strauss's *M362a* is opened (by the melting of a resin seal) is reminiscent of the burning of the beeswax at *He* House. When the wax is burned, it is said to release clouds of *werea* bees which are like the ants which gave rise to the first, long night. The burned wax also releases a powerful stench. If, as Lévi-Strauss argues (1973 : 361–422), in South American Indian thought din and stench are homologous, then the gourd of beeswax can be said to be an instrument of darkness. But as it is not truly a musical instrument, it is an instrument of darkness only in a metaphorical sense. However, it has close associations with noise both in that when it is used at *He* House, the person carrying the burning wax is followed by young men blowing trumpets, and in that, according to the Barasana, the bees released when the wax is burned make a loud buzzing noise.[18] But most important of all, instruments of darkness produce the long night: according to the Barasana, if the wax gourd were ever to be broken, a catastrophic flood would ensue; floods, as I have shown above, signify the long night.

Thus the Barasana wax gourd is a metaphorical instrument of darkness and, in addition, Lévi-Strauss's arguments concerning this instrument are confirmed: Lévi-Strauss states that the instrument of darkness is associated with honey − through *werea* bees (the wax gourd shows this link); that it is associated with 'honey smoke' − the burned wax produces this smoke; and that it is associated with a change of season − *He* House, when the wax gourd is used, takes place at the interface of two seasons, the end of the summer and beginning of the rains. However, it should be emphasised that if the wax gourd is an instrument of darkness, it is also an instrument of fire and light, for, identified with *Romi Kumu* and the Pleiades,

18 In the past, the Barasana used to have masked mourning rites exactly like those described by Goldman for the Cubeo (1963 : 219–52). During these rites, a man dressed in a mask representing the morpho butterfly would dance, accompanying himself by a rhythm made by hitting the inside of a hemispherical Crescentia gourd, held in one hand, with a leg rattle held bunched-up in the other. Here, at least, we have a gourd identical to the wax gourd (but without the wax) being used as a real musical instrument.

it signifies also the dry season which is associated with a universal conflagration.[19]

Menstrual blood, fire and water

In one version of M.1.C, when Old Star refuses to eat from *Romi Kumu*'s wax gourd (see M.1.C.11), he says, 'I will not eat of that which smells of the stuff that you exude from your vagina.' This would suggest that this wax has a specific association with menstrual blood. According to Lévi-Strauss (1973 : 366), 'South American Indians believe that the liver is an organ formed from coagulated blood and that, in women, it acts as a reservoir for menstrual blood.' While the Barasana made no definite assertion to this effect, their rather unelaborated notions concerning the physiological basis of menstruation would certainly be consistent with this idea. I have already established that the wax is identified with liver. When the wax is burned, it is transformed from a hard, dry substance to a molten semi-liquid and produces the smell of menstrual blood. The melting of wax is thus analogous to the 'melting' of coagulated blood (liver) which produces menstrual blood. It is therefore reasonable to argue that the wax is identified with menstrual blood.[20]

This adds a new dimension to the argument, set out in chapter 5, that shamans are like menstruating women. *Romi Kumu*, Woman Shaman, the prototype shaman from whom all shamans derive their powers, is identified with wax, in turn identified with menstrual blood. Her vagina is wide open in the following respects: she gives birth to the *He* People (see M.1.C); she is a menstruating woman; she is sexually voracious (see M.4.F.17) and she is called 'Vagina Woman'. Like her, shamans too are wide open. As the Pleiades she controls

19 Lévi-Strauss also finds that the instruments of darkness can signify *both* darkness and night (the rotten world) and fire and light (the burned world) when he writes: 'Consequently, according to whether the myth is thought of within the context of absolute space, or relative time, the same signifieds (conjunction and disjunction) will call for opposite signifiers.' And also when he writes: 'The bull-roarer and the instrument of darkness are the ritual signifiers of a disjunction and a conjunction, both non-mediatized, which, when transposed into different tessitura, have as their conceptual signifiers the rotten world and the burned world. The fact that the same signifieds, in so far as they consist of relationships between objects, can, when these objects are not the same, admit of contrasting signifiers, does not mean that these contrasting signifiers have a signified/signifier relationship with each other' (1973 : 421). See also pp. 237–8.

20 Lévi-Strauss (1973 : 255) argues that both honey and menstrual blood are 'naturally cooked' substances, honey being a product of the natural world and menstrual blood a product of the animal world. Beeswax too can be considered as a 'naturally cooked' substance.

the weather; according to the Barasana, shamans too control the weather.[21]

Romi Kumu's menstrual blood is quite explicitly identified with rain and her urine is also rain (see M.1.B.2). In one version of the myth in which heavy rain follows the death of Opossum (see M.7.K.7) it is stated that this rain was blood. This suggests a link between *Romi Kumu* and the opossum. The Barasana also state that the rainy season is itself the menstrual period of the sky (= *Romi Kumu*). These facts indicate that seasonal periodicity is associated with the physiological periodicity of women and that the major climatic features of the rainy season and the dry season are re-duplicated, at a physiological level, in the process of menstruation. Furthermore, the act of burning wax should, in a symbolic sense, both cause rain to fall and cause menstrual blood. This is precisely what happens at *He* House, for after it (and hence after the burning of wax which takes place during this rite) comes the rainy season and also after *He* House the initiates are confined in a special compartment. In chapter 5, I argued that this period of confinement was equivalent to the confinement of women during their menstrual periods and I shall present more evidence for this below.

It has been shown that both *Romi Kumu* and the Pleiades are associated with fire and water. It should therefore be expected that the wax gourd and the vagina are also associated with these elements. For the wax gourd, the association with water has already been shown above; the most obvious association with fire is the fact that, during a rite in which all contact with fire and heat is taboo, wax is ritually burned. The association of the vagina with water has again been already shown. The evidence for an association of the vagina with fire is as follows: the fire that the *Ayawa* stole from their grandmother was kept between her legs in her vagina (see M.2.C.1). To make fire, the grandmother squatted over a pile of urucú (*Bixa orellana*) branches (M.2.C.2). The red pigment from the seeds of urucú, used by women to paint their faces, is *Romi Kumu*'s menstrual blood (M.1.B.4). The story of the conception of *Kanea* (M.2.A) exactly parallels the story of the conception of Yurupary in M.8.14, suggesting that the grandmother of the *Ayawa* is the 'same' person as the mother of Yurupary who in turn can be identified with *Romi Kumu*. Finally, that fire and

21 They do this by wiping their hands in their armpits and then blowing the smell at the clouds whilst uttering a spell. Here again, as for the wax gourd, smell is used to control weather.

menstruation are linked is suggested by such expressions as 'she's boiling her pot, lighting her fire', etc., which are used by the Barasana as euphemisms to indicate that a woman is menstruating.

Beeswax and poison

The animals that come to eat from the wax gourd after the refusal by Old Star have two things in common: first, they are all poisonous or bite fiercely and secondly, they can all change their skins (see M.1.C.13).[22] This helps to clarify why, in some versions of the myth of the origin of night, the instrument of darkness (identified with the wax gourd) should contain ants. It also adds weight to the argument that, with regard to the wax gourd, the difference between bees and wasps is not of great significance. But the argument can be taken still further: the episode of the myth in which noxious animals come and eat from the wax gourd bears a strong resemblance to the episode in which these same animals come and steal poison from *Warimi*'s poison pot (see M.4.G.4). This suggests that there are grounds for linking the wax gourd with a pot of curare poison.

To obtain this poison, *Warimi* had to go inside the body of Poison Anaconda, the father of *Romi Kumu* (see M.4.F.22–3). The poison was in Poison Anaconda's gall-bladder, part of the liver which is itself identified with the wax.[23] Manioc-stick Anaconda's liver gave rise to wax in M.6.A.64; his gall-bladder gave rise to cultivated fish-poisons and a poisonous fungus in M.6.B.10–11.[24] *Romi Kumu*'s vagina ($\equiv$ wax gourd) was surrounded by barbasco fish-poison, her pubic

22 In a myth from the Tukano of the Río Paca, not far from the Pirá-paraná, a gourd containing coca is offered to people who refuse to eat from it because, in addition to the coca, it contains noxious creatures. These creatures then eat the coca and thus become immortal through the power to change their skins (Fulop 1954 : 113–14). This myth, a variant of M.1.C, is of great importance in that it is the only concrete piece of evidence I have found for supposing that people outside the Pirá-paraná area make use of the wax gourd. While it is true that the gourd in question is not stated to contain wax, it is nonetheless true that the Barasana wax gourd contains coca and that it is this coca, not the wax itself, that is eaten.

23 The story of *Warimi* getting poison from inside Poison Anaconda is very similar to the story of the young boy inside the belly of Yurupary (see M.8.40–6). This would suggest that Poison Anaconda $\equiv$ Yurupary. Like Yurupary, *He* Anaconda also swallows disobedient young boys and then vomits them up again (compare M.8.37–51 with M.5.A.1–9). This would suggest that Yurupary $\equiv$ *He* Anaconda. Finally, Yurupary, *He* Anaconda and Manioc-stick Anaconda are all burned alive and give rise to Yurupary instruments. Thus we have: Yurupary $\equiv$ Poison Anaconda $\equiv$ *He* Anaconda $\equiv$ Manioc-stick Anaconda.

24 According to a Baniwa Yurupary myth (Saake 1958a), when Yurupary was burned, the first species of poisonous plant grew up from his ashes and his liver gave rise to the first snakes and mosquitos.

hair (see M.4.F.15—16).[25] Finally, the Barasana consider that menstrual blood (≡ wax, see above) is poisonous. Thus the wax is identifiable with poison.

The identity of the wax with poison explains further why the Pleiades should bring the threat of sickness and death (see above), for the Pleiades are identified with wax and with the wax gourd.[26] Together with the fact that the *He* instruments have poisonous connotations, it also helps to explain why, during *He* House, the house becomes filled with poison.

Beeswax and immortality

The myth of the origin of night (M.2.B), which, as I have argued above, concerns the wax gourd as an instrument of darkness, can also be said to be a myth about the origin of man's mortality. Owing to the confusion between the words *nyami*, night, and *kami*, sores, sores and hence sickness and death were the consequence of obtaining night. Considering the death-dealing associations of the Pleiades and the identity of wax with poison, it is hardly surprising that the wax gourd should shorten human life. But M.1.B indicates that it is the wax gourd that is the key to *Romi Kumu*'s immortality and M.1.C indicates that it was precisely because the *He* People refused to eat from the wax gourd that they lost the power of rejuvenation and hence men became mortal. This poses two problems: why it is that the wax gourd symbolises immortality for some and mortality for others? And why did the first *He* People refuse to eat from the wax gourd whilst today's *He* People (the participants at *He* House are called '*He* People') eat the coca that this gourd contains?

According to Lévi-Strauss (1970 : 270) 'stench is the natural manifestation, in an inedible form, of femininity, of which the other natural manifestation, milk, represents the edible aspect. Vaginal odour is therefore the counterpart of the suckling function: being anterior to it, it offers an inverted image of it and can be considered its cause, since it precedes it in time.' In the present context this should imply that wax, clearly identified with stench and vaginal odour, should also be identified with milk. All versions of M.1.C

25 Lévi-Strauss (1970 : 270) argues that fish-poison is analogous to female filth.
26 For a discussion of the homology between fishing, poison and epidemics see Lévi-Strauss 1970 : 279—81 and of the death-dealing aspects of the Pleiades see Lévi-Strauss 1973 : 269—70 and 288.

put *Romi Kumu*'s offering of the wax gourd to the *He* People
immediately after their birth which in turn implies that, as the first
food offered to new-born babies, wax is like milk. Wax itself is a
totally inedible substance; what the participants at *He* House eat
is coca mixed in with it. The Barasana call coca and yagé by the
same term *kahi* (when relevant, a distinction is made by adding the
prefixes *bare*-, to eat, and *idire*-, to drink). Yagé is said to be *He*
milk and it is given to the initiates to make them live. The initiates
themselves are said to be soft and are explicitly compared to new-
born babies and in keeping with this, they must remain in a foetal
position throughout the rite. Though it is yagé that is being identified with milk I think there is sufficient evidence to extend this
identity to include coca.[27]

The stench of wax thus presents a paradox: it signals decay and
hence a shortening of human life, as does the opossum (Lévi-Strauss
1973 : 80–1) (Identified with *Romi Kumu*) but as milk it is the
source of life to new-born babies (and initiates). By refusing wax,
the *He* People refuse life and become the living dead, spirits from
the other world. *He* House is a dangerous game, for the living are
brought into contact with the dead and become one with them
but ultimately they must remain alive, so they eat wax. But the
wax gourd used at *He* House is not the real one but the left-over
gourd which gives life but not immortality (see M.1.C.10–16).

In spite of knowing that the wax gourd used at *He* House is
not the real thing, one informant said to me after the rite, 'We ate
from the wax gourd at *He* House so that we too could change our
skins.' For the Barasana, to change skins is a way to rejuvenation
and hence to immortality and this theme is stressed throughout
He House and the period following it.[28] The application of black
paint at the beginning of *He* House is designed to change the skins

27 Coca takes away hunger and people will never eat either whilst they are taking coca nor
soon after; as such it is an anti-food. Reichel-Dolmatoff makes this same observation
and also establishes that the Desana identify coca with milk (1971 : 46).
28 Lévi-Strauss argues that myths dealing with the loss of immortality view the problem
from two different angles: 'It is looked at prospectively and retrospectively. Is it possible
to avert death – that is, to prevent men from dying sooner than they want to? And
conversely, is it possible to restore men's youth once they have grown old, or to bring
them back to life if they have already died? The solution to the first problem is always
formulated in negative terms: do not hear, do not feel, do not touch . . . etc. The solution
to the second problem is always expressed positively: hear, feel, touch, see, taste. On the
other hand, the first solution applies only to men, since plants and animals have their
own method of avoiding death, which is to become young again by changing their
skins. Some myths consider only the human state and can therefore be read in one

of the initiates, and its disappearance at the end of the marginal period signifies that this has been achieved and that the initiates are ready to receive pepper blown by the shamans.[29] The stress placed on the initiates washing their faces during the marginal period is also connected with the theme of changing skin. Finally, whipping (see ch. 8) causes rebirth and a change of skin, and there are several episodes in Barasana myth in which the bones of a burned or cooked person are covered with leaves as a skin which is then whipped to bring the person back to life.[30]

According to the Barasana, women live longer than men because they menstruate. Menstruation, they say, is an internal changing of skin. This implies that immortality and periodicity are linked. This idea is confirmed in many different ways. Creatures that shed their skins, a sign of periodicity, are also immortal. The Sun, identified with the wax gourd never dies; in the rainy season he becomes old and less hot, then he sheds his skin and becomes young and hot again, which is the dry season. In the evening, *Romi Kumu* is old and ugly but in the morning she bathes and becomes young and beautiful again (see M.1.B.1). The wax gourd, as an instrument of darkness, is responsible for the regular alternation of day and night. As the Pleiades, it is responsible for the regular alternation between the dry and rainy seasons, an alternation which is homologous with that between day and night, for a period of heavy rain is part and parcel of the first, long night. In turn, the periodicity of the seasons is homologous with that of menstruation and it can be said that one reason for the burning of wax at *He* House is to ensure that this periodicity continues, a reason which also explains, in part, why

direction only – prospective continuance of life, negative injunction; others contrast the human state with that of creatures or entities that grow young again, and can be read in both directions – prospectively and retrospectively, negatively and positively' (1970 : 162). The myth about the refusal to eat from the wax gourd firmly supports this view.

29 The Cubeo apply black paint (genipa) to the bodies of new-born babies so that the foetal skin will be shed (Goldman 1963 : 169).

30 In the Tukano myth mentioned in n. 22 above, after giving a box containing night to humanity, *Yepa Huake* (represented on this earth by the Yurupary instruments) tells two people called *Cajta* and *Cajta Casoro* (two species of guan birds – compare M.2.B.8) to get up early in the morning to bathe. At the port they were to vomit, smoke tobacco and then whip themselves so that they could peel the skin from their heads down to their shoulders and then on down to their feet. After this they were to come back to the house and eat coca from a gourd. They both remained asleep in the morning but one of them wakes in time to peel his skin to his shoulders. *Yepa Huake* is angry at their laziness and makes the one who peeled to his shoulders put back his skin. Then he offers them the gourd of coca. They refuse to eat, as they are frightened of the noxious creatures mixed with the coca, so *Yepa Huake* curses man and tells them that henceforth they must die (Fulop 1954 : 122–5).

it is that *He* House is held at the end of the dry season and the beginning of the rains.

In chapter 5, I argued that the victory of the men who regained the stolen *He* (see also M.1.D) was double-edged, for the women retained a kind of *He*, their hair, and with it the ability to menstruate. M.1.C tells essentially the same story, for the men failed to get the true wax gourd back from *Romi Kumu*. In both cases, men lost the power to menstruate and with it they lost both periodicity and immortality. I have also argued that the initiates are in some ways like menstruating women. It would seem then that during initiation, an attempt is made to make the initiates menstruate in a symbolic sense and to make them periodic. Further evidence for this can now be given.

During *He* House, the initiates and others apply magically treated red paint to their bodies. This paint is identified with menstrual blood and should women have contact with it, it will make them menstruate; at this stage of the rite the initiates are still identified with women. More red paint, again identified with blood, is put on the initiates' bodies by women at the rite of taking a *henyerio*; this rite should take place two lunar months after *He* House. The black paint applied to the initiates' bodies is also associated with both menstruation and periodicity: this is the paint that *Meneriyo* wiped on the face of her brother the Moon (see M.4.A.3−5). This paint is said to be derived from liver, in turn identified with wax.[31] In addition to this can be added the stress on skin changing mentioned above.

Periodicity is also heavily stressed. The Barasana divide the major seasons shown in fig. 3 into a number of short periods, nearly all of which are called after the forest or cultivated tree-fruit that is in season at the time.[32] Fruits are thus used as time-markers and signal periodicity. These same fruits establish the timing of both *He* House and the different rites of Fruit House, so that, throughout the year, men take part in a series of rituals, each of which is an attenuated replica of *He* House. They are followed by a short period of restric-

---

31 This paint, together with red paint, is said to have come originally from inside the *He* instruments and is compared to the marrow of the *He*, which are bones.

32 The Indians of the Río Negro area believed that the Moon was the mother of fruit. The Sun fertilised trees and made them produce fruit which the Moon then ripened (Stradelli 1928/9 : 714, under the heading 'Yacy'). Here again fruits are linked with periodicity, this time represented by the Sun and Moon.

tions homologous with the marginal period after *He* House, which is itself likened to a menstrual period. The fruiting season of forest fruits, as opposed to cultivated tree-fruits, corresponds almost exactly to the major rainy season (see fig. 3) which is itself compared to a menstrual period.

It can also be argued that the initiates are themselves identified with these periodic fruits. During Fruit House men carry in baskets of fruit which the initiates then tip out on to the floor; during *He* House the men carry in not fruit but the initiates themselves. At Fruit House, after it has been tipped out, the trumpets are played directly over the fruit; at *He* House they are played over the initiates. It also seems likely that the green, unripe assai fruit, which is brought into the house at the Fruit House when pepper is blown for the elders after *He* House, represents the initiates. This is the only occasion on which green fruits are used and their greenness seems to represent the fact that, unlike the elders, the initiates are not yet ready to eat pepper. In chapter 8, it will be shown that the growth of the initiates is also linked with the growth of fruit.

In conclusion it can be said that at a cosmological level and in the natural world, the wax gourd is a symbol of immortality. In each case this immortality is consequent upon a regular alternation between two states: dry season and wet season, day and night. This alternation is explicitly compared to menstruation and to the physiological periodicity of women. Menstruation and cosmological periodicity are both compared to a process of changing skins. Throughout initiation, periodicity, skin changing and menstruation are all stressed, in particular with regard to the initiates themselves. At a cosmological level, regular alternation is a cyclical and reversible process, but at a human level it is irreversible for the generations must succeed one another by replacement. Women are the agents of this replacement at a natural level through their ability to bear children. This ability is dependent upon the ability to menstruate, a process compared to skin changing. Hence women are seen as being semi-immortal. At a social level men are the agents of this replacement for it is they who initiate boys into adult life, a change from one state to another.

It will be shown below that in all contexts the burning of wax is a symbol of disjunction. As such, it separates young boys from the world of nature and women, and separates child from adult. It thus signifies the succession of generations and consequently signifies human mortality.

The burning of wax

Before wax is burned, it must have spells blown into it by a shaman. It is then placed on embers in a potsherd and carried by a shaman or elder who fans the smoke in the four cardinal directions, using a woven fan. This action is called protective magic (*wanose*) and sending away sickness/disease (*nyase rohagu*).

Outside the context of *He* rituals, wax is burned on the following occasions: (1) When a woman returns to the house after giving birth which she must do in the manioc gardens. Before she returns, all food and material goods are taken out of the house on to the plaza to avoid their being polluted. The woman enters through a hole made in the side wall of the house at the rear. Wax is then burned in the house, after which the food and material goods are brought back into the house.

(2) After birth, the mother and father of the child must spend five days in confinement in their family compartment. Afterwards, they bathe at the port. As they return to the house, food and goods are taken out on to the plaza. They come in through the women's door and wax is then burned.

(3) At a girl's first menstruation she must be confined inside an enclosure. At the end of her confinement she bathes. Before she returns to the house, food and goods are taken out on to the plaza and after her return wax is burned.

(4) Dead people are buried inside the house. At death, all food is thrown away and all pots are emptied. Wax is burned to make the spirit (*wãti*) leave the body of the dead person. The burned wax is said to release a cloud of bees which drive out the spirit by biting it. In this context, the action of burning wax is called cutting off from death (*bohori tagu*).[33]

(5) Wax is burned at solar and lunar eclipses and when the moon turns red and 'dies' (see M.3). At such times, all household goods must be taken out on to the plaza and all food covered up. Loud noise should also be made.

(6) During epidemics, wax is burned to send away the sickness.

---

33 The Cubeo use burning chilli peppers for this same purpose (Goldman 1940 : 246). In Barasana myth both wax and chilli peppers are burned to send away spirits which suggests that pepper smoke and 'honey smoke' are equatable. In *Mythologiques* II (1973), Lévi-Strauss concludes that pepper smoke and 'honey smoke' both have the function of driving away spirits and that honey, the seductive power of nature, interrupts the communication between men and the supernatural.

Eclipses, especially solar eclipses, are believed to cause epidemics. When an individual is seriously ill, he is made to inhale wax smoke and to drink water into which molten wax has dripped. Wax is also burned after a snakebite. The affected area is bathed in wax smoke after which the other people in the house bathe themselves in the smoke so that they will not be bitten too.

(7) After burning off the felled trees, wax is burned in the gardens to cool them down.

(8) Wax is also burned in manioc gardens to send away plagues of caterpillars, etc. which threaten the crops.

(9) In myths at least, wax is burned to drive away malevolent spirits. Burning peppers are also used for this purpose.

Without entering into an extended discussion of all Barasana life-crisis rituals and other things besides, I think that it can be said that each of the contexts in which wax is burned, outlined above, have in common the features of disorder (natural, sociological or cosmological) and an excessive and undesirable conjunction (between nature and culture, pests and crops, the earth and the heavenly bodies, life and death and between the human and spirit worlds). In each case, wax is burned to cause a disjunction and/or to restore order from chaos.[34] I shall now apply this finding to an interpretation of the burning of wax at *He* rituals. I shall do so with reference to *He* House only but intend my interpretation to cover all *He* rites (Fruit House being considered to be an attenuated imitation of *He* House).

At *He* House wax is burned two times with certainty and possibly three. It is burned first outside the house on the plaza when the *He* arrive on the first night of the rite. The reason given for its burning is to send away disease and to prevent mystical attack on the participants. When the *He* are under water in the forest (in the natural world of animals and spirits), they are inactive and dead. When taken out on to land and into the clearing surrounding the house (the cultural world of people) they become active and alive. In myth, when the *He* People left the river and came on to land they changed from anaconda to human. In the same way, a baby is born in the

34 In all my reading of South American ethnography, I have come across only one systematic account of the ritual use of burnt beeswax, by Clastres, for the Guayaki. Lévi-Strauss, in *From Honey to Ashes*, makes very little reference to this topic and the few references he does make largely concern the Guayaki. The conclusions that Clastres reaches about the significance of burnt wax are the same as those that I reach for its significance among the Barasana (1972 : 166–8). Like the Barasana, the Guayaki burn wax at lunar eclipses and at male initiation.

gardens (semi-nature), taken to the river, and then brought from there into the house (the human, cultural world). In each case, the burning of beeswax creates a disjunction between one state and another, dead and living, spirit and human. When the *He* move from forest and river to house, from dead to living, a corresponding but reversed change occurs in the human world. The participants at *He* House are killed by having snuff blown up their noses. This snuff, obtained by Manioc-stick Anaconda from the Sun in the Underworld, is the Sun's fire, used to burn himself and his brother Macaw to death so that their bones became the *He* instruments (M.6.A). The participants also become *He* People. The burning of wax affects this change and also causes a disjunction between the world of women (on the side of nature) and the world of men (on the side of culture), for the screen that separates the sexes (see fig. 2) is drawn across the rear of the house at this point. Here again, the beeswax signifies death and mortality for the men.

The second time that wax is burned during *He* House is at midnight on the second night of the rite, after the initiates have been brought into the house. This time, the wax is burned inside the house and this action is seen as the climax and pivotal point of the whole rite. Again, according to informants, the wax is burned to send away sickness and disease and to protect the participants from shamanic attack. They say that it protects them from the dreams mentioned in chapter 3 and in particular from dreams of eating fish brought by the *He* People. They also say that the burning of wax prepares the participants to receive the coca and snuff from the wax gourd and tobacco gourd, which imparts strength and life. I think that it can also be said that the burning of wax causes a disjunction and separation of the initiates from the world of women and childhood. The initiates are in a liminal position between childhood and adulthood; they are both children and adults; burned wax separates these two states. The burning of wax also causes a final change in state in the *He* People who enter the house as the *He* instruments, for it is immediately after this that the process of fragmentation and differentiation, discussed in chapter 6, is fully reversed and Manioc-stick Anaconda and Macaw become alive and appear as *He* spirits.

The opening of the nut containing night, an instrument of darkness, is homologous to the burning of wax taken from the wax gourd, also an instrument of darkness. This act caused an interruption of the permanent day (see M.2.B) and was followed by the regular alternation

between day and night. It can be argued that the burning of wax at
He House ensures the continuance of this alternation. The permanent
day and the long night are homologous with the dry season and the
rainy season. The burning of wax at *He* House, held at the meeting
point between the two major seasons, thus ensures that, as night and
day follow one another in a regular alternation, so will the wet
season follow the dry season. I say it in this order because the original
state that was changed was a permanent day or dry season, not the
rainy season and permanent night (see M.2.B). In this sense, burned
wax symbolises that men must die, for the alternation of day and night
and dry season and wet season are made homologous with the succession of generations. Finally, it can be said that, just as the burning
of wax (as liver) brings on a menstrual period, so it brings on a period
of confinement closely paralleled by that of menstruation.

On the final day of *He* House, when the participants return from
the men's port after bathing, the women take all the food and
material goods out of the house on to the plaza before the men enter
the house. At the *He* House observed by me, this was not done and
I know about it only from informants' descriptions. Considering
that at all other occasions on which household goods are taken out on
to the plaza, wax is also burned, it would seem likely that it should
be burned on this occasion too.

In chapter 9 I shall argue that the bathing at the port, and in particular the vomiting that goes on there, can be seen as a symbolic
rebirth of the initiates. If this is so, then the removal of goods from
the house and also the burning of wax prior to the men's re-entry into
the house should be expected for this is what happens when new-born
babies are brought into the house. If in fact wax is burned at this
point, I would tentatively suggest the following interpretation: that
it re-establishes the normal order of things by causing a disjunction
between men and spirits. Immediately after the men return to the
house from their bathe, the shaman removes the feather head-dresses,
first from the two men who were the *He* spirits and then from the
other men who played the flutes. Men who wear the full feather
head-dresses are identified with *He* People, spirit people. Items of
ceremonial dress, especially the head-dresses, are strongly linked
with death and the people who wear them are symbolically dead,
i.e. spirit people.[35] By the removal of the head-dresses, the men once
again become normal human beings.

35 Feather head-dresses and other items of ritual equipment are buried with the dead

Explanation and analysis

I argued above that a change in the *He* from dead to living (water to land, forest to house) implies a reverse change in the human participants at *He* House – they become *He* people at the end of the rite. If the men are once again normal people, then the *He* should also become inactive and dead. This interpretation is entirely consistent with the fact that, immediately after the removal of the feathers from the heads of the elders, the atmosphere in the house changed from one of tense formality to one of jovial informality. Normal order is re-established in a variety of ways: the *He* are taken back and hidden under water in the river; the separation between the men and women is greatly diminished by the removal of the screen from the rear of the house; the men eat food for the first time since the start of the rite; and once again the initiates can sleep raised above the ground.

The *He* instruments and the wax gourd – a synthesis

The *He* instruments and the wax gourd are the most important sacred objects used at a Barasana initiation. The *He* instruments (Yurupary) have been frequently described in relation to Yurupary rituals from other parts of the Vaupés and most of the interpretations of these rites centre on them. Though there is internal evidence to suggest the use of the wax gourd outside the Pirá-paraná region, neither the gourd itself, nor its use or its significance has ever been described before.

The *He* and the wax gourd are symbols of mediation between opposed opposites: between childhood and adulthood, between life and death, between the human and spirit worlds, between fire and water and between the three basic divisions of the Barasana cosmos. Both are identified with shamans who are the human mediators of Barasana society. They are alike in that both are associated with creation and destruction, with life and death. They are both associated with poison and smell, and each combines an association with both fire and water. They are both musical instruments of a kind. Both express an opposition between container and contained, hard and soft; the element of container is associated with bone and the

(important men) and the Barasana describe the underworld river as being awash with the feather head-dresses of past burials (see also M.7.I.2, where the spider curses the bark-cloth aprons saying that they will be possessions of death).

The Cubeo also link feather head-dresses with death, and fear death from their possession (Goldman 1963 : 153).

element of contained with viscera. While the *He* are predominantly associated with men and the wax gourd predominantly associated with women, both combine an element of sexual ambiguity. Both have the same origins: either from the burned body of Manioc-stick Anaconda or from the body of *Romi Kumu*. *Romi Kumu* is the mother of the sky, Manioc-stick Anaconda is a manifestation (son) of *Yeba Haku*, the Primal Sun and father of the sky with whom both the wax gourd and *He* instruments are directly identified. Both are taboo to women.

In spite of the shared attributes and origins mentioned above, the *He* instruments and the gourd of beeswax are opposed to each other in the following ways:

He instruments	*Wax gourd*
male (+ female)	female (+ male)
————	○
(discontinuous shape)	(continuous shape)
bone	viscera
legs and arms	head
noise (+ smell)	smell (+ noise)
fire (+ water)	water (+ fire)
destruction + death	creation + life
jaguar	opossum
wet → dry	dry → wet
(taken from water to land)	(melts on burning)

The wax gourd is closely linked with the Pleiades; there is some reason to believe that the *He* instruments are associated with Orion. These two constellations are alike in that they appear and disappear within a few weeks of each other. Their appearance heralds the dry season and their departure heralds the rains — the rains following the Pleiades rains are called the Adze (*Sioruhu* ≡ Orion) rains. After they have gone, both constellations are said to fly back to the other side of the world in the form of small, migratory birds.[36]

The dry season is associated with male agricultural work, felling and burning of the forest, both of which presuppose dryness and fire. The wet season is associated with female agricultural work, the planting and cultivation of manioc, which involves wetness and water,

36 The Pleiades birds (*Nyokoaro minia*) are Bobolinks (*Dolichonyx oryzivourous*); I was unable to identify the Orion birds (*Sioruhu minia*).

for it is the rain that makes the crops grow (see fig. 3). The dry
season is associated with the Sun and with a universal conflagration;
the rainy season is associated with the sky from which the rain
falls, the rain being the menstrual period of *Romi Kumu*, the sky;
the first rainy season was a catastrophic flood (M.1.A.3—7). This
rain is also associated with the Moon: the period during which the
constellation Corona Borealis, the Armadillo, is visible corresponds
to the rainy season (see fig. 3). The Moon is identified with an
armadillo (see M.3.7). The true *He* instruments are used only at
He House which takes place in the dry season (albeit at its end).

Thus we have:

Dry season	*Wet season*
men	women
felling and burning	planting and cultivation
fire	water
Sun	Sky and Moon
universal conflagration	catastrophic flood
He instruments	wax gourd

At *He* House, two complementary opposites, the *He* instruments
and the gourd of beeswax, are brought into conjunction. This implies
simultaneously the conjunction of the sexes in reproduction, the
conjunction of men and women in productive activities, the conjunction of the two major seasons in an annual cycle, and the conjunction of the Sun and Sky, the two principles from which the
Barasana universe was created. Finally, the Barasana believe that
the human body is created in reproduction from the conjunction of
a hard, male element, bone, and a soft, female element, blood and
flesh, represented respectively by the *He* instruments and by beeswax.
Thus *He* House is not simply a rite of initiation; it has also a life-
giving and life-ordering function.

8

Open and closed:
the howler monkey and the sloth

Yurupary masks

In chapter 6, it was stated that the *He* instruments and the other items
of ritual equipment represent the animals of the world who have come
to dance at *He* House. One of the ornaments worn by the two men
who play the long flutes at the climax of the rite and who represent
the *He* spirits consists of hands of monkey-fur string worn on the
back.[1] This ornament, called *umaria yasi*, represents both howler
monkeys and sloths, sloths being the chiefs of all the various species
of monkey. In historical times, the Arawakan Tariana Indians of the
Vaupés region used elaborate masks, representing Yurupary, during
the second stage of their initiation rites (homologous with *He* House
as the second stage of Barasana initiation). There is evidence that
the Barasana hanks of monkey-fur string are homologous with these
masks.

The Tariana masks, called *Macacaraua* (*macaca-*, monkey, *-raua*,
fur), were made from monkey-fur string as their names suggest. This
in itself establishes a link with the Barasana ornaments. *Macacaraua*
is a name from Lingua Geral, the Tupian lingua franca once used
throughout the Vaupés region. In Tariana, the masks are called
putsumaka; I am unable to find a translation for *-maka*, but *putsu-*
appears to be derived from *putsaru* meaning sloth (Koch-Grünberg
1911 : 113, 131). If this derivation is correct, it suggests a further
link with the Barasana ornaments which represent sloths. The main
body of the masks was made from monkey-fur string, but the black
bands were made from string using the hair cut from young girls at
rites of first menstruation (Coudreau 1887 : 187; Koch-Grünberg
1909/10, vol. II : 253). According to the Tariana Yurupary myth

1 See Biocca 1965 : 181 for photograph. The ornament is also just visible in plate 4.

193

recorded by Coudreau, when the women stole the Yurupary instruments from the men, they also made Yurupary masks using hair cut from young *boys* at initiation. This would suggest that, like the Barasana, the Tariana considered male initiates and young girls at first menstruation to be equivalent. In other parts of the Vaupés region, young men used to collect the hair cut from girls at first menstruation rites and fasten it to the back of the headgear they wore at rituals (Koch-Grünberg 1909/10, vol. I : 181, 116). This suggests yet again a link between the hanks of monkey-fur string and the Yurupary masks, for, in the past, adult Barasana men wore their hair long and bound at the back in a pigtail; the pigtail was bound with monkey-fur string and from its base hung the fur ornaments.[2]

The Tariana Yurupary myth mentioned above also states that the child Yurupary wandered around dressed in a monkey skin and that it is for this reason that the masks are used as his symbol.[3] These masks, in male—female pairs, were considered to be even more taboo than the Yurupary instruments themselves. At the climax of Tariana initiation rites, two men dressed in the masks would come into the house (compare the *He* spirits that enter at the climax of *He* House) and jump around on all fours like monkeys, whipping the participants. Coudreau (1887 : 189) adds one very important detail to this account: the men who wore the masks had visible only four fingers on each hand and only three toes on each foot; both the fingers and toes were armed with long claws like the culture hero Yurupary of legend. Both the reduced number of digits and the long claws would suggest that the men represented sloths and this would seem to confirm my derivation of part of the Tariana word for Yurupary masks from the word for sloth.

The Barasana knew of the Tariana Yurupary masks but said that they had never used them themselves. In spite of this, I think that I have given sufficient evidence for saying that the Barasana hanks of monkey-fur string are homologous with these masks whether or not the Barasana ever used them. If this is so then the *He* spirits who

2 See Koch-Grünberg, 1909/10, vol. I : 328 for a photograph of a Tuyuka man with this hairstyle. Today Barasana men wear their hair short and in Western style but during dances they fix midribs from banana leaves to the backs of their heads. They then bind these with the monkey-fur string. See plate 4.
3 According to the Baniwa Yurupary myth published by Saake, Yurupary had a body covered in hair, the body of a monkey, but with head, hands and feet of a man (1958a : 273). M.8.29 states that his body was covered with dance ornaments.

come in at the climax of *He* House wearing the hanks of fur string (the only time that they are worn during the rite) can be considered homologous with the men wearing the Yurupary masks among the Tariana. In both cases, these men represent Yurupary or his equivalent Manioc-stick Anaconda and in both cases their appearance forms part of the climax of the rite. This demonstration opens up three interconnected lines of enquiry: sloths and howler monkeys in relation to Barasana cosmology, the relation between initiation and menstruation and the significance of hair.

Open and closed

According to Lévi-Strauss (1973 : 310), the howler monkey is a producer of filth: literally as a proverbial shitter and metaphorically as a producer of loud noise which is correlated with corruption. As such it is opposed to the sloth which produces a tiny whistle at night and defecates only occasionally, coming down to the ground to do so (1965–6 : 269–70). This can be represented as follows:

Howler monkey	*Sloth*
anal incontinence	anal continence
oral incontinence	oral continence

He also points out that both the howler monkey and the sloth are 'barometric animals' for the howler monkey howls when there is a change in weather and the sloth comes down to the ground and shits when it is cold. Finally he writes,

If we take into account the fact that, according to the Tacana myths (*M322–M323*), any attack on a sloth engaged in the normal exercise of its eliminatory functions would cause a universal conflagration – a belief which . . . is echoed in Guiana . . . where it is thought that any such attack would expose humanity to the perils resulting from the conjunction of celestial fire with the earth – it is tempting to detect, behind the acoustic aspect of the contrast between the howler monkey and the sloth . . . the contrast between the bull-roarer, a 'howling' instrument, and the instruments of darkness. (1973 : 429)

I shall now show that, in the Vaupés region, the sloth is associated with an instrument of darkness and that the contrast between the howler monkey and the sloth can be related to that between the

He instruments (homologous with the bull-roarers of Central Brazil) and the wax gourd, an instrument of darkness.

In the Vaupés region, almost every year there is an intensely cold period during which the sun is blotted out by thick clouds and a continuous fine rain falls from the sky. This period, called *aru* in Lingua Geral, comes right in the middle of the rainy season between the end of May and the beginning of July. The Barasana called this period *wɨhaɨ* and say that it is caused by a large toad (*Bufo marinus*) which stirs the water. The Bará call this cold period the sloth, and the fine rain, sloth rain, and they say that it is caused by a sloth who comes down to the ground at this time; according to Brüzzi da Silva (1962 : 262) the Tukano call the month of May, sloth. The Bará myth concerning this cold period tells of a special paddle with 'an unusually large handle' which the sloth takes with him on his once-yearly fishing trip (the *aru*) (Jackson n.d.).

Biocca (1965 : 426–7) has published a photograph of a special paddle, found in the lower Vaupés area, that has an elaborately carved handle in the form of an animal; this paddle belongs to a mythical character called *Aru*. *Aru* is the father of fish (both the Bará sloth and the Barasana toad are said to be fishermen) and he uses his paddle to cause the cold spell called after him (as does the Bará sloth). According to Stradelli (1928/9 : 380), *Aru* is a toad who changes into a handsome man and uses his paddle to travel upstream to visit the Mother of Manioc. He asks her to watch over crops and send rain at the right moment to fertilise them. Today, people sometimes find *Aru*'s paddles in the rivers and if they add a small piece of one such paddle to the fire when they burn off the trees from their garden, the *Aru*-toad will remain in the manioc garden and bring with it the Mother of Manioc who in turn brings rain (compare the burning of wax to cool down a manioc garden after burning – see ch. 7).[4] It seems clear from the above information that the paddle with 'an unusually large handle' belonging to the Bará sloth is the same kind of thing as the elaborately carved paddle illustrated by Biocca and that in some way the sloth and the toad are identified with one another.

In a myth from Guiana, recorded by Koch-Grünberg (cit. Lévi-Strauss 1973 : 451–2), a special paddle used in shallow water causes

---

4 *Aru*'s paddles are paddles occasionally found in the rivers of the Vaupés/Río Negro area. They are clearly very ancient, some being actually semi-fossilised (Stradelli 1928/9 : 380, under the headings 'aru' and 'aru-apucuita').

the river to dry up, whilst when used in deep water it causes a flood. Lévi-Strauss argues that this paddle is organologically connected to beaters and clappers, both of which are instruments of darkness. The sloth's paddle described above is also an instrument of darkness, and in a very real sense, for when it is used rainclouds blot out the sun and it becomes quite literally dark. Furthermore, the sloth's paddle can be connected with the wax gourd, another instrument of darkness: both are used to make rain and both wax and bits of paddle are burned in manioc gardens, one to cool them down and the other to bring rain. Thus, in the Vaupés region, there is good evidence to link the sloth with an instrument of darkness, a link suggested by Lévi-Strauss on quite independent evidence.

The story of the Tapir and the Howler Monkeys who swap voices establishes a direct link between the *He* instruments and the howler monkey, for the voice of each animal is its *He* instrument (see M.5.A. 18–22). Manioc-stick Anaconda, from whose bones all *He* instruments derive (M.6.A.63), is in particular associated with the trumpet Old Callicebus Monkey (*Wau Buku*). The howler monkey and the callicebus monkey can be considered to be 'combinatory variants', for both of them 'howl' at dawn and dusk and at changes of weather. They are furthermore associated together as Fire Callicebus Monkey and Fire Howler Monkey, two of the people who paddle the Sun's canoe up the Underworld River (M.6.A.16). It can thus be said that the *He* instruments are closely associated with both howler and callicebus monkeys and furthermore, in that both monkeys are associated with fire, the *He* instruments can also be associated with the dry season.[5]

From the above, it can be seen that Lévi-Strauss appears to be correct in tentatively seeing behind the (acoustic) contrast between howler monkey and the sloth, the contrast between the bull-roarer (homologous with the *He* instruments) and the instruments of darkness. For the Barasana context, this contrast can be represented as follows:

---

5 In the literature, I can find no information to indicate with which kind of monkey Yurupary is identified, but in view of the fact that both he himself and the instruments that represent him are characterised by noise, the howler monkey is an obvious choice. In support of this guess is the fact that *Warimi*, who can be identified with Yurupary, himself becomes a howler monkey at one point (see M.4.G.4). Yurupary can also be identified with *Kanea*, the youngest of the *Ayawa* (Thunders) (compare M.2.A.2–5 with M.8.14–18); it is *Kanea* who turns himself into a callicebus monkey, in order to steal fire from his grandmother. This in turn suggests an association between Yurupary and the callicebus monkey.

Howler monkey +	Callicebus Monkey	/ Sloth
oral incontinence	oral incontinence	/ oral continence
anal incontinence	—	/ anal continence

He Instruments	/ *'Instruments of Darkness'*
fire	/ water
dry season	/ rainy season

However, it must now be said that, for the Barasana at least, the correlation that Lévi-Strauss seeks to make between these two pairs of opposites is an oversimplification. In addition to its association with an instrument of darkness, the paddle, the sloth is also represented by a *He* instrument, the one called Old Sloth or Sloth Jaguar. Likewise, an instrument of darkness, the wax gourd, can also be linked to a 'howler' monkey (callicebus) insofar as it is identified with Maniocstick Anaconda who is himself identified with this monkey. Like the sloth, howler and callicebus monkeys also signal barometric change and if the wax gourd is a mediator between day and night, so too are the *He* instruments, for as monkeys they howl at dawn and dusk. These monkeys are associated with both fire and water; the sloth, who causes rain, also causes fire when attacked.[6] The *He* instruments are predominantly male symbols but have female associations, just as the wax gourd is primarily a female symbol but one which also has male associations. Similarly, the *Macacaraua* masks, which represent Yurupary himself, are in male–female pairs and appear to represent both howler monkeys and sloths.

Menstruation and initiation

According to the Barasana myth, the men punished the women who stole the *He* by making them menstruate; variants of this myth from elsewhere in the Vaupés region state either that the men raped the women or that they rammed the Yurupary up their vaginas (and thus made them bleed) (see M.1.D.7). These punishments have the common theme of opening up the women. The Tukano believe that

---

6 I have no data from the Barasana concerning the consequences of an attack on a shitting sloth, but if sloths cause rain and cold when they come to the ground (as they do to shit), then it seems reasonable that if they are frustrated in this endeavour they will do the opposite and cause fire.

Open and closed: the howler monkey and the sloth

Bisiu (one of the many characters identified with Yurupary) 'eats' (i.e. makes love to) girls at the time of their first menstruation (Brüzzi da Silva 1962 : 332). The Cubeo believe that it is the Moon who copulates with young girls and brings on first menstruation, a theme which is echoed in M.4.A; the Moon, they say, has such big teeth that he is unable to shut his mouth (Goldman 1940 : 245, 1963 : 180). Here again the idea appears to be that menstruation is caused by the opening up of a girl and it is significant that, in the Cubeo belief, the agent of this opening is himself marked by a wide-open mouth. According to a Tukano myth, menstruation was caused in the following manner: a paxiuba palm bore an unopened bunch of fruit upon which a strong wind blew, making it open and give forth sound. This sound came down with the wind and split two girls, sitting below, from the abdomen downwards causing them to bleed (Fulop 1956 : 343). This completes a full circle: the sound of the paxiuba palm causes menstruation: the *He* or Yurupary are made from this palm; the Barasana call this palm *besuŭ*; *Bisiu* causes menstruation.

It is clear from the above that, at the level of myth, a girl at first menstruation is opened up either by the Moon himself or by the *He*/Yurupary that are associated with him. At the level of ritual, among the Cubeo and Tukano, a girl was actually deflowered either by a shaman (Tukano) or by an old man (Cubeo) (Brüzzi da Silva 1962 : 440–1; Goldman 1963 : 179–80). I am not aware that this happens among the Barasana but the shaman still presides over first menstruation rites. Until a girl has undergone these rites she should not have sexual intercourse and if she fails to undergo the rites it is believed that her child would be unable to emerge from the womb so that she would die (i.e. she would be 'stopped up').

If by officiating at rites of first menstruation, a shaman is one who opens up girls in a real or symbolic sense, it is appropriate that he too should be marked by being opened up. This same feature of excessive openness characterises all the Yurupary heroes of Vaupés mythology. I have already mentioned the association of Yurupary with the howler monkey and of Manioc-stick Anaconda (≡ Yurupary) with the callicebus monkey, both of which are characterised by oral and anal incontinence. Yurupary and *He* Anaconda (≡ Yurupary) both eat up newly initiated boys through mouths as big as caves (M.5.A.3–6); M.8.40 presents a variant atypical of most Vaupés Yurupary myths: rather than eating them through his mouth, Yurupary

199

ingests the initiates through his anus (compare the behaviour of tapirs as Taking-in People); Yurupary belches and farts incessantly (M.8.42); Manioc-stick Anaconda is unable to control his farts (M.6.A.12); Manioc-stick Anaconda blows snuff from his mouth with terrible force (M.6.A.22, 57); *Uakti* (≡ Yurupary) had a body full of holes which sounded as the wind passed over them (Biocca 1965 : 230); Yurupary emits groans that spread over the land (Saake 1958a : 273); he sings loudly (M.8.32–3);[7] and he vomits up children through his wide mouth (see M.8.50 and M.5.A.11). This list could be extended with reference to other Yurupary myths but the point is already clear; Yurupary is excessively open.

The *He* (Yurupary) instruments which represent Manioc-stick Anaconda (≡ Yurupary) on earth, share this feature of openness: the trumpets produce a terrifying noise, compared to thunder; this noise is made by the player blowing with pursed lips ('raspberries') down an open tube and is thus like an amplified fart; like *He* Anaconda and Yurupary, the *He* instruments also vomit. These open instruments cause women to become opened up at puberty and if women happen to see the *He* they become yet more open. If the *He* can open up girls and women, they should also open up young boys at initiation. I shall now show that this is in fact what happens.

According to the Barasana, if a child should see the *He* instruments it would eat earth and suffer from violent diarrhoea until it wasted away and died. This illness, *wisiose*, is precisely that which afflicts the initiates who fail to keep the food and other taboos after *He* House; their anuses become so big that they literally drain away. The initiates are opened up; excessive openness will kill them. The consumption of yagé is reserved for initiated men; young boys are first given yagé at Fruit House as the first stage of initiation; at *He* House they are given yagé again, this time a much stronger drink and more of it; yagé induces violent diarrhoea and vomiting, especially in those, such as initiates, who are not used to its effects. Vomiting and diarrhoea indicate an open mouth and anus. After their first experience of Fruit House, great stress is placed on the young boys getting up early each morning to bathe and to vomit water; the theme of vomiting is particularly emphasised during the ritual bathe that takes place at the end of *He* House. Finally and more speculatively,

---

7 Milomaki, the Yahuna Yurupary, also sang loudly (Koch-Grünberg, 1909/10, vol. II : 292–3).

the use of black paint at *He* House can, I think, be linked to the
theme of opening up. The body of Yurupary was full of holes (M.8.
22) and it was full of flowers (M.8.29); these two facts suggest that
he was a container full of holes like a basket. The designs painted on
the bodies of the initiates and other men at the dance that marks
the end of the marginal period, like those painted for other social
dances, are clearly derived from the patterns of weaving. Thus they
could be said to transform men into 'baskets full of holes'. These
designs are called macaw, the name of Manioc-stick Anaconda's
brother and of the *He* flutes. At the start of *He* House the initiates
are painted from chin to toes in uniform black paint whilst the elder
men are painted only as far as their knees. It may be that the synchronic
opposition between the paint of the initiates and elders expresses
their relative degrees of openness (the initiates being almost totally
stopped up) and that the diachronic opposition between the initiates'
paint at the start and end of *He* House expresses the fact that they too
have been opened.

It can also be argued that the classic Yurupary myths can be taken
as stories about how Yurupary was initiated by being opened up. When
Yurupary was born, he had no mouth and could neither speak nor
eat and had to be fed with tobacco smoke that was blown over him.[8]
When asked questions he replied by shaking his head. (According to
Magalhães (cit. Bolens 1967 : 51) *yurupary* can be translated as 'to
hold one's hand over one's mouth'.) He grew very rapidly and at 'the
age of six' a mouth was cut in his face whereupon he let out a terrible
roar and soon after ate up the disobedient initiates in his cave-like
mouth (Saake 1958a). I will show below (ch. 9) that the story of
Manioc-stick Anaconda (M.6.A) can also be read as a story about the
hero's combined initiation and rebirth.

It can be seen from the above that the passage from childhood to
adulthood and the corresponding process of physiological maturation,
involves, for people of both sexes, a process of real and/or symbolical
opening up. The opening up of the digestive tube (mouth and anus)
is paralleled, at a sexual level, by the opening up of the vagina (girls)
or penis (boys); girls should remain virgins till first menstruation and
boys until after initiation. If the Moon opens up girls by copulating
with them (piercing with penis) and if *He* instruments rammed up

8 M.8, the Yurupary myth given in this thesis, does not describe this and is unusual in
 stating that Yurupary was full of holes as a baby. Other myths describe a progression
 from having no holes at all to a body full of holes.

their vaginas do the same, this would suggest that, at one level, the *He* instruments are penises. If this is so, then it can be said that, in one sense, the initiates are being equipped with new open penises. appropriately the smallest and shortest flutes.[9]

If girls are opened up at first menstruation they are also systematically taught to control the orifices of their bodies: they must control their mouths by *not* telling secrets, by *not* asking too many questions and by *not* talking too much. They must control their eyes by *not* seeing the *He* instruments and control their vaginas by *not* being licentious. The same can be said for young boys at initiation. These boys must get up each morning to vomit; the purpose of this vomiting is to get rid of waste food in the stomach. As such, it is an alternative to defecation and implies control over the digestive tube. During the marginal period after *He* House the initiates must (1) eat very little at all, (2) eat with very small mouthfuls and (3) cover their mouths with their hands as they eat. The initiates are also taught that they must not reveal secrets about men's ritual activities and are taught to control their sexual activities. All this implies control over bodily orifices.[10] Finally, Lévi-Strauss (1973 : 427–8) argues that those who are most stopped up and able to resist nature will be most gifted in cultural aptitudes, and that those most open will be most lazy. In chapter 4, I pointed out that initiates and menstruating women are considered to be inherently lazy and that the emphasis on weaving (for women) and basket-making (for men) was designed to counteract this.

Bolens (1967) has argued that the Yurupary instruments, fed on tobacco smoke (and snuff), like Yurupary without a mouth, and

9 I am fully aware that considerably more could be made of the association between the *He* instruments and penises. However, I have refrained, up till now, from mentioning the fact, partly because the Barasana emphatically deny any connection whatsoever (while freely admitting that the wax gourd is a vagina) but more importantly because I wish to avoid jumping to 'obvious' conclusions.

In addition to my statement in the text above, there is other evidence to suggest a homology between Yurupary instruments and the penis: the instruments are compared to (and sometimes identified with) fish; fish are equated with Fish Anaconda's penis. In some versions of the Yurupary myth, in order to give birth, Yurupary's mother was pierced by a fish and some versions state that the fish was a jacundá. This same fish was the one that showed the women how to use the stolen Yurupary instruments, by signalling with its *exaggeratedly large mouth* (Prada Ramirez 1969 : 131–2). Finally, the story of how the paxiuba palm was cut up into pieces and distributed among men as instruments can be seen as a transformation of the Tupi myth of Maira's long penis, which is cut up and distributed among women.

10 One of the things that instantly strikes visitors to the Pirá-paraná area is that the adult men delight in farting loudly, often modulating the noise with their fingers or cupped hands.

through which passes only air, represent a neutralised form of
Yurupary the cannibal with an excessively open mouth. While I
think that there is some truth in this, I think it is an oversimplification, for the essence of the *He* instruments is that they *combine*
the qualities of open and closed.[11] Like the other mediatory symbols
used at Barasana initiation, the *He* instruments are ambiguous in
that they combine complementary but opposed characteristics. I
will argue below (ch. 9) that the initiates are symbolically swallowed
and regurgitated just as *He* Anaconda swallowed and regurgitated
the disobedient initiates in M.5.A.1−11 (see also M.8.37−50). If
Yurupary (and *He* Anaconda) were really neutralised, this would be
impossible, and with it initiation also.

The significance of hair

According to Wallace (1889 : 191, 343), in the nineteenth century,
hairstyles among the Indians of the Vaupés area were as follows:
young men wore their hair in long, loose locks with a comb on top
and elder men wore their hair parted and combed on each side and
tied in a queue a yard long bound with monkey-fur cord, down their
backs, and with a comb on top. Women wore no combs. In the past,
Barasana women wore their hair tucked on the back of the head in
a bun (they now use combs) and elder men wore their hair in the style
described above. I have no data on the hairstyle of young men in
the past; at present, like the elders they wear their hair short. Today,
young boys, and even more so young girls, have their hair cropped
and at both rites of first menstruation and rites of initiation, their
hair is cut off completely. If it can be assumed that, in the past, young
Barasana men also wore long, loose hair, we can construct the series
in the accompanying table.

	Childhood	Puberty	Unmarried youth	Adulthood
Men	short hair	hair cut off	long, loose hair	hair in queue
Women	short hair	hair cut off	hair in bun	hair in bun

11 The fact that M.8.22 states that Yurupary as a *baby* was full of holes, whereas other
versions say that at this stage he was totally stopped up, may perhaps be a reflection
of this ambiguity at the level of myth.

Explanation and analysis

It can be seen from the table that, for both men and women, the difference between short and long hair signifies the difference between child and adult. Rivière (1969b) comes to the same conclusion regarding hair symbolism among the Waiwai. He shows that the blowpipe and hair tube are inversely distributed in Guiana but that both of them can be considered as energy transformers for the hair tube 'socialises' the free-flowing sexual energy represented by hair whilst the blowpipe directs breath, which can be used both to cure and kill, through a tube to propel a dart that converts game animals (nature) into meat (culture). He argues further that myths from the 'blowpipe area' link creation with the above, whilst those from the 'hair tube area' link creation with the below; and that in the 'blowpipe area', girls, at first menstruation, are raised as high from the ground as possible, whilst in the 'hair tube area', they are made to sit on or near the ground.

The Barasana do not use hair tubes as such, but like the Waiwai, they bind their hair with string (see above). Unlike the Waiwai, the Barasana use both blowpipes and *He* instruments; blowpipes are called *buhua* and *He* instruments are sometimes referred to by the same word. However, at all dances and at *He* rituals, the adult men wear tubes made from the leg bones of jaguars which represent the *He* instruments (Manioc-stick Anaconda was a jaguar, his bones are the *He* instruments). These bones are worn attached by monkey-fur string to the banana-leaf midribs which today take the place of hair queues. They are thus tubes-attached-to-hair but they are also 'hair tubes' in that they are stuffed with jaguar fur. According to M.1.B, women keep *their He* instruments in their hair. The conclusion is again that the *He* instruments are a kind of 'hair tube'. If hair tubes 'socialise' among the Waiwai so do *He* instruments among the Barasana, for here they transform young boys (on the side of nature) into young men (on the side of culture); the manner in which *He* instruments work, by modifying breath, is however more akin to the blowpipe.

Among the Waiwai all initiated men have constrained hair but unmarried men have long, undecorated hair tubes whilst married men have shorter, decorated tubes; only fully adult men may wear full ceremonial dress. This last feature is true of the Barasana also but the hair symbolism is more complicated, for young men have unconstrained hair whilst elders have bound hair (though both wear combs; Rivière argues that ornaments figuratively constrain hair and have the connotation of culture). Rivière also argues that the treatment of hair symbolises socio-sexual status. Among the Barasana this is true of women (who can have sexual intercourse and marry only after first menstruation when their hair has grown long) but for men sexual status and social status are differentiated. After *He* House young men achieve full sexual status but only on marriage do they achieve full social status (see ch. 5). This difference is signalled by the loose, long hair of the young men as opposed to the tightly bound hair of the elders. Rivière argues that marriage symbolises full adult status and also legitimate and socialised sexual intercourse which is creative. The constraining of hair in a tube amongst the Waiwai, like the binding of hair with cord amongst the Barasana, symbolises this. It is therefore highly appropriate that, among the Barasana, young men whose extra-marital sexual activities are potentially destructive, should have (or have had) unconstrained hair. After initiation, it is impressed upon young men that they should not attempt to sleep with their elder brothers' wives.[12]

Following Leach (1958), Rivière suggests that hair represents libidinous energy with an ambiguous power for both creation and destruction. Again, it is appropriate that young Barasana men (warriors) should have loose hair signifying potentially destructive energy. But here we are presented with a paradox: on the one hand, loose hair represents destructive energy (the Barasana say that hair is the seat of life and that those with long hair have much life-energy), but on the other hand it is loose unconstrained hair which, in women, brings on menstruation, a condition of laziness and inactivity (see M.1.B). Like the Waiwai, the Barasana say that hair is the seat of laziness.

This paradox lies at the heart of any interpretation of *He* House for on the one hand I have argued that this rite can be viewed as symbolic menstruation (and thus linked with laziness and inactivity) but on the other hand the rite also forms part of a warrior cult where aggression, energy and destruction are emphasised. The two men who enter the house at the climax of *He* House are fierce spirits (*guari wãtia*) who come to teach the initiates to be brave and to kill. Similarly, during the marginal period following *He* House, a period

12 In ch. 9 it is argued that Manioc-stick Anaconda can be identified as representing an initiate. It is around puberty that the sexual rivalry between brothers begins. The whole of the story of Manioc-stick Anaconda, the myth the Barasana give to explain *He* House, is centred on the destructive nature of extra-marital sex.

205

comparable to menstruation, in the past the initiates were made to drink blood to make them fierce and were taught the use of weapons of war. At *He* House, after eating coca mixed with beeswax to make them strong and fierce, the men are whipped to enhance these qualities; but beeswax also brings on menstruation. Again, the moon, who is the cause of menstruation according to some myths, is also the source of fierce magic (*guari*) (see M.3.14).[13] This paradox is also reflected in the ambiguous nature of the major symbols used at *He* House and it helps to explain why the *Macacaraua* masks, homologous with the fierce spirits who appear at *He* House, should be made from the hair shorn from young menstruating girls.

Rivière recognises this paradox when he writes: 'Hardness is a male virtue, but it is also, by its constraint and continence, a sterile one and cannot in itself lead to creativity which requires the help of women, incontinence and softness. Tubes are a means by which natural forces are directed towards cultural ends, but even when this is done, nature must still exert itself if the world is to go round' (1969b : 162).

The whips

The whips used at *He* rituals, called *heta waso* (*heta* = tocandira ant (*Paraponera clavata*), *waso* = long thin object), are made from peeled, branched saplings of a tree which is also used to make fishing rods.[14] According to a Baniwa Yurupary myth, the plant from which the whips are made grew up from the ashes of Yurupary together with the paxiuba palm and the first poisonous plants (Saake 1968 : 266). Another Yurupary myth, also from the Baniwa, states that mosquitos and poisonous snakes also came from Yurupary's ashes (Saake 1958a : 274). The tocandira ant is characterised by an extremely poisonous sting and bite. The connection between poisonous ants and whips is of great comparative interest, for in the Guianas, ant-frames are used in the context of puberty rituals and, among the Piaroa, ant-frames, whips and Yurupary instruments are all used together (Gheerbrant 1953 : 129–55).[15] It appears from this that where ant-

13 When told that the Yanomamö believe themselves to be the descendants of the blood of the Moon, the Barasana replied, 'No wonder they are so fierce.'
14 The Cubeo and Baniwa use bigger and more elaborate whips that draw blood and leave scars. The Barasana whips are thrown away after use; the Baniwa ships are kept. A photograph of a Baniwa whip can be found in Biocca (1965 : 49).
15 According to Prada Ramirez (1969 : 117–8), the Tukano use both whips and biting

frames are used in one culture area, the Guianas, whips called after or associated with ants are used in the same context in another, the Northwest Amazon.

The Barasana appear to use these whips rather less often than other Vaupés groups: most authors report the use of whips at all Fruit House rites whilst I only saw whipping during the Fruit House as the first stage of initiation and at *He* House itself. The Barasana also appear not to whip girls at first menstruation. According to the Barasana whipping has four interconnected purposes: to prevent the laziness associated with seeing the *He* instruments;[16] to promote a change of skin; to encourage growth and to make young men brave, fierce and aggressive.

Growth

The act of whipping during Fruit House and *He* House makes the initiates grow. The whips are first blown on by the shamans to impart power; this blowing is called putting in protective power through shamanism (*basere kunisāra*) and this power is then transferred in the act of whipping.[17] In the past, young boys were held by the hands and feet and then whipped in a horizontal position at the same time as being quite literally stretched.[18] This same stretching was also done to the initiates over the smoke of a fire at the end of *He* House. Small children may also be whipped to promote their growth.

At the age when boys first take part in Fruit House they are considered to be undergoing a period of growth and increasing maturity. This theme of growth is emphasised in the ritual of Fruit House. When asked the purpose of this rite, the Barasana reply that it is to make the fruit grow and mature so that it ripens in abundance. They say that they are giving life to the fruit (*katise isingu̶*) and that

ants during rites of first menstruation. The ordeal of stinging ants is known also to the Cubeo but they deny that it is connected with Yurupary rites (Goldman 1963 : 201).
16 Among the Saliva, to the north of the Vaupés, young men were whipped prior to the communal clearing of the forest. The whipping was to take away their laziness and to make them work hard (Gumilla 1963 : 160).
17 Among the Cubeo, whipping is also said to promote growth. There, the whips are first inserted into the far end of a Yurupary instrument and stirred round to draw power from it. The instrument is then rolled down the backs of the young boys (Goldman 1963 : 198). This is not done among the Barasana.
18 This stretching in connection with whipping is also reported for both the Tukano (Brüzzi da Silva 1962 : 356) and for the Cubeo (Goldman 1963 : 201).

if the rite were not done there would be no fruit (see M.2.F.17).[19] When the long flutes are played with their ends in the air during the rite this action is called encouraging or having the fruit. During *He* House, this same action promotes aggression and fierceness. The noise of the trumpets blown over the fruit at Fruit House says 'Have lots of fruit.'

The Tatuyo myth of Tree-Fruit Jaguar (M.2.F) also stresses the theme of growth and maturity. The fruits that are hung in the house and on the bodies of the participants (M.2.F.5, 6) are people (M.2. F.10) and the dance makes these fruit people ripen. The fruit are made to ripen by the magical act of changing their souls (*usu wasoase*) (M.2.F.7, 17), done by the shamans. Human beings also have their souls changed at birth and initiation; in each case the change causes a change from one state to another: pre-human soul to human baby at birth, from child to young man at initiation and from unripe fruit to ripe fruit at Fruit House. This change of soul is done by whipping.[20] Informants explicitly compare the fruit people of M.2.F.7 to the initiates at Fruit House, and the fruit leaving the house at the end of the rite (M.2.F.10) in a changed state is compared to the initiates who leave the house after Fruit House. The change of state of the fruit involves the application of body paint (M.2.F.10), just as at Fruit House, and even more so at *He* House, the change of state of the initiates is reflected in the application of paint. In each case this change of state is a change of skin. Finally, the fruit people of M.2.F are considered to be in a vulnerable state after their 'initiation' and must be protected by shamanism (M.2.F.9), just as the initiates after Fruit House and *He* House must be similarly protected.

From the above, it can be seen that young boys at initiation and

19 The Indians of the Atabapo/Inirida area, north of the Vaupés, used to sound baked-earth trumpets, called *botuto*, under palm trees to ensure an abundance of fruit (Humboldt and Bonpland 1966 : 273). The Cubeo also associate Yurupary rituals with the harvest of fruits and berries (Goldman 1963 : 192).

20 In M.2.F, after he is born Tree-Fruit Jaguar refuses to stop crying until his soul is changed by beating the walls of the house with sticks (M.2.F.4). According to Lévi-Strauss, the character of the 'crying baby' represents a baby 'who has (either) been abandoned by his mother, or has been born posthumously ... or he may consider he has been unjustly abandoned, even though he has reached an age at which a normal child no longer demands constant parental care'. He is 'the anti-social hero (in the sense that he refuses to become socialized) who remains obstinately attached to nature and the feminine world' (1973 : 378–81).

　　If this is so, Tree Fruit Jaguar could be said to represent the unwilling initiate who cries too much (compare also M.4.D.20 where *Warimi*, like Tree-Fruit Jaguar, removed from his mother by force, refuses to stop crying).

tree-fruit can be identified with one another. Fruit House promotes the growth of both fruit and young initiates.[21]

Aggression

Whipping not only encourages growth; it also imparts strength. It makes the body hard and strong and makes the initiates fierce and angry. It is for this reason that whipping is always followed by a display of aggression called acting-out spearing (*besuꝺ kesose*). As a generalisation, it can be said that whilst the growth aspect of whipping is emphasised during Fruit House, it is the aspect of aggression that is emphasised during *He* House. This stress on aggression and hardness is part of a much wider theme that permeates Barasana initiation. At initiation and especially at *He* House, the young boys become young men who are identified with warriors, marked by the qualities of hardness, wakefulness and fierceness, and after *He* House the initiates are systematically taught the arts of warfare. The eating of snuff and of coca from the wax gourd is also designed to impart the qualities of strength and fierceness and, like whipping, it is always followed by the action of acting-out spearing. Likewise, the burning of wax also imparts these qualities and is again followed by acting-out spearing. It seems then that for women, menstrual blood connotes fertility whilst for men it connotes aggression.

This cult of aggression is in particular associated with the use of the trumpet Old Star (the 'fierce *He*'), the sight of which is said to turn men into fierce animals.

According to the Barasana, each different variety of yagé vine came originally from the inside of a separate *He* instrument. Yagé vines are called vine from inside the *He* (*He guda hubea ma*) and they are compared to bone marrow (the *He* being bones). A variety of yagé called fierce yagé vine (*guari kahi ma*) came from inside the trumpet Old Star and it is this variety, mixed with yagé vine for seeing *He* (*He ĩaria ma*) that is consumed during *He* House. This yagé makes men fierce and aggressive and its consumption is followed by acting-out spearing.[22]

---

21 Goldman has come to much the same conclusion with regard to the Cubeo (Goldman 1963 : 194).
22 The Barasana say that in the past, people used to fight together when under the influence of yagé. Koch-Grünberg also notes that the use of yagé is related to a warrior cult and that its ingestion makes men brave (1909/10, vol. I : 352). See also MacCreagh (1927 : 373ff).

The action of acting-out spearing is also done at lunar eclipses and when the moon 'dies' and turns red (see M.3.14). It is done on this occasion to steal fierce magic (*guari*) from a spirit (*wãti*) identified with the moon. Occasionally the same action is also done outside of the context of ritual, when the men run up and down the house early in the morning. In this context the action is called hitting *Uma* spirit. There are strong grounds for identifying *Uma* spirit with the Moon for, like the Moon, he loses his feather crown when he comes to earth (see M.3.8—9).

Tobacco

Tobacco is considered to be a ritual 'non-food'. It is also the food of spirits and of the *He* People and it is for this reason that tobacco snuff is blown into the *He* instruments. The participants at *He* House and Fruit House become *He* People, spirit people, and as such they are given coca and tobacco to eat. Tobacco is also believed to establish communication with the supernatural and both snuff and tobacco smoke are said to have power; when blowing spells into the magical substances consumed at *He* rites, the shamans blow out puffs of tobacco smoke. Breath is seen as a manifestation of the soul and tobacco smoke is said to make the soul live.

During *He* rituals, a sacred gourd, similar in appearance to the wax gourd but containing tobacco snuff rather than wax, is used. The two gourds are kept together at all times and both are always used together. On the eve of *He* rites wax is burned outside the house next to the *He* instruments and, soon after this, tobacco snuff, taken from the tobacco gourd, is blown up the noses of the participants by the officiating shaman. The significance of this has already been discussed above. Again, at the climax of *He* rituals, after the burning of wax, the tobacco and wax gourds are placed in the middle of the house. Coca is eaten from the wax gourd and snuff from the tobacco gourd is wiped on the legs of the participants. (At Fruit House this snuff may also be eaten but at *He* House it is considered to be too powerful and dangerous to eat.)

It is clear that the wax gourd and the tobacco gourd form a pair. This can be seen from the above and it can also be seen from the myths: the wax gourd is the bottom half of Manioc-stick Anaconda's skull and contains wax identified with his liver (and tongue). The tobacco gourd is the top half of Manioc-stick Anaconda's skull and contains snuff identified with his brain (see M.6.A.64). In chapter 7, I showed that the wax gourd was identified with a vagina and beeswax with menstrual blood. According to M.6.A.64, the ceremonial cigar used at *He* House is identified with Manioc-stick Anaconda's penis and the little gourds that contain snuff with his testicles. This would suggest that the snuff that the gourds contain, like the tobacco contained in a cigar, is identified with sperm. This is confirmed by the fact that the word for brain (= snuff) is the same as that for seminal fluid.[23] Thus we have:

Tobacco gourd	*Werea gourd*
top of skull (high)	bottom of skull (low)
snuff	beeswax
brain	liver
sperm	menstrual blood
cigar	wax gourd
penis	vagina

If this analysis is correct then I think that it can be said that the ritual conjunction of a cigar with the wax gourd can be seen as symbolising sexual intercourse and that the conjunction of tobacco snuff (seminal fluid) with wax (menstrual blood from which, according to the Barasana, babies are made) symbolises fertilisation.[24] The same can be said for the conjunction, during the burning of wax, of the *He* instruments with the wax gourd; I have already argued that the *He* instruments can be seen as penises and the wax gourd as a vagina. Finally it can be added that the ritual cigars are constructed on the same principle as the *He* trumpets. The only direct evidence for saying that *He* House symbolises sexual intercourse comes from a statement from an informant that during this rite the men pretend to create children, the children being represented by the wax in the wax gourd.

If *He* rites can be seen as symbolic fertilisation at a physiological level, the same can be said at a cosmological level. Tobacco snuff

23 Further evidence for the association between cigars and penises comes from the fact that, in Barasana mythology, both are equated with fish. (See e.g. M.7.B.9.)
24 M.8.2–3 further suggests that tobacco smoke represents sperm, for it was smoke from a cigar placed between *Coadidop*'s legs that gave rise to the first men. *Coadidop* (identifiable with *Romi Kumu*) used her legs to make a cigar holder. Such cigar holders, made from carved red hardwood, were till very recently used by the Barasana during *He* rites and other dances. These holders (see Koch-Grünberg, 1909/10, vol. I : 282 for photographs) are stylised representations of men and when inverted with a cigar in place, they represent a man with an erect penis.

represents celestial and destructive fire (obtained from the sun and used to burn people to death, a burning equated with the burning of a manioc garden – see M.6.A, B): this fire comes from the mouth of the Sun – a man. Beeswax represents terrestrial and creative fire used for cooking and comes from the vagina of *Romi Kumu*, a woman. Beeswax also represents celestial water (the rain = *Romi Kumu*'s menstrual blood) whilst tobacco is on the side of terrestrial water (the original cigar, the origin of tobacco, was a fish – M.7.G.1–3), and during *He* rites tobacco applied to the body makes it safe for the participants to bathe. Thus we have:

Tobacco	*Beeswax*
celestial fire	terrestrial fire
(destructive)	(creative)
sun	sky (*Romi Kumu*)
man	woman
mouth	vagina
terrestrial water	celestial water

This can be interpreted at different levels: at the highest level, the conjunction between the sun and the sky is seen as the root-source of all creation, for the union between *Yeba Hakʉ*, the Primal Sun and *Romi Kumu*, the sky, gave rise to all things. The union between the sun and the sky, between fire and water, also represents the totality of seasonal continuity, the alternation between the dry and rainy seasons and *He* House, when the tobacco and wax gourds are used, is held at the conjunction of these two seasons. The destruction and burning of forest, a male activity done during the dry season, is a necessary preliminary for the planting of manioc, a female activity, done during the rainy season for manioc requires rain to grow. Thus, manioc is produced by the union of men and women, by the union of the dry and rainy seasons and by the conjunction of destructive, celestial fire and fertilising, celestial rain. This argument makes sense of the fact that Barasana myths accredit the origin of manioc to both a man, Manioc-stick Anaconda, and a woman, *Yawira*, and that, in the first instance, it is produced as the result of fire whilst in the second it comes from water (see M.6.B and M.7.C).

Finally, I think that it can be argued that terrestrial water associated with men is destructive (for in Barasana myths it is floods not rain that destroy) whilst the celestial water associated with women

Open and closed: the howler monkey and the sloth

is creative (for it is rain that makes manioc grow). Together with the two kinds of fire, this puts men on the side of destruction and women on the side of creation. I have argued already that this theme dominates *He* rites and their associated mythology.

9

Death and rebirth

High and low: myth and rite in time and space

In daily life, Barasana men go to great pains to avoid sitting on the ground. According to them, to sit raised up is to sit well; only women and children sit on the ground. To sleep on the ground is considered even more extreme, for only animals and Makú are said to do this. During *He* House, the initiates and younger men must sit on mats on the ground and on the last night they also sleep there. The shamans and elders sit on stools and on the last night they sleep in hammocks. After *He* House, the initiates can sleep in hammocks but a more general taboo on being raised above the ground applies throughout the marginal period.

At one level of analysis it can be said that by being made to sleep on the ground, the initiates are being identified with women and children on the side of nature; in Barasana society, there is a fairly consistent association of men and things that are relatively higher than things associated with women. The low position of the initiates is contrasted to that of the elders and their gradual raising up reflects their passage from the world of women to the world of men, from nature to culture. At the end of the marginal period, the initiates become people who sit on stools i.e. adult men.

At another level, the symbolic use of vertical space during *He* House can be analysed in terms of death and rebirth. The Barasana bury their dead in canoes in the floor of the longhouse.[1] The fact that both dead people and initiates are placed in extreme low positions suggests that the two are identified. In chapter 7, I argued that

---

1 In practice it is only the adult men who are buried in canoes though, in theory, all people should be so buried. Women are sometimes buried in the large canoe-like troughs that are used to contain beer.

214

when the *He* instruments are taken from the river on to land, a passage from low to high, they become active and alive and that this change causes a corresponding but reversed change for the human participants who become dead. For the initiates, this change is also associated with a passage from high to low.

Other things also confirm that the initiates are symbolically dead: the application of black paint is said to cause the body to rot and according to one informant, 'The paint reminds us that one day we too will die.' When *Meneriyo* put this paint on her brother, the Moon, his body rotted and he died (see M.4.A); at *He* House the initiates are covered in this paint. The extinction of fire and the taboo on contact with sources of heat during and after *He* House also indicate death: the Underworld River is said to be very cold and is opposed to the warmth of this world; the *He* instruments are also very cold. The Barasana say that a hot, sweaty body indicates life and vigour; a cold one indicates death.[2] The effects of yagé are also compared to death and when the initiates take the strong yagé used at *He* House they are said to cease to live. Finally, I have already argued that, by having snuff (= fire) blown up their noses, the initiates are burned to death in the same way that Macaw was killed by Manioc-stick Anaconda (M.6.A).

Once symbolically dead, the initiates become identified with unborn children. They sit throughout *He* House with their knees drawn up to their chests and their arms clasped round them – a foetal position. Immediately after being brought into the house, the initiates are given *kana* fruit, blown over by the shaman, to eat. *Kana* (*Sabicea amazonensis*) is a small vine that grows wild round human habitations. It bears small pink fruit with a sweet taste which grow singly along its length. Each fruit is a heart and the vine with fruit is compared to a series of hearts on a string. The hearts are those of each generation, connected together by an umbilical cord, the vine. This cord is said to extend out from the house to the port and then down the river to the east, the people's waking-up house where the sun comes from, the source of all humanity. By eating this fruit, the initiates become connected to the ancestral source of life by an umbilical cord, the river. The fruit in the shamans' gourd is compared to the heart in

---

2 This belief presents a paradox in Barasana ideology: men, especially young men, are ideally supposed to remain as cold as possible. Hardness, fierceness, strength and coldness all go together. But coldness also connotes sterility and death and is opposed to warmth and life. This relates to the discussion of creation and aggression, hard and soft and open and closed in ch. 8.

the space surrounding it; by blowing spells on the fruit, the shaman changes the heart or soul (*usu-wasoase*) of the initiate. *Kana* blown by shamans is also given to new-born babies and much of the shamanism treatment of mother's milk centres on this fruit.

In chapter 7 it was stated that the yagé given to the initiates is compared to mother's milk which suckles the new-born initiates. Like *kana* (the leaves of which are often used as an ingredient of yagé), yagé itself is compared to an umbilical cord that links human beings to the people's waking-up house and to the mythical past. Yagé is grown from cuttings and is thus thought to be one continuous vine which stretches back to the beginning of time. The common stock of all yagé vines is situated in the east. Yagé came from the east in the form of an anaconda which swam upriver. When people take yagé during *He* House this anaconda enters their bodies and establishes an umbilical connection with the past. The vomit that yagé produces is compared to the flickering tongue of the anaconda; it is also compared to a *kana* vine and the vomit on the ground is likened to a *kana* plant. Finally, the umbilicus itself is compared to the scars on the yagé vines left when yagé is cut for consumption at *He* House.

If death involves a passage from high to low then birth should involve the opposite. Certainly, in the myths of origin of humanity, this is so for the ancestral anaconda vomits the first people from the river up on to dry land. The people vomited forth were his children and it was at this point that they became fully human. This ancestral journey is repeated each time a child is born: the dead are buried in canoes (i.e. into the river); the Underworld River runs below the floor of the house, itself symbolically equated with the universe. The souls of the dead are believed to go either directly to the people's waking-up house in the east, or down the Underworld River and thence to the east. The souls of the dead return upriver from the east to be reincarnated as human babies. I think that the Barasana origin myth can be interpreted at one level as symbolising sexual intercourse; the anaconda vomiting out its children is like the ejaculation of sperm and it is significant that *ria*, children, also means sperm and is closely related to *riaga*, river.

Women give birth in the manioc gardens and then bring their babies to the house, entering through a hole in the wall near the women's door. This unusual entry may perhaps indicate the non-human status of the baby. Before they enter, all household goods are taken on to the plaza and all fires are extinguished. After entry, beeswax is burned round the house. After five days in the family compartment, the husband, wife and child go to the women's port to bathe and vomit. They are then covered in red paint and return to the house, entering through the women's door; in this sense, the baby is brought from the river. Before they enter, all goods are again placed out on the plaza and after their entry, beeswax is once again burned round the house.

At the end of *He* House, the initiates are taken down to the men's port at the front of the house. There, they and all the other men are made to vomit. This vomiting can I think, be interpreted as a symbolic act of birth.[3] One aspect of the Barasana interest in snakes centres on the fact that these creatures swallow their prey whole, a laborious act which one informant compared to birth backwards. Snakes can also regurgitate their prey, still whole, and it is presumably from here that the idea of ancestral anacondas vomiting up humans derives. According to M.5.A, *He* Anaconda ate up newly initiated boys and then vomited them out again as bones identified with *He* instruments. This myth is a close variant of M.8.37–51 but this latter myth adds one very significant detail: Yurupary ordered a painted enclosure/compartment to be built, into which he vomited out the bones. This compartment is clearly the same as that in which initiated boys are confined after *He* House. In myth, already initiated (and therefore adult) boys are swallowed (killed) and then regurgitated in a changed state (reborn) as bones or *He* instruments. In real life, uninitiated boys (children and the side of nature and women) are symbolically regurgitated as adults. In the first case the passage is from the fully human state to the *He* state; in the second, a passage from a human state on the side of nature and women to a fully human state.

In the last chapter it was stated that the name Yurupary has been translated as 'to hold one's hand over one's mouth', which relates to Yurupary's initial state of having no mouth. Another possible translation, favoured by Stradelli, is 'mouth in the form of a fish trap or barrage (*iuru* = mouth, *-pari* = fish trap/barrage)' (Stradelli 1928/9 :

3 The consumption of yagé can also be interpreted in this light. According to a Tatuyo myth, the ancestral anaconda stopped at a house called Yagé Mother's House, a place on the lower Vaupés. There, while the men danced and drank beer in the house, a woman gave birth to a child at the port. The labour pains of the woman made the men in the house feel the same effects as they now feel when they drink yagé. The child was yagé and it is the body of this child that the men now drink (see also M.8.25–6 and Reichel-Dolmatoff 1971 : 93–6, 1975 : 134–6).

498). The word *pari*, in Lingua Geral, not only means fish trap
but also enclosure/compartment, specifically compartments to
isolate menstruating women and initiate boys. Not only this: these
compartments are often actually made from such fish traps which
consist of splints of paxiuba palm woven together with vine into a
screen (see e.g. M.6.A.44). If my analysis of swallowing and regurgitation is correct, then 'compartment mouth' would be an apt name
for *He* Anaconda of M.5, who swallows initiated boys into a mouth
like a hollow log (or cave in other versions) and then vomits them
up into a compartment. The shamans at *He* House are identified with
Manioc-stick Anaconda, himself identified with both *He* Anaconda
and Yurupary; like Yurupary and *He* Anaconda, the shamans are
characterised at a symbolic level by having excessively wide-open
mouths. I would suggest that, by confining the initiates in compartments, the shamans symbolically 'swallow' the initiates and
then regurgitate them as adult men. It is above all the shamans who
must vomit at *He* House and it is they who go down to the port and
vomit with the initiates after the rite. M.5.A.19 states that the loud
voice (= *He* instruments) and open mouths of howler monkeys
(≡ shamans) should be used to open the *He* People's doors to make
men. The shamans are *He* People *par excellence*.

Immediately after the bathing and vomiting at the port, the
initiates are taken back to the house. Before they enter, all household goods are taken out on to the plaza. This sequence of events is
the same as that which takes place when a new-born baby is brought
to the house. Soon after this, the initiates are confined in a compartment, just as, soon after its birth, a baby is confined in a compartment together with its parents.[4] Immediately after the initiates
come from the river to the house (low to high), the *He* instruments
are taken back to the river and placed under water (high to low).
If when the *He* are taken from the river, the initiates die, then when
they are returned to the river, the initiates are reborn.

At the end of the marginal period, comparable to the five-day
period of confinement following birth, the initiates are taken back to
the river to bathe. They then return to the house and are painted all

---

4 At the *He House* that I observed, the *He* were taken back to the river at the end of the
rite. According to some informants, the *He* should have remained in the initiates' compartment for five days after the end of the rite. Considering the fact that the *He* are
said to adopt (*maso-*) the initiates, this makes the resemblance between the initiates
confined in their compartment and the baby confined with its parents even more striking,
for parents also *maso-*(adopt, make human, bring up) their new-born children.

over with red paint at the rite of taking a *henyerio*, just as a baby is painted red at the end of its period of confinement. The red paint is opposed to the black paint applied at the beginning of *He* House; black paint symbolises death; red paint symbolises life. The application of red paint is called *mamongu*, making new, and the paint itself expresses the newness of the initiates, now in the category *mamarã*, the new ones, young men. Black paint has connotations of separation (it is used to ward off spirits and was used in myth to send the moon away – see M.4.A); red paint has connotations of conjunction and social life and is used in particular at dances.

It was argued above that *He* House can be interpreted in terms of a symbolic death and rebirth and that the use of vertical space is crucial to this interpretation. I shall now show that the story of Manioc-stick Anaconda (M.6.A), given to me as an explanation of what happens at *He* House, can also be interpreted in this light. Manioc-stick Anaconda was the child of the Sun and the sky; he therefore comes from the highest of the three layers of the Barasana cosmos. At the start of *He* House, the initiates are carried into the house on the shoulders of the elders, also an extreme high position. Manioc-stick Anaconda falls to the Underworld through a pitfall trap; this fall is a kind of death, the trap being homologous with a grave. He is now in an extreme low position comparable to the initiates sitting on the ground during *He* House. The agent of Manioc-stick Anaconda's death is Macaw, a shaman tapir; the agents of the initiates' 'death' are also shaman tapirs. Manioc-stick Anaconda lands on top of an ingá tree, a mediator between cosmic levels. The ingá tree is also a mediator between seasons, fruiting at the start and end of each dry season; *He* House is held at the end of the dry season when ingá are ripe.

Once in the Underworld, Manioc-stick Anaconda travels upstream along the river; he therefore starts off in the west for this river runs from east to west; the initiates also start off in the west for they come from the women's end of the house.[5] Whilst in the Underworld, Manioc-stick Anaconda reveals his true identity to a kind of duck (*rĩa kumua*) by his inability to control his farts; according to Lévi-Strauss (1973 : 208–9), such characters are moving away from

5 The house represents the universe. The men's door is the east and the women's door is the west. The *He* are anacondas and they come from the east (and also from the river). They move towards the middle of the house; the middle of the house is the middle of the world, namely the Pirá-paraná region.

219

childhood too far or too abruptly; this suggests that Manioc-stick Anaconda is like an initiate. Manioc-stick Anaconda then meets the Sun, the possessor of shamanic snuff, who carries him through space and time to the top of the Underworld River. Barasana shamans are identified with the sun; both wear feather crowns and during *He* House the shamans are said to travel along the central beam of the house from east to west; this beam is the sun's path through the sky, the house being symbolically identified with the universe. The shamans effect a passage of the initiates from the women's world (west) to the men's world (east) and during this process they 'burn' the initiates with snuff just as the Sun burns Manioc-stick Anaconda in the Underworld. By refusing to eat the Sun's fish, Manioc-stick Anaconda behaves like an initiate, for these are the fish that the initiates must avoid at all costs.

At the top of the Underworld River (the east), Manioc-stick Anaconda meets another Tapir shaman who ferries him across a river; this passage across the river is a symbolic birth and during it, the Tapir shaman teaches birth shamanism and shamanism for mother's milk to Manioc-stick Anaconda. At the end of *He* House, the shamans (= tapirs) may symbolically give birth to the initiates. Manioc-stick Anaconda's passage across the river takes place immediately after he has moved from the Underworld to the Termite People's layer. This passage from low to high places him midway between earth and Underworld. At initiation, symbolic rebirth also involves a passage from low to high and, at this point in time, the initiates are also in an intermediary position, for after the bathe at the port at the end of *He* House, stools and hammocks are made safe to sit on but a general taboo on being raised above ground still applies.

Manioc-stick Anaconda then takes part in a dance, explicitly compared to an initiation at the end of which termites (also compared to initiates) leave the house. They have their souls changed by a shaman Tapir and are now termites that fly. Like initiates after *He* House, these termites are prone to attacks from jaguars. During this dance, the termites' initiation, Manioc-stick Anaconda refuses to have sexual intercourse with the shaman Tapir's wife: initiates too must not have sexual intercourse. Manioc-stick Anaconda finally leaves the termites' house, a passage from low to high; he leaves not through the door but through a hole in the side wall of the house, the same hole through which a new-born baby first enters the house.

He is met by young initiates, his children, out collecting termites, the food appropriate to their status. They take him back to the house where he enters through the men's door, the east − his passage from west to east now complete − and goes immediately to a compartment constructed just inside the men's door. At the end of *He* House, the initiates enter the house through the men's door and are then confined in a compartment constructed just inside.

I think therefore that it can be said that Manioc-stick Anaconda is identifiable with an initiate and that the structure of M.6.A.1−46, in terms of events occurring through space and time, parallels closely that of *He* House from its start to the beginning of the marginal period.

I have argued above that, in Barasana thought, a low position in space has connotations of immaturity, of relative youth and of an early stage in development. The passage from childhood to adulthood is seen as a passage from low to high. Consistent with this, the initiates are called people of another layer or level (*gahe tutiana*). They are this partly because they represent the next generation and generations pile one on top of the other like leaves and partly because, in symbolic terms, they come from another level of the cosmos, the river.

This passage from low to high is reflected in the food taboos that apply after *He* House. The first food that the initiates can eat consists of termites (*meka*), sauba ants (*mekahia*) and cassava bread, made only of starch − all things that come from markedly low positions in space. Ants and termites are very small creatures which are said to lack blood. In myth, termites, who live in holes in the ground, are presented as mediators between this world and the world below (see M.6.A.25−42) and as such they are entirely appropriate as food for reborn initiates. The order in which food is blown over for the initiates corresponds more or less exactly to the order in which it is blown over for a child but whereas for initiates this blowing occurs within the space of a few months, for a child it takes place over a number of years. The first food that a baby eats is its mother's milk; immediately after *He* House the initiates eat a variety of termites called *õhea*, breasts. The termites whose dance Manioc-stick Anaconda attends in M.6.A are *õhea*.

During the marginal period, the only animal food that the initiates eat consists of small insects, lacking blood, most of which live underground. After the blowing of pepper, they first eat the smallest kind of fish and then move on to progressively larger species culminating in the category large fish. Then they eat the smallest game animals, progressing on to larger species and culminating with tapir, the largest animal in the forest. From this it can be seen that the animal foods go in a progression from small to large, from low to high and from animals with no blood at all to those with progressively larger amounts. Adults are people who have progressed from low to high, small to large; the fact that game animals are called old/mature fish (*wai bukurã*) suggests a similar progression in the animal world. According to informants, in the recent past the Barasana did not eat very large animals like deer and tapir because these were considered to be the semi-human souls of the dead.

Fruit

I have argued above that *He* House can be interpreted as a rite in which the adult men symbolically give birth to the initiates. This idea was expressed by one informant who, after the rite of *He* House, said to me, 'the wax in the wax gourd is children in a womb. These children were created by the Sun. The men make as if they too create children but it's like a lie.' I think that this idea of adult men giving birth to the initiates can perhaps be related to the use of fruit at Fruit House. I must emphasise that my argument is tentative and requires a much more extended analysis than I can give here.

In shamanic language, women, as cultivators of manioc, are called food mothers and the manioc tubers that they produce are compared to their children. Women give birth to human children in the manioc gardens and bring them into the house through the women's door; they also bring tubers of manioc in through this same door. At Fruit House, the men carry fruit into the house through the men's door and at *He* House men carry the initiates into the house through this same door. I have argued that in some respects at least, the initiates can be identified with the fruit. I stated above that, in Barasana thought, men are associated with the high and women with the low and it is significant in this respect that in M.7.C *Yawira*, a woman, brings manioc from the river to land (low to high) whilst in M.7.I *Yeba*, her husband, takes fruit from trees down underwater to give to Fish Anaconda, *Yawira*'s father. In view of the above, it may be that tree fruits can be considered to be the 'children of men' in the same way that manioc tubers are the 'children of women'.

According to M.2.A, the youngest of the *Ayawa* (Thunders) was conceived after his grandmother had eaten a caimo (*kanea, Chryso-phyllum caimito*) fruit which the other *Ayawa* had filled with their sperm. In this sense, *Kanea*, the youngest of the *Ayawa*, was named after his 'father'. This story is a close variant of that of the conception of Yurupary: here Yurupary's mother, the Pleiades, was fertilised by the juice of a fruit, either caimo or cucura (*Pourouma cecro-piaefolia*) — see e.g. M.8.14–18. This suggests, among other evidence, that *Kanea*, the youngest *Ayawa*, can be identified with Yurupary and that his mother (who is also his grandmother) can be identified with the Pleiades, the mother of Yurupary (who is also his grandmother — see M.8). *Meneriyo*, Ingá Woman, is also identified with the Pleiades and her son *Warimi* can be identified with Yurupary.

If *Warimi* is identified with Yurupary then we should expect to find that caimo fruit played a part in his conception too. According to M.4.B, *Warimi*'s father was ~~*Umuaka Widau*~~, Little Sticky Man. Stickiness is a marked characteristic of caimo trees and fruit: the husk of caimo fruit contains a sticky latex which makes it almost impossible to eat the fruit without having one's lips gummed together, and caimo trees and those of related species produce abundant sticky latex sometimes used to adulterate rubber and gutta percha. This suggests that Little Sticky Man may be identified with caimo; unfortunately I did not realise the possibility of this till after I had left the field so that I cannot check the idea. However, further evidence comes from M.4.A: in this myth, the Moon is presented as *Warimi*'s father; immediately after the Moon had slept with his sister *Memeriyo*, she was catapulted up into the sky by a caimo tree (M.4.A.9). Thus, in one variant of the myth, Little Sticky Man (= caimo?) pulls *Meneriyo* up into the sky and then sleeps with her whilst in the other, the Moon sleeps with *Meneriyo* and then causes a caimo tree to send her up into the sky. Moreover, M.4.C makes it clear that the Moon and Little Sticky Man are one and the same person.

If the above argument is correct, it can be concluded that caimo fruit is a male principle (sperm) and ingá fruit a female principle and that the conjunction of these two fruits is an act of fertilisation: *Meneriyo* is identified with ingá fruit and after conjunction with the Moon, identifiable with caimo, she gives birth to *Warimi*. Similarly, it is caimo that fertilised *Siusi* (Pleiades), the mother of Yurupary. Unfortunately I can find no direct evidence whatsoever to link

Siusi with ingá. The only evidence comes from association: *Siusi*
is the Pleiades, so is *Romi Kumu*; *Romi Kumu* is the sky, so is
Coadidop, the mother of Yurupary in M.8; *Romi Kumu* can be
linked with the Pleiades, again by association.

The story of *Warimi*'s conception and birth can now be fixed in
time, and through this related to *He* rites. Ingá trees have two fruiting
seasons, one at the end of the short dry season and one at the end of
the long dry season. Caimo fruits only at the end of the short dry
season. *Meneriyo*, identified with ingá, is also linked to the Pleiades;
at the end of the short dry season the Pleiades appear on the horizon
at dusk. *Meneriyo* must therefore have conceived *Warimi* at this
time. As the Pleiades climb into the sky, so also *Meneriyo* goes into
the sky either just before or just after fertilisation (see M.4).

Prior to giving birth to *Warimi*, *Meneriyo* comes down from the
sky just as, at the end of the long dry season, the time of the second
fruiting of ingá, the Pleiades are setting (coming down) on the western
horizon. *Meneriyo* lands on an ingá tree (M.4.B.4 and M.4.C.3) and
soon afterwards she is dismembered by the Thunder Jaguars at the
foot of another ingá tree. Through this dismemberment, *Warimi*
is 'born', a birth that can be directly related to that of Yurupary
whose mother was cut open by the Thunders (compare M.4.D.14–15
with M.8.19–24). The story of *Warimi*'s conception and birth can
thus be taken at one level to be an account of the movements of the
Pleiades across the skies.

The timing of *Warimi*'s conception and birth can in turn be
directly related to Barasana *He* rites. At the time when the Pleiades
are rising on the eastern horizon at dusk, the time when ingá and
caimo are ripe, Fruit House is held in preparation for *He* House.
During this rite, ingá fruit are ceremonially brought into the house.
At the end of the main dry season, when the Pleiades are setting at
dusk and when ingá is again ripe, Fruit House is held again, this
time as a preliminary to *He* House, and is immediately followed by
He House itself. The relation between the movements of the Pleiades,
the fruiting of ingá and the timing of *He* rites can be seen in fig. 3.

It is clear from the argument above that the fact that it is ingá
fruit that is ritually taken into the house, both at the Fruit House
that prepares for *He* House and at the Fruit House that immediately
precedes it, is of considerable significance. It is tempting to see the
preparatory rite as a symbolic conception of the inititiates which is
then followed by their birth at *He* House. Unfortunately, my data

on the preparatory Fruit House is totally inadequate, as it was not held at all during the period of my fieldwork and it was only after I had left the field that I realised its potential significance.

In chapter 7 it was argued that the conjunction of the wax gourd, a female principle, with tobacco and the *He* instruments, male principles, could be interpreted as a symbolic act of fertilisation. As items of ritual equipment that are taboo to women, these objects are owned and controlled by men so that it is as if the men were trying to carry out the act of fertilisation without the aid of the women. This is reflected in the myths of origin of the *He* instruments; in one, *Romi Kumu*, a virgin, gives birth to the *He* instruments as her children, the *He* People. In the other, Manioc-stick Anaconda's body, burned with fire, gives rise to the *He* instruments, his sons. Today the men control both *Romi Kumu* (the wax gourd) and also Manioc-stick Anaconda (the *He*). The children that are believed to result from the conjunction of tobacco and the *He* with *werea* are not new-born babies but reborn initiates who, as *He* People, are identified with the *He* instruments.

This argument can, I think, be applied to tree-fruits: in myth, the conjunction of caimo, a male principle, with ingá, a female principle, represents an act of fertilisation. Both these fruits are controlled by men and used in a ritual context at Fruit House. The mythical characters *Warimi* and Yurupary, who have these fruits as one or both 'parents', are not ordinary people but *He* People; the initiates too become *He* People. The myths describe how these characters grew up in a very short space of time. In this sense they are like initiates who, after their rebirth at initiation, grow quickly into adults. I argued above that *Kanea* (caimo) of M.2.A can be identified with Yurupary; in M.2.F, *Kanea* himself gives birth to Tree-Fruit Jaguar, the master of tree-fruits. This successful act of male childbearing is reflected in M.8.14—15 where the Thunders try unsuccessfully to give birth to Yurupary – *Kanea* is himself a Thunder (*Ayawa*). Both *Warimi* and Tree-Fruit Jaguar have caimo fruit as a father and both are alike in being babies who would not stop crying (see M.4.D.20 and M.2.F.4). According to Lévi-Strauss (1973 : 378—84), the character of the crying baby, in South American mythology, is one who has an excessive longing for conjunction with his family; at initiation, a boy's close ties with his nuclear family, and in particular with his mother, are severed.

The arguments given above are tentative and incomplete; to carry them further would require both more data and an extensive analysis of Barasana mythology. I have included them to indicate that the analyses of the significance of tree-fruits presented in earlier chapters are by no means exhaustive.

10

The Sun and the Moon

This chapter, like the latter half of the preceding one, is exploratory
in nature and is intended as a pointer towards a fuller analysis of
the relation between *He* House and Barasana cosmology. In it I shall
try to show that the two figures, the *He* spirits who appear at the
climax of *He* House, are the Sun and Moon.

In daily conversation, the Barasana use the same word, *muhihu*, to
refer to the sun and moon. Where necessary, the two are distinguished
by the prefixes *nyamiagʉ*, the night being, and *ʉmʉagʉ*, the day
being. These two are in turn distinguished from another being called
Yeba Hakʉ, the Primal Sun, the source of creation and life. *Yeba
Hakʉ* is also frequently referred to as *muhihu*; the sun and moon
that we see today are said either to be his two sons, or to be two
manifestations of him. According to M.3.1 the Moon is the elder
brother of the Sun. In the beginning, the Moon was effectively the
Sun for it was he who had the power of both heat and bright light.
He threatened to abuse these powers by drying up the wombs of
women. His younger brother objected on the grounds that if he did
so there would be no seasons and no water – a situation reminiscent
of that described in M.1.A.7 and M.2.B.1 where the sun burns the
world, and there is an absence of periodicity between night and
day and also between the wet and dry seasons. The Sun (younger
brother) therefore takes away the heat from the Moon and replaces
the bright light of day with the diminished light of moonlight.
These sources of light are compared to feather crowns (see M.3.1–6).

He Anaconda, from whose burned body the *He* instruments were
made, is himself likened to the Sun and the place in which he was
burned to death is called the Sun's garden; the *He* themselves are
called the Sun's bones. *Yeba Hakʉ*, the Primal Sun, is both the
Father of Day and also the Father of Night (appropriately enough as

227

he is father of the Sun and Moon — see above) and it was from him that *Ayawa* obtained night (see M.2.B). *He* Anaconda, linked to the sun, heat and burning by the mode of his death, a death compared explicitly to the burning of a manioc garden in summer (M.6.B), is also linked with rain and floods; the storm and rain that preceded his eating of the initiates (see M.5.A.3–4) is compared to the catastrophic first night which the *Ayawa* caused when they opened the container of night given to them by *Yeba haku* (see M.2.B). I suspect therefore that the sun to which *He* Anaconda is likened is the Primal Sun, *Yeba Haku*.

After *He* Anaconda's death, the palm which grew from his ashes was cut into pieces and made into the *He* instruments. The Tapir, a terrestrial animal on the side of water, took the *He* instrument from the top of the palm whilst the Howler Monkey, an arboreal animal on the side of fire, took the *He* instrument from the bottom of the palm. The Tapir threatened to abuse his instrument by killing children and preventing them from being born. This threat can be interpreted as a threat to disrupt a kind of periodicity or alternation between the spirit, *He*, world and the human world, for human children come from the spirit world and return there at death. The Howler Monkey objected to this on the grounds that the Tapir's instrument should be used for the opposite purpose, to facilitate the birth of children. The Howler Monkey then took the Tapir's *He* instrument and replaced it with his own (see M.5.A.18–23).

There is thus a formal correspondence between the story of the Sun and Moon who swap the properties of heat and light (see above) and of the Tapir and the Howler Monkey who swap *He* instruments. This correspondence is the more striking for two reasons: firstly because the Tapir is on the side of water whilst the Howler Monkey is on the side of fire. The Barasana say that the Moon is the father of water and that when he came down to earth it became very cold, and rain blotted out the sun (see M.3.5–16). The moon is thus on the side of water and the sun on the side of fire. Secondly, the Barasana associate the head or top with seniority and the tail or bottom with junior status. Thus, by taking the top of the palm, the Tapir starts off as senior (elder brother) to the Howler Monkey and after the swap of *He* instruments the relative status of the two is reversed.

Let us now consider the story of Manioc-stick Anaconda and Macaw (M.6.A). Manioc-stick Anaconda and Macaw are children of the Primal Sun *Yeba Haku*. This immediately suggests that they are

the Sun and Moon. The *He* instruments are the bones of Manioc-stick
Anaconda and Macaw, created when they were burned to death in
fires equated to burning manioc gardens. This is clearly a variant of
the story of the death of *He* Anaconda, but whereas in the *He* Anaconda story, the *He* come from one body, here they come from two.
This in turn suggests that Manioc-stick Anaconda and Macaw are two
manifestations of *He* Anaconda just as the Sun and Moon are two
manifestations of the Primal Sun. Hence it appears that *He* Anaconda
is indeed the Primal Sun.

Manioc-stick Anaconda is the elder brother of Macaw. Initially
Macaw is aggressive towards Manioc-stick Anaconda and effectively
dominant over him: Macaw takes Manioc-stick Anaconda's wife and
then symbolically kills him by sending him down to the Underworld.
In order to do this Macaw turns himself into a tapir (M.6.A.1—7).
Initially then, Macaw behaves like the threatening elder brother
at the start of the Sun and Moon story and also like the threatening
Tapir of the Tapir and Howler Monkey story. But whereas, in these
latter stories, the aggressor is an elder brother (or like one), in the
Manioc-stick Anaconda story the aggressor is a younger brother. At
the end of the story however, it is Manioc-stick Anaconda who is
dominant over Macaw: Macaw tries to maroon Manioc-stick Anaconda
in the macaw's nest (M.6.A.47—52) but is outwitted by his brother.
Then Macaw tries to drown Manioc-stick Anaconda in a fish trap
but again his brother outwits him and very nearly drowns Macaw
instead (M.6.A.52—4). Whereas, at the start of the story, Macaw is
in a relatively high position (on the land while Manioc-stick Anaconda
is in the Underworld), by the end the situation is reversed (Manioc-
stick Anaconda is high in the macaw's nest while Macaw is down
below him and then Manioc-stick Anaconda is on the earth while
Macaw is underwater). Finally, Manioc-stick Anaconda's patience is
tried to the limit and he kills his brother by burning him to death
(M.6.A.54—60). Thus by the end of the story, though the relative
seniority of the two remains the same, their relative dominance is
reversed.

The key to this reversal between Manioc-stick Anaconda and Macaw
lies in the former's encounter with the Sun in the Underworld. There,
Manioc-stick Anaconda obtains the Sun's fire in the form of snuff
and it is with this that he ultimately kills his brother. The story of
Manioc-stick Anaconda's adventures in the Underworld (M.6.A.7—25)
is very clearly one of a set that is discussed in Lévi-Strauss's *Mytho-*

logiques III (1968: 109–60). Lévi-Strauss demonstrates convincingly that these stories, in which two (or more) characters travel by canoe, are stories about the sun and moon. If the Sun takes Manioc-stick Anaconda along with him in his canoe, it is reasonable then to suppose that Manioc-stick Anaconda can be identified with the Moon.

Initially, the Sun threatens to burn Manioc-stick Anaconda to death, but Manioc-stick Anaconda cools him down with shamanism (M.6.A.13): this suggests that Manioc-stick Anaconda, like the moon, is colder than the sun. The people in the Sun's canoe then tell Manioc-stick Anaconda to steal the Sun's snuff (fire) in order to avoid being burned to death (M.6.A.16). The Sun then tries to burn Manioc-stick Anaconda to death by blowing snuff at him, but fails. Then Manioc-stick Anaconda blows snuff at the Sun and hurts him so much that he tells Manioc-stick Anaconda to stop. While he tries to burn the Sun, he burns up his feather crown (M.6.A.20–4). Manioc-stick Anaconda (the Moon) therefore (1) diminishes the Sun's heat by cooling him down and by taking his fire (snuff) and (2) diminishes the Sun's luminosity by burning his feather crown. This is almost exactly what happens in the story given above in which the Sun and Moon change roles (see also M.3). It is appropriate that Manioc-stick Anaconda is described as being 'bright and shiny like the sun' (M.6.A.2). However, if Manioc-stick Anaconda becomes like the Sun, the Sun does not become totally like the Moon for later on he rises into the sky at dawn (M.6.A.24).

The relationship between the Sun and Manioc-stick Anaconda hinges on the meaning of the kinship term *hako makɨ*, mother's son. *Hako makɨ* (mother's son), *hako mako* (mother's daughter) and *hako rĩa* (mother's children) are kinship terms referring to ego's own generation. The Pirá-paraná groups have Dravidian-type kinship terminologies in which the terms in generations – 1, 0 and +1 are divided into those for members of ego's own patrilineal exogamous group and those for other like groups. The 'mother's children' terms are the only ones to occupy an ambiguous position here: people cannot marry their *hako rĩa* even though they may be affines of the correct generation. These terms are used reciprocally in three ways: (1) between individuals whose fathers are of different exogamous groups but who *either* share the same mother *or* have separate mothers belonging to the same exogamous group; (2) between men of different exogamous groups who are married to a pair of sisters or who are co-husbands to the same wife; (3) between strangers belonging to exogamous groups whose members do not usually interact. The implication here is that both are fellow Indians and that, indirectly, their respective groups are linked in marriage exchanges. These different usages may be represented diagrammatically as shown.

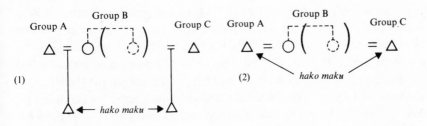

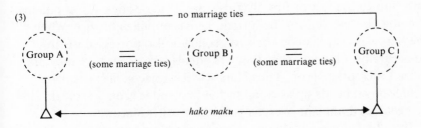

From these diagrams it can be seen that the term *hako maku* is used between those who, despite their being members of different groups, stand in the same relationship through marriage to a third group (usually represented by a single woman). It is the equivalence of his position to that of ego that makes a *hako maku* like a brother with whom women cannot be exchanged. But he also remains like an 'affine' in that he belongs to a different exogamous group from ego's own. Finally, it should be added that co-husbands to the same wife who belong to the same exogamous group are also seen as being *hako maku* to one another although they do not use this term between themselves.[1]

In M.6.A the Sun tells Manioc-stick Anaconda that if he really is his mother's son then he will be all right but that if he is not, he will be burned to death (M.6.A.20). Earlier Manioc-stick Anaconda

---

1 The principles of Barasana kinship classification, including the various uses of the term *hako maku* (mother's son) and their social implications, are dealt with in detail by Christine Hugh-Jones (1979).

231

argues that because he is the Sun's mother's son, the Sun's heat will not harm him (M.6.A.14). When the Sun sees that his heat does not harm Manioc-stick Anaconda and that instead Manioc-stick Anaconda can harm the Sun with his own heat, the Sun is convinced that they are related as mother's son (M.6.A.23). The implications of this are as follows: in Barasana kinship terminology there is no term for sibling of either sex which does not at the same time specify whether that sibling is senior or junior. Had Manioc-stick Anaconda called the Sun 'brother' he would automatically have had to say whether he was senior or junior to him. By claiming to be the Sun's mother's son he is claiming to be his equal: he is neither senior nor junior (brother) nor is he simply different (affine). Initially, however, his claim is false for in fact he is the Moon which means that he must be either senior or junior to the Sun. The Sun (rightly) doubts his claim and puts him to the test of fire. By this stage, Manioc-stick Anaconda has become like the Sun for, by a trick, he has obtained his fire. When the Sun sees that Manioc-stick Anaconda is also possessed of fire, he naturally concludes that they are equals and agrees that they are indeed each other's son. Thus Manioc-stick Anaconda starts off as the Moon and ends up as equal to the Sun and it is only after this that he becomes dominant over his younger brother Macaw.

If, as I have argued, Manioc-stick Anaconda starts off as the Moon, then Macaw should start off as the Sun. At the start of the myth, Macaw does indeed behave like the aggressive Sun at the start of M.3 and also like the aggressive Tapir of M.5.A. By the end of the myth the relative status of Manioc-stick Anaconda and Macaw is reversed just as that between the Sun and Moon and the Tapir and Howler Monkey is reversed. But if Macaw starts off as the Sun, then it should be Macaw, in the guise of the Sun, whom Manioc-stick Anaconda meets in the Underworld. This may at first sight seem absurd but it is in fact consistent with certain details of the story. If Manioc-stick Anaconda starts as the Moon and ends as the Sun, then Macaw should start as the Sun and end as the Moon; I have shown above that the Sun in the Underworld does in a sense end up as the Moon for he has both his heat and luminosity diminished by the actions of Manioc-stick Anaconda. Secondly, as effective co-husband to the same woman, Manioc-stick Anaconda and Macaw are indeed related to each other as mother's son.

I am aware that this argument raises almost as many problems as it solves but I do not propose to enter here into an extended discussion of the relative seniority of the different suns and moons of the Barasana cosmos. There are yet more myths concerning this problem which I have not presented here. If the reader feels confused his confusion is shared to some extent by the Barasana and their neighbours — the Barasana say that the Tatuyo are the children of the Moon whilst they are the children of the Sun. The Tatuyo dispute this and say that it is the other way round. Each side argues the case by manipulating the inherent ambiguities in the start of M.3 (see also above): in the initial situation, was the person who threatened to dry up the wombs of the women the Moon (his name was Moon) or was he the Sun (his qualities were those of the Sun)?[2]

In spite of the problems, I think that I have presented sufficient evidence to say that, as a pair, Manioc-stick Anaconda and Macaw are the Sun and Moon, also as a pair. The two *He* spirits that appear at the climax of *He* House represent Manioc-stick Anaconda and Macaw; if the arguments presented above are correct, they also represent the Sun and Moon. This would clarify certain details of what happens at *He* House. I have argued above that the two *He* spirits are homologous with the two characters, dressed in *Macacaraua* masks, who appear at the climax of Tariana Yurupary rites. If these two characters also represent the sun and moon, then it is entirely appropriate that the masks they wear should represent both howler monkeys and sloths, for howler monkeys, linked with fire and heat, are like the sun, whilst sloths, linked with rain and cold, are like the moon.

The *He* spirits are in particular linked with aspects of male aggression; when they appear, they play the long flutes with the ends raised in the air while the other participants act-out spearing; they teach the other participants to be aggressive. In chapter 8, I mentioned that acting-out spearing was also done at lunar eclipses when people try to steal fierce magic from the Moon. During lunar eclipses, the Moon is believed to come down to earth (see M.3); at *He* House too the Moon comes down to earth as a *He* spirit.

During *He* House, all contact with fire is prohibited, and after the rite, there is a general prohibition on contact with all sources of heat. After *He* House, the initiates must eat food which is either in a natural raw state (raw ants and termites, fruit, etc.) or which, though boiled,

2 See Lévi-Strauss (1967) for a discussion of the complexities involved in the analysis of 'Sun and Moon' myths.

has been allowed to become totally cold and has also been treated by the shamans to remove the harmful effects of the heat used in cooking. I have argued that the initiates are symbolically dead and also on the side of nature and it is entirely consistent with this that they should eat food which is either raw (on the side of nature) or that is as far removed from the cooking process as is possible. The end of the marginal period is marked by the initiates being made to chew smoked pepper and to drink boiling hot liquid. Clearly, the emphasis on contact with hot food and drink is opposed to the previous prohibition on contact with heat and it is significant that after the blowing of pepper, the initiates can not only once again eat hot food but can also once again have contact with sources of heat in general. The rite of the blowing of pepper is thus a rite of reintegration into normal social life and following it, the initiates can once again have contact with women.

Though the Barasana emphasise that contact with any source of heat is dangerous to the initiates, they place particular emphasis on the prohibition on contact of any kind with pepper. In chapter 8, I argued that tobacco snuff represents destructive, celestial fire and that this fire comes from the mouth. I showed that this fire is opposed to creative, terrestrial fire represented by beeswax and said that this fire came from the vagina. The fact that both wax smoke and pepper smoke are used to drive away malevolent spirits suggests that beeswax and capsicum pepper can be identified with one another. Like beeswax, pepper is also associated with the vagina for the Barasana jokingly refer to the vagina as a 'pepper pot' (*bia sotu*) a pot in which peppers are boiled up with scraps of fish — an example of this usage is found in M.6.A where the Tapir's wife asks him if he has been 'stirring her pepper pot', meaning, has he been making love to her? (see M.6.A.36). There is good evidence, then, to suppose that, just as tobacco is the cultivated, vegetable equivalent of celestial fire, so also is pepper the cultivated, vegetable equivalent of terrestrial cooking fire.

Everything indicates that during *He* House and the period afterwards the use of cooking fire is symbolically abolished, at least with regard to the male section of society. In an informant's description of *He* House it was stated that, at the start of the rite, all fires in the men's section of the house were extinguished. At the end of the rite, when the *He* were taken back to the river, the shamans blew spells over fire, after which old men rekindled fires in the men's section of the house. This did not happen at the rite I observed and I find it hard to reconcile this practice with the ceremonial burning of beeswax that takes place. However, the idea that cooking fire is symbolically extinguished is consistent with this statement.

In *Mythologiques* I (1970), Lévi-Strauss argues that cooking fire averts the threat of a total disjunction between the earth and sun, a situation he calls the 'rotten world'. Cooking fire also prevents the sun from approaching too close to the earth, a situation described as 'the burned world'. (The expression 'burned world' is also used to connote such things as the long day and the universal conflagration – see M.1.A.7 and M.2.B.1 and also M.5.A.11–12, M.6.A.59, M.6.B. 1–4 and M.8.59–62 where the burning of various Yurupary characters is likened to the burning of a manioc garden in summer and also to a universal conflagration. The expression 'rotten world' is also used to connote such things as the long night, catastrophic floods and solar and lunar eclipses – see M.1.A.3–6, M.2.B.7 and also M.3.1 where the Moon comes down to earth; when this happens there is a lunar eclipse and the moon causes rain to blot out the sun ≡ the long night.) Cooking fire thus mediates between the sun and earth, keeping it in a position which is neither too close nor too distant.

Lévi-Strauss argues that, in the myths he is discussing at this point, the acquisition of cooking fire demands a cautious attitude to noise. He states:

If the mediatory action of cooking fire between the sun (sky) and the earth demands silence, it is normal that noise should mark the reverse situation, whether it occurs in the literal sense (disjunction of the sun and earth) or figuratively (disjunction, as the result of a reprehensible union, of two people who were a potential married couple by virtue of their position within the normal marriage system): in one instance, the eclipse is greeted with a din; in the other, charivari is organised. However . . . the 'anticulinary' situation can occur in two ways. It is an absence of mediation between sky and earth, but this absence may be thought of as a lack (disjunction between the poles) or as a form of excess (conjunction). (1970 : 291–6)

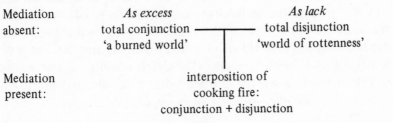

The situation of mediation requires silence, the situation of disjunction ('rotten world') requires noise and, he states, the situation of conjunction ('burned world') requires something half-way between silence and noise, either speech (profane) or chanting (sacred). I shall represent this as follows:

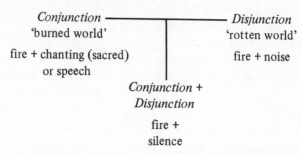

According to this scheme, *He* House appears to be a somewhat hybrid situation: cooking fire is abolished (i.e. mediation is absent), the *He* instruments make a deafening noise, normal speech is strongly discouraged but periods of chanting (the sacred alternative to speech) comes between the periods when the *He* are played. This hybrid situation is consistent with the fact that during *He* House the Sun and Moon come down to earth and appear as the *He* spirits. The 'burned world' is real enough, for if the initiates should expose themselves to the sun during the rite, they would be burned to death as Manioc-stick Anaconda burned up his brother Macaw with the Sun's fire. I have stated above that when the Moon comes to earth (eclipse) this threatens the long night, the 'rotten world'.[3]

In *Mythologiques* II Lévi-Strauss shows that the use of the instruments of darkness is associated with a period during which cooking is literally or symbolically abolished and during which direct contact is established between man and nature. This contact with nature is marked either by famine or by 'a lavish supply of substitute foods, such as wild fruits and honey, in a natural instead of a cultural form'. The state of famine corresponds to the 'rotten world' and the abundance of fruit to the 'burned world' (1973 : 403–14). Again, all this seems to correspond to the arguments presented above, including the fact that after *He* House (a contact with nature) the diet is very much reduced (like a famine – the 'rotten world') but also consists of raw, natural foods (the 'burned world') –again a hybrid situation

3 It should be noted that the Barasana view an eclipse as a *conjunction* and not as a disjunction.

consistent with the one mentioned above. I have shown in chapter 7 that the wax gourd is an instrument of darkness; the instruments of darkness are used when cooking fire is abolished and the Sun comes down to earth — as it does at *He* House as a *He* spirit.

As part of his argument concerning bull-roarers and instruments of darkness, Lévi-Strauss states that myths of the origin of day or night describe either an initial situation of permanent day or one of permanent night. Myths with a 'diurnal preliminary' describe an initial situation, the 'long day', in which though both day and night exist, they are *disjoined* from one another. (For example, in M.2.B night exists only within a house, Night House.) The 'long night' which precedes the regular alternation of day and night is caused by what Lévi-Strauss calls a 'subsidiary act' of *conjunction* (e.g. in M.2.B, when the *Ayawa* open the pot containing night, this night invades the day and causes the 'long night' and only afterwards is a regular alternation between night and day established). Here then, is a *disjunction* (between night and day) that corresponds to the 'burned world' and a *conjunction* (between night and day) that corresponds to the 'rotten world' whereas, in the myths discussed in *Mythologiques* I (1970) it is a *conjunction* (between sun and earth) that corresponds to the 'burned world' and a *disjunction* (between sun and earth) that corresponds to the 'rotten world'. Lévi-Strauss explains this apparent reversal by saying that whilst the myths of the origin of cooking discussed in *Mythologiques* I concern the notion of absolute space (the position of the sun relative to the earth), myths about the origins of day or night concern the notion of relative time (1973 : 419–20).

In myths of absolute space, mediation consists of maintaining the sun (or sky) in the right place, neither too close nor too distant. In myths of relative time, mediation consists of establishing a regular alternation between day and night. He goes on to say, 'Consequently, according to whether the myth is thought of within the context of absolute space or relative time, the same signifieds (conjunction and disjunction) will call for opposite signifiers.' (The 'signifiers' are the 'rotten' and 'burned worlds'.)

Lévi-Strauss writes:

The bull-roarer and the instrument of darkness are the ritual signifiers of a disjunction and a conjunction, both non-mediatized, which, when transposed into a different tessitura, have as their conceptual signifiers the rotten world and the burned world. The fact that the same signifieds, insofar as they consist of relationships between objects, can, when these objects are not the same, admit of contrasting signifiers, does not mean that these contrasting signifiers have a signified/signifier relationship with each other. (1973 : 421)

By which, if I understand him correctly, he means that the bull-roarer and instruments of darkness do *not* signify the rotten and burned worlds, nor do the rotten and burned worlds signify the bull-roarer and instruments of darkness. Finally he concludes,

it follows from what has gone before that the bull-roarer and the instrument of darkness do not effect conjunction or disjunction pure and simple. We ought rather to say that the two instruments effect conjunction *with* the phenomena of conjunction and disjunction; they conjoin the social group or the world at large to the possibility of these relationships, the common feature of which is that they exclude mediation. (1973 : 423)

If I have followed this intricate argument correctly, it would appear that empirical evidence from the Barasana suggests the same conclusions regarding the significance of the *He* instruments and the beeswax gourd, the former being homologous with bull-roarers and the latter being an instrument of darkness.[4] I have stressed throughout that both the *He* instruments and the beeswax gourd are inherently ambiguous symbols which combine in themselves complementary but opposed attributes, and I have argued above that, insofar as both the Sun and Moon come down to earth at *He* House, it is a hybrid situation that combines both the rotten and burned worlds. Finally, Lévi-Strauss argues that if both bull-roarers and instruments of darkness are associated with an absence of mediation, there must be a third instrument that represents mediation (1973 : 423). This instrument, he says, is the gourd rattle. In chapter 2, I stated that each kind of Barasana dance festival has its own associated dances and accompanying musical instruments. After *He* rites, the instruments used are gourd rattles.

4 Limitations of space do not allow for a full demonstration of the homology between bull-roarers and sacred flutes and trumpets. To do so would involve a comparative study of both the rites in which these instruments are used and also of their associated mythology. Such a study should not be limited to lowland South America but should include material from other parts of the world, notably from Australasia where secret men's cults show striking similarities with those of the Amazon region. For the purposes of this discussion, the reader will find that Lévi-Strauss's arguments concerning bull-roarers apply also to the *He* and other Yurupary instruments (cf. Lévi-Strauss 1973 : 411–22).

PART IV

Conclusion

11

Conclusion

I shall divide my conclusion into two sections. In the first, I shall place the description and analysis of Barasana *He* rituals presented in this book within the wider context of knowledge concerning the Yurupary cult throughout the Vaupés region as a whole. In the second, I shall discuss some of the broader issues concerning the interpretation of myth and ritual which emerge from my study of the Barasana.

Comparative

Throughout this book I have tried, where possible, to relate my description and analysis of Barasana Yurupary rites and myths to those of other writers whose works refer to the different Tukanoan and Arawakan groups of the Vaupés–Içana region. I have done this for three reasons. First, because I am convinced that a proper understanding of the Indian societies of Northwest Amazonia will only come when the different socio-linguistic groups or 'tribes' are seen as forming an open-ended regional system that spreads across cultural and linguistic boundaries and when their cultural differences are seen as variations on a common theme. Secondly, as the basic details of Yurupary rites and myths are broadly similar for all the groups of the Vaupés–Içana region, it is clear that they should be treated as variations or transformations of one another. Thirdly, I believe that the only people who can make effective use of the valuable but fragmentary data relating to the now acculturated Vaupés Indian groups, contained in the reports of missionaries, travellers and ethnologists, are those who have first-hand knowledge of similar but more traditional groups within the same culture area. Thus, I hope that this work will be treated as being of relevance not only to the Barasana and their neighbours in particular, but also to the Northwest Amazon region more generally.

Amongst the Barasana and their neighbours, the rites and beliefs that focus on the sacred flutes and trumpets are, without question, the most important and fullest expression of their religious life, and there is ample evidence that the Yurupary cult is, or was, of similar importance throughout the Vaupés region. But any attempt to compare Barasana Yurupary rites with those from elsewhere in the Vaupés is immediately made difficult by a problem of scale: I have devoted a whole book to a topic treated by other writers in the space of a chapter at most, and very often in less. Although a large body of Yurupary myths have been recorded from a number of different Indian groups in the Vaupés—Içana region, descriptions of Yurupary rites from these and other groups are highly superficial. One of the aims of this book has been to show that unless Yurupary rites and myths are taken together as the unit of investigation, and unless analysis of the rites is based upon an accurate and detailed account of their organisation that pays attention not only to the more exotic and salient features (such as Yurupary instruments, ritual flagellation, sexual antagonism, hallucinogenic drugs, etc.), but also to less striking but no less significant features (such as difference in dress, categories of participant, positions in space, sequence through time, etc.), the significance of this cult will not be fully understood.

Considering the importance attached to it by Indians and ethnographers alike, at first sight it seems surprising that so little serious attention has been paid to the Yurupary cult. One possible explanation for this relates to the distinction between the Barasana rites of Fruit House and *He* House. With few exceptions, virtually all the accounts of Yurupary rites from the Vaupés region describe a ritual that corresponds to Fruit House and not to *He* House. The Barasana attach relatively much less importance to Fruit House than they do to *He* House; it is the latter rite that is considered to be really important and sacred. The importance of Fruit House comes partly from the fact that it is an attenuated version of *He* House and partly from the fact that it forms the preliminary stages of an extended process of initiation that culminates in *He* House.[1] If, in other parts

1 Some informants dismissed Fruit House rites as mere play and claimed that in the past, when 'men were really men', and when people lived more by their traditions, these rites were never held at all and that instead *He* House was held several times a year. Whilst I find this hard to believe, it does give some idea of the relative importance attached to the two rites.

of the Vaupés area, there are, or used to be, two different kinds of
Yurupary rite, corresponding to the two different Barasana rites,
then this would explain a great deal, for whilst it is relatively easy
to explain the significance of many of the features of Fruit House in
the light of *He* House, it would be much harder to work the other
way round.

There is some evidence for supposing that something equivalent to
He House did take place elsewhere in the Vaupés. Amorim (1926/8 :
52–5) describes Wanano initiation as having two stages marked by
different rites: as amongst the Barasana, it was only at the second
stage of initiation that young men were shown the more sacred
Yurupary instruments, and Amorim's account of this rite has important points in common with the Barasana *He* House. Though the
details are less clear, the division of initiation into two stages, one
more sacred than the other, appears to have been true of the Tariana
also (Coudreau 1887 : 198ff). Finally, in the context of initiation,
Brüzzi da Silva (1962 : 438) describes the ritual eating of chilli
peppers amongst the Tukano; for the Barasana, this act forms part of
the terminal rites after *He* House.

A second point, related to the question of whether there are, or
were, rites corresponding to *He* House in other parts of the Vaupés
concerns the use of beeswax and the beeswax gourd. In my analysis
of the rites, I have placed great emphasis on the significance of
beeswax, an emphasis that reflects the importance that the Barasana
attach to this substance themselves. Again, whilst I know that the
ritual use of beeswax is common to all the Indian groups of the
Pirá-paraná area, I cannot find any direct evidence for its use in
Yurupary rites elsewhere. The Barasana burn beeswax on a number
of occasions outside the context of Yurupary rites (see ch. 7) and it
is significant that many other authors mention the use of 'smoke from
burning embers', 'resin and embers', 'burning resin', 'fumigation', etc.,
in exactly these same contexts. Considering that the beeswax in
question (cerumen) is made largely from resin, these references suggest
that its ritual use may be more widespread than might at first be
supposed. Whether or not beeswax is, or was, also used in the context
of Yurupary rites I cannot say, but there is evidence from myth for
the existence of something like the beeswax gourd amongst the
Tukano (see ch. 7, nn. 22 and 30). Finally, it must be pointed out
that the ritual use of beeswax is easily overlooked, especially during
Fruit House rites, partly because it is less eye-catching than Yurupary

instruments and ritual whipping, and partly because it looks and smells very like the resin that is used to light the house.

A third point relates to the connection between Barasana Yurupary rites and menstruation, a connection which rests in part on an understanding of the significance of beeswax and the beeswax gourds. But, as I have indicated in my analysis, there is evidence for this association, independent of that of beeswax, from elsewhere in the Vaupés region. This is especially true in relation to the *Macacaraua* masks which incorporate into their fabric the hair cut from girls at rites of first menstruation, but it is also implied by the widespread myth of the theft of the Yurupary instruments by women. In spite of this, with the exception of Reichel-Dolmatoff, the connection between Yurupary rites and menstruation appears to have gone unnoticed by other writers. Reichel-Dolmatoff states merely that Tukano initiates are called 'menstruation people', are compared with girls, and are in danger of menstruating if they do not follow the requisites demanded of them (1975 : 86).

The last point to be made about my accounts of Barasana Yurupary rites in relation to those from elsewhere in the Vaupés concerns the question of their timing. I have stressed that the timing of *He* rites and especially of *He* House is of crucial significance and I have demonstrated that this timing is related both to the movements of constellations and to seasonal subsistence activities. Although there is good evidence that timing is an important feature of Yurupary rites elsewhere, it has received virtually no attention.

Having tried to indicate the main areas in which my description of Barasana Yurupary rites appears to differ from those from elsewhere in the Vaupés, I shall now briefly consider two other interpretations of the Yurupary cult, by Goldman and Reichel-Dolmatoff, in relation to my own analysis. Goldman's analysis is particular to the Cubeo and he makes no claims for a more general applicability. He concludes that the flutes and trumpets represent the *Bekúpwänwa*, the Ancients, and that the Cubeo Yurupary cult is an ancestor cult. Young men are incorporated into this cult through a long-drawn-out process of initiation, a central part of which are the rituals that correspond to the Barasana rite of Fruit House. Goldman (1963 : 190–210) observed that the significance of the fruits used in the rites lies in their connection with growth magic that makes the young men grow fast and strong. These conclusions are all entirely consistent with my own regarding similar rites amongst the Barasana.

Conclusion

Reichel-Dolmatoff's interpretation is based upon data from the Desana but is intended to be of more general application to the Tukanoans as a whole. He writes: 'To the Tukano of the Vaupés, the *yurupari* rite represents the commemoration of an act of incest which the Sun Father committed with his own daughter in the time of creation, and the principal motivation behind the ceremony in which these trumpets are played is the promulgation of strict exogamous laws that are characteristic of the Tukano' (1972 : 94).[2] By 'Tukano', Reichel-Dolmatoff means the Tukanoan-speaking Indians of the Vaupés, a label that includes the Barasana. I am in no position to evaluate this interpretation as it applies to the Desana in particular, but certain points should be made concerning its more general application, especially with regard to the Barasana. The Desana Yurupary rite described by Reichel-Dolmatoff (1971 : 167–71), whilst basically corresponding to the Barasana rite of Fruit House, differs from it in a number of important respects.[3] The interpretation relies heavily upon the Desana myth of incest between the Sun and his daughter, a myth not told by the Barasana and not forming part of any Yurupary myth from elsewhere in the Vaupés region. Considering that very little of the evidence from the account of the Desana ritual, some of it relating to the Desana language in particular, applies to the Barasana material and, considering the fact that the Barasana lack the myth of the Sun's incest, it would seem that Reichel-Dolmatoff's interpretation could not possibly apply to the Barasana. Reichel-Dolmatoff rightly insists that attention should be paid to the Indians' own explanations of Yurupary rites: his own informant told him that 'Yurupary is a warning not to commit incest and instead to marry only with women of another phratry' (1971 : 171). No Barasana ever told me anything that could possibly be interpreted in this light.

In spite of these divergences, there are however certain points in

---

2 The evidence for this interpretation is set out in Reichel-Dolmatoff 1971 : 167–71.
3 Reichel-Dolmatoff's account of the Desana Yurupary rite is based on informants' accounts rather than on direct observation. The rite is held approximately once a year – much less frequently than its Barasana equivalent; fish and smoked meat are used as well as fruit – the Barasana, like the Tukano (Brüzzi da Silva 1962 : 353), use Yurupary instruments only in connection with fruit; meat and fish are exchanged at a different category of rite; the rite is held as a preliminary to marriage exchange, in a house where nubile girls are present – no such considerations are operative in the Barasana rites; ritualised sexual antagonism, prominent in Desana rites, is virtually absent in their Barasana equivalents; etc.

common: the Desana myth of the Sun's incest with his daughter forms part of a longer myth, the rest of which is a variant of the Barasana myth of the Sun and Moon (M.3) and it also resembles the start of the myth of Manioc-stick Anaconda and Macaw (M.6.A) (Reichel-Dolmatoff 1971 : 24). The Barasana also have a myth about incest, the story of the Moon who sleeps with his sister *Meneriyo* (M.4.A); the Barasana Moon, like the Desana Sun, is called *Abe*. On the basis of his analysis of myths concerning the journey of the Sun and Moon in a canoe, Lévi-Strauss (1968 : 137–8 has come to almost exactly the same conclusion as Reichel-Dolmatoff concerning the significance of the Vaupés Yurupary cult. We are thus faced once again with the problem of the identities of the Sun and Moon in Barasana myth (see ch. 10), a problem which would, it appears, be made yet more complex by attempting to relate Barasana myths to those of the Desana. In spite of this, whilst I would agree that the Barasana Yurupary cult, like other secret men's cults in the Vaupés and beyond, is bound up with relations between the sexes, I do not find that either Lévi-Strauss or Reichel-Dolmatoff presents convincing evidence to relate it to the specific theme of incest and exogamy. Finally, even if this interpretation is accepted, it cannot be said to account for anything like all that is known of the Yurupary cult in the Vaupés region.

Throughout this book, I have avoided giving a single, unitary interpretation of Barasana Yurupary rites because I do not believe that there is such a thing as one true and privileged interpretation of this, or any other, ritual complex. This point was made long ago by Richards (1956) in her analysis of female initiation amongst the Bemba. More recently, Lévi-Strauss has said of the interpretation of myth, 'A myth must never be interpreted on one level only. No privileged explanation exists, for any myth consists in an *inter-relation* of several explanatory levels' (1977 : 65). This statement can, I think, be applied with equal force to the interpretation of ritual and especially to the Yurupary cult, an elaborate complex involving both myth and rite. So far, most of the interpretations offered have stuck to one or two levels of interpretation. The cult has been interpreted variously as an ancestor cult, as growth magic, as a warning against the sin of incest, as a fertility rite, as a means whereby men dominate women, as the commemoration of Yurupary the culture hero, etc. But none of these interpretations taken on their own, whether right or wrong, provides a satisfactory explanation of the supreme importance of the cult in the religious life of Vaupés Indians.

One thing is certain: Yurupary rites provide the context for the initiation of young men into adult male society, a theme that I have stressed throughout this book. But these rites are much more than simply rites of initiation: the young men are initiated into a cult that has an existence and receives expression quite independently of rites of initiation. Goldman's (1963 : 190–1) portrayal of the Cubeo ancestral cult as involving a number of different rites in which the ancestors are invoked, of which initiation rites are but one example, would certainly apply to the Barasana also. The focus of the Barasana cult is the concept of *He*. At its narrowest level of meaning, *He* refers to the sacred instruments and to the ancestors that they embody; more widely, it refers to a state of being that existed prior to contemporary society and that now exists as another dimension of everyday reality. This *He* state is known indirectly through myths or *bukurã keti*, the stories of the ancients or ancestors, but it is also experienced directly. This direct experience comes, in dangerous and uncontrolled form, through dreams, illness, childbirth, menstruation and finally through death. Direct experience is achieved, in a controlled and beneficial way, through ritual and shamanism and through the use of the hallucinogenic yagé: this experience is made accessible only to initiated men. The essence of Barasana shamanism is both the profound and detailed knowledge of myth, and also the ability to enter into contact with the *He* state at will. Other men, with the help of shamans, enter into this contact by dancing, chanting and by wearing feather ornaments or *He* possessions (*He gaheuni*) at each communal dance or ritual. *He* House, the model for all these dances, represents the culmination and highest point of this experience.

The Barasana conceive of the *He* state frequently in terms of spatial metaphor: initially life existed in an undifferentiated *He* state, in the form of *Yeba Haku*, the Primal Sun, outside the world or cosmic house, beyond the Water Door in the east. Today, the *He* state, represented by the *He* instruments, exists outside the house in the forest; the *He* state is on a par with, though not identical to, the world of nature – both are external to everyday human society. Transitions between these states are also represented in spatial terms: by entering the world and ascending the rivers, the ancestral anacondas, as manifestations or sons of *Yeba Haku*, transformed both their bodies and state of existence and gave rise to human beings; ontogeny repeats phylogeny when human babies, born outside the house and coming from the *He* state, are brought into the house and made human by the intervention of the shaman; at *He* House, the *He* instruments, as ancestors on a par with jaguars and anacondas, are taken from the rivers and forest and brought into the house where they change their state from dead to living, from spirit to human; when shamans enter into contact with the *He* state, their souls leave their bodies and travel between the layers of the cosmos; and when chanters recite the myths of origin, their souls leave their bodies and repeat the ancestral journeys. What is separated in time is seen as being separated in space; transitions in space effect transitions in time. At *He* House, categories that are normally kept separate are merged and confounded: the house become the universe, the past and present are merged so that the dead are living and the living are dead, present time becomes mythic time, a time when human beings, animals, and ancestors are as yet un-differentiated. The major ritual symbols, the *He* instruments and the gourd of beeswax, which combine opposed but complementary attributes, are the means by which this merging of categories is brought about.

Barasana myths describe the establishment of a differentiated cosmos from an undifferentiated life principle, and describe the establishment of order from chaos. This ordered cosmos, implied by the concept of *He*, and established as changeless in the mythic past, is seen by the Barasana as being the 'really real' (Geertz 1966) of which the human social order is but a part. When Barasana tell myths which refer to the creation of this order, to the division of the cosmos into layers, to the alternation of day and night and of one season with another, to the regular succession of the constel-lations across the sky and to the establishment of human society, they continually emphasise its goodness, perfection and changeless-ness. The social order, projected out into this wider cosmic order, is seen as having been created independently of human agency. The human world is seen as being ordered by principles established in this mythic past when society itself came into being. In the beginning, there was only one house, the universe, with one father, *Yeba Haku* and his sons, the ancestral anacondas. These in turn became fathers in their own houses, with their sons, the *He* People, as the sib ancestors of different exogamic groups. In each case, society is presented as being only two generations in depth. The maloca

248

community reproduces this structure in miniature; its core consists of a group of male siblings, united as the children of one father.

But human society is in danger of becoming separated from, and out of phase with, its generative source. Through time, a maloca community grows big and splits up. In simplified terms, a man's sons grow up, get married and have children of their own. As these children grow up, their parents hive off and establish new maloca communities, the splitting usually occurring at the death of the last surviving member of the senior generation, the unitary focus of the group. The continuity, implied by an ideology of patrilineal descent, between the social order of the mythic past and that of the present, also implies an increasing separation in time and space. By comparing the succession of generations to the leaves that pile on top of one another on the forest floor, the Barasana show themselves to be aware that descent implies time-depth and separation. They say that *He* House 'squashes the pile' of generations so that each generation of initiates is brought into direct contact with, and adopted by, the first ancestor. Barasana men inherit the name of a dead patrilineal kinsman in the second ascending generation, the names being those of the *He* People or first ancestors. Related to this, there is an ideology of 'soul recycling' such that new-born babies receive their souls from dead grandparents and are seen as being reincarnations of them. This again suggests a society of two generations in depth. At *He* House, such a society is brought about, for the anaconda ancestor, the father of the group, adopts the participants as his sons. Thus, in each generation, the mythic order is re-established and society is created anew.

Barasana myths make it clear that the continuity and differentiation of descent also imply death. Only when the anaconda ancestor was burned to death could his sons, the Yurupary instruments, be made from the palm tree that sprang from his ashes and by extension, when the anaconda ancestor gave rise to the *He* People by the segmentation and transformation of his body, he himself died. The origin myths of Yurupary are also myths of the origin of death: because Yurupary, the first ancestor, died, so all men must die; because the *He* People refused to eat from *Romi Kumu*'s gourd of beeswax, they lost the power to shed their skins and with it their immortality. In myth, the death and destruction of a single source lead to the segmentation and continuity of its parts: the body of the anaconda ancestor gives rise to sons who live on through their descendants, or to the

Yurupary that live on in the *He* world. In the maloca community, men give rise to sons who in turn give rise to their descendants. As the senior generation dies off, their sons split up and form new communities. But the myths of Yurupary and the rite of *He* House also concern immortality. The myths suggest that death is not final and that through death immortality is achieved: the *He* ancestors live on in another world. At *He* House, the ancestors are brought back to life and come to adopt the living.

The metaphor that underlies these myths is taken from slash-and-burn agriculture, a metaphor of repetitive and reversible time. Through the destruction and burning of the forest, the death of one plant generation, new life is created as plants spring from the ashes. Two modes of creation are suggested, one involving the alternation of death and life, the other involving the continuity of life through replacement. These two modes involve the two sexes who stand in a complementary relation to one another. Male creation, involving destruction, is linear and progressive through time; female creation, involving replacement, is repetitive and reversible. In agriculture, as in hunting and fishing, men destroy life in one sphere to enable its continuity in another. In reproduction, women create life with their bodies and in agriculture they tend crops which they plant in the soil. The complementary relation between the sexes in reproduction, in agriculture, in seasonal activities, and by extension in the ordering and creation of the cosmos, is given expression at *He* House. But *He* House is considered to be not merely expressive, but also instrumental in establishing and perpetuating this order.

Female creativity is seen to be natural and uncontrolled; women do not dominate nature by destroying it, but rather they manipulate it in agriculture and become dominated by it in reproduction. Female reproduction and agriculture are intimately associated in Barasana thought so that manioc tubers are referred to as 'the children of the women'. The Barasana say that women are semi-immortal: through menstruation, they continually renew their bodies by an internal shedding of skin − hence they live longer than men − and through childbirth they replace themselves with children. These processes are thought of as being akin to the succession of seasons and the growth of animals and plants in the natural world. The key to female creativity is seen to lie in the fact that women, like the world of nature, are periodic and cyclical. The periodicity of women, and the immortality it suggests, are emulated by men

during the rites of Fruit House and *He* House, themselves closely
linked to a periodic seasonal cycle. Perhaps the ultimate secret of
this exclusive men's cult is not the *He* instruments themselves, about
which the women know a great deal, but what lies behind them in
terms of their esoteric significance. Women are excluded from *He*
rites but not from contact with the *He* world. At menstruation, and
more especially at childbirth, an occasion from which men are
systematically excluded and about which they profess to know nothing,
the women enter into contact with this world and thereafter must be
ritually protected like the men. But this contact, and the creation that
it makes possible, is not controlled by the women themselves; rather
it is they who are seen to be controlled by their nature and their
bodies. Their *He* is in their bodies and in their hair whilst that of
the men is embodied in cultural symbols. In one sense, the women
are seen as being closer to the *He* world than the men, but this world
is on the side of nature and beyond the control of human society.
Material birth is distinguished from spiritual birth. Women give
birth to children, but only men give birth to men. In this perspective,
women and children are spiritually unborn, and only initiated, reborn
men are truly spiritual beings. Men, through ritual and through the
possession of cultural symbols, such as the *He* instruments and the
gourd of beeswax, seek to dominate and control the *He* world. At
a social level, this involves the dominance of men over women; at
a more general level, it involves the dominance and control over the
cosmos through shamanic activity.

There are many possible ways of understanding the religion of an
alien culture. In this book, I have not attempted a general description
and analysis of Barasana religion. To do so would require a more
thorough and extended analysis of their mythology, a more detailed
treatment of rites of birth, naming, first menstruation and death, and
a more extensive treatment of shamanism and many other things
besides. Instead, I have focussed attention on one particular ritual
complex, set selectively in its wider context. But by doing so, I have
not only given an extended and detailed analysis of Barasana initiation, but have also shown that through such an approach, important
insights can be gained into their religion and cosmology as a whole. I
have sought to show not only that *He* rituals have many meanings
and can be explained from a number of different perspectives, but
also to show how these different explanations are interconnected —
what, with reference to myth, Lévi-Strauss calls 'an inter-relation of

several explanatory levels'. Ritual is a multidimensional phenomenon: a number of different activities and events, involving different individuals and groups, happen simultaneously through time, and the participants (and observer) receives information simultaneously through a number of different sensory channels. Any description and analysis of ritual must therefore be correspondingly multi-dimensional.

Myth and ritual

Although this book is first and foremost a monographic study of the Yurupary cult amongst the Barasana and their neighbours, certain points emerge which bear upon anthropological analyses of myth and ritual more generally. Without assuming either that myth is indissolubly linked with ritual or that myth, as a statement in words, necessarily 'says' the same thing as ritual, as a statement in action, I have taken a complex involving both myth and rite as my unit of analysis. This complex involves, not simply one ritual overtly related to one myth in such a way that the myth is a recounted rite and the rite an enacted myth, but a number of different rites and myths, many of which bear no apparent or superficial relationship to each other. Up till now, no *systematic* effort has been made to relate Yurupary rites to their associated mythology: either the myths have been analysed more or less in isolation from the rites (see e.g. Bolens 1967; Lévi-Strauss 1968 : 137–8), or, more usually, the rites have been analysed with only haphazard reference to the myths (see e.g. Reichel-Dolmatoff 1971; Goldman 1963). What I have shown is that many aspects of these myths and rites, obscure when considered in isolation, are clarified when related together as a set. I would emphasise that this applies not only to relations between myths and rites but also to those between one myth and another and between one rite and another.

Anthropological discussions of the relationship between myth and ritual generally focus on two separable but interconnected issues: the first concerns the way in which myth can or should be used to elucidate the meaning of ritual (and vice versa); the second concerns the relationship between myth and ritual in terms of formal organisation, structure and function. A full discussion of this topic, which has a long history and about which a considerable amount has been written, is beyond the scope of this work. In what follows I want

Conclusion

merely to raise some points, emerging from my study of the Barasana, which relate to some recent contributions to this debate.

In his writings, V. Turner adopts a rather contradictory attitude to the use of myth in the interpretation of ritual. On the one hand, in discussing the role of native explanations of ritual and ritual symbols, he notes that such explanations may take the form either of myths or of piecemeal exegesis and that these two forms may be found together or separately in different societies (1969a : 11–12); on the other hand, some of his writings imply a critical attitude towards those who interpret ritual with reference to myth: 'My method is perforce the reverse of those numerous scholars who *begin* by eliciting the cosmology, which is often expressed in terms of mytho-logical cycles, and *then* explain specific rituals as exemplifying or expressing "structural models" they find in the myths' (1969b : 15), and 'There are no short cuts, through myth and cosmology, to the structure – in Lévi-Strauss's sense – of Ndembu religion. One has to proceed atomistically and piecemeal . . . if one is properly to follow the indigenous mode of thinking' (1969b : 21).

Lévi-Strauss, in reply to this criticism, distinguishes between two modalities of myth:

Either it is explicit and consists in narratives whose importance and internal organisation makes them fully fledged works. Or, on the contrary, mythic representations exist only in the form of notes, sketches or fragments; instead of being joined together by a connecting thread, each one remains linked to one or other phase of ritual; it provides a gloss for it, and it is only on the occasion of ritual acts that these mythic representations will be evoked. (1971 : 598; my translation)

This position is not so different from that of Turner when he states that piecemeal exegesis (implicit myth) and (explicit) myth are equivalent to one another.

To some extent at least, the anthropologist must adapt his approach to suit the particular idiom in which his informants choose to explain their rituals. When the Barasana discuss, comment upon or attempt to explain their rituals to each other or to outsiders, they do so sometimes in terms of piecemeal exegesis and sometimes in terms of connected narratives. No distinction is made between these two forms of ex-planation: all esoteric knowledge of this kind is classified as *bukurã keti* (*bukurã*: ancestors, ancients; *keti*: myth, stories, news, etc.). The Barasana told me repeatedly that if I wished to understand their rituals, I should first understand their 'myth' in this wider sense. At

first sight, there would appear to be a difference in what constitutes
an understanding of exegesis in each case. When exegesis is produced
in the form of piecemeal glosses for particular symbols or actions in
ritual, it would seem that the anthropologist has a ready-made
explanation or, at least, that he can know whether or not his own
understanding corresponds to that of his informants. But when
exegesis is offered in the form of connected narrative, matters become
more complicated. Very often, such narratives as produced by the
Barasana bear no obvious or apparent connection with the rites,
symbols or ritual acts that they purport to explain; further questioning
often fails to clarify the connection beyond statements like 'It's
obvious.' Either such narratives must simply be accepted as 'charters'
without any clear understanding of how or why they are so used, or
they must be analysed to establish a connection at a deeper, structural
level. But having carried out such an analysis, it is often difficult to
tell how the anthropologist's interpretation and understanding
relate to that of his informants. But I think that this difference is
(or should be) more apparent than real, for all too often anthropologists accept informants' interpretations of ritual as their own,
especially when such interpretations are offered as piecemeal exegesis.
I would rather take the position that all native explanations, in whatever form they are given, should be treated as part of the data to be
explained and not as anthropological explanations in their own right,
a point made long ago by Radcliffe-Brown (1964 : 235) and echoed
more recently by Sperber (1975).

Lévi-Strauss is concerned not only to take Turner (and others) to
task for their failure to distinguish between implicit and explicit
myth, but also, and more importantly, for treating exegesis or
implicit myth as part of ritual and thus failing to distinguish between
myth, in whatever form, as an essentially verbal phenomenon, and
ritual which is essentially non-verbal (1971 : 598). Nonetheless,
Lévi-Strauss both claims the right to make use of any manifestation
of the mental or social activities (including ritual) of a given community that allows him to complete or explain their myths (1970 : 4),
and also emphasises that myths can clarify the nature and existence
of beliefs, customs and institutions that appear incomprehensible
at first sight (1971 : 571). This view of myth and ritual, as separate
but closely linked entities that shed light on one another, is one
shared by many contemporary analysts and one that I have adopted
throughout this book. But, with few exceptions, notably that of

Tambiah (1970), this view has neither been explored in sufficient depth nor applied in a systematic way.

Leach, in his analysis of the Tongan kava ceremony, sees myth as a charter for ritual performance in such a way that what is symbolised in ritual can only be understood with reference to what is 'said' in myth, the message being conveyed not by the superficial content, but by the structural patterns embedded in the myth (1972 : 240). I have taken the same line in showing that the story of Manioc-stick Anaconda (M.6.A) only makes sense as a charter for the rite of *He* House when both are reduced to their structural elements. But the set of myths that Leach chooses for analysis is defined largely in terms of their superficial content, i.e. their explicit reference to kava and the kava ceremony and by the fact that these myths are offered by the Tongans as charters for their rites. What I have tried to show in this book is that the myths offered by the Barasana in explanation of their rites are themselves only fully comprehensible in the light of other myths which make no explicit reference to these rites and which are never offered as explanations for them, and that, at a structural level, some of these other myths show a clear relation to the rites which is not apparent from their superficial content. In other words, the set of myths taken as relevant to the understanding of a particular rite must be defined by criteria other than those of superficial content and of their use as explanations by native informants. As one of his three rules for the interpretation of myth, Lévi-Strauss states: 'A myth must never be interpreted individually, but in its relationship to other myths which, taken together constitute a transformation group' (1977 : 65). Myths given as explanations for ritual must be analysed not only in their narrow relation to the rite in question, but also in relation to other transformations of these myths. As the Barasana give myths not only as charters for their rites as wholes, but also as explanations for particular objects and actions that occur in these rites, such an exercise involves the examination of something approaching the entire corpus of their myths. In this respect, the analysis presented in this book is incomplete.

One of the aims of this book has been to lay the groundwork for a more extended treatment of Barasana ritual, and in particular of their rites of passage, which would see such rites as a set of transformations. I have shown that the rites of Fruit House and *He* House, homologous in terms of basic structure and following one another in time as part of an initiatory process, are only fully comprehensible when taken together as a set. More generally, I have tried to show that certain aspects of Barasana initiation can only be understood in relation to other rites of passage such as birth, first menstruation and death. Since the work of Van Gennep (1960) it has become almost an anthropological cliché that rites of passage typically involve three stages of separation, liminality and reincorporation and that rites of initiation frequently involve a symbolic death and rebirth. Yet few, if any, analyses of such rites attempt to compare and interrelate rites of symbolic death with real mortuary rites or rites of symbolic birth with those of real birth. In my analysis of Barasana initiation, I have taken a step in this direction, a line of research I hope to follow up later. One of the main points of significance that I see emerging from my work so far is that rites of initiation, which combine 'birth' and 'death' and which are conceptually half-way between these two uncontrollable natural processes, recreate them, through the use of symbols, in a controlled and ordered fashion. By doing so, they seek to confer power on those who undergo them, a power that is believed to enable adult men to control the processes of life itself. The real secret of the Barasana men's cult is not the secret items of ritual equipment themselves but the power that they imply. To some extent at least, this is made explicit by informants' statements, but it is even more explicit when the rites are seen in conjunction with the myths that are said to explain them.

Finally, I should like to offer some comments upon Lévi-Strauss's analyses of Amerindian mythology as a whole. One of the objectives of our field of research was to examine some of Lévi-Strauss's ideas in the light of a detailed body of ethnography, including a corpus of myth, collected with this end in mind. Although the primary focus of this book is on ritual and not on myth and although a more thorough analysis of Barasana mythology remains to be done, certain preliminary conclusions can be offered on the basis of this study of the Yurupary cult. Throughout this book, in the text and in notes, I have tried to indicate where my findings on Barasana mythology are in accord with those of Lévi-Strauss, based on the study of myths outside the Vaupés region. In particular, Lévi-Strauss's intricate argument, arrived at deductively through a comparative study of myths from a large number of different societies, concerning the relationships between the rotten and burned worlds, and between bull-roarers and the instruments of darkness, appears to be confirmed directly by empirical data from the Barasana. Again, though the

Conclusion

Barasana gourd of beeswax is not a musical instrument in strict organological terms, the discovery of this 'instrument' adds weight to Lévi-Strauss's arguments concerning such instruments in a South American context, for the only such instrument that he was able to find, outside the realm of myth, was the Bororo *parabára* about which there exists only sketchy ethnographic data (Lévi-Strauss 1973 : 369–70).

On the basis of the analogy that he draws between mythic thought and language, Lévi-Strauss argues that there can be no such thing as a finite corpus of myths from a given society: the myths of a society are like sentences (*parole*), or expressions of an ordered system of mythic thought (*langue*) that operates above the level of a particular social group. Just as new sentences are continually produced in a given language, so, through time, new myths are produced and old ones become transformed or disappear. Myths, at the level of *parole*, are an open set, whilst Myth, or mythic thought, at the level of *langue*, is a closed system (Lévi-Strauss 1970 : 7–8, 1971 : 565–6). But whilst it is in some ways true that each and every telling of a myth will produce a new variant, variants at this level are without significance for Lévi-Strauss's analysis which is carried out at the level of the gross features and elements of the story as a whole. Because the significance of myth lies at a meta-linguistic level, it is resistant to distortion at the level of language itself (1971 : 580). And although it is also true that, through time, new myths are produced and old ones varied and transformed, changes in myth, at the level at which Lévi-Strauss analyses them, are also unlikely to occur over relatively short periods of time; when they do occur, they are likely to be correlated with other changes in the societies that produce them, as is the case for variations of myths that occur between different societies in space. But in any case, the significance and extent of variations through time of the myths of a given society must be decided on the basis of empirical enquiry and not assumed *a priori*.

During our field research we attempted to obtain as full and detailed a corpus of myths as we could. Working with check-lists, we obtained versions of the same myths from different informants, versions of different myths from different informants, and versions of the same myth from the same informant on different occasions. By the end of our stay, we had more or less exhausted the repertoire of myths that the people with whom we had contact were able (or willing)

257

to tell us. Two things emerged from this work: first, there was
surprisingly little variation between versions of the same story as
told by the same or different informants on different occasions:
when telling myths, the Indians of the Pirá-paraná region both aim
for and achieve consistency and correctness at a level well below that
of the gross features of the story. Secondly, within this known
repertoire of stories, informants were well able to distinguish between
stories that are considered to belong to the common culture of the
area (involving in particular the Barasana, Bará and Tatuyo) and those
that are alien (mostly stories from the Arawakan groups to the south).
Thus, at least in this area, there is something that approximates to a
finite and relatively closed corpus of myths at a particular point in
time.

Two points follow from this. If it is possible to demonstrate
empirically, and without straying beyond the confines of a particular
cultural group, what Lévi-Strauss arrives at deductively on the basis
of a massive cross-cultural comparison of myths from a number of
different societies widely separated in space, one is led to wonder
if, for some purposes at least, he is not making a virtue out of a
necessity. Throughout the four volumes of *Mythologiques* there
seems to be a progressive tendency away from analysing myths in
relation to the social context of the societies that produce them,
towards analysing one myth in terms of another and working out
the relations of transformation between them. I do not question
the value of the comparative exercise *per se* but when it is claimed
that myths from one society can only be fully understood by
reference to myths from other societies widely separated in space,
I would ask if this may not be so much a methodological principle
as a necessary and inevitable by-product of the fragmentary nature of
much of the ethnographic data on which the analysis is based. To
quote T. Turner (n.d.), 'I simply question the tendency to substitute
[comparative analysis] for, or to regard it as prior to, the compre-
hensive analysis of the structures of individual myths and their
relations to their particular social and cultural contexts of reference.'

The second point, related to the first but of greater importance,
concerns the significance of the myths within their social and cultural
context. Lévi-Strauss is frequently criticised for ignoring the social
context of the myths that he analyses. Such a criticism is largely
unfounded, at least at the level of methodology but not always at
the level of practice, if by context is meant the ethnographic back-

ground of the myths. Although ethnographic data on some of the
societies whose myths he analyses is highly fragmentary and sometimes misleading, Lévi-Strauss's interpretations of Amerindian
mythology depend upon knowledge of their social context and
consist in relating the myths to details of the ecology, economy,
kinship and political structure, ritual, etc. of the societies from which
they derive (see also Lévi-Strauss 1977 : 65). But if by context is
meant the role and significance of the myths in question in the
function and organisation of the societies from which they derive,
then the criticism carries some weight. By shifting progressively
from the question of *what* myths mean to *how* they mean and how
they are organised internally, and by shifting from the study of myths
in relation to their specific social and cultural context to the study
of myths from one society in relation to those of other societies, he
is left with a vast self-contained and self-enclosed system which relates
to nothing but itself, a set of signifiers with no signifieds – 'myths
which operate in men's minds without their being aware of the fact'
(Lévi-Strauss 1970 : 12). For my part, unless the myths of one
society are seen as a relatively bounded and self-contained system,
and the evidence suggests that they can be, then we must indeed 'see
in these *Mythologiques* the description of a language of which each
Indian society knows only bits which have been assembled by Lévi-
Strauss' (Sperber 1975 : 72). I hope that I have shown in this work
that it would be neither possible nor fruitful to study the signifiers
of Barasana myth and ritual without at the same time studying their
signifieds, and also that such a study is only possible when the rites
and myths are seen within a specified social and cultural context.

In the concluding section of *Mythologiques* vol. IV, Lévi-Strauss,
apparently going against some of his earlier statements concerning
the relationship between myth and ritual (1963 : chs. X and XII;
1973 : chs. V and XIII), appears to reduce ritual to a spin-off from
myth, a vain endeavour to re-establish and reassert the continuum
of experience that has been fragmented by the polarising procedures
of mythic thought: 'whilst myth resolutely turns its back upon
continuity to cut up and dismember the world by means of distinctions, contrasts and oppositions, ritual moves in the opposite
direction: starting with discrete units which are imposed upon it
by this prior conceptualisation of the real, it chases after continuity
and tries to catch up with it, although the initial split brought
about by mythic thought makes the task for ever impossible' (1971 :

607; my translation). Such an idea might appear to be confirmed by my discussion of Barasana Yurupary rites, for in them, as in so much religious ritual elsewhere, can be seen an attempt to overcome the unpleasant consequences of a manner of thinking that sets up life and death as polar opposites. But at the same time, these rites, in harmony with mythic thought, build upon and emphasise differences of age and sex and establish a fundamental cultural distinction that permeates every aspect of Barasana society. Ritual is thus foremost amongst the various mechanisms that amplify and convert distinctions in thought to produce divisions in society.

Rather than reduce one to the other, I would see myth and ritual as drawing upon a common set of cultural categories, classifications and ideas, expressed not only in the myths and rites themselves but also in the activities of daily life, and producing transformations of a common set of elements. But ritual is not the same as myth for it stands half-way between thought and action. It is through ritual that the categories of thought can be manipulated to produce effects. Myth may exhibit order in thought, but it is through ritual that this order is manipulated to produce order in action and in society at large.

PART V

The Myths

Leaving aside stories about spirits (*watía*), most Barasana myths can be divided into five major cycles, each of which centres on the activities of one or more principal characters. Most of the myths presented in this book are drawn from these cycles (M.1, M.2, M.4, M.6 and M.7). With the exception of the story of Manioc-stick Anaconda (M.6), I have never heard any of these myth-cycles told right through from start to finish at one sitting. Usually, part of a cycle is told as a discrete story with the rest either left out altogether or briefly summarised at the beginning or end. As presented here, the longer cycles are divided up into numbered sections. These sections correspond to the way in which informants might divide up the myths but it must be emphasised that the divisions are in no way fixed. Different people will divide up the myths in different ways according to the particular circumstances of telling.

In order to save space, in most instances I have had to reduce the myths to their bare essentials, often reducing to a few lines whole sections that might take an hour or more to tell. I have also had to leave out whole sections of the myths which contain material that is not of immediate relevance to my argument. The only myth which is anything like complete is that of Manioc-stick Anaconda.

With the exception of M.8, all the myths were recorded in the Pirá-paraná region. In most cases the sections of each myth presented are based on a number of different versions collected from both Barasana and Bará informants; M.2.F and M.5.A are based on versions from a Tatuyo informant. M.8 is an abridged version of the Yurupary myth recorded by Biocca from a Tariana informant living at Jauareté on the Vaupés river.

M.1

Romi Kumu

M.1.A *Romi Kumu* makes the world

1. In the beginning the world was made entirely of rock and there was no life. *Romi Kumu*, Woman Shaman, took some clay and made a cassava griddle. She made three pot-supports and rested the griddle upon them. The supports were mountains holding up the griddle, the sky. She lived on top of the griddle.

2. She lit a fire under the griddle. The heat from the fire was so intense that the supports cracked and the griddle fell down on the earth below, displacing it downwards so that it became the Underworld; the griddle became this earth. (Variant: the griddle fell through the earth below and became the Underworld.) She then made another griddle which is the layer above this earth, the sky.

3. She made a door in the edge of the earth, the Water Door, in the east. There was lots of water outside and when she opened the door the waters came in and flooded the earth.

4. The waters rose inside the house. All the possessions in the house became alive. The manioc-beer trough and the long tube for sieving coca became anacondas; the post on which resin is put to light the house became a cayman and the potsherds and other flat objects became piranha fish. These animals began to eat the people.

5. The people made canoes to escape the flood but only those in a canoe made from the *kahuu* (unidentified sp.) tree survived. Everyone else and all the animals were drowned.

6. The survivors landed on top of the mountain called *Ruriho* near the Pirá-paraná. There they began to eat each other as there was no food and the animals that survived ate each other too.

7. Then the rains and floods stopped and it was summer. The sun stayed high in the sky and it became hotter and hotter and drier and drier. This went on till the earth itself caught fire. (Variant: *Romi Kumu* set fire to the earth.) The earth burned furiously and everything was consumed. The fire was so hot that the supports of the layer above cracked and it came crashing down (see 2. above).

M.1.B The nature of *Romi Kumu*

1. *Romi Kumu* is very old. In the evening she is old and ugly but in the morning when she has bathed she is young and beautiful. She changes her skin. She has the old beeswax gourd up there with her in the sky so that she can do this.
2. When *Romi Kumu* urinates it is very cold; her urine is the rain.
3. She has fire in her vagina.
4. Urucú (*Bixa orellana*) is her face paint; it is her menstrual blood; it is her *He*. She puts the paint on her face and then removes it again taking off a layer of skin so that her face becomes white. This is what women do today.
5. Her body has *He* within it; she has *He* here in her hair. When shamans blow spells on food for a menstruating woman, they hide her hair back behind her head. The hair stays there for a month and then falls back in front of the woman's face; then she sees the *He* and menstruates once more. When the hair is behind her head she cannot menstruate.
6. *Romi Kumu* is the mother of the sky or day (*Umuari hako*). She is the grandmother of the *He* People, all peoples' grandmother.

M.1.C *Romi Kumu* creates the *He* People

1. *Romi Kumu* was a virgin; she had no husband. She made two daughters, the Women-that-squeeze-manioc-in-a-press (*Buhe Romia*).
2. She created all *He*, all the *He* People. They had no father, they simply came into being. The people were inside that palm, that womb.
3. *Romi Kumu* was a shaman, she was like a man. She turned the *He* People into beings like women; they were like women in that they menstruated.
4. *Romi Kumu* was going to give the *He* People shamanised substances from the gourd of beeswax.
5. She made manioc beer and then made the *He* People sit out on the plaza in front of the house.
6. The *Meni Masa* were like wild beasts, like warriors and killers. They went into the house, greeted *Romi Kumu*, then out again and round and round the house.
7. She offered them one gourd but they gave it back to her without eating from it; she offered them another but they gave it back angrily.
8. Anacondas and snakes came and ate from the gourd that they had refused.
9. At midnight, *Romi Kumu* did protective blowing for the *He* People. They went round and round the house looking for her gourd.
10. They came back into the house and she offered them a gourd of shamanised substances; it was the gourd of beeswax.
11. 'Take that gourd away, you filthy beast', said Old Star (*Nyoko Baku*), the fierce one, their warrior, 'I'm not going to eat from your vagina, it is very bitter and smells.' He ran off again.
12. She put the gourd between her legs and took out another gourd and offered

it to them. Old Star saw her do this. 'That's not the right gourd. You have hidden it from us', he said as he ran behind her to look.

13. There was nothing there. Snakes and spiders had come and eaten from the gourd and then the white people had come and taken it away.

14. The white people had taken the gourd for changing skins. With this gourd, when you get old you slough off the skin and become young again. The priests have this gourd, it is their incense. That gourd was for us but they cheated us and took it away.

15. As the *He* People put on the head-dresses to dance, *Romi Kumu* escaped from them and ran away. They chased after her. First they went round the edge of the world and then down the middle but they could not find her.

16. They went to the east and found her there. She gave them the gourd that we have today, the one that we use during *He* House. They were going to kill her for taking away the good gourd.

17. As she gave them the gourd, she went through the Water Door and climbed up into the sky, up to the layer above. She became the Pleiades (*Nyokoaro*) and she is there today.

18. Cubeo and Siriano men still menstruate today; *Romi Kumu* made them like that.

19. The *He* People returned to the Pirá-paraná. People tried to give them fish to eat as they were initiates. That is why when we see the *He* we dream of eating fish caught with poison.

20. They were the *He* People, our people. That is why we have *He*. There was Guan (*Kata*) and Cotinga Jaguar (*Rasuᵾ Yai*) – they all had names like jaguars. There was Sloth Jaguar (*Kerea Yai*); he is Old Sloth (*Kerea Buku*). Old Callicebus Monkey (*Wau Buku*) was their shaman like *Romi Kumu*. We don't see that one; it stays inside the shamans' enclosure together with their gourds. There was Manioc-squeezing Woman (*Buhe Romio*), two of them, short trumpets, and *Kana* Flower (*Kana Goro*), a short trumpet. There was *Wenandurika*, two of them. There was Old Star (*Nyoko Buku*), the fierce one, the warrior. Their protection was the whip and the sword-club. The snail-shell snuff holder was their shamanism.

M.1.D *Romi Kumu* steals the *He*

1. *Romi Kumu's* father, Poison Anaconda, told his sons to get up early and go down to the river to bathe, vomit water and to play the *He*.

2. In the morning the sons stayed in bed but *Romi Kumu* got up early and went down to the river where she found the *He*.

3. (Variant: the women/woman did not know what to do with the Yurupary. They put them over all the orifices of their bodies but not in their mouths. Finally a fish, jacundá (*Crenicichla* sp.), showed them what to do by signalling with its big mouth – Fulop 1956 : 361–2; Prada Ramirez 1969 : 131–2.)

4. The father was at first pleased when he heard the noise of the *He* but when he saw his sons still asleep he realised what had happened and was very angry.

5. The men ran down to the port but *Romi Kumu* had already gone, taking the *He* and all the other sacred equipment of the men with her.

6. They chased after her, following the sound of the *He*, but each time they got near she ran off again. She walked along the rivers and one can still see her footprints (carved) on the rocks in the Pirá-paraná area. She came to Yurupary Cachoeira (*Sunia Hoero*), on the Vaupés river. There the men caught up with her and took back the *He* and ritual equipment.

7. The men punished *Romi Kumu* and the other women by making them menstruate. (Variant: When the women stole the Yurupary they talked a lot and were drunk. The men attacked the women and rammed the instruments up their vaginas — Fulop 1956 : 366.)

8. When the women stole the *He* from the men, the men became like women: they worked in the manioc gardens producing manioc, they had a bend in their forearms like women and they menstruated.

M.2

Ayawa, the Thunders

M.2.A The *Ayawa* create their younger brother

1. In the beginning there was no earth and no trees, only a hard land made of rock. There were no people, only the *Ayawa*, Thunders. There were three of them: *Bosuɨ Waimi*, the eldest, *Bo Ayawa*, the next, and *Masame*, the youngest. They did not know who their parents were so they concluded that they must be the children of the sky.
2. They came to a *kanea*, caimo (*Chrysophyllum caimito*) tree with lots of fruit. They ejaculated into the fruit and then gave it to their grandmother to eat.
3. Another woman, *Hatao*, warned her not to eat the fruit telling her that the *Ayawa* had put their sperm in it. The grandmother ignored the warning and after eating the fruit she became pregnant.
4. The grandmother gave birth to a son. The *Ayawa* decided that the child must be their younger brother and they called him *Kanea* after his 'father'. He grew up very fast and became a very powerful shaman. His elder brothers were ignorant — today too, it is the youngest brother who becomes the shaman.

M.2.B The *Ayawa* obtain night

1. The sun stayed high in the sky all the time and there was no night. The *Ayawa* complained that there was no beginning and no end to their day and that their life was not ordered and regular. Especially important to them was the fact that there was no established routine for the picking, processing and eating of coca.
2. They went to Night House where Day Father (*ɨmuari Hakɨ*), Night Father (*Nyamiri Hakɨ*), *Nyami Sodo*, lived. They stayed in his house.
3. In the afternoon they went with their host to pick coca; in the evening they processed the coca and at night they ate the coca as they sat and talked in the centre of the house. When they went to bed at Night Father's bidding they woke up in the morning refreshed instead of feeling tired as they had done after the fitful rests to which they were accustomed. Only at Night House was day and night ordered in this way.

267

4. They decided to ask Night Father for night. They said to him, 'Mother's son, give us night.' He gave them a box telling them not to open it without first carrying out the appropriate blowing.

5. They went home and after blowing spells on the box, they opened it. A resin-like substance fell out and covered their bodies with sores. They were angry with Night Father saying that they had asked for night (*nyami*) not sores (*kami*).

6. They went back to Night House and asked once again for night. Night Father gave them a pot and told them not to let the women see it. He told them also that they must blow spells against the night animals and against the illness of women, the latter because they would sleep with the women at night. He also warned them not to open the pot until they got back to their house.

7. They were very suspicious of the pot, thinking that it too would contain sores. When they reached the edge of their manioc garden they decided to open the pot and see what was inside. As they opened it, the lid flew off and covered the eyes of the sun. Everything became pitch black with heavy rain falling and wind whistling through the trees. The rivers rose and flooded the land and the *Ayawa* were very frightened. The night was very long.

8. Finally, *Kanea*, the youngest, went up into the sky and, using his powers as a shaman, found dawn. During the night the *Ayawa* had turned into night animals; they became douroucouli monkeys, owls, potoos, etc. As dawn broke they became *umamu* frogs (*Hyla* sp.) that croak after heavy rains. They also became *kata rihoa borea*, white-headed guan (*Pipile cumanensis*) and *kata maha*, rufous-breasted guan (*Penelope jacquacu*), both dawn-feeding birds.

9. *Buko*, Anteater, then began to laugh at them, teasing them about the catastrophic night that they had caused. They told him that they would deal with him later.

10. They went to Anteater's house and began to prepare tobacco snuff. When they had finished they blew the snuff up each other's noses and then offered some to Anteater. They blew the snuff at him making his two nostrils. *Kanea* had blown spells into the snuff to make it strong. Anteater became very dizzy and the *Ayawa* then chased him out of the house. As he ran off, they threw a flowering arrow cane after him which hit him in the rear and became his tail.

M.2.C The *Ayawa* obtain fire

1. The grandmother of the *Ayawa* owned fire which she guarded jealously between her legs as she squatted on the ground. (Variant: She kept the fire in her vagina.) When she blew on the fire, huge sparks came out with loud bangs. Without this fire the *Ayawa* could not have thunder. They asked their grandmother for the fire but she refused to give it to them.

2. The youngest *Ayawa*, *Kanea*, turned himself into a callicebus monkey (*wau*) which the other *Ayawa* then killed. They took the monkey to their grandmother and asked her to singe the hairs off so that they could eat it. She took urucú

branches and squatted over them and made a fire. As she did this, the other
Ayawa ran up, grabbed the fire from her, and ran away.

3. The grandmother told Fire Cayman (*Hea Guso, Caiman sclerops*) that she had
lost the fire and he promised to get it back for her.

4. The *Ayawa* ran till they came to a big river. There, Fire Cayman offered to
ferry them across in his canoe. They put the fire in the prow of the canoe which
was Fire Cayman's nose. In the middle of the river Fire Cayman ate the fire and
then dived under the water leaving the *Ayawa* to swim.

5. The *Ayawa* then turned themselves into *umamu* frogs (*Hyla* sp.) and
began to croak. Fire Cayman came along to eat the frogs and as he came near,
the *Ayawa* turned back into people, grabbed Fire Cayman and cut him open.
They looked for fire in his guts but couldn't see it. They called Macaw Wasp to
fan the fire with his wings until it glowed. They took the fire from the belly of
Fire Cayman, then wove a palm-leaf mat to put over the hole. Then they filled
his belly with stones and put him back in the water.

M.2.D The *Ayawa* seek water

1. The *Ayawa* were very thirsty but all the water in the world was poisonous so
that they could not drink. Their grandmother owned water so they went to ask
her for some.

2. Their grandmother told them that they would find water inside a tree. They
went and cut down various trees without success.

3. Finally, she revealed the right tree to them. After many adventures, they
succeeded in cutting it down. Its trunk and branches gave rise to all the major
rivers in the area and all fishes came from the water inside its trunk.

M.2.E The *Ayawa* steal thunder

1. The *Ayawa* went to Thunder Chief's (*Buho Boku*) house to steal thunder
from him. They turned themselves into macaws and flew into the house and flew
out again carrying the thunder-club; Thunder Chief was asleep. As they flew into
the air, Thunder Chief awoke and tried to kill them with another club. The
thunder that the *Ayawa* stole was tree thunder that makes a loud noise (forked
lightning); the thunder that Thunder Chief had left was distant rumbling thunder
and sheet lightning.

2. The *Ayawa* went back to their grandmother's house. She was outside weeding
the cleared space round the house. They struck her with the thunder-club in
order to try out their new possession. The thunder-club killed their grandmother
but the *Ayawa* brought her back to life.

M.2.F The *Ayawa* and Tree-Fruit Jaguar

1. *Kanea*, the youngest *Ayawa*, ate sabalo fish (*huwai*) without having bathed after working at clearing the forest to make a manioc garden.
2. The fish inside him grew big and he became pregnant. The child inside him was Tree-Fruit Jaguar (*He Rika Yai*). *Kanea* became very ill as he was unable to give birth to the child.
3. The *Ayawa* called two shamans; one was the little woodpecker that cries 'ruputuru ruputuru', the other was a big woodpecker, spotted like a jaguar. They made a hole in *Kanea*'s body and delivered the baby. They were helped in their work by their women, *ria tüha* frogs (*Leptodactylus* sp.).
4. The baby would not stop crying. They tried shamanism to change his soul but he went on and on and would not stop. Finally they beat the walls with sticks and he stopped. He was a jaguar, one who eats people.
5. Tree-Fruit Jaguar told the *Ayawa* to decorate the house with tree-fruit. They hung uacú (*simio*), iauapischuna (*toa*), gubotea, pataua (*nyomu, Oenocarpus baccaba*), assai (*Euterpe oleracea*), wahu (*Hevea* sp.), rubber (*biti, Hevea* sp.) and *bubi*, all the tree-fruit, on the posts and beams of the house.
6. They hung tree-fruits on their bodies; all their dance ornaments were tree-fruits.
7. They were making the tree-fruits ripen; they were changing the soul of the tree-fruits.
8. They asked, 'Who will be the tree-fruit feather crown?' Blue-crowned Motmot (*Utu, Momotus momota*), whose cry is 'utu utu utu', replied, 'I will be that (*yu ti, yuti, hutu*).'
9. Fearing that people might eat the tree-fruit people, protective blowing was done with tobacco to make them smell and become poisonous.
10. After the dance, the tree-fruit people began to leave the house; this was the maturation of the fruit. Some of them had black paint on only one part of their body, others were covered all over. The pataua were black all over. The iauapischuna were covered in red paint. The tree-fruit spread out over the land.
11. There were two Guans in the house, *Kata Maha*, Red Guan, and *Kata Rihoa Borea*, White Guan (see M.2.B.8 above).
12. Red Guan wanted to show that he was a true shaman; he put White Guan under a basket.
13. Up on the roof beams of the house were tocandira ants, snakes and scorpions. If Red Guan had been a real shaman he would have got rid of these creatures by knocking them off the beams with a whip but he failed to do this.
14. They called White Guan out from under the basket. He took a whip and after blowing spells on it, cleared all the noxious animals from the beams.
15. Red Guan called his daughter to bring cassava bread for him to eat together with the tree-fruit but as he was afraid of the poisonous animals he flew off. White Guan ate up all the tree-fruit.

16. After dawn, Tree-Fruit Jaguar left the house and went to look at all the fruit dispersed throughout the forest. Then he went to *He hɯdoa wi* in the east where he is today.

17. It is because of Tree-Fruit Jaguar that tree-fruits are well shamanised and have their souls changed. By doing this, the fruit never finishes and there is always more. Today, because people do not do this properly, there is less fruit. If they hold Fruit House, do the right shamanism and burn beeswax then there is lots of fruit. They do that so that the soul of the fruit does not become exhausted and stop.

18. Uacú (*simio*) fruit is yagé, that is why the fruit is so bitter. It is tree-fruit yagé.

M.3

Sun and Moon; day and night

1. The Sun and the Moon were brothers. The Moon, the elder of the two, said, 'I am going to heat up and dry the wombs of the women. I shall be the day.'

2. His younger brother, the Sun, thought about the need for seasons, and the need for water for drinking and cooking. He said, 'No, I shall be the one who owns the day.'

3. He took the day from his elder brother and gave him night. Then he went away to escape from his elder brother.

4. The Moon had a very feeble light, the thing that he thought would be the day. His younger brother, the Sun, shone bright and clear.

5. The Moon's body then turned to blood. That is what really happens when people tell you that the moon is 'dying' (the conventional explanation of lunar eclipses and of the red moon in a red sky). The whole of the Moon's place turned to blood and he appeared as a little red lump like a lump of red paint.

6. The Moon came down to the earth and arrived at an abandoned house where all the inhabitants had died. As he went in, the house was filled with light from his feather crown. He took off his crown and hung it on the lighting post in the middle of the house.

7. Then the Moon became an armadillo and began to eat the bones in the grave in the floor of the house.

8. A Siusi man had come into the house earlier and had hidden up on a shelf and gone to sleep. Seeing the crown on the post, he took it and put it under a pot and then got back up on the shelf. The house went dark.

9. The Moon stumbled around looking for his crown. At last he saw a chink of light and, lifting up the pot, put his crown back on his head and then left the house. He climbed back up into the sky.

10. The Moon comes down to the earth to eat the bones of dead men who made love to menstruating women when they were alive. As he comes into the house he says, 'was it so good to make love to a woman like that, son-in-law?' This is why men are afraid of menstruating women and avoid looking at them.

11. Today, when the Moon 'dies', if there is any food in the house it becomes filled with blood. All the objects in the house become covered in blood. To

avoid this, all food and all possessions must be taken on to the cleared space outside the house.

12. If we sleep when the Moon 'dies' our arms and our mouths become filled with blood so everyone must be woken up. The blood is the Moon's blood, menstrual blood.

13. When the Moon 'dies', the shamans do protective shamanism with beeswax. Everyone must be outside the house. The shamans blow on red paint and then wipe it on the people's bodies.

14. The men act-out spearing; they go to steal the fierce magic of a spirit who appears at this time. They hit him hard and steal his magic.

15. The sky is like a gourd around which the Sun travels. He owns and holds us all; he is our father. When he goes high in the sky it is summer; when he is not so high it is the rainy season. When it is summer down here it is the rainy season up above. In the beginning the day was the summer and the night was the rainy season. The seasons are good.

16. When the Moon 'dies' people call out; if they are going to die soon the spirit of a dead relative answers them. If the spirits do not reply they will live longer.

M.4

Warimi

M.4.A *Warimi*'s conception (1)

1. The Moon, *Abe*, had a younger sister called *Meneriyo*, Ingá Woman.
2. The Moon used to come to his sister's hammock at night and make love to her. *Meneriyo* did not know who it was that came to her and she decided to find out.
3. She prepared a pot of black paint and during the night she painted her lover's face.
4. In the morning, the Moon looked in a mirror and saw that his face was covered in paint. He tried many different ways to wash off the paint but he could not get rid of it.
5. The paint on his face made the Moon ill and he died. His body rotted and turned to water. Bats that live by the riverside came and ate his rotting flesh. This gave them diarrhoea so today they hang upside down to stop their food from running out.
6. The Sky People brought the Moon back to life by shamanism after tying his body together with string. The dying Moon and his subsequent revival was the beginning of the moon's periodicity.
7. *Meneriyo* was by this time pregnant and very frightened. When she returned to her father *Meni Kumu*, *Meni* Shaman's house, he was very angry with her.
8. Outside the house was a parrot (*weko*, *Amazona* sp.) sitting up on a caimo tree. *Meni* Shaman told his daughter to go and feed the parrot.
9. As *Meneriyo* pulled the branch on which the parrot was sitting down towards her, it sprang back and catapulted her up into the sky. There, lots of bees came and buzzed round her head.
10. *Meneriyo* had a tame japú (*umu*, *Icteridae* sp.) bird. He looked into a pot of water and saw *Meneriyo*'s reflection high in the sky. He flew up to join her.
11. *Meneriyo* sent the bird back down to the house to bring her her work-basket containing the string she used to weave garters. She then climbed down the string back on to the ground.
12. She set off in search of her father. She came to a fork in the path; one fork

274

was marked by blue-crowned motmot tail feathers, the other by a macaw tail feather. She asked some people which path to take. They told her to take the one marked by the macaw feather, but her child *Warimi*, from inside her belly, told her to take the other path.

13. She arrived at a house. Inside there was a huge pot covered in white mould. The pot was a woman, White Worm (*Wasi Bomo*). *Meneriyo* laughed at the pot saying that it was horrible. The pot replied, 'You come from on high, you are a beast. Your mother went that way.'

14. She set off again and arrived at the house of *Oa*, Opossum. In the house was another huge pot, this time a man. There was a hammock above the pot and Opossum's mother told her to sleep in it as it belonged to her son. The floor under the hammock was covered in water so *Meneriyo* spread ash to make it dry.

15. As she lay in the hammock, a huge 'worm', a *yokeri masɨ* (Amphisbaena) came and lay in the hammock with her. The ropes broke and the hammock fell, breaking the pot. The mother said, 'Oh! My son is broken.' *Meneriyo* went off in disgust.

M.4.B *Warimi*'s conception (2)

1. Little Sticky Man (*Umɨaka Widaɨ*) lived up in the sky. He used to catch people to eat by letting down a line baited with brightly coloured objects. When people picked up the objects to see what they were, they stuck fast and were hauled into the sky. He caught lots of people in this way and ate them.

2. One day he caught *Meneriyo* who at this time was menstruating. He was frightened of her in this condition so he put her on a shelf and waited. She became pregnant by him.

3. When Little Sticky Man went out to pick coca, his mother warned *Meneriyo* that unless she escaped she would be eaten too. She brought her the line that her son used to go down to earth; on the end was a kind of seat like the ones that Vaupés Indians use to teach their children to walk. *Meneriyo* got into the seat and was lowered to the earth below.

4. Just as she came down on top of an ingá tree, Little Sticky Man arrived back in his house up above. Seeing that *Meneriyo* had escaped on his line, he pulled it upwards so that *Meneriyo*'s thighs were jerked into the air and she fell to the ground.

M.4.C *Warimi*'s conception (3)

1. Sky Anaconda (*Umɨa Hino*) lived in the roof of the Moon's house.

2. He would come down to the ground, catch people and then take them up into the roof and eat them.

3. One day he caught a woman who was menstruating. He put her aside to

eat when her period was over but she escaped from him. She came down and landed at Ingá Mountain.

M.4.D *Warimi*'s birth

1. After her return from the sky, *Meneriyo* came to the house of the Thunder Jaguars (*Buho Yaiya*, *Ho Yaiya*) (also called *Jaguar Tooth Sea*) at Jaurareté on the Vaupés river. Jauareté, meaning 'jaguar' (rapid), is the home of the Tariana.
2. There was only one old woman in the house – all her children were out felling the forest to make a manioc garden. *Meneriyo* addressed this woman as '*mekaho*', father's sister.
3. After listening to *Meneriyo*'s story of her adventures in the sky, the woman told her that she must hide from her children who would otherwise eat her.
4. The woman hid *Meneriyo* under a basket up on a shelf, telling her that her children were about to hold a dance and that on no account should she show herself.
5. When the Jaguars returned, they asked their mother who had come to the house. She told them that no one had come but they knew that she was lying as they had seen *Meneriyo* through their special eyes.
6. The Jaguars started to prepare for the dance and again their mother warned *Meneriyo* not to show herself.
7. As the Jaguars began to dance, *Meneriyo* peeped out from under the basket. The Jaguars were her *tenyua*, potential husbands, and she found them very attractive.
8. As soon as she looked, the Jaguars began to sing, '*Meneriyo* is watching us, we've seen her, there's food around.'
9. Convinced that she had been seen, *Meneriyo* said to the woman, 'They've seen me, I'm coming down.' The Jaguars' mother told her to stay where she was, but she insisted and came down.
10. *Meneriyo* began to paint the legs of the Jaguars with red and black paint. Their mother told her to paint the eldest first but instead she painted the youngest, whom she found most attractive. The eldest Jaguar began to get angry and his mother warned *Meneriyo* again that if she ignored her advice, the Jaguars would eat her.
11. When the Jaguars were all painted, *Meneriyo* went out to dance with them. Their mother told her only to dance with the eldest who was the lead dancer but instead she danced first with the youngest and then with the others in the dance line. Only just before dawn did she dance with the eldest Jaguar. Again the mother warned her to dance only with him.
12. The Jaguars were dancing with hollow bamboo stamping tubes. One of the tubes hit *Meneriyo*'s toe and knocked off the nail. The tube ate the toe-nail and then sucked out her soul through the hole in her toe.

13. At dawn the Jaguars danced in a circle round *Meneriyo*. Suddenly the eldest Jaguar killed her by biting her in the back of the neck.

14. The Jaguars took *Meneriyo* outside the house to singe the hairs off her body before cooking and eating her (Variant: to roast her body under an ingá tree). They cut off her head and began to eat her.

15. The Jaguars' mother asked them for *Meneriyo*'s viscera to boil separately. She took them down to the river to wash them. She opened the womb and saw a male child. He jumped out of her hand and into the water. She told him that the Jaguars had killed his mother. He had a tiny, feeble voice and simply said, 'we we we we'.

16. There was a dam where *Warimi*, *Meneriyo*'s child, had escaped into the water. The Jaguar children came there to play with him. They tried to catch him with sieves and nets but he slipped through them as if he was made of water.

17. The Jaguars urinated on the sand near the water and butterflies came to drink there. *Warimi* caught the butterflies and drew designs on their wings.

18. *Meni* Shaman came to visit his sister, the mother of the Jaguars. He brought his children and they too tried to catch *Warimi*.

19. They dug a hole in the sand and buried their young, pre-pubertal sister in it with her legs apart. Then they urinated on the sand on top above her heart. When they had gone away the butterflies came to drink the urine and *Warimi* came out of the water to play with them. As he stood above the girl's vagina, she slammed her legs shut and caught him in her legs and arms.

20. *Warimi* then turned into a little baby who cried and cried and refused to stop. He only stopped crying when he had been blown over to change his soul and when the little girl carried him.

21. They took *Warimi* back to *Meni* Shaman's house where he grew very fast into a boy.

22. *Meni* Shaman's wife, a Jaguar woman, went one day to visit her own people to get manioc. She took *Warimi* along with her. In the manioc garden he turned himself into various species of small bird. Each time he did this, a Jaguar girl would chase him. Suddenly he would turn himself into a grown man, make love with her and then turn back into a child.

23. On the way back home, *Warimi* was in a canoe with his grandmother, *Meni* Shaman's wife. He dived into the water saying that he was going to fetch a hollow log full of fish. Instead he came up with an anaconda full of fish which he tipped into the canoe. His grandmother fainted with fright but *Warimi* revived her with medicine taken from the anaconda. By this time *Warimi* was an adult man though he still looked like a child.

M.4.E *Warimi* returns to the Jaguars' house

1. *Warimi*'s grandfather, *Meni* Shaman, made lots of basketry to take to his

affines the Jaguars. *Warimi* asked to go but was told that the Jaguars would eat him.

2. *Meni* Shaman told *Warimi* to go and see if there were fish in a trap for him to eat while he was away. As he went to look, *Meni* Shaman set off, leaving him behind. *Warimi* cooked the fish very quickly and after eating, he went after *Meni* Shaman.

3. *Warimi* followed *Meni* Shaman as a little bird, *kuri*. *Meni* Shaman kept trying to catch him to send him home. He warned him that if he came, the Jaguars would eat him just as they had eaten his mother.

4. They arrived at the headwaters of a stream where there was a canoe waiting. *Meni* Shaman filled the canoe up with basketry so that there was no room for *Warimi*. *Warimi* then stacked the baskets neatly and got into the canoe.

5. As they got near to the Jaguars' house, *Meni* Shaman rubbed the bitter juice from a leaf on to his head. This is why *Warimi* is also called Bitter (*Sɇe*).

6. He followed his grandfather into the house. He looked like a young boy. After greeting *Meni* Shaman, the Jaguars asked who was with him. 'That's Bitter, my grandson.'

7. The Jaguars wanted to eat *Warimi* and in order to find out if he really was bitter, one of them gouged out some flesh from his head and tasted it. 'He really is bitter', said the Jaguar. Another Jaguar suggested that he might be less bitter underneath so he dug deeper into *Warimi*'s head. Quickly *Meni* Shaman squeezed more bitter juice into *Warimi*'s head and the Jaguars finally decided that he was not fit to eat.

8. The Jaguars held a dance during which they began to play football with *Warimi*'s mother's head. The head rolled towards him and when he saw it he began to cry. *Warimi* then played football too and was very popular with the Jaguar children.

9. *Meni* Shaman then returned home leaving *Warimi* with the Jaguars; *Warimi* assured him that he wanted to stay.

10. *Warimi* began to ask the Jaguars how his mother died. They told him a number of different stories about her death but *Warimi* did not believe them, as he knew that it was they who had killed her.

11. *Warimi* slung his hammock over the cassava griddle at the back of the house. He swung so violently in his hammock that the ropes broke and he fell on to the griddle, breaking it. He put it all back together but kept some of the pieces aside.

12. He then told the *horoa* ants to cross a big river and return with the scales of the miritı́ fruit belonging to the Miritı́ Tapir (*Rẽ Wekɇ*). The ants brought the scales; *Warimi* made piranha fish out of the bits of pottery and used the scales to make their teeth.

13. *Warimi* made a bridge across the river and went to visit Miritı́ Tapir. Miritı́ Tapir did not recognise him but told him that there was a character called *Warimi* around and that if he met him he would kick him to death with his big feet.

14. On the pretext of extracting jiggers from Miriti′Tapir's feet, *Warimi* lifted them up and filled them with jiggers and then made them very sore by clumsily trying to extract them again.

15. *Warimi* then challenged Miriti′ Tapir to a race. The outcome was that Miriti′ Tapir ran headlong into the river and was eaten by the piranhas that *Warimi* had put there. This was a trial run and *Warimi* was pleased with the results.

16. *Warimi* went back to the Jaguars' house and told them to hold another dance. During the dance they again played football with *Meneriyo*'s head. *Warimi* kicked the head high into the air so that it went across the river and landed in the crook of a *hou* tree. It became a wasps' nest.

17. *Warimi* made a bridge across the river in order to get the head back. He cut assai palm logs and bound them together with vine. The logs were anacondas and the vines were snakes.

18. On the first day of the dance, *Warimi* told all the Jaguars that they were to dance across the river on the bridge.

19. When all the Jaguars were on the bridge, at a signal from *Warimi*, the bindings of the bridge came undone and all the Jaguars were thrown into the water. The piranhas in the river ate them all up and the water turned red with blood.

20. Only one Jaguar, Steel Tapir (*Kome Weku*), survived, as he already had one foot on the opposite bank when the bridge collapsed. The piranhas ate his other leg but he managed to scramble ashore. He is the ancestor of the white people.

21. *Warimi* went back to the Jaguars' house, turned all the household possessions into people and then bashed them to pieces with a club, carefully making it look as if there had been a bloody fight.

22. Then he went back to *Meni* Shaman's house and told him that other people had come and killed all the Jaguars and that they should go and bury them. *Meni* Shaman went back to the Jaguars' house with *Warimi* and realised that it was in fact *Warimi* who had killed his affines. In anger, he stuffed *Warimi* into a coca mortar and pounded him to death. Then he poured out the powder and *Warimi* flew off as a small parrot, *butu kiri*. Then *Meni* Shaman went home and mourned his affines.

M.4.F *Warimi* obtains poison

1. *Rame*, a man-eating eagle, ate up many of the first people. One day he picked up a man by his belt and carried him off to his nest to give to his children to eat.

2. The man killed *Rame*'s children and then climbed down the tree from the nest. He took the down from the fledgling eagles for use in shamanism.

3. The man then went and told *Warimi* about *Rame* and *Warimi* decided to kill him. *Warimi* made some poison but found that it had no strength; he decided to obtain poison from Poison Anaconda.

4. He stood on a hill and soon a big flock of Wood Ibises (*Ēoroa, Mycteria*

americana) came past on their way to give ants in a ceremonial exchange of food to their *umaniko*, mother-in-law, *Romi Kumu*.

5. *Warimi* greeted the birds, calling them *hako maku*, 'mother's son', but they told him that his *hako maku* was following along behind. He greeted other Ibises in the same way but again they told him that his *hako maku* was following behind.

6. Finally one of the birds answered his greeting and *Warimi* asked him if he would take him along with him. The birds made many excuses in order to dissuade *Warimi* but each time he assured them that he would manage to overcome the obstacles they told him about.

7. The Ibises put down on *Warimi*'s body and feathers on his arms. They began to teach him to fly. At first he could only go a short distance before crashing to the ground. Finally he learned to fly properly and set off with the Ibises on their journey.

8. Soon they arrived at fire-manioc garden, where flames shot high in the air and blocked their path. *Warimi* made rain which put out the fire so they could go past. This made the Ibises very pleased with him.

9. They had to pass through other obstacles, first a strong wind and then two mountains that crashed together and threatened to kill them. *Warimi* overcame both and made it safe for the others to pass.

10. They arrived at *Romi Kumu*'s house; as they came in through the door, Pouncing Jaguar (*Taho Yai*) began to kill them. He was a deadfall-trap placed in the door of the house which fell on the Ibises. Pouncing Jaguar ate the birds as for him they were all the different kinds of game birds.

11. With his shamanic powers, *Warimi* fixed the trap so that it no longer fell. Pouncing Jaguar became angry and asked the Ibises if there was anyone with them. They told him that they were alone. *Warimi* was invisible to both Pouncing Jaguar and *Romi Kumu*.

12. The Ibises danced all night and in the morning they presented their mother-in-law *Romi Kumu* with the packets of ants.

13. After the dance, *Romi Kumu* and Pouncing Jaguar kept noticing that, though they could see no one eating it, small pieces of cassava bread kept disappearing. Again they asked the Ibises if there was anyone with them but they denied that there was. Finally the Ibises flew off home, leaving *Warimi* behind.

14. As *Romi Kumu* began to sweep the floor of the house after the dance, she felt someone tugging at her pubic hair. She could see no one so she felt around on the floor looking for him.

15. *Romi Kumu* had a huge crop of pubic hair; it was *ēho misi*, fish-poison vine (*Lonchocarpus*), and covered with flowers.

16. The more that *Warimi* tugged at her hair, the more excited *Romi Kumu* became. *Warimi* became a green bee, *berua buku*, who came and drank from the flowers on the poison vine. Then he began to make love to *Romi Kumu* and went inside her body. He was looking for poison with which to kill *Rame*.

M.4 Warimi

He could find no poison so he came out through her head as a poison lizard
(*rima yau, Uracentren flaviceps?*).
17. By this time *Romi Kumu* had become sexually voracious and made love to
Warimi again and again, raping him.
18. *Romi Kumu*'s father, Poison Anaconda, lived nearby in a stone house. *Romi
Kumu* took *Warimi* into the house with her and left him there, shutting the
stone door behind her so that he would not escape.
19. Poison Anaconda was asleep but she woke him up, saying, 'Father, here is
someone who will be your servant and blow your fire up for you.'
20. *Warimi* jumped up on to the lighting post in the centre of the house. Poison
Anaconda began to look for him on the floor of the house; he wanted to eat
Warimi. He called *Warimi* to come and blow the fire so that he could catch him
but *Warimi* used his powers to blow the fire from afar, still sitting up on the post.
21. *Warimi* climbed to the roof of the house and drilled a hole in it. A sunbeam
came through the hole and lit up Poison Anaconda's body; this was *Warimi*'s
blowpipe. Poison Anaconda then went to sleep.
22. *Warimi* turned himself into a flea and after biting Poison Anaconda on the
back to distract him, went inside his body to look for poison. He tied a string
round Poison Anaconda's heart and another round his gall-bladder. Poison
Anaconda cried out in pain, 'It's Father of the Sky, it is *Warimi*, she left him with
me, that stupid bundle of pubic hair.' *Warimi* took poison from the gall-bladder.
23. *Warimi* tried to get out of Poison Anaconda's body; he went down to his
anus but Poison Anaconda blocked it with his hand; he went up to his mouth
but Poison Anaconda clamped it shut and gritted his teeth. Then *Warimi* tickled
the inside of Poison Anaconda's nose; he sneezed and *Warimi* escaped.
24. *Warimi* went out through the hole in the roof that he had made, turned into
a parrot, *tói*, and flew off. Then he turned into a moriche oriole (*nyaho mini,
Icterus chrysocephalus*); he carried the poison round his neck, which is why this
bird has a yellow throat. As he flew above *Romi Kumu*'s manioc garden she
threw a club at him to kill him. He dodged the club and flew on.

M.4.G *Warimi* makes curare poison

1. *Warimi* flew off to *Rame* mountain where he began to distil the poison he
had taken from Poison Anaconda.
2. As the poison boiled, froth rose to the surface. He flicked the froth off with
a feather and it gave rise to *emoa*, tiny red ants with a burning sting, and to *roe*,
another ant with a painful sting.
3. Then Lizard Woman (*Yuo*), came along and began to laugh at him, saying,
'*Hako makɨ*, mother's son, your poison is not very strong.' *Warimi* shot her with
his blowpipe.
4. As the poison boiled, fumes rose up and went into *Warimi*'s nose and mouth.
He began to suffocate and choke, going 'hu hu hu hu hu', the noise of the howler

281

monkey. Then he fainted. While he was unconscious all the snakes, spiders, centipedes and other creatures that have poison came and drank from the poison pot. Not all the snakes managed to drink before he woke so some are not venomous.

5. *Warimi* put the poison in a poison pot; the spatula used to put poison on the arrows was the scorpion, the string that tied on the cover was a poisonous spider, the string round the top of the pot was the centipede and the cover of the pot was a nest of poisonous wasps.

6. *Warimi* then made all the different kinds of blowpipe, selecting for his use the one made from two concentric tubes of palm wood.

7. He made all the different kinds of blowpipe dart and all the different kinds of cotton used to wind round the end. Then he put poison on the darts and set off to kill *Rame*.

M.4.H *Warimi* kills *Rame*

1. *Rame* sat on top of *Rame* mountain, and from there he swooped down and ate up all the people.

2. *Warimi* looked through his blowpipe and saw him sitting there. He shot one dart but it missed. Where it landed, poison vines grew up. He shot another dart and the same thing happened.

3. Then he shot a dart that went high in the sky, turned over and fell and pierced the top of *Rame*'s neck.

4. *Rame* flew all over the Pirá-paraná region trying to escape from *Warimi* but he kept cutting off his retreat. As he flew and as the poison began to kill him, he sang *Rame*'s dance-song. For each of the places he flew to, he sang a different section of the song.

5. Finally *Rame* fell dead. The Tukano and Desana came and took poison from him and took his down. This is the stuff they use for shamanism and it explains why they have so much poison.

6. From *Rame*'s body, the Tatuyos obtained all their ceremonial equipment. For them *Rame* is called Eagle Jaguar (*Ga Yai*), and also Round Gourd Jaguar (*Tuga Yai*). They took his wing feathers – these are the strings of yellow feathers they wind round their *He* instruments. They took his bones which are their *He* instruments; these instruments are called the Sun's bones, Eagle Father Bones. They took his other bones to make the jaguar bones that they tie on their feather head-dresses. They took his skull and made their sacred gourds, the beeswax gourd and the tobacco gourd. They took his blood to make the red paint used to anoint initiates. *Rame*'s shadow was deer (*nyama*); from this they made the tapir-skin screen behind which the shamans sit at *He* House.

7. *Rame*'s brain was their shamans' tobacco and his liver their beeswax. His down was the down they use in shamanism.

8. The Letuama and Tanimuka came and obtained their shamanic substances

from him also. They took his eyes, the quartz crystals that shamans use for seeing. They took his down too.

M.5

He Anaconda

M.5.A *He* Anaconda (1)

1. *He* Anaconda's grandsons had seen the *He* for the first time in their lives.
2. He climbed a uacú (*simio*, a tree with large, green pods which are bitter but edible when roasted – unidentified sp.), picked some of the fruit and dropped them into a fire he had lit at its base.
3. The children smelled the fruit, took them from the fire and ate them.
4. *He* Anaconda came down from the tree and immediately the world went dark and a terrible thunderstorm with heavy rain came up.
5. *He* Anaconda lay on the ground like a huge hollow log with a wide opening at one end.
6. The children, seeking shelter from the rain, ran into the hollow log and thus into *He* Anaconda's mouth.
7. With a noise like thunder, *He* Anaconda went off to the east, to the river mouth, to *He hɨdoa wi*, to the Water Door. There the children died.
8. Later it was time to show the *He* to others of his grandchildren who had grown up. *He* Anaconda told his son to prepare beer, coca, tobacco and yagé for the rite.
9. On the appointed day, *He* Anaconda arrived. As he approached, the *He* sounded; the sound of the *He* was *He* Anaconda himself.
10. In the afternoon he arrived; he went round and round the outside of the maloca.
11. Then his son blew tobacco snuff into his nose. *He* Anaconda lost consciousness and then vomited up the bones of his grandchildren. They were the Sun's bones, the bones of the son of the Sun. He vomited the bones into an enclosure.
12. Then he told his son to light a fire and burn him on it so that there would be more *He*. His son lit a fire, dragged *He* Anaconda round and round the house and then out of the front door on to the plaza. There he put him on a big fire till he burned to ashes.
13. In the place where the fire had been, tobacco, caraiuru, fish-poison, calaloo and a paxiuba palm grew up, first tobacco and then the palm. They grew very

fast making a 'tɨ tɨ tɨ tɨ' noise as they went upwards. When the palm reached the sky, it stopped growing.

14. From the place where *He* Anaconda was burned, the people came and obtained all kinds of magic substances used in shamanism.

15. White Toucan Woman (*Rase Bomo*), *He* Anaconda's daughter, came and sat on the top of the palm mourning her father. She said that because they had killed her father, from then on all people would avoid seeing the *He* as it would be an unpleasant experience.

16. The paxiuba palm bore fruit. The Toucan began to eat the fruit and it fell from the tree to the world below. From these fruits, the paxiuba palms of the world grew. The fruit of this palm makes one ill if eaten as it comes from the palm of *He* Anaconda.

17. Red Squirrel came and cut the palm trunk into sections, making *He* instruments for all people.

18. Tapir came and took the instrument made from the very top of the palm. With it he made a loud, deep noise, saying, 'I shall suck in the people, the children of the people, and kill and eat them, I shall be the one that does not like people.'

19. The Howler Monkeys heard him say this and told him, 'No, that's not what that instrument is for. That is for shamanism to open the *He* People's doors to make men.'

20. They told the Tapir to bring his instrument over to them so that they could try it. The instruments that the Howler Monkeys had came from the very bottom of the palm and made a tiny, squeaking whistle, 'owi owi owi owi', like that of the tapir today.

21. They gave their instruments to the Tapir and when he gave them his, they ran immediately up a tree so that he could not catch them.

22. They left the Tapir with their instrument; now it is they who have deep, loud voices. They do well by making men.

23. The tapir is an animal that does not like his instrument and stamps his feet in anger.

M.5.B *He* Anaconda (2)

1. Toucan landed on top of the *He* palm. He let fall a fruit which fell and grew up into another palm. It grew very fast and touched the sky.

2. The toucan then cut the palm up into sections, making *He* instruments for all people. The Toucan is *He* Father.

3. He gave the *He* to all people: to the Yukuna, Tanimuka, Makuna, Letuama, Bará, Tukano, Makú, Cubeo, Baniwa, all of them.

4. The very bottom of the palm was *He Bohori Yageomɨ*, the *He* instrument used at mourning and death rites. This instrument belongs to the Siriano. It was the one that belonged to the Toucan and had death inside it.

5. It sounds 'pu poe he he he' and is crying and mourning.

6. This is why today the Siriano have death *He* (*bohori He*).

7. They said, 'That bone will become a man.' This is why they drink the water from the top of that palm; it is why they scrape the bones of their dead parents and drink them in manioc beer. They are the 'bottom end' of the *He* People.

8. The instrument Fish Anaconda's Son (*Wai Hino Makʉ*) fell into the water. The Bará people fished around in the water for it. This is why they have the instrument Old Water Thrower (*Oko Yue Bʉkʉ*), their shaman.

M.6

Manioc-stick Anaconda

M.6.A Manioc-stick Anaconda and Macaw

1. Manioc-stick Anaconda, also called Cross Eyes (*Kahe Sawari*) and Old Gourd
(Koa *Bʉkʉ*), was the child of *Yeba Hakʉ*, the Primal Sun, precursor of the sun
and moon today. His mother was the sky.
2. Manioc-stick Anaconda was bright and shining like the sun.
3. He did not know who his parents were and this made him very sad. *Yeba Hakʉ*
came and told him that he was his father. He said that though he was going to leave
the world, Manioc-stick Anaconda was to stay to bring people into being.
4. Macaw was Manioc-stick Anaconda's younger brother. Manioc-stick Anaconda
was married to Jaguar Woman, and they had children. Macaw had no wife. He
seduced his brother's wife and told her not to obey her husband any longer.
5. Macaw decided to kill Manioc-stick Anaconda. He turned himself into a
tapir and ate the crops in their manioc garden. Then, turning back into a man,
he suggested to his brother that they went to catch the tapir in a pitfall trap.
6. As they cut stakes to line the bottom of the pit, Macaw tried to stab Manioc-
stick Anaconda but Manioc-stick Anaconda outwitted him.
7. They dug the trap and when it was deep, Macaw told his brother to jump in
to finish the digging. Manioc-stick Anaconda jumped in and fell through the
bottom down to the Underworld below. He landed on an ingá tree by the side
of the Underworld River.
8. As he sat by the river, the Moon came by. '*Hako makʉ*, mother's son', called
Manioc-stick Anaconda but the Moon replied that his mother's son was following
on behind.
9. Then Morning Star, Morning Venus, came past. Manioc-stick Anaconda called
out to him too but he went by without answering; he was going up into the sky
to shine in the morning.
10. Then a striped water snake (*rĩa neri*) came past. Manioc-stick Anaconda
greeted him as '*Hako makʉ*, mother's son', but he too went by without answering.
11. Then the giant otter and small otter, the Sun's canoe paddlers, came down
to the river on their way to fetch the Sun to take him up to the headwaters of

the Underworld River. 'Take me with you, mother's son', called Manioc-stick Anaconda. The otters replied that his mother's son would be following behind.

12. Then Sun Grebe came by catching spiders and grasshoppers to use as bait. 'Mother's son', called Manioc-stick Anaconda. 'Yes, who is it?' replied Sun Grebe. Manioc-stick Anaconda asked him to take him in his canoe and the grebe agreed on condition that he did not fart at all. Manioc-stick Anaconda agreed and got in. After a short distance he could contain himself no more and let out a tiny little fart. Immediately Sun Grebe's canoe split asunder throwing Manioc-stick Anaconda into the water. He became a spider and bounced along the water to a tree stump. Sun Grebe flew off upriver.

13. Manioc-stick Anaconda sat by the river and after a time the Sun approached in his canoe. His heat spread out in front and threatened to burn Manioc-stick Anaconda to death. Manioc-stick Anaconda cooled him down with his shamanic power.

14. 'Mother's son?' called out Manioc-stick Anaconda. 'Yes', replied the Sun, 'what do you want?' Manioc-stick Anaconda asked the Sun to take him with him in his canoe. The Sun told him that it would be too hot but Manioc-stick Anaconda argued that because he was the Sun's mother's son, he would be all right. The Sun agreed and they set off upstream together.

15. At midday (in the Underworld, midnight on this earth), the Sun told Manioc-stick Anaconda to dive down under the water and to bring up a hollow log full of fish. Manioc-stick Anaconda dived down but all he could find was a huge anaconda. He came up and told the Sun that there was no log there. The Sun told him to try again. The same thing happened. Then the Sun, not believing Manioc-stick Anaconda, dived down himself.

16. While the Sun was under the water, the Sun's canoe paddlers, Fire Callicebus Monkey (*Hea Wau*) and Fire Howler Monkey (*Hea Ugu*), Red Squirrel, Giant Otter and Small Otter, told Manioc-stick Anaconda to take snuff from the Sun's bag as the Sun would try to burn him to death.

17. The Sun blocked up the mouth and anus of the anaconda log and then tipped it out into the canoe. As many fish as have names in the Barasana language came out from that log. The large fish, the Sun's fish, Underworld River fish, disease fish, evil shamanism fish, came out of this log. They must be carefully blown before they are eaten.

18. They went on upstream to an otter's feeding place on the bank of the river. The Sun told Manioc-stick Anaconda to gut the fish but he refused. The Sun's paddlers did so instead. The Sun sent Manioc-stick Anaconda off to fetch his cooking pot. Manioc-stick Anaconda went off but all he could see was a fer-de-lance snake lying coiled up. He went back and told the Sun. The Sun sent him to try again. The same thing happened. The third time the Sun went off and brought back the snake, his cooking pot. He put the fish in the pot and put it on to boil.

19. Manioc-stick Anaconda refused to eat the fish. When urged on by the Sun he

pretended to eat but let the fish drop from his mouth. He knew the fish were harmful, they were anaconda-body fish (see 17 above). They set off upriver again.

20. The Sun was not happy with Manioc-stick Anaconda as he doubted that he was really his mother's son. He said to Manioc-stick Anaconda, 'It's no good, we cannot approach one another closely. Are you really my mother's son?' Manioc-stick Anaconda assured him that he was. The Sun then told him that if he was his mother's son he would live but that otherwise he would be burned alive.

21. The Sun tipped out some snuff, put it in his mouth and then blew it out in a cloud of fire. Manioc-stick Anaconda became a spider, jumped over the side of the canoe and then got back in when the heat had passed. The Sun tried again and the same thing happened. Each time he blew out the snuff, the Sun called out, 'Mother's son?' and Manioc-stick Anaconda answered, 'Yes', in a confident voice.

22. After two tries, the Sun told Manioc-stick Anaconda to try burning him. Secretly, Manioc-stick Anaconda put the snuff he had taken from the Sun into his mouth and then blew it out in a cloud of fire. The Sun's feather crown caught on fire and the heat was so intense that the Sun cried out, 'Stop, stop.'

23. Then the Sun said to him, 'You really are my mother's son. I care for you very much. You are a man. Your brother thought that he would get rid of you but you will not disappear, you will not die.'

24. They went on upstream till they arrived at the Sun's landing place, a big log sloping into the water. The Sun told Manioc-stick Anaconda that there were lots of fire ants (*emoa*) around and that he should shut his eyes to avoid being stung. As Manioc-stick Anaconda shut his eyes, the Sun rose up into the sky and left him. Manioc-stick Anaconda tried to hit the Sun with his club but missed. He used his club to vault upwards but only got as far as the *Ka* People's layer, the home of the maniuara termites (*meka*).

25. Manioc-stick Anaconda arrived at a place looking like an abandoned manioc garden. He saw Tapir there collecting cecropia leaves to make ash to mix with coca. Manioc-stick Anaconda called out, '*Nikɨ*, grandfather', to him. Tapir told Manioc-stick Anaconda that he was going to the *Ka* People's house where he was to be the shaman at a dance.

26. Manioc-stick Anaconda asked Tapir if he would take him with him but he replied that there was a large river that Manioc-stick Anaconda would be unable to cross.

27. Manioc-stick Anaconda told him that he would become his tick and lodge behind his ear. Tapir agreed and they set off together. When they came to the river, Tapir told him that when he was out of breath he was to bite him hard and he would come up to the surface to breathe.

28. Tapir set off across the river, walking along the bottom. After he had gone a quarter of the way across he came up for air. He set off again and came up when

he was half-way across. Then he came up three-quarters of the way across and the next time he came up they were on the other bank.

29. Each time that Tapir came up for air, he recited a piece of shamanic chanting to Manioc-stick Anaconda. The chanting is that used at the birth of babies and for blowing spells into the mother's milk.

30. On the other bank, Tapir shook himself violently and Manioc-stick Anaconda fell to the ground. Tapir told him to take a path in the distance and that a fork in the path he would find Path Fork Dancer (*Ma Hido Baya*), a kind of lizard also called *sebero* (*Plica plica*). Tapir set off leaving Manioc-stick Anaconda behind.

31. Manioc-stick Anaconda went along the path indicated and found Path Fork Dancer. He split a stump of wood down the middle and jammed Path Fork Dancer into the fork by his neck so that he was trapped. Manioc-stick Anaconda then set off again for the house.

32. When he got to the house, the termites asked Manioc-stick Anaconda if he had seen Path Fork Dancer, who was coming to be the lead dancer at their dance. Manioc-stick Anaconda told them that he had seen him back along the path. Later on Manioc-stick Anaconda slipped out of the house and went back and released Path Fork Dancer. Then he came back.

33. Soon after, Path Fork Dancer arrived in the house with a sore, flabby neck (the *sebero* lizard has a red, erectile pouch under its neck). After greeting the termites, Path Fork Dancer got very angry, saying that there was an imposter in the house who had treated him very badly. The termites reassured him and he began to lead them in dancing.

34. Tapir sat on a stool doing the protective shamanism for the termites who would leave the house in the morning.

35. Tapir's wife, asleep in her hammock, suddenly let out an enormous fart. Manioc-stick Anaconda was sitting next to Ant Bird (*Meka Mini, Formicaridae*), who said to him, 'Mother's son, did you hear that? Off you go and make love to her.' Manioc-stick Anaconda declined so Ant Bird went instead.

36. When he had finished, Tapir's wife said 'Tapir, have you been stirring my pepper pot? It's all wet.' Tapir denied that it was him and went over to see if what she said was true. He became very angry.

37. Lighting a taper, he went round each of the termites in turn, making them pull back their foreskins to see if there was sperm underneath. Termites must have spells blown on them before they are eaten otherwise they make one waste away and die. They are shamanised for the initiates to stop them from vomiting. This is related to this incident.

38. Ant Bird began to panic but Manioc-stick Anaconda told him to put white ash from the fire on his penis. When Tapir inspected him, the ash dropped on to the floor and Tapir was satisfied. He said to his wife, 'None of my grand-children did it, you must have done it yourself.'

39. The termites danced all night and at dawn they crowded round the door of the house ready to leave. Tapir told the worker termites to go and see if the way was clear. They went out and immediately a jaguar (a termite-eating bird) ate them. This made the other termites very frightened.

40. Manioc-stick Anaconda wanted to urinate badly so Ant Bird led him out through a hole in the wall at the side of the house.

41. Manioc-stick Anaconda found himself on the termite hill near his house where he used to come to get termites. He heard the sound of the *He* instruments played by his children. They had been initiated by Macaw and were coming to collect termites, their diet after initiation.

42. Manioc-stick Anaconda became a katydid (*diro*) and clung to a tree. His daughter followed his footprints and found him there. He told her that he was still alive though his brother had tried to kill him.

43. He told his children to make two termite traps, one in the east and another in the west. Then he blew spells on the termites to make them safe to eat. He told his children that the termites had been drinking yagé all night and that if they ate them without being blown they would be harmed by the drug.

44. They set off back home. Before they got there, Manioc-stick Anaconda told his daughter to go on ahead and make a compartment just inside the men's door using a fish trap. She was to sling his hammock there. He told his children not to tell their mother or uncle that he was alive and then slipped into the compartment unnoticed.

45. As they ate the termites, one of them bit the daughter's finger, making it bleed. The blood fell on to her mother who began to beat her. For protection she revealed the presence of her father in the compartment. The mother was pregnant by Macaw and became very ashamed and subdued.

46. Macaw told his brother that he had initiated the children and suggested that he and his brother went to get a young macaw to teach the initiates how to make feather head-dresses.

47. They set off together for Macaw Mountain, where the macaws were nesting. They made a scaffold to reach the nest and Macaw told his brother to go up and bring down the macaws. By magic, Macaw turned himself into an anaconda inside the hollow where the macaws were nesting. He was going to kill Manioc-stick Anaconda. Manioc-stick Anaconda turned the anaconda back into a macaw. Then Macaw took away the scaffold, leaving Manioc-stick Anaconda stranded.

48. Manioc-stick Anaconda took the young macaws and rubbed them all over with yellow ochre to make their feathers grow yellow.

49. He called the snake *badi rẽ guhia* (*Oxybellis*) to stretch across from a nearby tree but he was too short and fell down. Manioc-stick Anaconda called other kinds of snakes all of which were too short and fell down. The snakes draped over the tree and became lianas.

50. Then Manioc-stick Anaconda called the snake *wakʉako* (*Clelia clelia clelia*?).

He stretched high into the air and toppled over on to the place where Manioc-stick Anaconda sat. He pulled himself taut and Manioc-stick Anaconda slid down his body. As he slid, the snake's body resounded 'ma'tooooor'.

51. Manioc-stick Anaconda returned to the house, much to the displeasure of his brother Macaw then suggested that they should go and trap fish for the initiates to eat.

52. At the river, they put the traps in position. Macaw then told Manioc-stick Anaconda to dive down to check that there were no gaps under the traps. While Manioc-stick Anaconda was under the water, Macaw opened the doors to the world below, hoping that Manioc-stick Anaconda would go through and be drowned. He failed, so he sent him down again but with no success. Then Manioc-stick Anaconda sent Macaw down — he was testing him to see how strong were his shamanic powers. By now he had begun to plot to kill his brother. Manioc-stick Anaconda opened the doors to the world below and Macaw went through. He did not come back, but finally Manioc-stick Anaconda went down and saved him. Macaw came up again as a small otter with red eyes who panted, 'kara kara kara'. Lots of fish went into the traps and the next day they went and took them out to smoke them.

53. In the dry season, when the rivers are very low, Macaw suggested that they went to poison fish. They went first to collect the poison vines. Manioc-stick Anaconda went to the Sun and got vines from him. His bundle of vines was small, whilst that obtained from the manioc garden by Macaw was large. Macaw laughed at him for having such a small bundle.

54. They rinsed the vines in the water and lots of fish died. At midday, Manioc-stick Anaconda called his wife to come and cook fish for him. Macaw told her not to go and told Manioc-stick Anaconda to cook the fish for himself. This happened twice and then Manioc-stick Anaconda got really angry. He decided to kill his brother and wife but to try and save his children.

55. He told his children to go and collect leaves to cook the fish in. He told them to get the leaves from a long way away but they refused to listen and remained nearby.

56. Then Manioc-stick Anaconda once more tried to persuade his wife to cook fish for him. Macaw told him that he could cook for himself and that his wife would not come.

57. Manioc-stick Anaconda became furious. He put the snuff he had obtained from the Sun into his mouth and then blew it out in a cloud of fire. Everything burned up like a burning manioc garden. Macaw and Manioc-stick Anaconda's wife flew up into the air as macaws. Macaw cried out, 'agu gagu agu gagu agu gagu' (the cry of the macaw but also translatable as 'ow, elder brother, ow, elder brother . . . ').

58. Manioc-stick Anaconda went up into the sky and cut off their retreat. He burned them again. They began to come down and he cut off their retreat to

the world below. Then they fell, dying. They cried, 'aa aa aa aa aa aa', fell into the river and sunk under the water.

59. Manioc-stick Anaconda's children were burned up too. As they burned they cried out, *'hea soekoa, hea soekoa*, the fire has burned', and turned into birds called *Hea buekoa*. Manioc-stick Anaconda said to them, 'You will not disappear. You will become the birds that keep the food mothers (women) company as they work in the manioc garden. You will make them happy as they work.' They went off to the tree people's layer.

60. Manioc-stick Anaconda went to the river and felt around under the water; lying there were *He* flutes, the ones called Old Macaw (*Maha Buku*). The longer flute was Macaw and the shorter one was Manioc-stick Anaconda's wife.

61. Manioc-stick Anaconda was very sad and began to mourn his wife and brother. He said, 'You will not disappear. You will be *He*. You will be shown to each generation of children and adopt them as your own.'

62. Then Manioc-stick Anaconda went to Jaguar Path House and married Jaguar Woman. She bore him a son called *Yeba*. The story of *Yeba* is another 'line' (story), it is more alive and more living (see M.7 below).

63. Then Manioc-stick Anaconda went to the east. His bones became the *He* instruments. They became Dance Anaconda (*Basa Hino*), Manioc-squeezing Woman (*Buhe Romio*), Old Callicebus Monkey (*Wau Buku*) and *Kana* Flower (*Kana Goro*).

64. The top of his skull became the tobacco gourd and the bottom became the beeswax gourd. His liver and tongue became beeswax; his heart became a snuff gourd and his brain became tobacco snuff. His eyes became *kahe makuri*, small pieces of polished brass worn on sticks over the ears. His penis became the ceremonial cigar and his testicles became little gourds of snuff and red paint kept in the feather box and used at initiation. His elbow became the elbow ornament (*rika sāria yasi*) and his ribs became the sacred shell belt called *hino waruka*, anaconda ribs.

M.6.B Manioc-stick Anaconda burns himself

1. Manioc-stick Anaconda was angry with himself. He put snuff in his mouth and then took it out and put it in a little heap on the ground. It began to burn and a spark landed on his neck.

2. Manioc-stick Anaconda burned and everything round him caught fire. The whole land was white from the ash of the fire.

3. His soul left his body and became another man, also Manioc-stick Anaconda. He was a man like us.

4. Manioc-stick Anaconda's shadow lay on the ground burned to ash. From the charcoal on the ground grew up manioc, all the manioc there is today.

5. From his liver grew up green calaloo (*au sumeriku, Phytolacca* sp.)

and from his lungs grew red calaloo (*au sūarikɨ, Phytolacca* sp.); it is red from the colour of his blood.

6. *Kɨma au*, an edible fungus, grew up on the charred logs, Manioc-stick Anaconda's bones. Then *wahe riti* and *wahe riti abase*, other edible fungi, grew there.

7. *Wati Kome*, an edible bracket fungus, grew up from his skin.

8. Then *mɨte au*, an edible fungus, and another inedible one grew up.

9. The *taga*, an edible fungus, grew up from his body-fat. The *osoa*, another fungus, also called *ehaga*, grew up from the lining of his stomach and guts.

10. From his bile grew a poisonous fungus looking like *wahe riti*. Worms came and ate his rotting liver; these are the insects that eat holes in calaloo leaves.

11. From his bile grew *nimi hũ* and *wai rima*, two cultivated fish poisons. *Taro bɨkɨ rima*, another fish poison looking somewhat like a pineapple plant, also grew from his bile.

12. Because of the fire and burning, if we eat fish caught with cultivated fish poison but not first made safe with spells, our bodies become hot and our fingernails rot.

13. All the plants came from the liquid parts of Manioc-stick Anaconda's body. The myth underlies the spells blown on calaloo to make it safe for the initiates to eat. If not treated in this way, it causes violent stomach pains.

14. The order in which the plants grew from Manioc-stick Anaconda's burned body is the same as that in which they grow after the vegetation has been burned off a new manioc garden.

15. The myth underlies the spells used to cool down a manioc garden after it has been burned. The shamans blow spells on beeswax which they then take to the garden.

M.7

Yeba

M.7.A *Yeba*'s birth and early childhood

1. *Yeba* was the first man. His mother was Jaguar Woman, and his father was *Yeba Haku*, the Sun, the Primal Sun.
2. The Sun told his wife to cook food for him but she refused to do so.
3. *Yeba*'s mother could not, or would not, suckle him. He lived off white water, stone water, the origin of milk. His mother would not tell him who his father was. He asked the animals but they could not talk.
4. Finally the Sun came and told *Yeba* that he was his father. The Sun created *Yeba* in a gourd of beeswax which was the world itself. The Sun went in circles round the earth so that *Yeba* knew that he was there.
5. *Yeba* grew up fast and when he was a boy *Romi Kumu* took him away and initiated him. She had a big gourd of beeswax which she was able to take on and off like clothing.
6. *Yeba* began to look for a wife. The animals were his people and he made tongues for them so that they could speak. When they could talk he asked them where he could find a wife. They offered him one of their women but he refused, saying that he was a man not an animal.
7. *Yeba* made people by blowing on earth or clay. These were the Makú. He asked them where he could find a wife. They offered him one of their women but again he refused, saying that he was a true man not a Makú.

M.7.B *Yeba* meets *Yawira*

1. *Yeba* went out hunting with a blowpipe. He came to an ucucí (*Pouteria ucuqui*) tree with lots of empty fruit shells lying underneath — clearly the remains of someone's meal.
2. Blue Morpho Butterfly (*Emu*) was sitting on one of the fruit shells, licking it. *Yeba* said to him, '*Niku*, grandfather, where are the women?' The butterfly replied that he didn't know. *Yeba* squashed him under the end of his blowpipe

295

and asked again. Morpho told him that there were Fish Women around who had been eating the fruit.

3. *Yeba* climbed up the ucucı́ tree and hung down from a branch as a double, testicle-shaped fruit. The Fish Women came back but were very frightened as they could smell *Yeba*. *Yeba* dropped to the ground among them.

4. One of the women, *Yawira*, picked up the fruit to eat it. Immediately *Yeba* grabbed her with a length of thorny, creeping palm.

5. *Yawira* thrashed around trying to escape. She was a big anaconda and lots of fishes came into being from her body.

6. *Yeba* took *Yawira* back to his house at Manao Lake. She lay under his hammock and as *Yeba* felt with his hands he could feel a huge anaconda. He could not make love to her as his penis was in the wrong place, up on his belly like that of a jaguar.

7. *Yawira* changed her skin and became human. She sloughed off one skin and became a boa constrictor, then she sloughed off another and became a woman.

8. *Yawira* would only eat the winged form of the termites called *bʉkoa*.

9. *Yeba* went fishing to catch something for them to eat. He brought back Jacundá (*Mʉhabuhua, Crenichichla* sp.). *Yawira* protested saying, 'That's my father's penis.' He brought *Wena* and again *Yawira* protested, saying that they were her younger brothers. He brought back *Rasowai* and she said that they were her grandparents; he brought Acará (*Wani*, Cichlid sp.) and she said 'They are my cousins', and of Sarapó (*rike, Gimmotidae*) she said, 'That's my father's cigar.' She refused to eat any of them.

M.7.C *Yawira* brings cultivated crops

1. *Yeba* told *Yawira* to go and bring his 'manioc', a fruit called *ibisa*, from his garden, the forest. She went off but came back soon after saying that *ibisa* was not manioc and that *Yeba* was an ignorant beast. He sent her to another garden to bring bananas. She went and came back saying that wild bananas (*Yeba oho; Heliconia bihai*) were not bananas at all and she refused to eat any.

2. As *Yawira* sat in the doorway of the house weaving garters, some rubber fruit (*biti, Hevea* sp.) that Small Black Squirrel (*Kahebua, Wahʉha he rika*) had hung above the door, dehisced explosively so that the nuts inside landed on *Yawira*'s lap. She called *Yeba* over and told him that the nuts were food.

3. *Yeba* told Squirrel to go and get rubber fruit with *Yawira*. They set off together and as Squirrel threw down the fruit from the tree, *Yawira* told him to wait at the tree while she went to visit her father Fish Anaconda (*Wai Hino*).

4. She went to the river and went under the water to her father's house, taking rubber fruit with her. Squirrel, thinking that she was drowning, ran into the water to save her.

5. When she got to the house, *Yawira* told her father her news about how *Yeba* had captured her and married her and how he was very uncivilised.

6. After a while they heard a rustling in the roofing leaves – it was Squirrel looking for *Yawira* under the water. They brought him into the house wet and cold and Fish Anaconda blew spells on him to bring him back to life. *Yawira* said to Squirrel, 'Niku, grandfather, I told you to wait at the tree.'
7. Fish Anaconda gave his daughter all the different kinds of cultivated crops for her to take back to *Yeba*. He blew spells on them so that *Yeba*, eating new food for the first time, would not be harmed.
8. *Yawira* went back to *Yeba*'s house and gave him the crops, telling him that in fact it was he who was uncivilised and who knew nothing.

M.7.D *Yawira* creates coca

1. *Yawira* told *Yeba* that she was going to make him something good to eat but that he should not care too much about his younger brother *Nyake*.
2. She told *Yeba* to go and make a proper garden by felling the forest and burning the trees. Then she asked *Nyake* to help her carry manioc sticks there to plant. In the garden she made love to him so violently that he died. He lay spread-eagled and his body became the rows of coca bushes in the garden. The coca was *nyake* coca, a variety that belongs to the Barasana.
3. *Yawira* was pregnant by *Nyake* and had a son from whom the *Nyake Hino Rĩa*, a Barasana sib, are descended. She cut off the baby's umbilical cord and planted it in the ground and from it a gourd vine sprang up. From the gourds, the *Koamona*, another Barasana sib, are descended.
4. *Yeba* could only make love to *Yawira* with his finger as his penis was in the wrong place. From doing this, the Barasana sib *Roe Masa* and *Yeba Masa* came into being.

M.7.E *Yawira* plants manioc

1. *Yawira* called her younger sisters to help her plant manioc. *Meneriyo* was *mene-ruku* and *Hatio* was *hatio-ruku*, varieties of manioc, *Wakuo* was *wakubu* (*Cecropia*), a garden weed, and *Widio* was all the other weeds. *Yawira* told *Yeba* not to watch them as they planted the garden. They went off and their chatter became the birdsong that accompanies women's work today.
2. As they worked, *Yeba* lifted a section of the roof of the house and peeped out at them. Immediately the women started running around and in the confusion, *Wakuo* and *Widio*, who had been told to stay at the edge of the garden, ran into the middle so that today weeds grow amongst the manioc plants.

M.7.F *Yawira* changes *Yeba*'s penis

1. When the manioc had grown, *Yawira* called her sisters to help her process it. As they did so, they began to tease *Yawira* about the way that *Yeba* made love to her. She decided to alter the situation.

2. She cooked some tapioca flour in the fire to make a heavy, sticky lump. *Yeba* was sitting in the doorway weaving a basket to give to his mother-in-law. She gave him some toasted manioc starch to drink and then came up behind him and hit him on the back of the neck with the lump of tapioca flour. His penis dropped down to the place where it is on men today, leaving a scar on his belly, the umbilicus.

3. *Yawira* then made love to *Yeba* to try out his penis. At first it hurt *Yeba* very much but *Yawira* pared down the end making the glans. Then she tried again and *Yeba* liked it.

M.7.G The origin of tobacco

1. *Yeba* and *Yawira* went off together to visit Fish Anaconda. Fish Anaconda was very angry with *Yeba* for marrying his daughter without first asking his consent. He ordered *Yeba* to bring him meat and tree-fruit at a dance. He told him that if he failed to bring the food he would eat him. *Yeba* went off to get the food.

2. Fish Anaconda gave *Yawira* tobacco to give to *Yeba*; the tobacco was in the form of a cigar looking like the sarapó fish. He told *Yawira* to tell her husband not to eat the cigar.

3. She took the cigar to *Yeba* and told him not to eat it. *Yeba* said that it was clearly a fish and ate it. His belly swelled up and he had violent diarrhoea. He went out of the house and defecated violently; from his faeces grew tobacco plants.

M.7.H *Yeba* gives meat to Fish Anaconda

1. *Yeba* went out and shot lots of animals and birds with his blowpipe. He killed guans, and Uacarí Monkeys (*Rŭtŭa*), his own people. Then he took the meat to Fish Anaconda and gave it to him at a dance.

2. As *Yeba* handed the meat over, Fish Anaconda cast off his skin and became a man. His shed skin became the tipiti (manioc-squeezing tube). He lunged forwards and grabbed the meat from *Yeba*, making him very frightened. *Yawira* reassured her husband, saying that this was how anacondas normally behave.

M.7.I *Yeba* gives fruit to Fish Anaconda

1. *Yeba* told all his people, the animals, to go and collect tree-fruit for him. The Monkeys were the people who carried the fruit.

2. *Yeba* ordered Spider to make painted bark-cloth aprons for the dance. Spider went and brought back a tiny bundle of aprons and gave it to *Yeba*. *Yeba* was angry with him, telling him that he had not made nearly enough. He undid the bundle and more aprons than he could possibly use flew out in all directions.

M.7 *Yeba*

Yeba, in anger, had hit Spider in the teeth. Spider now became angry with
Yeba and cursed the aprons and other ritual ornaments, saying that from henceforth they would be death possessions.
3. All the animals began to assemble for the dance. The Peccaries carried all
the fruit, blowing the trumpets as they went. The sound of the trumpets is their
grunting. The Woodpeckers carried the box of feathers which is why today
they have white patches on their backs. The Woolly Monkeys were the elbow
ornaments used at the dance. The shaman was Callicebus Monkey, and Jaguar
and the Otters were also shamans. Sloth (*Kerea*) was the bundles of animal
fur worn on the back (*umaria yasi*) and Agouti (*Bu*) was the women making
for the dance.
4. Red Squirrel (*Timoka*) sat secretly chewing on a tucum palm nut. He was
carving designs on the nut to make part of the special elbow ornament that the
Barasana use at initiation. The other animals asked him what he was doing and
he told them that he was chewing his tail. All the animals began to copy him
which is why today some animals have no tails.
5. All the birds began to paint themselves for the dance which is why today they
are all different colours. Blue Crowned Motmot was one of the feather crowns.
Musician Wren was one of the long flutes and Cotinga was another. Macaw was
their dancer and he was the feather head-dresses. Egret (*Yehe*) was also part
of the feather head-dresses.
6. All the birds began to chant; the sound of their chanting is the sound of the
He flutes.
7. *Yeba* gave Fish Anaconda the fruit and then began to dance. He did not know
how to dance but *Yawira* and her sister *Nacuo* danced with him and taught him.
He sang rubber-fruit dance, the dance that the Barasana and Bará sing after
Fruit House rites.
8. After the dance. *Yeba*'s brothers-in-law (*tenyua*) wanted to kill him in revenge
for his having killed and eaten fish, their people. *Yeba* and most of the animals
left the house in a hurry, but a few of the animals were left behind, which is why
some animals, like capybara, now live in the water.

M.7.J *Yeba* and Tapir

1. During a dance, Fish Anaconda gave *Yeba* and Tapir some Umari fruit (*Wamu*).
The fruits were people, women.
2. Both *Yeba* and Tapir planted their fruit; from Tapir's fruit grew a huge umari
tree with lots of fruit but from *Yeba*'s fruit grew a tiny tree with no fruit at
all. *Yeba* decided to get umari fruit from Tapir.
3. Tapir was very jealous of his umari fruit. *Yeba* asked Tapir to come to a dance
where Tapir would present *Yeba* with fruit. Tapir asked what kind of beer
would be served and on hearing that it would be made from *rutu* (*Xanthosoma*),
he refused. *Yeba* asked him again, this time offering beer made from arrowroot

299

(*ngalia*), but again Tapir refused, as he did when offered beer made of yam (*nyamo*). Only when offered beer made from coca yam (*kaho*) did he agree to come.

4. Tapir came to the dance bringing lots of rotten little fruit. *Yeba* decided to steal the umari fruit from Tapir instead.

5. With the aid of Red Squirrel and Small Agouti (*Boso*) *Yeba* finally obtained the fruit. Tapir tried to kill Small Agouti but failed.

M.7.K *Yawira* seduced by Opossum

1. During a dance, Opossum (*Oa*) and Tinamou Chief (*Ngaha Ʉhʉ*) were dancing in the dance line. While *Yawira* danced with Tinamou Chief, he made a tryst with her but Opossum overheard their plans.

2. After the dance, *Yawira* went along the path from the house till she came to a fork. Tinamou Chief had told her to take the path, marked by the tail feather of a japú bird, which led to his house and he warned her not to take the path marked by the tail feather of a blue macaw. Opossum had however switched round the feathers so that *Yawira* took the wrong path.

3. She arrived at the house and Opossum's grandmother told her that she should go and lie in her grandson's hammock. As she approached the hammock, clouds of flies flew off it; Opossum stank and all his possessions stank too.

4. *Yawira* did not like living with Opossum so she resolved to escape. Opossum had told her not to look up- or downstream while she was bathing at the river. The next time she bathed she looked downstream and saw the handsome Tinamou Chief, bathing at his port. She swam down to join him.

5. At first Tinamou Chief would not accept her, as she stank so much after having slept with Opossum.

6. Later on Opossum came down to Tinamou Chief's house looking for *Yawira*. *Yawira* hid and Tinamou Chief denied that she had been with him. Opossum had told his grandmother that if he should ever be killed it would immediately start to rain.

7. After a quarrel, Tinamou Chief did kill Opossum and immediately it started to rain heavily (a rain of blood according to a Tatuyo informant).

8. Tinamou Eagle (*Ngaha Ga*) saw the rain and began to mourn Opossum, saying '*yʉ hako makʉ* oa oa oa oa oa' ('My mother's son, oa oa oa oa oa' – this bird cries 'oa oa oa oa oa oa' on a descending scale).

9. In revenge, Tinamou Eagle killed Tinamou Chief and from his bones the Cubeo obtained their *He* instruments.

M.7.L *Yawira* seduced by the Vulture

1. After having been seduced by Opossum and Tinamou Chief, *Yawira* then ran off

M.7 Yeba

with Vulture Chief (*Yuka Bokɨ, Sarcohamphus papa*) and went and lived with
him in the sky.
2. *Yeba* followed her to the Vultures' house and after a series of adventures he
waged war on the Vultures and killed all except Vulture Chief.
3. He set off with *Yawira* once more and on a path they came upon Irara (*Wasoɨ
Wehero, Tayra barbara*) sitting in a tree drinking honey. *Yeba* went up to join
him and *Yawira*, still down on the ground, implored *Yeba* to let her come and
drink honey too.
4. Finally *Yeba* allowed her to come up and drink but warned her to drink
very carefully and slowly. She came up and began to gulp the honey down in
big mouthfuls, making *Yeba* very angry. He pushed her head down into the
honey so that she gasped for breath and drowned. As she died she cried, 'ẽo
ẽo ẽo ẽo'.
5. *Yawira* became the cunauaru frog (*ẽhoka, Phyllomedusa bicolor*). *Yeba* told
her that she would not disappear and that instead she would become *He* mother,
the mother of feathers and dance ornaments. (The cunauaru frog lives inside
water-filled hollow trees. There are very often bird feathers floating in the water
and the Barasana use the juices of this frog for tapirage, a process whereby tame
birds' feathers are plucked out and the new ones made to turn yellow. The
yellow feathers are used in head-dresses. The frog also makes brood cells using
the collected resin of *Protium heptaphyllum* – von Ihering 1968 : 267.)

M.8

The Thunders and Juruparí [1]

1. Before the earth existed, a young virgin girl lived alone in empty space; her name was *Coadidop*, grandmother of the days.
2. She made a cigar holder from her left and right legs. She made tobacco from her body, squeezed milk into it from her breasts and put it in the holder. She smoked the cigar and took coca.
3. The smoke produced thunder and a thunderbolt and a figure of a man came and then went. She smoked again and the same thing happened. The third time she smoked, the smoke became a human body. She said, 'You are the son of Thunder, you are Thunder; you are my grandson. You will have all powers and do what you want in the world.' The Thunder was called *Enu*.
4. She said, 'I made you as a man; you can do what you want, all things, both good and bad. I am a woman; I order you to make companions for yourself to live well. I will make my own companions too.'
5. The Thunder made a man from cigar smoke. He said to the man, 'You are my brother, my son; we are brothers and have the same name: Thunder, son of Thunder, emerged from the blood of Thunder'. He blew tobacco smoke again; the smoke made thunder and lightning which went up and down. He made more smoke; the third time, a third man appeared.
6. The first Thunder said, 'You are my brothers, the blood of my blood, you come from my being. The second Thunder will be the Thunder which guides the day, son of the days, *Enu Koana*. The third Thunder will be *Enu Pokurano*, and the fourth, the Thunder which does not give rise to hunger.'
7. The Thunders said to the Virgin, 'Our mother, our mother, our aunt, our blood, we will do whatever you want.' The Virgin replied, 'You are men, I cannot remain with you; now I will create women, I must have women by my side.'
8. The Virgin made a woman in the same way as she made Thunder. 'Your name will be *Caiçaro*.' Then she made another woman, *Paramano*. Now there were four Thunders and the three women. The Thunders lived on tobacco and coca. They all lived in a stone house in the sky.

1 Tariana; abridged and adapted from Biocca 1965 : 269–81.

9. The time came for the maidens to become ill (first menstruation). The Virgin remained alone to show them what they should do. The Thunders did not understand: they wondered what to do to make the women well again. The youngest Thunder said, 'You, my elder brothers, are so old you don't know what to think. In the same way as she created us, she will teach us the things to do.' He went to the Virgin and said 'What should we do with you?' She replied, 'You, my grandson, are the last one; the last of each generation will be the wisest and most able. Your elder brothers could not even think.'

10. She taught them to make an enclosure (*pari*) painted with urucú and charcoal. 'With this enclosure you will enclose me.' She taught songs, prayers, everything. She said, 'I've got an enclosure, I've got tobacco, I've got genipapo for painting, I've got caraiuru.' She made all these things with milk squeezed from her breasts. 'I have told you all this as you are the cleverest and most able. Go and teach your brothers these things', she said.

11. He enclosed and isolated the Virgin in the enclosure to blow on her and exorcise her. The four Thunders took the bark of a tree (*paiuma* – they use this scraped bark to wash a girl entering puberty), painted her, blew on her, exorcised her as she had told them, and after five days they were already bathing her.

12. After this she asked the other women if they were well. 'We are hungry; we want to eat, we have nothing', they replied. The Virgin said, 'Your life will be different; you won't be like the Thunders who only smoke and take coca. You will work. I will give you the earth.' This is why people must work to eat.

13. She took a rope, wound it round her head, took it off and divided it in half and then squeezed milk from her breast into the circle and made the earth. The next day a big field had formed in the earth. She gave the earth to the women, saying, 'With this you can live.' The women came down there too; the Thunders remained in the air; they made only thunder.

14. The two women wanted to make many people so that they would be happy. The Thunders said, 'We are four; we must make another person appear.' They blew on coca. There was a ball of *abil*, caimo (*Pouteria caimito*), juice of *cucura* (*Pourouma* sp.) and of *cuma* (*Cuma* sp.) They wanted to see if, by eating those things, yet another person could be born. They tried to become pregnant. They made the thigh and arm muscles but it was ugly.

15. The women saw this and said, 'These old shamans are mad! Look how they have made the belly grow in their arms and legs! The Thunders resented this teasing and said, 'Let us do the work on them. Becoming pregnant is for them not us!'

16. The Thunders came down to earth. They called the young girls and spread perfume to attract them and went to the river to bathe. The girls were curious as to what the Thunders were doing. There was a huge cigar with a nice smell of tobacco; there was a beautiful ball of *abil* and there was coca. The three Thunders had done this; the first had remained to one side.

17. One of the girls took the *abil*, licked it and ate it and then smoked. The other took coca. The first one said, 'You too eat, it's delicious.' She opened the ball of *abil*, inside it there was a child. The other girl said, 'There is something in there, I won't eat it.' They became very sad; it was as though they had had contact with a man. They began to feel different. 'Let's run away, the Thunders are coming', they said, and ran off.

18. After some time, the girls were already swollen and pregnant. The Thunders, who were keeping watch on them, said, 'Where will they go for the delivery?' The Virgins were writhing in pain: they were not like women today. Their bodies had the hole to pass urine but no vaginas.

19. The first Virgin walked writhing in pain near a stream called the stream of pains, till she arrived above Jauareté. There she found some other women and said to them, 'My grandmothers, look after me for I am fainting and the Thunders are coming. Don't let them take my baby.' Then she lost consciousness.

20. (Even today one can see the place where she put her buttocks, her sides, her hips and all her parts. One must not look at this place; if one does one will have many enemies and will become blind very soon. Only old people can see that woman's body in the waterfall. They say it is really the body of a woman.)

21. The Thunders, who had taken the form of monkeys, followed the women to Jauareté. When they arrived the Virgin was as if dead; the other women were caring for her body. The Thunders opened her body from the navel downward using the point of the cigar holder. They took out the baby. Then they put *cucura* and *cuma* juice in the Virgin's mouth. It ran down on to the wound from which the baby had emerged and healed it. The Thunders took the baby to their house in Irapoí waterfall.

22. The baby was full of holes.

23. When the Virgin awoke she saw that the baby had vanished. The Thunders had made the women who were to guard her fall asleep.

24. This was the time when the Tukano, Wanano, Pirá-Tapuyo, Arapaço and Tuyuka came in the shape of fishes swimming up the river. Their canoe was a snake. They drew the canoe to the bank, got out and became people.

25. They saw the other two sisters, who were resting, and said, 'This one must have a baby.' The son of the first girl was brought up by the Thunders; the son of the second was brought up by these people; he was the father of yagé. They made yagé from him and everybody drank it.

26. The Thunders brought up the first child. He was of another race, of another kind. He had come to give laws, to instruct.

27. The Thunders created many people; the Tariana and Baniwa. Nobody had seen the child; he was now a man. He had grown very fast; in a few days he was a young boy, in one moon he was a man. He was *Koe* or Juruparí, the son of a Virgin and the Thunder.

28. He went to dances and taught the people how to sing and dance. He was the chief of each dance that he attended. No one knew he was the son of that woman.

29. His body was full of flowers but no one saw them as his body was covered with dance ornaments.

30. His mother was among the other women but she did not know that he was her son. He said to her, 'You thought I had disappeared from the world; but I am here, I am a man.' He sang for her, 'I am your son, I have made all the sacrifices for you.' He was the leader of the dancers.

31. The two sisters sat on a bench. His aunt said, 'My sister he is singing for you, why don't you listen?' She had been dozing but then she opened her eyes. He was so handsome, so perfect that one couldn't even look at him with one's eyes. He said, 'Mother, don't look at me; no one must look at me.'

32. He gave his mother the plant that prevents madness and made her tear off a small branch. Then he said, 'Come and accompany me with your singing.' While he sang to his mother, a great noise of Jurupari instruments could be heard outside the house.

33. Outside, the chief of the dance, called Deer, sang so loud that the earth shook. It was still Jurupari; inside, the mother sang; outside the noise reverberated terribly. He said, 'My animals have come to the feast; it is myself who is here, myself who is out there.'

34. In the morning the dance was ending. He said, 'When I am no longer here on this world, you will continue to do like this. These instruments, which play out there, are my bones.' The whole tribe said, 'Let us give our children to this man so that they learn to do what should be done.'

35. The dance ended and he went back to his stone house in the mountains of the Rio Aiari.

36. He had three generations of children with him to whom he taught everything. They were very many, they were Tariana and Baniwa; already they sang as he sang.

37. He took the children to make a fiesta of uacú (it was the season of this fruit). He forbade them to eat roast uacú. The children did not listen: the fruit fell from the tree into the fire and they smelt the pleasant smell. They roasted the fruit and ate it.

38. He then threw a huge stone hook to kill them with. It fell in their midst. In the waterfall of Irapoi one can still see this stone hook.

39. He called wind and rain and said, 'Run, look for shelter.' While the children looked for leaves to shelter with, he lay on the ground and opened his huge arse; 'Hide in here', he said. The children saw a dry cave and ran in. The last one had cleaned his mouth with cassava bread. Juripari thought that he had not eaten the fruit and closed his arse before he could enter.

40. From the house they saw the thunderstorm and said, 'He's been angry recently, he has eaten all our children.' The women shouted, 'Look, we have no children any more.'

41. Jurupari took the last child to his stone house and closed the door. Jurupari slept, leaving the child alone.

42. The children inside him began to rot. He belched terribly and asked the boy, 'Does it smell bad?' The boy, being afraid of being eaten himself, replied, 'No.' He farted terribly from belly and mouth. 'Is it a bad smell? It is the smell of children who are stubborn and disobey; it is their smell', he said.

43. The child thought to himself, 'I can't stay here long, I must escape.' He became a small parrot with a long tail and began to peck a hole in the roof of the house. He tried to go out; he was weak from hunger and the smell. He went out and came back in again.

44. Jurupari awoke, farted again, and again asked about the smell. 'It is not good, it stinks. You are horrible', replied the boy; 'You were brought up by my fathers, the Thunders, and you swallowed all my brothers and now you want to kill me with this putrid smell.' Jurupari tried to grab him but the boy escaped through the hole.

45. He flew home singing. There were only old men there. The boy arrived and told the terrible news.

46. The men plotted to kill Jurupari. They made beer with burnt cassava and sugar-cane juice (*payaru*). They sent the parrot to invite Jurupari to the dance but he replied, 'I don't drink *payaru*, it smells of fart.'

47. They sent the parrot to invite him again. Jurupari replied, 'Your fathers want to kill me. They will not be able to. I will come and talk with your fathers. I will tell them that I did not kill the children willingly. They themselves wanted it as they provoked me.' He closed the door and went out.

48. He arrived at their maloca; it was the day of the feast and they were afraid of his strength. They greeted him properly.

49. Jurupari said, 'I've come to tell you that you are the fathers of stubborn children, children who don't obey, inquisitive children and children who act against the wishes of the elders. It is your fault that your children are guilty as you have not brought them up properly. I will now give you back their bones. Make an enclosure.'

50. They made an enclosure and painted it with urucú, charcoal and caraiuru. He squeezed his belly, opened his mouth and vomited out the bones. Then he said, 'Throw away the bones. I'm going away; I won't drink beer with you.' He went away.

51. He lived in his stone house without ever coming out. They made different kinds of beer and sent for him again. The small parrot invited him. He said, 'Why do they call me? I'm quiet here.' Then he said, 'All right, I'll come but I don't drink beer as I did when I was with you. They want to kill me with poison; poison is in my body. They want to kill me with arrows; arrows won't kill me. All this is nothing to me. Tell them to plant ingá, lots of it. When the plants are grown they must skin the fruit so it dries. Tell them to plant bananas so that there are lots of bunches hanging inside the house. When they are ripe they must peel and cook them. This will be my beer; I have never drunk it before; I know all the others. I want just banana beer. The ingá plants must be put on a fire,

only thus will I be able to die. I can only die by being burned.' He really wanted
to die.

52. They made a big fire with the ingá. They made banana beer and then sent
the boy to invite him saying, 'He made us do this, now he must come.'

53. Jurupari replied, 'I will come, I have never had that beer before and have a
great desire for it.'

54. He came out. Snake bones were his collar. As he went out, the holes in his
body produced sound. The sound was the songs of all the animals. He arrived
with that loud music at the house of the dance.

55. The three old Thunders live there; they were the chiefs. They had created
the Baniwa. The Tariana had married the Baniwa and they had many children
and grandchildren. That night they did not dance but drank lots of very strong
beer. The day passed, the night passed and by morning Jurupari was drunk.

56. They had prepared caves underground stocked with food, provisions and
seeds. They said to the women, 'You can go in now, we are already close to the
moment.'

57. Early in the morning they danced with Jurupari, from one side to the other,
singing his song. When he was completely drunk and when a huge fire was
burning, they put all the ornaments, the bird feathers and the rest into the body
of Jurupari.

58. Then they threw the whole lot on the fire. The feathers and ornaments
burned immediately and the fire spread till all the earth was burning.

59. They jumped into the caves with all their possessions but even there lots of
ash fell in.

60. They stayed in the caves a long time and then sent one of the men out to
see if the fire was out. He became a cricket, the one with the black head that
makes its nest underground. The cricket got his feet burned as the soil was still
hot. This is why this cricket has black feet. He came back and told them the fire
was not yet out. They stayed under the ground for a long time.

61. When they came out the earth was bare with no trees or houses. They planted
seeds in the ashes and lived in Tururi rapid.

62. Jurupari turned into a paxiuba palm which grew up where he had been
burned. It made a noise as it grew. It was his body. Before going up he said, 'I
leave you this paxiuba; divide it in pieces. Each piece will make a different
sound.' He gave the measurements of all the instruments. He went up and up
and then disappeared.

63. When the palm fell, the fruit flew in all directions to the different waterfalls
along the rivers. The fruit grew into new palms from which the flutes were
made. Jurupari had said, 'You will do all this in my memory.' In the memory
of him who had gone up they made the masks and the dances. He is the chief of
the dancers and leads the dancing. Those who do not want to dance are whipped.
He is also the chief of the instruments.

64. The women must not see the instruments. From the time that Jurupari

had to keep the secret of that music, the women never saw the instruments. The men kill them if they do.

65. They didn't want to live where Jurupari had died; they dispersed and built their houses on the banks of the rivers. This is why they live in different parts.

66. In the place where Jurupari was burned, near the waterfall on the Aiari, a beautiful place, there is still lots of charcoal. The smell of the charcoal is poisonous. There are lots of poisonous plants there. Fruit cannot be taken from there. If Indians go there they die. Only the children of the Tariana and Baniwa can go there – they know what to do to stop being killed. This is why the Baniwa possess lots of poison; they get it from there; it is for killing their enemies. When they walk on that ground, a noise like a drum is made. They sing, 'I'm coming to ask for poison, I want poison to kill my enemies.' They can take it.

APPENDIX 1

Descriptions of Yurupary rites – a list of sources

Source	Indians referred to
Acebes (1954)	Desana
Allen (1947)	Cubeo?
Amorim (1926/8)	Wanano
Biocca (1965)	Vaupés in general
Boeldeke and Hagen (1958)	Yąnomanö – Río Cauaburí
Boje (1930)	Tuyuka
Brüzzi da Silva (1962)	Tukano (Vaupés in general)
Coudreau (1887)	Tariana
Galvão (1959)	Baniwa
Gheerbrant (1953)	Piaroa
Giacone (1949)	Tukano
Goldman (1963)	Cubeo
Gumilla (1963)	Saliva
Humboldt (1966)	Baniwa
Jackson, Jean (unpublished field notes)	Bará
Jacopin, Pierre-Yves (personal communication)	Yukuna, Tanimuka
Koch-Grünberg (1909/10)	Baniwa, Bará
Langdon, Tom (personal communication)	Barasana (Caño Tatú)
MacCreagh (1927)	Upper Tiquié (Tukano?)
McGovern (1927)	Pirá-Tapuyo
Reichel-Dolmatoff (1971)	Desana
Rozo (1945)	Puinave
Schultz (1959)	Makú (Paraná Boá-Boá)
Silverwood-Cope, Peter (personal communication)	Makú (Makú Paraná)
Terribilini (1961)	Makú (Jauareté)
Wallace	Wanano

Yurupary myths – a list of sources

Amorim (1926/8)
Barbosa Rodrigues (1890)
Biocca (1965)
Brüzzi da Silva (1962)
Coudreau (1887)
Fulop (1954, 1956)
Galvão (1959)
Giacone (1949)
Goldman (1940, 1963)
Koch-Grünberg (1909/10)
Orico (1937)
Prada Ramirez (1969)
Rozo (1945)
Saake (1958a, 1968)
Stradelli (1890b, 1928/9)

The playing of Barasana *He* instruments

Trumpets during Fruit House

Players standing still
Ends held close to ground. Playing starts when ends circled clockwise (CW) from player's point of view. Both simple and complex rhythms played. At end, trumpets held still, then ends raised upwards with playing stopped as trumpets are 45° from horizontal. Playing ends with long fading note.

Players moving in horseshoe pattern (done most of the time)
Trumpets are laid at base on edge of dance path by post 1 or 2, mouth ends towards centre of house. Play standing still (as above), facing in towards middle of house (a). Then players turn as pair to face along dance path (b); walk round dance path (c) moving ends up and down and playing simple rhythm; arrive at point opposite start (d); stop facing end wall, play complex rhythm with ends circled CW. Players then turn inwards towards each other and walk back round the dance path to (a) and repeat stationary playing and turn. Go back and forth round dance path many times. Finally, on coming back to original starting point, turn and face middle of house. Turn made by inner of pair walking across front of outer player as turn made towards middle of house. Stand, play complex rhythm and stop circling ends of trumpets. Then stop as described above. Trumpets then replaced in base (see diagrams 1 and 1(a)).

Trumpets played with short flutes
Trumpets lead flutes going away from base; flutes lead trumpets on return (see diagram 2). The same pattern applies when two pairs of trumpets are played from the same base.

Trumpets blown with ends circled over fruit
See diagrams 3, 4, 5, 6, 7. Details of playing as above.

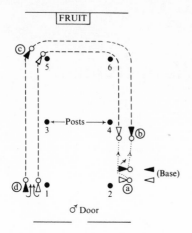

Diagram 1 The trumpets played in horseshoe pattern at Fruit House

Diagram 1a The turn of the trumpets

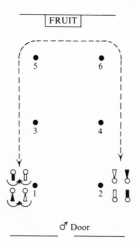

Diagram 2 Trumpets played with short flutes

Diagram 2(a) Trumpets played with short flutes — the start

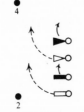

Diagram 2(b) Trumpets and flutes at the end of playing

Trumpets

Flutes

Key

Appendix 3

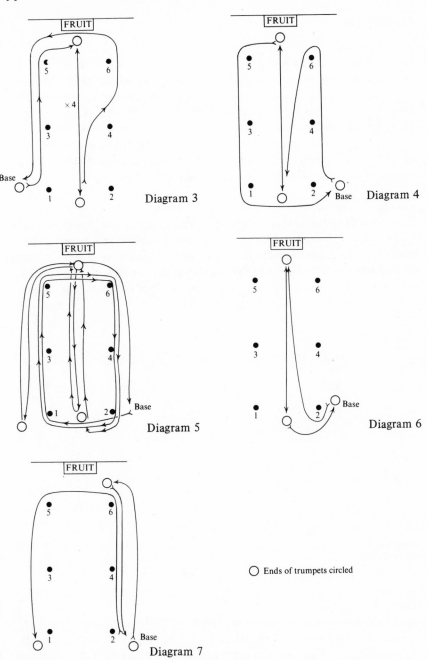

Diagram 3

Diagram 4

Diagram 5

Diagram 6

○ Ends of trumpets circled

Diagram 7

Diagrams 3–7 The paths taken by the trumpets when blown with the ends circling over the fruit

Appendix 3

The long flutes

Normal playing
Players stand just beyond posts 1 and 2 facing in towards middle of house. Start playing and move ends of flutes in CW circle. Walk as pair up middle of house, now keeping ends of flutes stationary. At posts 5 and 6, pause momentarily, turn inwards towards each other, then back down the house. Repeated many times. At end, players remain standing in 1, 2, 3, 4 space till next session.

When one pair has finished playing, flutes leant against male door (or placed on sticks by post 3 during *He* House), players return to seats. At start of next session, players raise flutes in their hands and salute the men sitting.

The slow sacred dance of the flutes
Players start playing as above. Then walk *very* slowly up and down house, leaning slightly backwards and walking in rhythm together. At each end, very sudden turn made. Turn done by both turning in the same direction so that they remain side by side and facing in same way. As turn is made, high sustained note played which coincides with sweeping circular motion of ends of flutes (see diagram 8).

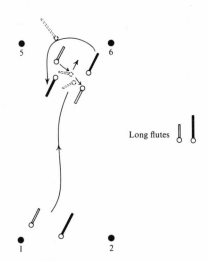

Diagram 8 The slow dance of the long flutes

Ends in the Air
Start at male end facing down house. Raise ends of flutes to near vertical above head, then, playing 'toooo tooo too to t t ttt', run with very smell steps with emphasis in right foot, down to other end. Return to male end in slow dance, then repeat end raising as above. Finally stop by fruit and play with ends raised but without moving feet. Then continue with slow dance.

314

Appendix 3

He House

The parade
One individual takes the instruments from the base near the dance path on the right of the house and lays them in pairs down the middle of the house (see diagram 9). Younger men then pick up trumpets and stand in long line along the dance path, facing away from middle of the house. Then do 'swing × 3' action: swing the ends of trumpets first to left, then to right, then to straight out in front of player, each time blowing as near to the ground as possible. Then pair nearest men's door walk round dance path × 2, round post 5 and down the middle of the house, followed by the rest, all in pairs. At male door: go out, round house × 1, back in men's door, round dance path × 2, round post 5, down middle till leading pair reaches men's door. Then stop with 'swing × 3', replacing trumpets in pairs on ground. Or: on reaching men's door, go out again and twice round the house, then repeat the ending as above (see diagram 10).

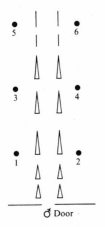
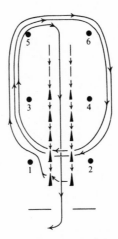

Diagram 9 The *He* laid along the length of the house

Diagram 10 The path taken for the parade of trumpets

Going to make the tree-bark low
Start with parade as above going round house × 2. Then come into house, straight up middle with lead pair stopping beyond posts 5, 6. Pairs form into two *lines* which turn inwards to face each other. Then 'swing × 3'. Whole line then walks to men's end with rear leading and repeat 'swing × 3', then back to female end and repeat 'swing × 3'. Then leaders go round post 6 followed by rest of line now again in pairs. Round dance path × 2 (CW) then back down middle after going round post 5. As leaders arrive at men's door, do 'swing × 3'

315

but this time first swing to right, then to left and then out to front (i.e. reversed order), then stop.

Named instruments

(1) *Wenandurika* always leads parades of trumpets.

(2) Old Deer: basic pattern of playing same as for other trumpets but when played has to be supported by man walking in front holding the end of each of the pair in his hands. As he walks he lifts up the ends one after the other in unison with the alternation of the playing. Generally accompanied only by a pair of short flutes, Old Parrot.

(3) Old Sloth: the only flute taken on the parades with the trumpets and not played very much at all. Should go in middle of line of players. Generally preceded by Old Star and followed by Manioc-squeezing Woman.

(4) Old Macaw: only very occasionally taken on parade round the house. When taken, always on the end of the line.

BIBLIOGRAPHY

Acebes, H. (1954) *Jungle Explorer*. London.

Allen, P. H. (1947) Indians of southeastern Colombia. *Geographical Review*, vol. 37, pp. 568–83.

Amorim, A. B. de. (1926/8) Lendas em Nheêngatú e em Portuguez. *Revista do Instituto Histórico Geográfico Brasileiro*, tomo 100, vol. 154, no. 2 (1926).

Bamberger, J. (1974) The myth of matriarchy: why men rule in primitive societies, in M. Z. Rosaldo and L. Lamphere (eds.), *Woman, Culture and Society*, pp. 263–80. Stanford.

Barbosa, Rodrigues, J. (1890) Poranduba amazonense. *Anais de Biblioteca Nacional de Rio de Janeiro*, vol. 14, 1886–7, fasc. 2.

Beksta, C. (1967/8) Experiências de um pesquisador entre os Tukâno. *Revista de Antropologia*, vols. 15/16, pp. 99–110.

Bidou, P. (n.d.) Mythologie Tatuyo Histoire de Hungue Warimi. Unpublished ms.
 (1972) Représentations de l'espace dans la mythologie Tatuyo (Indiens Tucano). *Journal de la Société des Américanistes*, vol. 61, pp. 45–105.
 (1976) Les Fils de l'Anaconda Céleste (les Tatuyo): étude de la structure socio-politique. Unpublished thesis for Troisième Cycle, University of Paris.

Biocca, E. (1965) *Viaggi tra gli Indi. Alto Río Negro – Alto Orinoco: Appunti di un Biologo*, vol. 1: *Tukâno – Tariâna – Baniwa – Makú*. Rome.

Bödiger, U. (1965) *Die Religion der Tukano*. Kölner Ethnologische Mitteilungen no. 3. Cologne.

Boeldeke, A. and Hagen, L. (1958) *With Graciela to the Headhunters*. London.

Boje, W. (1928) Am Río Tiquié. *Welt und Wissen*, vol. 17, no. 111, pp. 57–65.
 (1930) Das Yurupari-fest der Tuyuka-Indianer. *Der Erdball*, year 4, no. 10, pp. 387–90. Berlin.

Bolens, J. (1967) Mythe de Jurupari: introduction à une analyse. *L'Homme*, vol. 7, no. 1, pp. 50–66.

Brüzzi Alves da Silva, A. (1955) Os ritos funebres entre os tribos do Uapés (Amazonas). *Anthropos*, vol. 50, pp. 593–601.

317

Bibliography

(1956) Morte do chefs indígena da tribo Tucano. *Revista do Instituto Histórico a Geográfico de São Paulo*, vol. 53, pp. 119–24.

(1961) *Discoteca etno-ligüistico-musical das tribos do Ríos Uaupés, Içana e Cauaburi.* São Paulo.

(1962) *A civilização indígena do Uaupés.* São Paulo.

(1966) Estrutura da tribo Tukano. *Anthropos*, vol. 61, pp. 191–203.

Butt, A. J. (1956) Ritual blowing. *Man*, vol. 56, pp. 49–55.

Chagnon, N. A. (1968) *Yąnomamö: The Fierce People.* New York.

Clastres, P. (1972) *Chronique des Indiens Guayaki.* Paris.

Colini, G. A. (1885) La provincia delle Amazzoni: secondo la relazione del P. Illuminato Guiseppe Coppi, missioniario francescano. *Bolletino della Società Geografica Italiana*, vol. 22, pp. 136–41, 193–204.

Coudreau, H. A. (1887) *La France equinoxiale*, vol. II: *Voyage à travers les Guayanes et l'Amazone.* Paris.

Emst, P. van. (1966) Indians and missionaries on the Río Tiquié, Brazil–Colombia. *Internationales Archiv für Ethnographie*, vol. 50, pt 2, pp. 145–97. Leiden.

Fock, N. (1963) *Waiwai: Religion and Society of an Amazonian Tribe.* National Museum of Denmark, Ethnographic Series, vol. 8. Copenhagen.

Fulop, M. (1954) Aspectos de la cultura Tukana: cosmogonía. *Revista Colombiana de Antropología*, vol. 3, pp. 97–137.

(1955) Notes sobre los términos y el sistema de parentesco de los Tukano. *Revista Colombiana de Antropología*, vol. 4, pp. 123–64.

(1956) Aspectos de la cultura Tukana: mitología. *Revista Colombiana de Antropología*, vol. 5, pp. 335–73.

Galvão, E. (1959) *Acculturacão indígena no Río Negro. (Boletim do Museu Paraense Emilio Goeldi, Antropologia*, no. 7.) Belém.

Geertz, C. (1966) Religion as a cultural system, in M. Banton (ed.), *Anthropological Approaches to the Study of Religion.* ASA Monograph no. 3, pp.1–46. London.

Gheerbrant, A. (1953) *The Impossible Adventure.* London.

Giacone, A. (1949) *Os Tucanos e outras tribus do Río Uapés, affluente do Río Negro-Amazonas: notas etnográficas e folclóricas de um misionário salesiano.* São Paulo.

Goldman, I. (1940) Cosmological beliefs of the Cubeo Indians. *Journal of American Folklore*, vol. 53, pp. 242–7.

(1948) Tribes of the Uaupés–Caquetá region. *Handbook of South American Indians*, vol. 3, pp. 763–98. Washington, D.C.

(1963) *The Cubeo: Indians of the Northwest Amazon.* Illinois Studies in Anthropology, no. 2. Urbana.

(1964) The structure of ritual in the Northwest Amazon, in R. H. Manners (ed.), *Process and Pattern in Culture: Essays in Honor of Julian H. Steward*, pp. 111–22. Chicago.

Gourlay, K. A. (1975) Sound-producing instruments in traditional society: a

Bibliography

study of esoteric instruments and their role in male–female relations. *New Guinea Research Bulletin*, no. 60. Canberra.

Gumilla, P. José. (1963) *El Orinoco illustrado y defendido*. Caracas. (First published Madrid, 1741.)

Hugh-Jones, C. (1979) *From the Milk River: Spatial and temporal processes in Northwest Amazonia*. Cambridge.

(1977) Skin and soul, the round and the straight: social time and social space in Pirá-paraná society. *Proceedings of the forty-second International Congress of Americanists*. Paris.

Hugh-Jones, S. P. (n.d.) Why shamans are jaguars. Unpublished ms.

(1977) Like the leaves on the forest floor: ritual and social structure amongst the Barasana. *Proceedings of the forty-second International Congress of Americanists*. Paris.

Humboldt, A. de and Bonpland, A. (1966) *Personal Narrative of Travels to the Equinoctial Regions of the New Continent*, vol. V. New York.

Ihering, R. von. (1968) *Dicionário dos animais do Brasil*. São Paulo.

Instituto Geográfico Agustín Codazzi. (1969) *Atlas de Colombia*. Bogotá.

Izikowitz, K. G. (1934) *Musical Instruments of the South American Indians*. Göteborg.

Jackson, J. E. (n.d.) Unpublished field notes.

(1972) Marriage and linguistic identity among the Bará Indians of the Vaupés, Colombia. Unpublished Ph.D. thesis, Stanford University.

(1973) Relations between semi-sedentary and nomadic Indians of the Vaupés, Colombia. Unpublished paper presented to annual meeting of the South-Western Anthropological Association, San Francisco.

(1974) Language identity of the Colombian Vaupés Indians, in R. Bauman and J. Sherzer (eds.), *Explorations in the Ethnography of Speaking*, pp. 50–64. Cambridge.

(1976) Vaupés marriage: a network system in the Northwest Amazon, C. A. Smith (ed.), *Regional Analysis*, vol. II: *Social Systems*, pp. 65–93. New York.

(1977) Bará zero generation terminology and marriage. *Ethnology*, vol. XVI, no. 1, pp. 83–104. Pittsburgh.

Kloos, P. (1971) *The Maroni River Caribs of Surinam*. Assen.

Koch-Grünberg, T. (1906) Die Indianerstamme am oberen Río Negro und Yapura und ihre sprachliche Zugehörigkeit. *Zeitschrift für Ethnologie*, vol. 38, pp. 166–205.

(1909/10) *Zwei Jahre unter den Indianern*. 2 vols. Berlin.

(1971) Aruak-sprachen nordwestbrasiliens. *Mitteilungen der Enthropologischen Gesellschaft*, vol. 41, pp. 33–153, 203–52. Vienna.

(1912/16) Betoya-sprachen nordwestbrasiliens. *Anthropos*, vol. 7, pp. 429–62; vol. 8, pp. 944–77; vol. 9, pp. 151–95, 569–89, 812–32; vols. 10/11, pp. 114–58, 421–49.

(1922) Die Völkergruppierung zwischen Río Branco, Orinoco, Río Negro

Bibliography

und Yapura, in W. Lehman (ed.), *Festschrift Eduard Seler*, pp. 205–66. Stuttgart.

Krickeberg, W., Trimborn, H., Müller, W. and Zerries, O. (1968) *Pre-Colombian American Religions.* London.

Langdon, T. (1975) Food restrictions in the medical system of the Barasana and Taiwano Indians of the Colombian Northwest Amazon. Unpublished Ph.D thesis, Tulane University.

Leach, E. R. (1958) Magical hair. *Journal of the Royal Anthropological Institute,* vol. 88, pp. 147–64.

(1961) *Rethinking Anthropology.* London School of Economics Monographs on Social Anthropology, no. 22. London.

(1972) The structure of symbolism, in J. La Fontaine (ed.), *The Interpretation of Ritual: Essays in Honour of A. I. Richards*, pp. 239–75. London.

Lévi-Strauss, C. (1943) The social use of kinship terms among Brazilian Indians. *American Anthropologist*, vol. 45, no. 3, pp. 398–409.

(1963) *Structural Anthropology.* New York.

(1965/6) Résumé de cours de 1964–1965. *Extrait de l'Annuaire de Collège de France*, year 65, pp. 269–70. Paris.

(1967) Le sexe des astres, in *To Honor Roman Jakobson: Essays on the Occasion of his Seventieth Birthday*, vol. II, pp. 1163–70. The Hague.

(1968) *L'Origine des manières de table* [*Mythologiques*, vol. III]. Paris.

(1970) *The Raw and the Cooked*, tr. J. and D. Weightman. London. [*Mythologiques*, vol. I: *Le Cru et le cuit.* Paris, 1964.]

(1971) *L'Homme nu* [*Mythologiques*, vol. IV]. Paris.

(1973) *From Honey to Ashes*, tr. J. and D. Weightman. London. [*Mythologiques* vol. II: *Du miel aux cendres.* Paris, 1968.]

(1977) *Structural Anthropology*, vol. II. London.

MacCreagh, G. (1927) *White Waters and Black.* Garden City, N.Y.

McGovern, W. M. (1927) *Jungle Paths and Inca Ruins.* London.

Maybury-Lewis, D. (1967) *Akwẽ-Shavante Society.* Oxford.

Moser, B. and Tayler, D. (1963) Tribes of the Pirá-paraná. *Geographical Journal,* vol. 129, pp. 437–48.

Murphy, R. and Murphy, Y. (1974) *Women of the Forest.* New York and London.

Nimuendaju, C. (1948) The Tikuna. *Handbook of South American Indians*, vol. 3, pp. 713–25. Washington, D.C.

(1950/5) Reconhecimento dos Ríos Içana, Ayari e Uaupés. *Journal de la Société des Américanistes*, vol. 39, pp. 125–82; vol. 44, pp. 149–78.

Orico, O. (1937) *Vocabulário de crendices amazônicas.* São Paulo.

Paes de Souza Brazil, T. (1938) *Incolas selvícolas.* Rio de Janeiro.

Prada Ramirez, H. M. (1969) Frente a una cultura: los Tukanos del Vaupés, en Colombia, Suramerica. *Boletin de Antropología del Universidad de Antioquía,* vol. 3, no. 2, pp. 107–38. Medellin.

Radcliffe-Brown, A. (1964) *The Andaman Islanders.* New York.

Bibliography

Reichel-Dolmatoff, G. (1971) *Amazonian Cosmos: The Sexual and Religious Symbolism of the Tukano Indians.* Chicago.
(1972) The cultural context of an aboriginal hallucinogen: *Banisteriopsis Caapi*, in P. Furst (ed.), *Flesh of the Gods*, pp. 84–113. London.
(1975) *The Shaman and the Jaguar.* Philadelphia.
Richards, A. I. (1956) *Chisungu: A Girl's Initiation Ceremony among the Bemba of Northern Rhodesia.* London.
Rivière, P. G. (1969a) *Marriage among the Trio.* Oxford.
(1969b) Myth and material culture: some symbolic inter-relations, in R. F. Spencer (ed.), *Forms of Symbolic Action*, pp. 151–66. Proceedings of the 1969 Annual Spring Meeting of the American Ethnological Society. Seattle.
(1971) Marriage: a reassessment, in R. Needham (ed.), *Rethinking Kinship and Marriage.* ASA Monograph no. 11, pp. 57–74. London.
Rozo, J. M. (1945) La fiesta del diabolo entre los Puiñave. *Boletin Archaeología*, vol. 1, no. 3, pp. 241–7.
Saake, W. (1958a) Die Juruparilegende bei den Baniwa des Río Issana. *Proceedings of the 32nd International Congress of Americanists*, pp. 271–9, Copenhagen.
(1958b) Aus den Uberlieferangen der Baniwa. *Staden-Jahrbuch*, vol. VI, pp. 83–91. São Paulo.
(1968) Mythen über Inapirikuli, den Kulturheros der Baniwa. *Zeitschrift für Ethnologie*, vol. 93, pp. 260–73. Berlin.
Schaden, E. (1959) *A mitologia heróica de tribos indígenas do Brasil.* Rio de Janeiro.
Schauensee, R. M. de (1964) *The Birds of Colombia.* Narberth, Pa.
Schultes, R. E. (1972) New data on the malpighiaceous narcotics of South America. *Botanical Museum Leaflets, Harvard University*, vol. 23, no. 3, pp. 137–47. Cambridge, Mass.
Schultz, H. (1959) Ligeiras notas sobre os Makú do Paraná Boá-Boá. *Revista do Museu Paulista*, vol. 21, pp. 109–32. São Paulo.
Schwartz, H. B. (1948) *Stingless Bees (Meliponidae) of the Western Hemisphere. (Bulletin of the American Museum of Natural History,* vol. 90.) New York.
Silverwood-Cope, P. L. (1972) A contribution to the ethnography of the Colombian Makú. Unpublished Ph.D. thesis, University of Cambridge.
Smith, R. (n.d.) *Southern Barasano Grammar.* Summer Institute of Linguistics Language Data Microfiche, AM3.
Sorensen, A. P., jun. (1967) Multilingualism in the Northwest Amazon. *American Anthropologist*, vol. 69, no. 6, pp. 670–82.
Sperber, D. (1975) *Rethinking Symbolism.* Cambridge.
Stanner, W. E. H. (1960) On aboriginal religion: sacramentalism, rite and myth. *Oceania*, vol. 30, no. 4, pp. 245–78. Sydney.
Stradelli, E. (1890a) L'Uaupés e gli Uaupés. *Bolletino della Società Geografica Italiana*, 3rd ser., vol. 3, pp. 425–53.

Bibliography

(1890b) Leggenda dell'Jurupary. *Bolletino della Societ'a Geografica Italiana,* 3rd ser., vol. 3, pp. 659–89, 798–835.

(1900) Iscrizioni indigene delle regione dell'Uaupés. *Bolletino della Società Geografica Italiana,* 4th ser., vol. 1, pp. 457–83. Rome.

(1928/9) Vocabulários da Lingua Geral, Portuguez–Nheêngatú e Nheêngatú–Portuguez. *Revista do Instituto Histórico e Geográfico Brasileiro,* tomo 104, vol. 158, no. 2 (1928), pp. 5–768. Rio de Janeiro.

Tambiah, S. J. (1970) *Buddhism and the Spirit Cults in North-East Thailand.* Cambridge.

Terribilini, M. and Terribilini, M. (1961) Enquête chez des Indiens Makú du Vaupés, Août 1960. *Bulletin de la Société Suisse des Américanistes,* vol. 21, pp. 2–10. Geneva.

Torres Laborde, A. (1969) *Mito y cultura entre los Barasana: un grupo indígena Tukano del Vaupés.* Bogotá.

Turner, T. (n.d.) The fire of the jaguar. Unpublished ms.

Turner, V. (1967) *The Forest of Symbols.* Ithaca, N.Y.

(1969a) Forms of symbolic action: introduction, in R. F. Spencer (ed.), *Forms of Symbolic Action,* pp. 3–25. Proceedings of the 1969 Annual Spring Meeting of the American Ethnological Society. Seattle.

(1969b) *The Ritual Process.* London.

Van Gennep, A. (1960) *The Rites of Passage.* London.

Wallace, A. R. (1853) *Palm Trees of the Amazon and their Uses.* London.

(1889) *A Narrative of Travels on the Amazon and Rio Negro.* 2nd edn. London.

Whiffen, I. (1915) *The Northwest Amazons: Notes on Some Months Spent among Cannibal Tribes.* London.

Ypiranga Monteiro, M. (1960) Cariamã, pubertatsritus der Tucano–Indianer. *Zeitschrift für Ethnologie,* vol. 85, pp. 37–9. Berlin.

INDEX

323

Index

fire 13
  attitudes towards, after *He* rites 88, 233
  in myth 161, 179, 228, 232, 235; *see
    also* M.2.C, M.5.A, M.6.A,B, M.8
  symbolic significance of 123, 179–80,
    197, 233–5
fish
  and *He* House 81
  in myth *see* M.2.F, M.4.E, M.6
  as ritual food 34, 60, 95–6
fishing 22, 30, 35, 86, 106, 175
fish poison 29
  in myth 180
food 30
  cooking, symbolic significance of 112–13
  in confinement (seclusion) 85, 90,
    221–2
  hierarchy in 60, 90–1, 93, 220
  restrictions 17, 30, 32, 61, 66–7, 83,
    84, 85
  ritual use of 34, 60
  shamanism of 32–3, 60, 83, 90–1, 99
frog, in myth 173; *see also* M.2.B, C, M.7.L
fruit 28, 29, 30, 41, 85, 184
  in myth 223–6; *see also* M.2.F
  ritual use of 5, 30, 34, 35, 51, 55, 57,
    60, 141, 207–8, 222–3
  see also plants
fruit, ritual
  assai palm 94, 185
  ingá 65, 66, 171–2, 223–4
  kana 63, 77, 215–16
  pupunha 66
  umari 66
  see also plants, ritual

garters 112, 202
gathering, of forest fruit 22, 30, 47
girls 109, 131
  see also children; rites, first menstruation
gourds 163–4
guests, at rituals 43, 55, 57, 62, 132–3

hair
  at *He* rites 77, 203
  in myth; *see* M.1.B
  symbolism of 13, 87, 131, 132, 184,
    195, 204–6, 251
  styles of 203, 204
He, concept of 9, 138–40, 247
He instruments (sacred flutes and trumpets)
  12, 34, 37, 100, 138ff, 159–60,
    187, 242
  and beeswax gourd 12, 175, 190, 195–6,
    238

and coca 59, 210
definition of 7, 144, 197, 229
description of 134–8, 155, 157–8
at Fruit House 46, 47, 51, 52–3, 55,
  94, 100, 130, 133, 150, 155–7
function of 10, 12, 41, 128, 154, 157–9,
  251
at *He* House 38, 61, 64, 67, 72–3,
  76–7, 78, 79, 81, 82, 83, 107,
  118–19, 133, 134, 142–9, 153–5,
  188, 189, 215, 248
and initiation 61, 70, 78, 80, *83*, 87,
  94, 147
and menstruation 87, 125, 130–1,
  198, 199, 200
and monkeys 197
in myth 127–8, 132, 139, 149, 152–3,
  157–9, 198, 217, 225, 227–8,
  229, 244; *see also* myths, elements
  of: origins; myths, characters in;
  M.1.D
names of: Manioc-squeezing Women
  148, 160; Old Deer 143, 149, 160;
  Old Guan 143; Old Callicebus Monkey
  81, 121, 143, 147, 197; Old Macaw
  67, 73, 76, 79, 80, 81, 82, 143,
  144, 146, 148, 154, 155, 160; Old
  Parrot 143, 160; Old Star 119, 143,
  144–6, 149, 159, 209; Old Sloth
  198
and prohibitions 88
and social status 116, 118–19
and specialist-role system 146–9
symbolic significance of 13, 38, 142–9,
  150, 153, 156, 159, 190, 197, 200,
  201–3, 204, 211, 238, 247
and tobacco 210
and women 12, 31, 38, 51, 72, 100,
  125, 128, 129–31, 148, 155
and yagé 209
see also Yurupary instruments
He rites 10–11, 12, 16, 37–8, 100, 141,
  145, 150, 217, 241–7
  frequence of 144
  Fruit House 11, 16, 41–68, 132, 140,
    141, 243; and initiation 61–4, 106,
    200, 202, 207–8; interpretation of
    141–2, 150, 155, 185, 207, 211,
    224; and myth 156
  v. *He* House 69, 100–2, 156, 165,
    208, 222, 242–3
  He House 11, 17, 61, 65–6, 69–100,
    132, 150, 175, 187–92, 200, 242–3;
    confinement during 84–8; dancing
    at 97–9; frequency of 69, 184;
    function of 37–8, 106–7, 120,
    132, 139, 140, 144, 179, 182, 183,

Index

Index

as rebirth 114, 132, 182, 189, 201, 217
and Yurupary instruments 7, 64, 107,
    202
see also initiates; *He* rites
insects
    as food 30
    in myth 206; *see also* M.1.C, M.2.F,
        M.4.E, F, G, M.6, M.7.B
    as ritual food 34, 60, 67, 83, 85, 88, 90
'instruments of darkness' 13, 15, 176–8,
    180, 181, 183, 188, 195–6, 197,
    198, 236–7, 256

jaguar
    He 76, 79, 83, 90, 146, 151
    in myth 170, 204, 220, 224; *see also*
        myth, characters in
    as predator 92, 124
    and shamans 124
    symbolic significance of 125, 157, 204

kinship
    affinal v. agnatic 36, 110, 230–1
    and communal rituals 37, 133
kinship, ritual 77, 80, 96, 112–15
kinship terminology 27, 111; attitudes
    towards 106; and myth 2, 30

language 21–2, 23, 24, 26, 27, 168
laziness, Indian concept of 87, 127, 202,
    205, *207*
life-cycle, beliefs concerning 10, 141
    see also immortality
longhouse (maloca) 4, 5, 22, 27–30
    community 26, 30–1, 35, 36, 42, 43,
        154, 248–9
    organisation of, and symbolic significance
        107–9, 151
    symbolism of 216, 219, 248

male/female polarity
    in daily life 31, 105, 106, 111, 191
    in *He* rites, 38, 72, 100–1, 109, 160,
        190–2, 212
    high/low 214ff, 221, 222, 228
    hot/cold 89–90, 110–11, 158, 215,
        228, 230, 233
    in longhouse 28, 108
    wet/dry 192, 228
maloca *see* longhouse
manioc
    as beer 42, 46–7, 51, 52, 59, 65, 72,
        76, 90

production of 22, 28, 30, 42, 46, 105,
    175, 222
manioc garden 28, 96, 111, 139, 175
manioc juice 95
manioc starch 52, 76, 83, 85, 90, 134;
    see also cassava
marriage
    and longhouse community 26, 27
    and male/female relations 111–13
    rules of 23–4, 27, 230; and Yurupary
        cult 245
    and social status 111–12
meals, communal 28, 30–1, 108
    at Fruit House 56, 60
meat 30, 34
    see also animals, as food; food
men
    daily life of 28, 29, 214
    hairstyles of 203–4
    ritual role of 10, 141, 225
    social organisation of 31, 51
    status of 38, 42, 141, 205; and *He*
        rites 118
    and women 111–14; in myth 6, 127–8, 132
men, unmarried (*mamarã*)
    hairstyles of 203–4
    at *He* House 107–15
    kinship relations among 110
    obligations of 31, 111
    ritual role of 47, 109, 116
menstrual blood
    attitude towards 84, 178, 181, 209
    in myth 178, 179, 211; *see also* M.1.B,
        M.3, M.4.B
    red paint as 184
    see also menstruation
menstruation 10
    attitudes towards 12, 32, 87, 127,
        131, 178–9, 183, 185, 247, 250
    confinement during 112, 127, 132
    and hair 205
    and *He* instruments 87, 125, 131, 198
    and initiation 195, 201, 244
    and myth 127, 179, 184, 198–9; *see also*
        M.1.C, M.4.B, C, M.8
    and red paint 76, 179–80
    and shamanism 125, 178
    and weather 179
missionaries
    attitude of, to Yurupary cult 4–5,
        9, 129–30
    effects of 5, 21, 241
monkey-fur string, as ritual ornament 79, 193
monkeys
    and *He* instruments 197, 233
    in myth 123, 228; *see also* M.4.G, M.5.A,
        M.6.A

Index

masks of see Yurupary masks
symbolic significance of 122–3, 193–5, 199
Moon see myth, characters in
myth
  animals in 124, 141, 142, 144, 156–7, 169, 180, 197; see also M.1.A, M.1.C, M.2.B, F, M.3, M.4, M.6, M.7
  birds in, as He 140–1; see also M.4, M.6; He instruments
  chronology in 168
  and concept of predator 124
  and He 9–10, 13, 139, 156–7
  and male/female polarity 38, 125, 127
  nature of 6, 9, 139, 247, 257, 258
  and ritual 15, 37, 252ff
  punishment in 131
  stars in 65, 144–6, 168; Adze constellation 145; Morning Star, see M.6; Orion constellation 144–6, 191; Pleiades 144, 168, 169–70, 171, 223, 224
  and shamanic power 33, 120ff
  teaching 106
myth, characters in
  Ant Bird see M.6.A
  Anteater (Buko) see M.2.B
  Aru 196
  Coadidop 211 see M.8
  Cotinga Jaguar see M.1.C, M.7.1
  Dance Anaconda see M.6.A
  Eagle (Rame) 125 see M.4.F, H
  Fire Callicebus Monkey 123, 197, see M.6.A
  Fire Cayman see M.2.C
  Fire Howler Monkey 123, 197, 228, 229, see M.6.A
  Fish Anaconda 100, 124, 156, 202, 222, see M.7.C, G, H, I, J
  Fish Woman Anaconda see M.7
  Guan see M.1.C
  He Anaconda 122, 131, 157, 169, 171, 197, 203, 217, 218, 227–8, see M.5
  He Jaguar 95
  Jurupari see M.8; see also Yurupary
  Kana Flower see M.1.C, M.6.A
  Little Sticky Man 171, 223, see M.4.B
  Lizard Woman see M.4.G
  Macaw 83, 123, 228–33, 246, see M.6.A
  Manioc-squeezing Woman 148, see M.1.C, M.6.A
  Manioc-stick Anaconda 15, 88, 95, 113, 120, 121, 122–3, 125, 139, 147, 153, 161, 165, 171, 180,

197, 205, 218, 219, 228–33, 246, 255, see M.6.A
Meneriyo (Ingá Woman) 169, 170, 171, 215, 223, see M.4.A, B, D
Meni Shaman see M.4.D, E
Miriti Tapir see M.4.E
Moon 199, 201, 206, 210, 215, 219, 227–33, 236, 245–6, see M.3, M.4.A, C, M.6.A
Morning Star see myth, stars in
Old Callicebus Monkey 95, 122, 197, see M.6.A
Old Star 149, 167, 178, 180, see M.1.C
Old Sloth see M.1.C
Opossum 169–80, 172–4, see M.4.A, M.7.K, L
Pleiades see myth, stars in; Pleiades
Poison Anaconda 180, see M.1.D, M.4.F, G
Pouncing Jaguar see M.4.F
Red Guan see M.2.B, F
Red Squirrel (Timoka) 100, see M.5.A, M.6.A, M.7.I, J
Romi Kumu (Woman Shaman) 95, 125, 127, 128, 144, 149, 152, 167, 168, 169, 173, 175, 176, 177, 178, 183, 224, see M.1.A, B, D, M.4.F, M.7
Sky Anaconda 125, see M.4.C
Sky People 157, 168, see M.4.A
Steel Tapir see M.4.E
Sun 88, 152, 161, 165, 183, 220, 227–33, 236, 245–6, 247, see M.3, M.6.A, M.7
Tapir 197, 228, 229, 232, see M.5.A, M.6.A, M.7.J
Thunder Jaguar 224, see M.4.D, E
Thunders (Ayawa) 117, 123, 126, 170, 176, 179, 197, 223, 228, 237, see M.2, M.8
Tinamou Chief see M.7.K, L
Tinamou Eagle see M.7.K
Toucan see M.5.B
Toucan Woman see M.5.A
Tree-Fruit Jaguar 208, 225, see M.2.F
Vulture Chief see M.7.L
Warimi 146, 168, 170, 171, 180, 223, 224, 225, see M.4.A, D, E, F
White Guan see M.2.B, F
White Toucan Woman see M.5.A
White Worm see M.4.A
Woman Jaguar see M.6.A, M.7
Wood Ibises see M.4.F
Yawira 156–7, 169, 172–3, 222, see M.7
Yeba 100, 125, 156–7, 168, 222, see M.7

Index

Index

INDEX OF NAMES